Maverick's
Progress

*

James Thomas Flexner in his twenties.

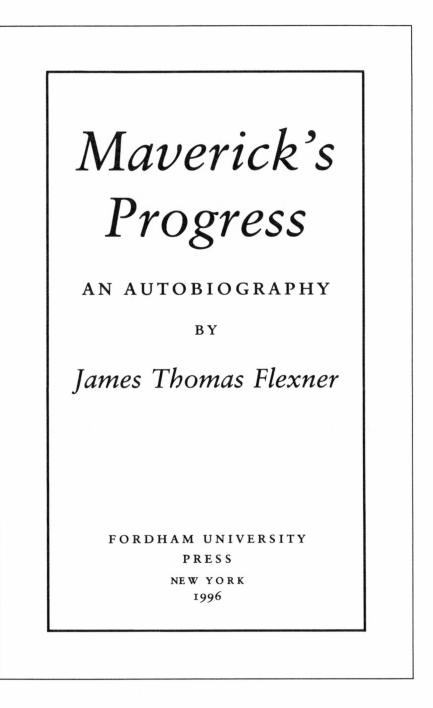

Maverick's Progress

AN AUTOBIOGRAPHY

BY

James Thomas Flexner

FORDHAM UNIVERSITY
PRESS
NEW YORK
1996

Library of Congress Cataloguing-in-Publication Data

Flexner, James Thomas, 1908–
   Maverick's progress : an autobiography / James Thomas Flexner
     p.   cm.
   Includes index.
   ISBN 0-8232-1660-8
   1. Flexner, James Thomas, 1908–   . 2. Historians—United States—
Biography. 3. Art historians—United States—Biography. 4. Biographers—United
States—Biography. 5. Biography as a literary form. 6. Authorship. I.
Title.
E175.5.F549A3   1995
973.9'092—dc2   95-10132
[B]   CIP

To
Ruth Flaherty
who has helped me along
for some twenty years

Contents

*

CONTENTS

OUTREACH

Illustrations following pages 132, 324, and 452

Acknowledgments

*

The staff of Fordham University Press—Saverio Procario, Mary Beatrice Schulte, Loomis Mayer, and Margaret Van Cott—have been so warm and helpful that I have almost felt myself a member of their fellowship. I have thanked Ruth Flaherty in the dedication to this volume. The New-York Historical Society, which has been hospitable to me for more than sixty years, has continued their hospitality. The American Philosophical Society, which I made the custodian of my mother's and father's papers, have been extremely helpful. I have relied, as always, on the New York Public Library, of which I am an honorary trustee. I have often had recourse to the library of The Century Association.

Sunshine and
Shadow

*

I

HERITAGE

*

THE peculiar situation of the family into which I had been born was brought home to me when I was very small by a terrifying circumstance. Our brownstone house in New York's East Sixties was saturated with tension. Father, although it was broad daylight, was hidden away in his bedroom behind a closed door through which I was not allowed to pass. I was told that I must be very quiet because Father was very sick. When Mother went in, she came out again in tears. Strange men hurried up the stairs carrying small black bags. They were let into Father's room. They would reappear looking frightened, and cluster in the halls. Mother told me not to be afraid of them: they were doctors come to help.

Different men were clamoring from outside the house. They were lounging on the steps of the high stoop that rose from the street to our front door. They invaded the vestibule, and I could see their silhouettes through the frosted glass. When the doorbell rang, it would sometimes be one of them. The maid would try to block his way as he shouted a question. Mother would appear, her tears changed to rage. The intruder would retreat, but the ominous shadows remained on the frosted glass.

This terrifying assault on my home and my endangered father remained alive in my memory. But only as time passed was I enabled to understand.

I learned that, although a doctor, my father, Simon Flexner, was not like the men who had rushed upstairs with their black bags, or the doctors Father apprehensively called in whenever I had a sore throat. He did not attend on sick individuals, but in what was called a laboratory made discoveries that helped cure diseases for all mankind.

When our house had been besieged, the United States was being ravaged by infantile paralysis, an epidemic that seemed the more horrible because it attacked children and often left its victims, if they survived, crippled. Father had, during a previous epidemic, this one of cerebrospinal meningitis, created the "Flexner serum" which had cured a high proportion of those infected. Now he was seeking a cure for infantile paralysis. In a time of hysteria it is necessary to find something to cling to, and the vision of Dr. Flexner, in his laboratory, surrounded with test tubes, staring into his microscope, seemed across the United States a dawning of hope. And then there appeared on the front pages of the newspapers horrifying news. The savior was himself on the verge of death.

Day after day, the newspapers ran stories reporting what they could discover of his condition. But they could discover little, since he was immured in his own house and no one was available to keep the press informed. Supposing he should die? That would be front-page news. To keep from being scooped, each newspaper and wire service had to take its own precautions, which meant having its own reporter watching the house, twenty-four hours a day, for any indications of tragedy.

Father returned to his laboratory. He was to make several important discoveries, the most significant being that infantile paralysis was caused not by germs, as cerebrospinal meningitis had been, but by a mysterious agent just then emerging into the ken of science. Germs could be caught in the very finest of filters, but the lethal cause of infantile paralysis passed through, being therefore known as a "filterable virus." However, no one knew what viruses were or had any hints of how to deal with them. Years were to pass before Jonas Salk discovered the cure that Simon Flexner so passionately sought in 1911.

*

Fortunately for my education as a future biographer, my father's career had many facets, starting out with a sensational leap from one basic aspect of American life into another.

[4]

Simon Flexner was born on March 25, 1863, at Louisville, Kentucky, to German-speaking Jewish parents who had reached the United States some dozen years before. His father, who now called himself Morris Flexner, had arrived almost penniless, had become a peddler first on foot and then with a wagon, and then partner and star salesman in a wholesale hat business. Some prosperity followed, but in 1872, in one of the periodic depressions, the business went bankrupt. For the rest of Simon's childhood, the family direction was downward, moving to poorer and poorer locations in Louisville. They had joined those anonymous people whom academic historians, scorning biography as "elitist," represent as digits on the tables they wield to write "people's history." But Father's adventures as a boy and young man seemed by no means impersonal people's history as he described them to me in my own younger days.

In a large and energetic family, six boys and two girls, Father was considered the dunce and the misfit. He was miserable in the successive schools which followed the family descent into tougher and tougher districts where Jews were not welcomed.

As an example of the humiliating situations into which he had been placed, Father told me how his mother, who had difficulty in winter keeping her large brood warm, had got hold of a secondhand tail coat which, although it was much too large, she placed over Simon's shoulders. When he appeared in school, he was greeted with cries of derision. Particular attention was paid to the tails drooping down. During recess, the boys formed themselves into two lines, one attaching itself to each tail. They pulled, ripping the coat up to the collar.

Learning almost nothing, Simon suffered from the teachers' continual punishment, often corporal; was made to repeat the seventh grade; and dropped out before he had finished the eighth, bringing his formal schooling forever to an end.

Simon's duty was now to contribute what pittance he could to the family income. The family's mainstay was a brother-in-law, Edward Klauber, who owned a successful photographic studio, and employed the Flexner boys as they came along. Simon was put under an older brother in the developing department, his task being to watch over enlargements lest they become overexposed as they ripened in sunlight. But the boy had somehow got possession of a jigsaw and some wooden cigar-box tops. Paying complete attention to sawing out fascinating designs, he allowed enlargement after enlargement to be ruined. Fired as incompetent by his uncle, Simon was expelled from the family progression. His despairing family hired him out to shop-keepers too unsuccessful to pay more than a few pennies, but even those most lowly and demeaning jobs in the most sordid circumstances Simon could not keep.

Simon was so bad at baseball that he was always, during street games, put in the farthest outfield. But in that isolation he dreamed so intently of being triumphant before cheering multitudes in a great stadium, as a pinch hitter when the bases were loaded, that he forgot he was supposed to be keeping an eye on his younger sister. A voice interrupted from the outer world, "Where's Mary?" She had disappeared. His mother's screams alerted the neighborhood. That Mary was eventually found did not mitigate Father's guilt. It was then that his father took him to the county jail to show him where he would end up.

Father enjoyed telling stories of his early mishaps and indignities, preserving always the comic tone made possible, I suppose, by his eventual triumphs. But tears would sometimes appear in Mother's eyes as she listened beside him.

*

Father's savior proved to be such a germ as he was later to try to eradicate. He came down with typhoid fever, and his life was despaired of. But instead of dying, he was in effect born again.

Resurrected as it were from death, Simon, who had always been regarded as a family liability, became an object of family solicitude, particularly attracting the attention of the mother whom he adored but who had formerly, as she labored heroically to keep the family afloat, pushed him aside. And in his convalescence he for the first time experienced quietude. He had always been pushed around by unsympathetic teachers, hostile classmates, and despicable employers. The family's latest move (the older boys were earning more) had been to a house with a little garden, and there Simon could sit, hour by hour, undisturbed. Louisville having no public library, he had no access to books, which may have been just as well. Other people's thoughts might have interfered with the voyage of exploration he was taking within himself. He found within himself surprising mental strength, increasing self-confidence, a growing conviction of inner potentialities to be realized.

Toward defining these potentialities, he received almost no hints from his parents' backgrounds in Europe. They had come to America to bury their past in a new world. Themselves pursuing Jewish traditions, they made little effort to indoctrinate their children. When they spoke German, their children answered in English. Now, as Simon Flexner dreamed out a future, he determined to understand what was best in American life and, if he could achieve it, make a contribution of his own. No man was ever more devotedly American than the father by whom I was raised.

*

Paying attention at last to their reincarnated son, Simon's family apprenticed him to a highly respectable druggist. The first adult gentile Simon had known treated him with scrupulous fairness. Simon's indentures required sending him to the Louisville College of Pharmacy for two annual three-month sessions. The mind of the former elementary school dropout moved like a race horse, outdistancing all others. To the amazement of his family—his dying father shed tears of joy—Simon brought home the college's gold medal. His mother treasured the medal as a family icon. When Father became engaged, she sent it to his fiancée with a little note, saying that she was sure Helen would treasure it as she had done. The medal now graces my own household as a family icon.

Working now as a registered druggist, Simon gained access to a microscope used for routine studies of specimens. He had found his Aladdin's lamp that fostered an Horatio Alger adventure that became a cornerstone of my existence.

Having started by playing with the microscope as a hobby—he carried it home, working surrounded by his many brothers and sisters on the kitchen table under the one gas jet—Father soon got hold of books and taught himself, before the subjects were even recognized by American medical schools, the rudiments of the sciences, inaugurated in France and Germany, that were the bases of modern medicine: pathology and bacteriology. He published little papers in local medical journals, and planned to found his own laboratory in Louisville serving the local practitioners and making discoveries. But the time came when he found that he could not carry his studies any further all by himself, with his rudimentary equipment and no instruction beyond the few books he could procure. He had never set foot outside the environs of Louisville, but he would have to seek instruction elsewhere.

He quickly set his sights on a just-founded university, the Johns Hopkins, where a teaching laboratory had been established as the first step toward a medical school. But to enroll in what were considered postgraduate courses, he would need a medical degree. His local admirers included the leading practitioner who ran, as an almost private venture, the Medical School of the University of Louisville. They made him a present of an M.D. degree. His brother Abraham, who was running a successful school in Louisville, having lent him $500, he launched out into the great world.

*

It did not take long for Dr. William Henry Welch, who became famous as "the Dean of American Medicine," to realize that a prodigy had emerged from the boondocks into his laboratory. This little man, dressed in crude provincial clothes, speaking in uneducated accents, this self-educated druggist, began almost at once setting up his own experiments and reaching significant results. Flexner stayed at the Hopkins for eight years, becoming a full professor and demonstrating himself, in Welch's words, the most important young pathologist in America.

Despite opposition, a mixture of anti-Semitism, and distrust of the modern scientific medicine being pioneered at the Hopkins, Flexner was called to America's oldest and most venerable medical school, the University of Pennsylvania. The conservatives in the faculty had not altogether got over their feeling that they had condescended when Flexner was to their chagrin called away to such a promising appointment as had never before existed in the United States.

The Rockefellers, John D., Sr. and Jr., had, after soliciting much advice, decided to undertake the revolutionary experiment of founding an independent institution devoted exclusively to medical research. Flexner was offered the directorship. Acceptance was risky, since his professorship at Pennsylvania was a prestigious lifetime appointment, while the Rockefellers, proceeding cautiously, had agreed to support the project for only ten years. No one was sure that enough talent in the new sciences could produce justifying results. In 1901, Flexner took the plunge that brought him to New York City, where I was born seven years later.

By the time I was able to comprehend, the Rockefeller Institute for Medical Research was firmly established as one of the major medical institutions of the world. Since Father got his exercise walking back and forth, we always lived in Manhattan's East Sixties, within walking distance of the augmenting number of buildings which rose fortress-like on the crest of an extensive hillside. The grounds backed on a high bluff dramatically overlooking the East River, and rose in front at a gradual slope over Avenue A (now York Avenue). A stone wall surmounted by a high iron fence ran for several blocks along the avenue. Access was through a high ornamental gate presided over by a watchman with a thick German accent who always greeted me with enthusiastic deference as I grew older and older.*

*

As Dr. Welch gradually retired, Father stepped into his shoes as the leader of the American scientific medical establishment. Under successive governors he served as chairman of the Public Health Council of the State of New York, an advisory body to the Board of Health that had administrative powers of its own. For my brother and me, it was particularly delightful that the very low number of our automobile license plate indicated a high state official who it was wise for the police not to tangle with.

The Rockefeller philanthropies reached out widely, not only across the United States but in many other parts of the world. According to Raymond Fosdick, a longtime director of the Rockefeller Foundation, Father became "the accepted dean of the board, not only its chief scientific adviser, but its 'Knowledgeable Man' to whom one looked for the final nod of approval. It was fascinating to watch him in action. His slight build, his soft voice, his gentle manner, were all in striking contrast to the steely precision of his reasoning. His mind

---

*Long after Father had retired, the name of the Institute was changed to Rockefeller University.

was like a searchlight which could be turned at will on any question that came before the trustees."

How widespread were Father's activities and reputation is signaled by his being elected to seven learned bodies in France, five in Germany, three in England, one or more in Italy, Belgium, Holland, Sweden, Denmark, Venezuela, Argentina, Ecuador, Japan, Russia. He received Japan's highest award, the Order of the Rising Sun, and became a Commander of the Legion of Honor which, we were told, would entitle him to a regiment at his funeral if he were buried in France.

*

Among my mother's attractions for my father was his realization that as inheritor of mature and elevated American traditions she could assist him as a role model. And great as was my pride in Father's leap from humble beginnings, my view of America was broadened because my mother represented another major aspect of our national experience. Her Thomas family had arrived, indirectly from Wales, on the banks of the Chesapeake in 1651. With the other first settlers they had patented the best land to create the aristocracy of Maryland.

The Thomases had come as Puritans, but soon they were converted during a missionary trip by the founder of Quakerism, George Fox. This was so determining an event that almost three hundred years later my mother called an autobiographical book *A Quaker Childhood*. In 1810, Mother's great-great-grandfather broke the family's prosperity by, as a matter of conscience, freeing his some hundred slaves, thus banning himself from plantation life. The family built a new life in Baltimore. There, my grandfather, James Carey Thomas, although a practicing physician, played important roles in the development of American education. He was a founder of Bryn Mawr College, which my aunt, M. Carey Thomas, was to invigorate into a great force in women's education. Dr. Thomas was also one of the founding trustees who, against the advice of the presidents of Harvard, Yale, and Cornell, revolutionized American education by organizing the Johns Hopkins as a graduate university. And Dr. Thomas was so influential in getting going the Hopkins medical school, which introduced scientific medicine into America, that on hearing of the death of the great scientist, the faculty of the medical school marched into his funeral as a body.

*

Mother's mother's family, the Whitalls, were outstanding for religious zeal, feminine power, and—by far the most influential on me—literary interest and achievement. They came to America in the seventeenth century, settling in West Jersey, Quaker territory across the Delaware from Philadelphia. Mother's grandfather, John M. Whitall, captained ships in the China trade, founded a glass manufactory that made him rich, and, as a mystic, spoke twice daily to God. His oldest daughter, Hannah Whitall Smith, my mother's aunt, brought with her own children, to whom Mother was very close, concern and achievements that were directly apposite to what was to be my career. Hannah was an internationally successful writer. Her religious books are currently published in multiple editions. Her oldest daughter, Mary, was to become the wife of Bernard Berenson. Her second daughter was to be the first wife of Bertrand Russell, who became my mother's inspiration and friend. Her son, Logan Pearsall Smith, was to be the highly admired precious essayist whose book *Trivia* is still regarded in some circles as a masterpiece.

Mother herself had passionate literary ambitions. She taught composition at Bryn Mawr. She filled notebooks with eloquent descriptive writing, mostly of nature. After her marriage but before I was born, she finished a novel, somewhat in the manner of Edith Wharton. The one publisher to whom she submitted it was interested enough to make suggestions for changes but they over-discouraged her. She had dreams of a daughter who would fulfill her literary ambitions. But nature presented her with two sons. She tried to indoctrinate my older brother, but his preferences were to make him a mathematician and master statistician. Her efforts with me were so successful that I thought of myself as a writer before I was old enough to learn the alphabet. Only once in my lifetime, as far as I can remember, did I deviate from this ambition.

I was in the cellar of our New York City house, the lair of the coal furnace, where it was against the rules for so small a child to be. From a chute that extended up through a hole to the sidewalk, coal was rushing noisily into a bin beside me. This was in itself worth watching, but my delight came when a man appeared with a shovel to hurry the coal along. He was the dirtiest man I had ever seen, the color of coal from head to foot. My conclusion was instantaneous: he never had to wash! I was perpetually forced by grown-up females to wash. I resolved then and there to be a coal man. Great was my disillusionment when I was told that coal men had women of their own who made them, when they got home, wash. I gave in.

I would have to be a writer after all.

2

THE TWIG IS BENT

*

MY name was first written in my mother's diary for 1908: "James Carey Thomas Flexner was born on Monday morning, January 13, at four o'clock in the morning." The birth took place at home, 105 East Sixty-second Street, my parents' rented brownstone house in New York City.

When I was a month old, I fell out of my crib on my head. Mother wrote Father, "He seems none the worse for it," a verdict which would have been denounced by the pedants and particularly the establishment of academic art historians with whom I was to feud in later years.

*

Mother wrote Father that, as she was breast-feeding "my alert little boy," she thought, "Please God, he will be a happiness to us both down the long years." That was to be a considerable task. Few children have been tossed into so demanding an environment.

Our parents, as they well knew, had nothing tangible, except modest savings, to hand on to their two sons: no hereditary title or honor or clan position except locally in Baltimore, no wealth, no family business, no estate in the country, not even a house they owned in New York. If we were not to have an Icarus-like fall, were to continue to fly in the rarified atmosphere they had attained, it would have to be on our own wings. Helping us to grow wings strong enough to support us was the main objective of our upbringing. It was perpetually brought home to us that what was adequate achievement for others would be disgraceful for us. I was so indoctrinated that this requirement seemed to me an innate part of my nature. When as a young man I was propelled, because I was prevented from living up to this need, by the icy grip of writer's block, to the verge of a nervous breakdown, it never occurred to me to lay any blame on my upbringing.

*

When I was less than two years old, my family moved to 150 East Sixtieth Street, slightly east of Lexington Avenue, another brownstone whose stoop rose from the sidewalk in procession along the street. My earliest remembered reaction to this house came back to me when I first saw the Eiffel Tower in Paris, embroidered with its zigzag of iron stairways. Our house rose from basement to roof five stories, and every step of the stairs was, at first, almost half my height. Although that proportion shrank, the house comes back to me as primarily vertical.

My childhood was imbued with the sounds of New York. The beat of horses' hooves, the shouts of carters, the grinding of iron wheels came in through the windows, silencing at nighttime until it was human footsteps I mostly heard.

Automobiles had only begun to infiltrate the streets. Because one of Father's many medical anxieties was having his children sit in school with wet feet, my earliest automobile rides were an aspect of rainy days. Taxis were called with such frequency that, to my subsequent embarrassment, I supplied the telephone number of the taxi company to my teachers as my own. The high-ceilinged, windowed cabs, where we sat separated by a partition from the drivers, seemed child-sized houses, and I loved to pass in them through the rain-swept city.

Unlike modern escarpments of parked automobiles, the horses tethered beside the sidewalks offered interest and possible companionship to a small child. Among my proudest memories is learning to hold the palm of my hand so completely flat that I would not get bitten as a horse nuzzled for a piece of sugar. Police horses were regarded by my elders as the most reliable, but there were also fascinating creatures attached to wagons. I once saw a horse fall on an icy street but was dragged away by an unfeeling nurse before I could be comforted by seeing it on its feet again.

Horse droppings sustained cheerful inhabitants of the streets: flocks of English sparrows who filled the atmosphere with chirpings and the movement of little wings.

*

Afternoon tea was the only regular occasion when I was allowed to be with both my parents. Leaving Fräulein (my German governess) upstairs, I would join Mother in the parlor where she would be waiting, silver vessels on the table before her, for Father to return from the Institute. There were cakes and sandwiches, and I was allowed very weak tea with a lot of cream and sugar. Since after Father had arrived the conversation was usually beyond my interests, I would look out of the window that was only a half-storey above the street. During winter evenings, when the dusk came early, I would watch for the appearance of a man carrying a long stick on the end of which a little light flickered. He would stop beside each of the evenly spaced lampposts, turn a little spigot, and then touch the end of his pole on the frosted globe overhead. It would spring into luminance. His rhythmical progression, brightening carts and pedestrians as the light reflected from the rows of windows on the opposite side of the street, is still vivid behind my eyes. But there was a sadness in it, since it meant that I would soon be hustled off to bed.

*

I was so active a baby that my parents were worried that I might prefer physical to mental expression, but their fears that I might become an athlete were dispelled by my failure to grow at a normal rate. How small I was was dramatically brought home to me as soon as I was sent to school at the age of four. Every morning, all the students gathered for prayer in the assembly room, the boys marching through one door in single file, the girls through another. When I was chosen to lead the male procession, I was proud of my responsibility to get the ceremony going at the exact moment when a teacher began to tinkle on a piano. But soon the realization came over me that the lines were arranged by height, and I was being daily displayed as the smallest boy in the school. Even in what was primarily a girls' school, boys would scuffle, and I was the smallest of them all.

I was never able to reach five foot six. Years later, when I finally gave in to consulting a psychiatrist, I tried to impress him, vainly as it did not suit his theories, with the importance in my life of the conviction that I could not hold my own in a fistfight. I lacked not only height but reach: the shortest sleeves procurable on ready-made shirts had to be shortened for me. I had to disarm opposition with talk, a task requiring assessment of character. And there was no way for me to express aggressions except through words.

I compensated to some extent for lack of size by intensity of behavior. Stories I came to be told, about how passionately I stared out of my baby carriage, are corroborated to a comic degree by an old picture that must have been taken by one of the photographers who wandered Central Park and its environs trying to lure someone to pose. Judging by my expression, which could be called a basilisk stare, the photographer must have amazed me by ducking under the cloth behind his camera. My brother, three and a half years older, takes it all calmly, as a man of the world.

That I always walked on tiptoe bothered my parents. Father, who had strings of physicians at his beck, took me to a variety of specialists. Having failed to find a physical cause, they diagnosed overeagerness. They assured my parents that when I grew older my weight would bring my heels down to the ground. Mother tried to hurry the change along by repeating a command we had heard given a dog who jumped up on people: "Down, Ponto!" Eventually, my body weight did mend my walking, but at dances I always went up again on my toes. When in much later years I became physically unable to do this, I was at a loss how to dance.

*

I had been born bald, but my head soon sprouted with a growth that was to have a major effect on my life. Red fuzz appeared and then began to twist. My head became topped with curls so far from carrot-color that I was never, except by an occasional stranger, called by the common appellation "Red." The skillful artist who painted my portrait as a boy detected in shadows between the curls a hint of purple. The deep red curls were so tight that the need for a haircut was revealed not by trailing locks but by over-expansion of the explosion above my ears and my forehead. A single strand of hair, if unraveled, could be pulled down to the tip of my nose.

Until it faded when I was in my forties, my red hair made an instantaneous favorable impression wherever I went. I was only four when Mother wrote Father concerning my entrance into a hotel dining room: "As always, he attracted smiles and admiring glances." When I was five, she wrote Bertrand Russell, "Jim is at the moment in a very beautiful stage, but fortunately quite deaf to the praises that echo around him." I would, indeed, have been glad to get out from under my red thatch that attracted "old ladies." Although my definition of an old lady was any female beyond girlhood, the composite picture in my memory of my tormentors was middle-aged, blowsy, and given to drooling sentiment. They were not necessarily people I had ever seen before. As, in Central Park, I ran desperately to make a rescue in a game of prisoners' base, one would appear, block my path, run her hand through my hair, and try to kiss me. Having experienced wet smacks that even in retrospect revolt me, I developed the skill as a sprinter that enabled me at Harvard, despite my short legs, to get on the Freshman track team by running a hundred yards in ten seconds flat.*

Mother became worried lest the attention I always attracted have a deleterious effect on my character. "Everyone smiles who looks at Jimmie, whatever he is doing," she complained, adding that it was "a smile of pleasure not mere amusement. If he combines with this quality gifts of energy and intelligence, he may be both happy and useful in the world. . . . In any merely personal rivalry, his personal power will give him the victory, but the future will hold many struggles of a different sort."

*

Struggles of a different sort! As I entered the age when I should learn to read and write, I failed to do so. There could be no greater

---

*That this, though not sensational for a male, was then faster than the women's world record enabled me to tease Aunt Carey, then president of Bryn Mawr. Her reply was that as soon as women were given a choice, they would run a hundred yards twice as fast as any mere man.

dereliction in such a household as ours. Mother and Father had the choice of considering me frighteningly retarded or inexcusably lazy. While not discounting the first of these possibilities, they preferred to act on the second. There remains a series of snapshots of Mother trying to teach me to read. She is leaning over affectionately, applying to me, as I wiggle in my chair, all the blandishments of a loving and very charming woman. My father's method was the opposite. Inefficiency angered him, and he expressed disapproval with a vehemence that made major scientists quail even in anticipation. He would not shout at me with anger, or rant in a way that a child could in retrospect mock as ridiculous. His resentment was icy, dominated by a lethal glare in his green-gray eyes. To avoid such encounters was a major policy of my childhood. However, there was no way around the fact that I could not read or write. When not under active attack, I did try to pass the dereliction off lightly. My brother's responding hoot of derision engraved on my memory one of my lame sallies: "I won't read until I am twenty-one and then I'll read the newspaper." Such seeming frivolity on so serious a subject deepened my parents' disapproval.

A generation or so later, the cause of my inability to read would have been clear to any informed person because of my parallel difficulty with writing. As I laboriously inscribed capitals in preparation for longhand, there were several letters which, however much I was admonished—even while the scolding was going on—I could not help reversing. Among these were J and F, both essential for writing my name.

I was suffering from a type of dyslexia now known as mixed dominance. It is ruled to be associated with confusion between the functions of the left and the right hand. I have searched my memory in vain for indications that I was corrected when I favored my left hand, but such training could have occurred before memory started recording. I do remember that when I got puzzled about directions, I was taught to orient myself by putting my right hand on my left breast, which I could identify because it was where my heart was supposed to be. My dyslexia waned as the years passed, but has to some extent returned with age: unless I have them firmly written down before me, I cannot help scrambling telephone numbers.

Despite my problem, I felt a need to express myself on paper.

In communications between my parents, a sheet covered with non-representational scribbles was enclosed as my message. Had I become an abstract painter rather than a writer, these would undoubtedly be scanned for deep significance. As it is, they seem random. However, I produced a book, laboriously titled (undoubtedly with adult help), "The Puss and the Rabbit," with a text altogether made up of scribbles.

*

I could still take you to the very spot. In front of the old Arsenal Building in Central Park there is a sunken plaza reached by steps that descend from Fifth Avenue at Sixty-fourth Street. On the downtown side of the plaza, there used to be a bench on which, some eighty years ago, I was sitting holding open in my hand a book about Peter Rabbit. Whoever had been reading to me had temporarily vanished, leaving a terrifying crisis unresolved: Peter Rabbit's little son had been cornered by the wicked fox! Peter was dashing to the rescue, but what could a rabbit do against a fox? After I had discovered, to my great relief, that Peter, inspired by father love, had beaten up the fox, I realized that something even more miraculous had happened. I had read, without hesitation or difficulty, a page all the way to the bottom! The evil spell was broken! This achievement seemed to me so sensational that in my imagination the buildings rising along Fifth Avenue were leaning forward the better to see and admire.

A sequel to this drama became part of the folklore of the Rockefeller Institute. The director is to deliver a speech and his little son is brought in to hear his father. It is observed that I am brandishing in my hand a book about Peter Rabbit. Naturally, I am asked why. Not wishing to tell the truth—that the book was a boast that I could now read to myself—I answered that I thought it a good idea to have it handy in case Father's speech was dull.

My ability to read having unblocked my ability to write, a deluge followed. I even became my own first publisher. Preserved is a small notebook with a professional cover. The title: "Bedtime Stories," with below it a drawing of a little animal, then the author's name with the J reversed but the F firmly in place. "Illustrated by ʃames Flexner"; the publisher given as "ʃames Flexner Co." The forty-two pages include a preface, a table of contents, a list of illustrations, and eight stories each following a half-title. The handwritten text, all in capital letters, is so misspelled, reversed, smudgy, and sparsely punctuated as to preclude adult supervision.

There is perhaps a hint of a biographer's approach in a six-page pamphlet titled "The Jolly Puppy." Opening paragraph (here repunctuated and respelled): "Puppy was born in a nice little house in a beautiful garden. In the same house lived his father, Growler, and his mother, Blacky. The first thing he remembered was that a boy put a collar on him. [Small drawing of collar.] You know that a puppy can understand what you say. So, he heard what he said. 'What can I call my puppy? Of course, Woof Woof. Yes, that is what I will call him.' And puppy said in dog language to Blacky, 'I am not his dog. What does he mean?' And Blacky said, 'You are his dog. I am his father's dog. You must not bite him for if you are bad he will hurt you. And now your name is Woof Woof.' 'Yes,' said Woof Woof, 'but it is so strange.' 'That may be so,' said Growler, 'but you will get used to it.'"

For my all-staff-written magazine, "The Show," I lettered an advertising poster stating ambitiously that it would be "issued twice a month or oftener," the price, fifty cents a copy, subscription a dollar. My parents insisted that I could not charge money as the subscribers would all be relations or family friends. I would have to accept pins as token money. I had no use for pins. However, my concern was not with gain but with art.

Eight issues were published between March and September 1917. I often had to apologize in "Editor's Notes" for falling behind schedule: I had been sent to bed early or the hectograph had failed to work.

My printing office was the boys' bathroom, the press was the hectograph, an oblong frying pan containing a flat, waxy substance. Using special ink, I would prepare a page—illustrations, titles in caps, text in longhand—and then press the paper, face down on the hectograph. Enough ink was supposed to be absorbed so that when a blank page was subsequently pressed down the image would appear. Commercial hectographs were available. However, since brother William enjoyed such operations, he mixed the chemicals. The great scientist, Dr. Simon Flexner, acted as consultant, yet some pages came out hardly legible.

As editors of literary magazines discover to their chagrin, quality is less likely to make a smash hit than topicality. Mother was active in the campaign for the Woman Suffrage Amendment, and I was encouraged to stop adult women in the park. If they confessed to being "antis" (as those opposed to the amendment were called), I would sententiously ask, "Madam, don't you believe in yourself?"

The publication in "The Show":

> Hark, hark, hear the lark
> Singing so merrily
> In a tree so tall
> "Woman suffrage over all"
> Trittree, twittree.
>
> I sing of the free
> Yes, you and me
> Singing a song
> Of the antis who are wrong
>
> I am singing way up high
> In the sky
> Yes, I, yes, I
> Twittree, twittree.

My subscriber, the president of Bryn Mawr College, had the poem typed up, and wrote my mother that she was going to send it to various Women's Suffrage leaders. My reaction was dismay at having my privacy thus violated. Aunt Carey then wrote me with a respect for my childish dignity surprising for that tartar to her faculty, "Your mother tells me *The Show* is quite confidential." She was glad that she had not yet dispatched any copies, and was sending me all the typed versions. Should I feel like forwarding one to Anna Howard Shaw (the president of the National American Woman Suffrage Association), "I think she wouid be pleased." I have no memory of whether or not I did send a copy.

*

Poems written by a child, like much of what is now called "folk art," are of very uneven quality because the creator is not in conscious control of his medium. He cannot revise without muddying. Inspiration has to strike true in the initial blow. But if it does so strike, the result displays the purity and profundity of innocence.

My flooding nine-year-old poetic *oeuvre* is mostly just immature, but there remains this plea written in a year of terrible war:

> Oh sun!
> You know of wealth untold
> Oh, orb of glittering gold
>   Sailing across the sky
> Give us, oh sun, the light
> That will make the dim world bright
>   Make peace that can never die.

3

DIVIDED LOYALTIES

*

WHEN, as an old man, I was walking along Broadway, I saw a legend raised high on the marquee of a movie theater: "A million light years from the world and all alone." My heart contracted to see my lifelong fear thus displayed.

When I was a child, I was walking with my governess beside me in New York's Central Park. I can still see the broad asphalt walk that curved to the right as it wound gradually upward. On the rising surface, children were running, old people pacing along. There was much sound of voices. But suddenly I was struck with the horrifying realization that everything I was seeing and hearing, even the pavement beneath my feet, was not really there. All could in an instant vanish, leaving me all alone in utter emptiness.

It has been a major sorrow of my life, which I have, alas, inflicted on the people I have loved, that when one of them is away from home I am tortured by anxiety lest the absent one disappear forever. If there were a carpet in the front hall of my long-inhabited apartment, it would have a track worn in it where in anguish, for hours on end, I have passed back and forth, listening for the stopping of a midnight elevator. With what anxiety have I met trains and planes to be filled with despair when among the first-appearing faces was not the one I sought. I cannot sleep for several nights before I myself set out on a trip for fear that I will never again find my way home.

When I was a child, my parents observed that I became frightened when left by myself for more than a few minutes. They attributed this to my having received too much attention from my successive German governesses (who were all designated "Fräulein"). It was ruled that I should remain alone in the playroom for half an hour every day. This, all the more because I was ashamed of my need, was torture. My toys lay untouched as, in despair and with a sense of degradation, I listened, it seemed interminably, for the sound of the governess's returning footsteps. My parents must have realized that their experiment had boomeranged since the enforced sessions were soon abandoned. However, this situation and its outcome could not have pleased Father, and was probably among the reasons he considered me so inferior in my development to my brother.

*

Mother had never been a happy woman. Long before she had met her husband, she had, as I was in my turn to do, sought sanctuary from the ills her nerves were heir to in the pursuit of her chosen career as a literary writer. But that weapon (as I was to learn almost too grievously) turns in your hand and points itself against your own breast if the ideas and words will not come, if the paper before you becomes a desperate scramble or remains blank. Thus, it engenders further self-doubt, frustration, despair.

When Mother met Father she was deep in writer's block. Part of her hope for her marriage was that her husband's continual creativity and strength of purpose would help her get going with her own career. But it had not worked out that way.

*

It was the norm in my parents' world to employ as governesses foreign women who would, in addition to their nursing duties, inoculate their charges, at an early age, with a second language. The choice was between Fräuleins and mademoiselles. My parents' decision, as subsequent events were to exemplify, was not a product of any loyalty descending from Father's background. Since Germany exerted a major influence on American science, scientists employed Fräuleins.

Fräuleins came and went until shortly before the outbreak of World War I there appeared the woman who was to cast such a shadow over my life. A vivid memory depicts my trying to pay attention to playing with my toys while keeping watch on the door for the emergence of the new Fräulein who I knew was expected. What she was like would be of tremendous importance since I would spend in her presence almost all my hours, waking and sleeping.

There appeared a short narrow woman holding herself very upright, with a long neck and a small shield-shaped head under mouse-colored hair. Her eyes behind rimless glasses were serious and intent, her mouth drawn in a firm line. Her manner was very ingratiating, and I was not put off at seeing so powerful a person, since Fräuleins were from day to day my security. They comforted and dispelled, as far as they could, my terrors; they protected me from my older brother's attacks; they were my refuge outside the house; they were my reliance in my chronic anxiety that I would find myself all alone in an alien world.

Elizabeth Hoch proved to be a super Fräulein. When Father was called to China to help establish the Rockefeller-endowed Peking Union Medical College, Mother despaired of going along until she persuaded herself that Fräulein could handle the boys and the servants in her absence. No mishaps having resulted, Fräulein became a fifth, if auxiliary, member of the family of whom Mother was very fond.

When World War I broke out in Europe, Fräulein was strongly in favor of her homeland. As early as September 1914 domestic trouble was presaged. Mother wrote Father of being "in high spirits yesterday. I only hope today's paper will confirm the German retreat. Fräulein is bearing up very well . . . and really tries, I think, not to worry about the war."

Whether or not Fräulein tried, she certainly did not succeed. As my perpetual companion, she indoctrinated me with pro-Germanism. I celebrated with her German victories, mourned German defeats as a matter of course.

The date was May 7, 1915. As Mother and I were waiting by the tea table in the ground-floor drawing-room for Father to come home from the Institute, male voices from the street were crying "Extree! Extree!" However, I paid little attention as during the war the sale of evening papers was often enhanced with such shouts. The sound of Father's key turning the lock was routine, but then the situation became wild. Father did not approach at his usual measured pace but entered the room at a run, a newspaper dangling from his hand, his face working with emotion. He yelled—I remember the exact words—"The *Lusitania* has been sunk. Wilson will have to stop stalling." After I had run upstairs to consult Fräulein, she told me the Kaiser had been absolutely justified in sinking the *Lusitania*.

Like their whole world, from the Rockefellers down, my mother and father were inflicted with a sense of shame that the United States was not standing beside Great Britain in saving the world from "barbarism." Of this it was impossible for me to remain ignorant or indifferent. My classmates in school reflected the attitudes of their parents. The multitudes of American flags that were augmenting in our view from our bay window looking up and down Madison Avenue spoke of war—and there was I, sharing with Fräulein our little two-room apartment on the top storey of our house, hearing from my mainstay and perpetual companion, and being expected to agree with, blasts of praise for the Kaiser and joy at German victories. The storm was approaching the breaking point when on February 3, 1917, President Wilson severed diplomatic relations with Germany. My family hailed this as the final step toward war between Fräulein's Germany and my own native land.

On February 8, Mother noted in her diary, "Little Jim has been having a hard experience with Fräulein. . . . He made up his mind that the Germans had become 'too vicious,' as he phrased it, for him to uphold them any longer, and being a firm little person he made his opinion clear to Fräulein in his quiet way. . . . She was greatly upset by the break with Germany and no doubt feels the lack of Jimmie's customary sympathy. Be that as it may, she has spent two days in crying and poor little Jim feels he cannot bear it any longer. I spoke to Fräulein this morning, recommending she go over to stay with some German friends on Sunday for I cannot have little Jim's life darkened by her emotionality. Poor creature, it is not that I am not sorry for her. I realize how bitterly hard the situation is, but it has to be borne for there is no way out." When Fräulein returned after two days' absence, Mother assumed that "little Jim's life" would no longer be darkened by her pro-German "emotionality."

The United States soon declared war. Then, almost everything around me fed my sense of guilt, my resentment at having been led into supporting the enemies of my country. I had been betrayed into betrayal! Although still in her company and still acutely dependent on her, I began, without conscious avowal, to hate Fräulein.

*

So totally that I must have known, Father was devoting his energies and his Institute to the medical problems of the war. He was perpetually in Washington conferring with the Surgeon General. He was a member of the National War Board and the Medical Advisory Committee of the American Red Cross. He labored to bring sanitation to the exploding army camps. Two constant visitors in our house—Dr. Alexis Carrel and Dr. Henry M. Dakin—had developed a cure for the gangrene that otherwise made minor battle-wounds fatal. To teach the medical officers how to apply the "Carrel–Dakin solution," a base hospital was erected on the Institute grounds. I visited there, and saw the damaged soldiers lying under treatment with their limbs trussed up in the air.

Father was commissioned a major (he rose to colonel). To give leverage to his inspections of military camps, he needed to wear a uniform. However, he ordered one with reluctance and, after he had tried it on, noted, "Cannot say I am particularly pleased with the result." He was never at ease in his uniform, lowering his eyes when he saw approaching him a soldier who would salute him and have to be saluted in turn.

*

We took off to New Hampshire for the summer, but in the country as in the city the Fräulein crisis gnawed at me like a damaged nerve. Even Mother, who saw her so much less often, found her elation at German victories, her depression at German defeats, "very tiring," although "one sympathizes." Then Fräulein sneered that Father was "busy playing soldier." William asked what she meant, and Mother said, "Yes, Fräulein, what do you mean?" She smiled and said, "Everybody is playing soldier now." At first, Mother was "very angry over her insolence, and then I forgave her. She dreams of her delicate niece going hungry, and then dying of insufficient food, and cannot be judged strictly, poor thing."

A few days later: Fräulein was "extremely disagreeable at breakfast," Mother wrote. "She makes conversation almost impossible, poor woman." "It would be a relief to get rid of her, yet one must be kind and self-controlled. [As a German, Fräulein could not get another job.] I take pleasure in our big flag which still hangs among the trees."

If Mother needed comfort herself for Fräulein's occasional outbursts in her presence, where was I, who was in effect to Fräulein a perpetual prisoner of war, to find release? I collected enamel pins featuring shields with stars and stripes, American flags, and other patriotic symbols, pinning them on my clothes in such profusion that when I stooped I clattered. I pestered Father to wear his uniform, threatening otherwise to call him a "mock-major," and when he put it on, I followed him around with my child's box camera, clicking and clicking. My anxiety as the films were being developed was extreme, and I stuck the three most satisfactory results up on my mirror where, when I looked in, they surrounded my face. "Jim," Father noted, "has never been so intimate with me. Almost before he is dressed in the morning, he tiptoes into my room with questions and plans."

On a family spree, a day-long motor excursion deeper into the White Mountains, something happened that Father noted briefly in his diary: "Poor Jim was carsick." This was the first recorded physical symptom of the nervous ailments that were to darken my life.

*

The effect of my wartime traumas was long lasting. Well after peace had returned, I was still writing poems that placed me in the middle of the horrors of war:

Over the Top

We charged, we charged, and I fell
We charged into the center of hell
And here in the shell hole I lie
Listening to the wounded cry.
There around me lie the brave
Destined to an early grave.
I saw a man hit clean in the head
Down he fell, stone, stark dead.
The heroes' hearts' blood

Makes the field red.
Machine guns spit their murderous lead.
There flies Old Glory high
Every man for it would die.
Then I heard a frightful roar
I felt a pain
I knew no more.

To rid myself of the guilt of my pro-German treason, I forced myself to stop being bilingual. Taught German since infancy, I had spoken it almost as fluently as English. My resentment of this knowledge was amplified by my discovery in school that Schiller had, in his play *Die Jungfrau von Orleans*, utterly altered Joan of Arc's character by inventing a romance with an English officer. That the author Germans considered their "national poet" should have been guilty of such venality was the straw that broke the camel's back. My knowledge of German vanished from my conscious mind. I assume that it is still hidden in some cranny of my brain since an occasional German phrase sometimes automatically appears on my lips.

Why in all the years that have passed have I continued to suppress my German? How significant is it that my childhood sense of guilt engendered a compensating passionate pride in the United States? To what extent this influenced the eventual direction of my career it is impossible to say. But there can be no doubt that the strains created by my relationship with Fräulein had made me more vulnerable to the outside pressures that were to throw me into what would be diagnosed today as a nervous breakdown.

*

Mother had noted while the war was still flaming and Fräulein was still at my throat that my habitual gregariousness had altogether disappeared. "Never has there been so exclusive a person as little Jim. He likes no outsiders of any sort. Were he not so attractive personally, I should be greatly bothered by this obsession of his, but I feel that when he does wake up to the delights of outside companionship, he will find no difficulty in obtaining it. However, I try to influence him to like people as much as I can. Forcing him at this stage would only deepen his distaste, I fear."

4

PARIAH

*

THE Lincoln School of Teachers College was the brain child of my Uncle Abraham Flexner, who, often in consultation with Father, secured from the Rockefeller-supported General Education Board the necessary funds. Its object was to revolutionize American primary and secondary education with a curriculum "better suited to modern times." Abe expressed scorn for all tradition for which "an affirmative case could not be made" for communicating "real situations." No grammar, no memorizing of historical facts, no "obsolete and disgusting" classics. Reflecting the freedom of the individual, the school would discard "all formal discipline."

On April 1, 1917, when I was nine, Father noted in his diary with "great satisfaction" that both his boys had been accepted for the school. He expressed no concern that in its first year the school would have no class suitable for me. Did not the prospectus promise that "proper provision will be made for all admitted"?

Father had to be in San Francisco during the opening of the school and for a month thereafter. He wanted Mother to be there too, and overruled her when she expressed concern at leaving Fräulein in complete charge at so crucial a time. "I don't want to be indifferent to their [the boys'] point of view, but I don't want to be over-impressed by it."

Mother did her best by having her college roommate Lucy Donnelly, whom we called "Aunt Lucy," come to New York to take me to the Lincoln School for the first day. Forced to return instantly to

Bryn Mawr, where she was professor of English, she was worried into sending Mother a modified S.O.S.: "Fräulein is most competent practically but spiritually unstable. . . . I am particularly glad that you are in California and not in China." But Mother might as well have been in China. Father had no intention of pampering his younger son.

The opening of the Lincoln School had been a whirlpool of confusion, so much so that Uncle Abe, finding himself a target for clamoring, considered it prudent to flee. Every arrival was given a slip with the number of a room on it. But there was no method for finding the numbered room except by traipsing around the halls, wading through a sea of other bewildered seekers. Little by little the confusion subsided, but Aunt Lucy and I, when we did find our number, could not believe that we were in the right room. It was filling up with boys and girls so much my senior that my small figure was submerged like a sapling in a forest.

It developed that the "proper provision" made for the fifth-, sixth-, and seventh-graders, for whom specific classes had not been organized, was to throw them all together in one middle-sized room with a single classroom teacher. Not only small for my age but a year younger than even my fellow fifth-graders, I was surrounded with boys and girls sometimes four or even five years my senior.

This might seem a return to the old one-room schoolhouse of American tradition, but the differences were profound. Then, the children, whose parents knew each other, all came from the same background, and the teacher kept order even if she had to wield a ruler. New York was a various city—I had never before seen even one of my fellow pupils—and the mix had been enlarged for idealistic reasons by bringing in boys from extremely tough neighborhoods. Since I had previously been eduated in a tiny and gentle class in what was primarily a girls' school dedicated to good manners and decorum, my plight was that of a half-grown housecat thrown into a jungle.

My tininess and obvious ill-ease attracted the bullies, perhaps because they felt themselves personally insulted by being grouped with something so puny. The attacks were basically different from those I had been inured to by my brother. He wished to express his irritation and demonstrate his power. My new assailants wished to inflict pain. One who had picked me out as a victim had a way of twisting my arm which was excruciating. And I was as helpless as a rabbit caught in a snare.

In school there was no hope of intervention since no effort was made to restrain the behavior of anybody. At home, I had only Fräulein with her repulsive pro-German ardors. She, of course, was anxious to protect little Jimmie, but she could think of nothing except coming and sitting beside me in the classroom, which, however for the moment reassuring, filled me with shame, and made me when she was not there all the more an object for attack.

*

When my parents finally appeared in late October, Father wrote, "Now that we are in New York again, the boys' problems loom large. The new school is still unorganized and not completely staffed. . . . We can make little or nothing out of Jim's work. It matters less this year for him, as he is on the whole developing more slowly than William did. . . . I've seen Abe who looks tired. He has many things on his hands. The addition of the school—his own pet project—may be too much."

Considering me, in contrast with his own beleaguered childhood, a "spoiled darling," Father had no sympathy with my plight.

A month later, on November 28, Mother wrote Bertrand Russell concerning the Lincoln School: "If you were here, I could make you laugh over some of the things that have happened, for the management, with its head in the rarified atmosphere of theories, overlooked some of the most obvious necessities. Also, a belief in allowing the children great freedom in conduct has unfortunately resulted in little Jimmie's being badly terrorized by some of the older boys. . . . The little fellow has suffered greatly and is not likely to have a much pleasanter memory of the freedom of the Lincoln School than Shelley had of the tyranny of Eton. This has been a great source of anxiety to me, and even yet Jim has not recovered his normal spirits. However, we are sticking it out and still hope for good results."

Also in mid-November, Mother wrote Father, "Poor little Jim began the day by wanting to escape school . . . and actually cried after breakfast and was nauseated to the point of vomiting a little."

In response to a similar letter, Lucy wrote that it had "distressed me greatly for little Jim. . . . I hate to hear of the child suffering so cruelly, though I realize with you the necessity of his not being too softly treated and for learning to make his way in the world. . . . I do hope Miss Hall can help."

Miss Jennie Hall was my classroom teacher. Aunt Lucy had described her as "a thoughtful, kind woman," but she was clearly overwhelmed by the chaos in her classroom and indeed in the whole school. When invited to tea by Mother, "to talk Jim over," Miss Hall said, "'He seems to be unable to concentrate and is distracted by everything!' I told her his teachers had never before made such a complaint. . . . She seemed distressed to hear that Jimmie suffered so much."

Miss Hall alleviated her distress by assigning to me a project that got me out of the classroom and out of her sight. The school had a print shop with shelves of type and a hand-powered press. I was to set up "The Charge of the Light Brigade" and print a copy for each member of the class. At arranging the individual letters in proper sequence and then going on to another line I could succeed, however slowly. But before a block of type could be put on the printing press it had to be locked in a case which was tightened on all four sides by screws. The resulting pressure was supposed to hold in position the thousand or so individual pieces of type. The instructor explained to me that for success the edges of the type block had to be made altogether even. If one line was only a tiny bit too long, when I picked up the case all the type would fall through.

Finally, the whole poem was set up. Then I attended to the edges with all the care the tremor of my nerves and hands allowed. It was with a sense of triumph and relief that my drudgery was almost over that I raised the case from the table and started to carry it toward the printing press. The case seemed to jump in my hands as, with a crumbling crash, all the type fell out and scattered across the printing room floor.

I was now further behind than at the very beginning, since every piece of type had to be picked up from the floor and sorted into its correct alphabetical box. This I achieved, and then I began to set up again, laboriously, probably more slowly than before, line by line. Eventually, the whole poem lay again on the table. How hard I worked to get everything even! Finally, I put the case around the block and I tightened the screws. I twisted them as tight as my small boy's hands would allow. Gingerly, I raised the block an eighth of an inch. An unevenness appeared on the surface, so, dropping the block back onto the table, I unscrewed the case, identified (as I thought) the type line that was an iota too long, shortened it an iota, and screwed the case up again. This time a timorous trial showed no irregularity. I picked up the case to carry it to the printing press, it leapt upward in my hands, and the type scattered all over the floor.

How often, during the long semester when I was assigned nothing else, I went through these maneuvers I do not know. But the frustration, the horror, and the fear are still alive in my mind. Was this to be my entire life? Would I never escape? I could not foresee that this experience, with others as traumatic that were to follow, would make possible my career as a wide-ranging biographer.

I suppose that the shop instructor finally took pity on me and evened the edges himself. In any event, as the school year was drawing to an end, I did have a printed copy which I was enabled to distribute to the rest of the class. Miss Hall was, of course, full of praise and compliments, but recipients made no pretense of being impressed, and I was deeply humiliated by this pitiful result of a year's labor. Not only was I an utter failure, but I was the class pariah, and I knew it.

As for Miss Hall, she justified herself by urging Father to accept and act on the realization that he had a son with a subnormal intelligence.

Had Father not lived through as disastrous a childhood, been considered the class dunce and a subject of mockery, had to repeat the seventh grade in school and failed to finish the eighth, been unable to hold even the most demeaning job, and been shown the jail as his ultimate destination, and had not his ultimate destination been greatness and fame, he would undoubtedly not have sent me back to the school where I had been considered subnormal. But Father's fear was of my being made a weakling by overindulgence in a childhood so different from his.

In September 1918 I found that the worst hazards of my first year at Lincoln existed no longer. My class had become an entity. No more rough older boys. Miss Hall had vanished. A new teacher did little more than preside over study periods. We went to rooms where other teachers expounded, and I trouped along with the others.

Buoyed up by a new gym teacher, Mr. Goucher, I came to enjoy roughhousing with the other boys. I was delighted to find that despite my small size, I did not fare too badly. But the teacher created for me a new impediment.

The gymnasium roof was supported by an iron beam about seven feet above the floor. It was about eight inches wide. Although there was nothing to hold onto except occasional struts rising at an angle, Goucher lined up the boys to prove their manhood by walking in procession across the beam. But when my turn came I was unable to step out. I had to push my way back to the ground through mocking faces.

I know now that this was an aspect of my fear that, if I lost control, "reality" would vanish. This fear made me as a child dread snowstorms, since custom would require that I go sledding, and, once the sled was off, there was no way it could be stopped. I could not even turn somersaults because I dreaded the moment when my body would proceed on its course whatever my will. At an older age, when I went out with girls on a multiple date, I resisted, as far as I could without explaining, plans to visit amusement parks lest I be humiliated by my inability to ride on roller coasters. However, my phobia has done me the service of protecting me, although I enjoy drinking, from drunkenness. As soon as I feel myself beginning to lose control, I draw back.

Goucher had no sympathy with my difficulty concerning the beam, which he regarded as cowardice not to be condoned. He re-created the situation again and again. My reiterated failures made any assimilation with other members of the class impossible. But the resulting isolation was nothing compared to the trauma of the previous year. I did not enjoy school, but I did not fear it.

*

It was during my third year, when I was not yet thirteen, that my father noted in his diary an amazing change. I could not get off for school quickly enough, came home late, and chattered endlessly— Father's major complaint against me was my talkativeness—about what had taken place at school.

A miracle had happened. The gym teacher was still making the boys walk the beam, but it was now accepted that when I got to the stepping-off place, I would be unable to go on. The boys behind me would routinely make space for me to flee down the ladder. Then one morning I found myself walking without tremor across the beam.

Almost immediately, Alan Boles and Breading Furst asked me to join them in an empty classroom. Tall and strong, Alan was the star athlete; he had bats' ears, was noisy, loyal, somewhat insensitive, jocose, and very good-humored. Breading, although showing equal high spirits, was basically of a dark temperament, over-sensitive, and subtle. They were the leading and liveliest boys in the class, and I looked up to them with admiration. They told me they had long considered making me a third in their relationship, but only when and if I proved myself by walking across the beam. They did not doubt that I would be eager to join them, as indeed I was.

But I still had to pass an examination. Breading enunciated and Alan wrote on the blackboard, "Father Uncle Cousin Kate." Underlining the capital letters they achieved "FUCK." Did I know what the word meant? I did not. They told me to find out and when I knew I could join their fellowship.

The word was not in any dictionary (which was probably why it seemed so magic to my potential new friends). I had to ask Father. He replied that it meant love between unpleasant people. I carried this definition back to Alan and Breading, who accepted it as demonstrating that I had enough sophistication to be a third in their fellowship. This was among the most significant happenings in my life. Through the rest of my school career, Alan and Breading remained my staunch friends. My role as pariah was completely reversed. The three of us came to establish over student life in the school a virtual hegemony.

5

HOME FIRES BURNING

*

THE autumn of 1918, when I was ten, I journeyed down a single flight of stairs: from the top floor suite where I had been imprisoned with Fräulein to a small room next to Mother's bedroom. This signaled my acceptance in the household as more than just a small child.

The relationship thus established with my parents was to be the sustaining force of my developing years. Never sent to a summer camp or going elsewhere except for a short visit, I was constantly with my mother and father until at the age of seventeen I went off to Harvard. After that, as long as they lived, I continued in town with my parents. New York City was our common home ground, and we often spent the summers with or near each other.

Our associations were from day to day placid. Even when I was young my parents enforced few restrictions that I found irksome; we never confided to each other to any depth that could engender conflict. Perhaps the even tenor of our way was made more feasible because my older brother, William, created concern and spice. Concern because he was haunted by respiratory difficulties that threatened tuberculosis. Spice because of his perpetual fights with Father, whom, as the older son, he felt he had to challenge. Father found intimacy in the battles. His diary abounds with speculations about William's states of mind, but never wonders about mine. William was Father's favorite; I was Mother's.

*

Close friends of my parents were Christian and Susan Herter, each rich. Christian's father, a colleague of Louis Tiffany's, had made his fortune as interior designer for the grand mansions being built by the very rich. Father's intimate was both a scientist and a financier, a member of the Rockefeller Institute and its treasurer. The Herters had built a modest mansion on Madison Avenue between Sixty-eighth and Sixty-ninth Streets, designed by the architects of the New York Public Library, Carrière and Hastings. When the spacious but not elaborate house next door became vacant, the Herters bought it for real estate reasons, and offered it to my parents for a rent they could pay. Bigger than we needed, we rattled around in it with our three Irish maids. This was my home from young boyhood until after I had graduated from college.

Mrs. Herter, whom I called "Aunt Susan," gave my parents for me a hundred dollars (now more than a thousand) when I was born and for every succeeding birthday until I was twenty-one, a fund to which my parents periodically added. Although about my mother's age, she was my first love. As with the many older males whose wives found her worrying, she was charming to me, but on my own childhood terms. I remember my great pride when, after I had wondered if there was a First Street, she sent me downtown alone like an adult on the back seat of her chauffeur-driven limousine.

The most fascinating aspect of our house was a second-storey bay window which offered a more than 180-degree view up and down Madison Avenue. Year after year it revealed New York to my sight: wagons gradually replaced by automobiles; girls, as I became more interested, open to view in ever-varying costumes for every season; streetcars rumbling by, evenly spaced up and down the avenue, or so stalled during snowstorms. Add that I lived within a short block of Central Park, where I was first taken by Fräulein to play and then flirtatiously escorted girls who grew older as I did. The total result was that despite the time I spent in New England and my stays in Europe, I have always been a New Yorker at heart.

*

Since I had been raised in comfortable affluence, I came to be treated with great snobbishness by professional proletarians. Actually, the view of the underprivileged presented to me through the memories, instincts, and behavior of my father was the fruitful biographical view. I was to write of other self-made men. The poor who do not escape can appear only as statistics in sociologists' tables or as generalizations in political diatribes. They do not generate those personal documents that are essential to the biographer.

No religious conflicts troubled my upbringing. Father, having been born with the mind of a scientist, was unconcerned with matters undemonstrable. At an early age, he lost what Jewish faith he had imbibed from his immigrant parents. The Reformed rabbis he had met as a youth had wished to make Judaism a world religion and were thus forced to abandon the conception of a Jewish race separate from the gentiles. According to their doctrine, a person was a Jew, whatever his background, if he believed in "the religion of Moses." It followed that a person who did not believe was not a Jew. Although he was plagued by anti-Semitism, Father never thought of himself as a Jew, preferring to throw all his loyalty, beyond his primary dedication to science, into being a patriotic American. This American patriotism I inherited from him, along with his lack of concern with Judaism.

Mother's upbringing was many times as religious as Father's. As we have seen, she called her autobiography *A Quaker Childhood*. After her own mother had killed herself by relying on God to cure her of the breast cancer, Mother broke away from the Society of Friends, but it was too deep a part of her nature to be expelled. She remained a profound believer in the Christian virtues.

Once he had left Louisville, Father never moved in Jewish circles, although, of course, he employed Jewish scientists at the Institute, some of whom became our friends. Mother had never moved in Jewish circles. The world in which William and I were raised was Christian in ethic and behavior, although only rarely devout. With Father's approval, Mother prepared us to be at home in that world. Somewhat of a crisis was raised when John D. Rockefeller, Jr., invited my parents to send me to the Baptist Sunday School class he himself taught. Despite Father's desire to please his benefactor and friend, the invitation was refused. But Mother took us occasionally to church so that we would know how to behave there, and read to us passages from the Bible as examples of great literature. As for synagogues, I did not know enough to keep my hat on when first assigned there in my twenties when on the *Herald Tribune*.

In all the hundreds of letters between my parents I have read, in all the thousands of diary references, I have never come on a single mention of their difference in religious background. None of their variances of attitude of which I was conscious came over to me as being religious or racial. The "Jewish question" lay altogether outside of our family circle. Yet my parents knew that their children would, to a greater or lesser degree, experience anti-Semitism. We would have to be prepared to encounter it, and were thus warned. As it turned out, although there were flurries, I can recall no occasions when any path I wished to follow was seriously blocked.

*

Although Father had plenty of self-confidence to operate powerfully in his professional world, he always relied on Mother's instinctive understanding of social behavior within the environment to which he had not been born. He concluded that educating their sons in the ways of the world should be entrusted to Mother. Her basic definition of courtesy, mingled with my natural gregariousness, was to enable me to find my way in almost any civilized social situation.

Mother was always loving, gentle, and kind, far from a depressing companion. She kept her inner darkness so well hidden that I was amazed, when examining family papers decades later, by the melancholy in her diaries and by her sometimes desperate letters to Father. Within my range of hearing she complained that she was prevented by the interference of household duties from achieving the results she sought in her writing. Father assigned her a room at the Institute with a beautiful view over the East River where she could work in solitude, but that did not suffice. The emphasis during my upbringing on writer's block as a destroyer may have encouraged my eventual desperation when engulfed in the same malady.

Although Mother could not, as her evangelical background made her feel she should, remedy any deep social wrongs, she was active in the Women's Suffrage Movement and perpetually concerned with the inner workings of what was going on at Bryn Mawr. To her family circle she never applied the expletive "Outrage!" which we teased her for applying so often to exterior events. She was amused by family contretemps, enjoyed jokes even on herself. She smoothed over difficulties. Although never hilarious, she was often high-spirited.

She paid her compliments to New York's rich society in her diary description of a dinner party given by the Rockefellers: "A gathering of many rich people with many shining jewels adorning old ladies, inappropriate as it seemed to my unworldly eyes. Mrs. Harriman would have looked the charming, intelligent, benevolent person I am sure she really is had it not been for the circle of diamonds about her white hair, and the great pearl on her wrinkled forehead. Mrs. Cornelius Vanderbilt is, of course, a great goose but handsome, so that her jewels fitted her better, and the untidy mop of white hair she had encircled with sparkling jewels did somewhat suggest a French marquise. In these conditions, the men were obviously outshone. John Rockefeller, looking like the determinedly-minded good boy and Cornelius Vanderbilt like the narrow-minded fool of the party. General Gorgas' face does not suggest his ability, but Mr. Crane's does his vacuity. Only genial old Mr. Morse was a pleasure to see, a human being he and a lover of horses. The Mayor has a fine upstanding figure and a sharp intelligent face and Simon's distinction always shows. Mr. Ed Robinson, who came in for the music, brought up the level of the men. But oh! the vulgarity of Mrs. Walter James and her sister, a hideous, dumpy creature in turquoise velvet and a diamond tiara a foot high. . . . The old music played on the old instruments was enchanting, but how in such a company was one to enjoy such a fine and delicate thing?"

Mother kept such rebellious comments to herself. Her southern graciousness combined with her Quaker simplicity and brightened by her red-headed beauty made her very attractive to the conservative social group to which many of my parents' friends belonged. She enjoyed pleasing with her soft manner and her tact, while secretly applying her critical faculties. One of her games was to experiment on whether it was possible to flatter a man too much: her skill was so great that she concluded that it was not possible. Roger Fry, Bloomsbury's anointed art critic, ruled that Helen Flexner was the most delightful American woman he had ever met.

*

The family's concern with the arts in New York City was, except for the theater, conventional for their social circle. They subscribed to the Philharmonic Orchestra. They took me to the Metropolitan Museum but by no means as assiduously as they would visit museums in Europe. Their closest painter friends were well-off and well-bred: Adele and Alfred Herter.* Adele was a highly accomplished pastelist who worked for that medium on a tremendous scale. Father arranged for her to do for the University of Pennsylvania the full-length of him standing in his laboratory (illustrated in this volume). He had a yen for Adele even as Mother had for Bertrand Russell.

Mother's friendship with two of the founders of the Museum of Modern Art, Lillie Bliss and Abby Rockefeller, did not lead her far toward such advanced taste, although we attended the historic opening of the museum. We did subscribe to the *Dial*, the avant-garde literary magazine that was often contributed to and sometimes edited by Mother's former pupil at Bryn Mawr, and still her friend, Marianne Moore.

I was encouraged, when a young man, to take some of my short stories for criticism to the flat in Brooklyn where Moore lived with her mother. The stories depicted the world I knew, with its liquor and sexual freedom. Moore, instead of giving me literary advice, disapproved of my stories on moral grounds.

I never saw Marianne Moore again, but sent her Christmas cards which she regularly acknowledged with little handwritten notes, making agreeable comments on the pictures I had sent her.

*

Father relished the theater, while my mother's interest and mine were heightened by its dependence on words. It was, of course, impossible to foresee that, half a century and more later, I would be much involved with the writing of dramas for a medium not yet dreamed of: television.

My parents started taking me to plays when I was so young that, if the action on the stage got racy, our little trio was stared at disapprovingly, all the more because, due to Mother's deafness, we always sat in a front row.

Since my parents were unconcerned with Broadway, it was at the Provincetown Playhouse in Greenwich Village, the haunt of Eugene

---

*The couple's son, Christian Herter, was to become Secretary of State. The painters were brother and sister-in-law to our neighbors and landlords.

O'Neill, Robert Edmund James, and Paul Robeson, that I saw my first professional plays. I remember particularly Robeson in O'Neill's *Emperor Jones*, and a performance of Ibsen's *Peer Gynt* with music by Prokofiev.

As the Provincetown Playhouse faded, the Theatre Guild became so successful as a subscription theater in presenting on Broadway plays of artistic merit that it was a major cultural force. Theresa Helburn, a founder and director, had been another of Mother's pupils. A ticket was subscribed for me until I went away to Harvard, after which Mother would use her pull to get me tickets during my holidays. In all this, the family had only been appreciators, but in even more forward-looking directions they had played an active part.

It began with the appearance of the Moscow Art Theatre in New York when I was fifteen. I was taken to see Chekhov's *Three Sisters*. Although unable to understand the lines that were delivered in Russian, I was moved by the depth and intensity of the performance, and can still remember the sight and sound of the three sisters, forever isolated on their decaying estate, crying out in despair as the final curtain fell.

Konstantin Stanislavski, director of the Moscow Art Theatre, was the creator of what came to be known in America as "the Method," a technique of acting which was eventually to conquer the American stage so thoroughly that it is still dominant as I write these lines. Stanislavski returned to Paris with his company, but his disciple Richard Boleslavski and a great actress, Mme Ouspenkaya, stayed in the United States. For them a family friend, Mrs. Richard Stockton, organized the American Laboratory Theatre, an acting school, with a small playhouse attached. With this seedling, from which the Method was slowly to spread across the United States, my family became closely involved. Father served as a trustee and Mother solicited funds.

As a stripling, I hung around the Laboratory Theatre enough to consider it part of my environment. The Method did not really enter my consciousness until some ten years later when, through the friendship of a leading lady, Margaret (Beany) Barker, I became familiar with the Group Theatre that finally and triumphantly brought that acting reform to Broadway. But I remember with great vividness a classroom exercise that inculcated in me a principle that was to be of major importance to me as a writer. The students were asked to deliver ordinary phrases—"Good-bye" or "How nice to see you"—in ways that expressed various, even contradictory, emotions. This started me on a realization that words, like painters' colors, have in themselves only generalized meaning. They gain strength and luster and sharp significance from the way they are used, from the contexts and the rhythms in which the writer imbeds them.

*

Another long-range influence came from the opposite theatrical extreme. After the Lincoln School had moved to 123rd Street, near Columbia University, we were within two blocks of Herdick and Seaman's which, when renamed the Apollo Theatre, became a showplace for the Harlem Renaissance. Then it was a burlesque theater. That we were forbidden to go there increased the allure. A little group of medium-sized boys could be seen nervously, but bravely, sneaking in.

There was the usual "runway," a narrow continuation of the stage that extended almost to the back of the orchestra. Here, female entertainers, underclad for those days, pranced in the midst of and only slightly above the patrons. A singer who seemed to us middle-aged, with a much-painted harpy's face and vast bosoms bursting from tiny restraints, came along bellowing, "When my sugar walks down the street, all the little birdies go tweet, tweet, tweet." Seeing below her our little line of fresh-faced boys, she dropped on her knees, and reached out to kiss Alan. He recoiled in horror, and she drew back a hefty arm and socked him on the jaw. The audience cheered. We fled, but we came back on other afternoons.

Burlesque gave a whole generation of brilliant comics to Broadway. Although this I would have denied in protection of my emerging manhood, I was less taken by the women and the lewd implications than by the way that humorous dialogue was developed to a climax which struck like a whip. The instant the whip had been cracked, the theater was thrown into darkness. The lights went on again to a different sequence.

What in burlesque was called a "blackout" became an important part of my writing technique. Fabricated transitions bring in superfluous words. Better when you get to the end of a subject to break off sharply (as I am now going to do), relying on the general flow of conceptions to produce continuity.

*

Every summer, I went off with my parents to communities where, as that was their taste, there was little active social life. I did swim with the neighbors' children and play tennis, drive the car when the family finally got one, and, when the time came, flirted not too seriously with the not too unattractive girls. I went for long walks with my Irish terrier. But my principal activity, to begin with under Mother's guidance and then with her cooperation, was reading English literature.

When on the English faculty at Bryn Mawr, Mother had complained to Bertrand Russell that her efforts to impart an appreciation of literature were being frustrated by demands that she induce pedantic scholarship, Bertie replied what she in essence communicated to me: "The American devotion to pedantry is very unfortunate. They have not realized that the ultimate aim of every dignified study is *emotion*. They never enquire concerning ends but pursue means so completely as to assure non-attainance 'of the ends.'" This conviction, which Mother applied to our innumerable hours of reading together, was to be a touchstone of my entire literary career.

*

Mother and I did not go backward in time before Shakespeare— but what an opening gun! Well before I was able to understand the complexities and the characters, I was ravished by the magical effectiveness and variety of his use of words. From the simple lightness of "Under the greenwood tree / who loves to lie with me," to the majesty of "When I consider every thing that grows . . ." I have bowed at Shakespeare's feet for all my career.

In the succeeding period of English classicism I did read, but with less relish: Pope and Spenser. It is in my memory, although somehow I doubt it, that I waded all through *Paradise Lost*. I could take Donne or leave him alone. Lovelace and Herrick I had a taste for. But my excitement really kindled with the romantic movement. I believe that if my biographies were judged on such a scale, I would be considered, despite the grounding in fact, a romantic writer.

Seventeen ninety-eight, the publication of the *Lyrical Ballads*, was then as important a date to me as 1776 was to become. I wallowed, as did Mother, in romantic poetry which we would read to each other. I memorized. I can still lure from the back of my brain poems by Wordsworth—"A violet by a mossy stone," etc.—and Coleridge's "Kubla Khan." Byron, too: "When we two parted in silence and tears. . . ." Shelley and Keats fired rockets in my brain, Shelley first; but when I was a little older, I assumed that Keats was, as a lyrical poet, the greatest in the world. And then there was Swinburne, closer to Shelley than Keats, more flamboyant and seductive, amoral. Glib or no, I could once recite by heart the whole *Garden of Proserpine*. Although in subsequent years I heard much sneering at Tennyson as Victorian and stuffy, my loyalty to those of his poems that I loved remains. I learned by heart his "Sir Galahad" and much of "The Lotus-Eaters":

> There is sweet music here that softer falls
> Than petals from blown roses on the grass,
> Or night-dews on still waters between the walls
> Of shadowy granite, in some gleaming pass;
> Music that gentlier on the spirit lies,
> Than tired eyelids on tired eyes.*

From the later nineteenth century I picked out poems rather than poets: Thompson's "The Hound of Heaven"; Dowson's "Cynara," that revelation of emotion communicated almost altogether by the sound of words. Mother was unable to indoctrinate me with Browning despite her impassioned rendering of "A Last Ride Together." Her admiration for Rossetti was encouraged, I suppose, by his role as a painter in making such red hair as hers, previously despised, the height of esthetic fashion. For my part, I was excited by his depiction in his sonnet "Body's Beauty" of Lilith, the witch the Devil created for Adam before God got around to making Eve.**

---

*A tangible gift that you can give to old age is memorizing poems which can be called back to soften the rigors of sleepless nights.

**At a much later date I was amused, after I had discovered that a Welsh genealogist had descended Mother's family from the witch at King Arthur's court, Morgan le Fay, to learn that "my ancestress" was considered by students of mythology to be the same as Lilith.

Among American poets, I was fascinated by Poe, my favorite being "Ulalume": ". . . the dank tarn of Auber, in the ghoul-haunted woodland of Weir." "The Raven" seemed to me good fun. I was later to dream of teaching a crow to say "Nevermore" and letting him loose at a meeting of the Modern Language Association. I have never been attracted to Walt Whitman's ungainly vociferations.

*

Although I then read no books of biography, what I did read contributed greatly to the art of biography as I was to practice it. I immersed myself in narratives showing the development of character in their environments and through time. Told that it was the first real novel in English, I read Richardson's *Pamela* from beginning to end, although I cheated by reading his *Clarissa Harlowe* in an abridgment. Fielding's more masculine *Tom Jones* interested me more. I developed a passion for Scott's *Ivanhoe* and *Quentin Durwood* (Scott's poetry for some reason passed me by). Dickens became my favorite novelist all the way from the comic *Pickwick Papers* to the darkest novels. Trying to read again the dark ones during my later years, I felt them in their delineation of event and character too bitter and exaggerated, giving so terrible a view of the human animal that I had to shut the volumes. But as a boy and young man I was fascinated, finding his savage denunciation of the human race in some way life-enhancing. Although I very much enjoyed *Vanity Fair*, I found Thackeray on the whole too milk-and-water compared to Dickens. I cannot remember having read Jane Austen, although my approaches to character through small deeds and reactions were occasionally to be compared by critics to hers. The group of serious English novelists at the end of the century—Hardy, Meredith, Bennett, etc.—I read with interest and I am sure to my profit, although memory brings them back as ponderous. I preferred Stevenson and Conrad. The only novel Mother urged on me which I found too irritating to finish was Pater's *Marius the Epicurean*. Oscar Wilde dazzled me. I still feel a deep resentment against the composer Strauss for having drowned the poetic subtleties of Wilde's *Salome* in a perpetual melodramatic yowl.

In American literature, Mark Twain was our hands-down favorite, all the more because my Kentucky-bred father so relished his humor. I had my own personal passion for Washington Irving, not only his

American folktales, but those in his *Alhambra*. I have always felt some affinity between his style and mine. It may have been some mystic foretaste of writing *Mohawk Baronet* that made me resent Cooper's Indian characterizations: natural philosophers if pro-British in the French and Indian War, sadistic devils if pro-French. Hawthorne did not appeal to me as much as he did later, and I somehow skipped Melville. Poe's lurid tales would have curled my hair if it had not already been so curly.

*

As director of the Institute, Father had a concern, paralleling a biographer's, with individual genius. I remember sitting in on an argument between Father and the celebrity-aviator Charles Lindbergh, who had just returned, somewhat bemused, from a visit to Russia. Lindbergh held forth with enthusiasm on how the Communist government would fight a medical problem by mobilizing hundreds of workers. Father demurred, stating that the best recourse was to find the right man and put all the resources behind him.

The plan of the Rockefeller Institute had no resemblance to that of a college or university. There were no established departments that added up to a coherent whole. Following the broad spectrum of medical research in America and across the world in periodicals and conversations, Father was perpetually on the watchout for achievements that revealed outstanding ability. He dug out from some obscure hole in Chicago Dr. Alexis Carrel, whose discoveries were to make blood transfusion and organ transplants possible. He induced his trustees to widen the scope of the Institute by calling in Dr. Jacques Loeb whose concern with experimental biology of the cell seemed then far afield of medicine. I remember Father's pointing out to me on the Institute grounds the stooped, elderly figure of Loeb, telling me to remember that I had seen a very great man.

When Father got his man, he would build a department around him. Should the scientist drop out, the department would be eliminated. Should two men appear in the same field, if their efforts could be separated to prevent overlapping, there would be two departments. This made administration an aspect of personal relationship. To hold what Father called his "prima donnas" together as part of a single enterprise covered by a single budget, working cooperatively side by side without feuding, was a task of legerdemain in which Father perpetually called for advice from Mother [Year after year I would listen in.] Often I had at least some personal experience of the individuals involved.

*

I was never allowed over the threshold of Father's laboratory because of the toxic materials that were being dealt with there. (I was impressed by how many times and ways Father cleansed his hands after he emerged.) However, I became conscious of basic principles of research that were to throw light ahead on my labors in other fields.

Before launching into the unknown, it was necessary for a scientific researcher (as for an historian or biographer) to be master of what was already known. Imperfect preparation was punished by a force infinitely more imperious than any Ph.D. supervisor or "learned" reviewer: Mother Nature herself. To peep into the unknown from a base that is shaky or askew is to fall down. I learned from Father the importance of completely accurate research.

To avoid confused results, so Father told me, it is necessary to set an experiment up with a minimum, preferably only one, variable. Because this is impossible for examination of human behavior on any but the tiniest scale, I learned that there can be no such thing as truly scientific history or biography. The door was opened wide to my gleeful acceptance, when the time came, that history and biography are in their essence not science but art. Although, of course, I prefer my own results to those of others, I know that the conception of a "definitive work" is pure moonshine.

6

THE BIOGRAPHICAL ZONE

*

It was my tremendous good fortune to have been born into and raised in what I came to call "the biographical zone," that area of human experience that is inhabited by persons significant enough in their own right, and generating the necessary records, personal and historical, to be available for biographies of length, interest, and depth.

Take Alexis Carrel, who had been an obscure French surgeon practicing in Chicago until he published an article in the magazine *Science* that caught Father's eye. Called to the Institute just as the first building was being planned, he was encouraged to design his own laboratory. Surgeons through history had wished that there were some way of rejoining blood vessels after they had been severed. Carrel invented the technique that freed surgery and made blood transfusion possible. He also invented ways for keeping organs alive outside the body so that they could be transplanted by methods he also engineered. He founded the science of tissue culture, enabling cells from a chicken heart to live and produce more cells year after year in apparatus he designed. He was awarded a Nobel Prize. The medical historian George Washington Corner regarded Carrel's advances in the practice of biology and surgery as commensurate with Edison's advances in the practice of electricity.

Carrel was short, stocky, and very military in bearing. He was an impassioned royalist—his wife, who was twice his size, stemmed from an old French aristocratic family—and a devout Catholic. He horrified his fellow scientists by accepting the miracles of Lourdes. His genetic theory—down the generations the most able had mated to create the aristocracy—made him conclude that Father, whom he tremendously admired, must somehow have inherited royal blood. I, as Father's son, had to be similarly endowed. Dr. Carrel treated me with respect and was always my supporter and friend.

*

In Japan, Father had done no more than smile politely when an obscure laboratory worker said he would like to join Dr. Flexner in America. What was Dr. Flexner's amazement when, after he had responded to a knock on his door at the University of Pennsylvania, to see in the hall the diminutive Japanese standing there, bowing and grinning.

Hideyo Noguchi had brought along many presents, each of which he handed Father with many gestures, but he proved to have almost no money. Father's first act had to be buying him an overcoat. It had never occurred to Noguchi that the America of his dreams might be cold.

Since no job could be found for Hideyo Noguchi except as a waiter in a Japanese restaurant, Father had to take him into his laboratory. The upshot belongs in a fairy tale. It was quickly demonstrated that the stray was a scientist of true genius. Noguchi was to discover the causes and cure for syphilis and yellow fever. He became famous in America, and is in Japan a national hero.

Short, quick, and slight, Noguchi was as exuberant as any of my classmates at school. After he had given my brother and me opera glasses for Christmas, he posed at the far end of the room with his mouth open to see if we could focus on his tonsils.

When he was working with Father on the relationship of snake venom and bacterial poisons, Noguchi brought to our house in the country a good-sized dead snake. His conference with Father over and the weather being hot, he did what seemed to him natural: he curled the snake upon the ice in our old-fashioned ice box. The next morning we were awakened with screams as the cook disappeared down the hillside.

Father came to love Noguchi as almost another son, but he remained elusive. This is still brought home to me by phone calls, several a year. Writers of biographies or television scripts, mostly Japanese, clamor for information about Noguchi's wife. He did have a wife. He never introduced her to Father. Father knew only that Noguchi got his salary paid in two separate checks, one to hand on to his wife and the other to keep so that he would have something to spend. Father assumed that she was some disreputable, lower-class woman who had taken advantage of Noguchi's innocence. But no information exists about the wife of this major scientist.

*

On a more intimate scale were my relations with an uncle and an aunt—Father's brother Abraham Flexner and Mother's sister M. Carey Thomas. Both major figures in the development of American education, they were as stupendous a contrast as supplied by any of Father's prima donnas.

Abraham Flexner was utterly different in temperament from Father. He was not a conciliator but a fighter, preferring to overwhelm an enemy rather than make a friend, delighted with his brains, drive, and subsequent power which forced others to submit to—and sometimes admire—his own outrageous behavior. He achieved fame with an act of destruction, the "Flexner Report" that killed off a great many inadequate proprietary medical schools. Subsequently, he used Rockefeller money and also funds he himself raised—he had an affinity with financial robber barons—to endow scientific medical institutions spaced across the United States. Eventually, he became so heady that, despite Father's efforts to hold him in check, he forced his discharge from the Rockefeller philanthropies. However, he was much too buoyant to remain down. Raising the money himself, he founded the Institute for Advanced Study at Princeton and set it off on its continuing course stormy with controversy.

I hated my Uncle Abe. Possessed of great intuitive insight into people's minds, he used this gift when I was a child to say and do what he knew would most hurt my feelings and demean my pride. Any effort to talk back he would repel as lack of respect to an elder of great importance.

Among my happiest memories is my brother's and my successful revenge. One afternoon, Uncle Abe stopped off at our house to glean admiration for how handsomely he was dressed for an important lecture he was about to deliver. We boys had been cultivating skill as pickpockets: we handed people their watches which they had thought were in their pockets. It was child's play for us to extract Uncle Abe's handkerchief and substitute a long, greasy rag. During his lecture, he reached for his handkerchief to wipe his brow with results that convulsed his audience. He was soon pounding into the Simon Flexner household demanding that Father inflict severe punishment. "Abe," Father said, "if you play jokes on my boys, they can play jokes on you."

But to play such a trick on our Aunt Carey would have been horrifying beyond the realm of belief.

*

Miss M. Carey Thomas, the president of Bryn Mawr College, Mother's oldest sister, was almost as domineering as Uncle Abe, but her explosions, however much they riled her faculty, were to me congenial as they resembled the outpourings of a gifted child. As I grew older, I wondered how, with all her vagaries, she managed to get done so much of importance, to wield so much power, and I concluded that she was like England's famous Queen Elizabeth I, who was said to have been sober and effective in council while much given to extremities in her private life.

As a growing girl, Aunt Carey had been a tomboy resenting every implication that women were inferior to men. Overcoming thickets of administrative and social handicaps, she became one of the first women to secure a Ph.D. (*summa cum laude*, no less!). It was from the University of Leipzig. While she was away, her father and other relations had been engaged in founding a Quaker college for women. Although in her twenties, Aunt Carey assumed that she would automatically be made president of Bryn Mawr. But the majority of the trustees considered her a wild woman, and her relatives succeeded only in having her appointed dean. She overwhelmed the poor elderly Quaker preacher who was titularly president, and when he died no one could prevent her succeeding him. Aunt Carey immediately set about acting as the conservatives had feared: she changed a parochial Quaker college into a national institution that pioneered in opening to women the highest education already available to men. Her support for many women's causes has made her a favorite subject for "Women's Studies."

Carey's close friend, Mary Garrett, had been considered the richest single woman in the United States. When Carey's father was engaged in the struggle to get the Johns Hopkins Medical School started, his daughter and Miss Garrett, by conditionally offering the needed funds, forced admission of women and such high entrance requirements that Dr. Welch said to Father, "It's lucky we are faculty because we would not have got in as students."

When Miss Garrett died—I was a small child—Aunt Carey inherited her fortune, which she spent with gusto. She had to an extreme the panache, the grand manner, that, before these egalitarian tunes, was preferred in college presidents. Yet, she established, to utilize the college dormitories during summers, a pioneering "School for Women Workers in Industry." Factory girls were offered, during the two weeks of vacation which was all they were permitted, specially designed courses to open to their enchanted eyes the desire and the possibilities of self-education.

Her own summers Aunt Carey spent traveling the world. She took along so much baggage (it included a bathtub) that in oriental ports she would be followed, on her way from the dock to the hotel, by a parade of coolies balancing bundles on their heads. As she proceeded on her tour, the possessions augmented and the processions enlarged. Wherever she was, she bought artifacts and curios, indiscriminately mixing valuable finds with junk. It is recounted that when in Arabia a donkey kicked her down a sandy slope, she hurried back up despite a leg partly crippled in a childhood accident, and returned the kick. This is hard to believe, but after long experience I would not put it beyond her.

During our school vacations, Mother habitually took my brother and me to stay with Aunt Carey at Bryn Mawr. The campus being part of a rural countryside, it was during these visits that I first saw nature in other moods than summer. I remember my excitement at finding under dead leaves spring's first tiny flowers. I also remember my satisfaction when, as a small boy, I entered a classroom with Aunt Carey, all the girls stood up.

With Miss Garrett, Aunt Carey had built on the campus an art nouveau mansion which was (although Bryn Mawr has barbarously torn it down) the most architecturally distinguished building I have ever considered almost my own. Life in these extensive halls had for me two facets. On the adult occasions at which I came increasingly to be present, the most careful behavior was required. Perfect decorum had to go with the perfect service, elegant furnishings, and delicious food. But at other times I was allowed to roam by myself, engaging in high jinks which, if they were not destructive, Aunt Carey encouraged. I lived with Whistler etchings; with reproductions of pre-Raphaelite paintings; with a combined swing and couch from India decorated at the four corners with bronze elephant heads; with a small mummy Aunt Carey had picked up in Egypt and put on top of a chiffonnier. Aunt Carey's celebrated "English garden" was the size of a city block. In a pool surrounding one of the fountains, I reinvented jet propulsion. I discovered that if I blew up a toy balloon, put the outlet under the water, and then released the air, the balloon would scuttle rapidly over the surface of the pool.

Out of her vast store of bibelot, Aunt Carey showered me with presents. As I look back, what seems most remarkable about her behavior toward me was her solicitude never, as we shared jokes, to bruise my childish or boyish self-respect. Aunt Carey, that doughty fighter for feminism and dictator of Bryn Mawr, behaved toward me in a flirtatious manner between a female and a male.

As a boy and as a young man, when I considered myself first a poet and then a novelist, I could have had no conception of how valuable my early experiences being brought up among suitable subjects for a biographer would be for me. Constant association not only fed me valuable insights and intuitions, but made me feel at ease with the eminent persons I was to depict, free of any personal need to debunk or engage in hero-worship, any eagerness to define my own position in the world by clinging onto my protagonist's coattails.

*

Not only was my understanding deepened by birthright-intimate insights into the biographical zone, but I was immunized against the biographer's disease of trying to enlarge your own personality and worldly position by self-identification with your protagonists. This can nurture opposite results: either exaggerating the achievements and virtue of your self-appointed alter ego, or trying to tear him down to your own size.

However, in my real-life association with the self-important, my lack of awe does not always go down well. I remember particularly John Kenneth Galbraith who I had often disagreed with when he was president of the American Academy of Arts and Letters. As vice president for literature, I was amazed when, as we shared a taxi for the long trip from the Century Club to the Academy, Gilbraith occupied the half to three-quarters of an hour by, without pause, enumerating his achievements and the honors he had been awarded. I listened silently and, although what he had to boast of was impressive, I cannot say that I was overawed.

My principal falling out with Galbraith took place when the American Center of P.E.N. (where I had once been president) hosted an annual convention of that international writers' association. Galbraith had arranged that the American Academy would sponsor the opening session, and had (without consulting his board of which I was a member) agreed with P.E.N.'s current president, Norman Mailer, that the keynote address be delivered by the American Secretary of State, who had no literary qualifications whatsoever. When I got wind of this, I went through the roof. One of the main principles of P.E.N. was that the national centers should refuse to be politically manipulated by their governments, and George Schulz was the kingpin of the American efforts during the Cold War. Galbraith pushed my protests aside by saying it was too late to rescind the invitation. As it turned out, the delegates from the various centers who had been self-righteously preached to by us, concluded that the American P.E.N. was the worst of all.

What had been Galbraith's intention I do not know—whether he had actually intended to kidnap the American writing profession— but I do know that forever after he treated me with minimal courtesy.

7

LANDSCAPE PROPHECIES

*

IT was then routine for a mother and her children, taking the maids along, to spend summers in the country, husbands arriving for their vacations. Usually, the Flexners migrated to Chocorua, New Hampshire. The magnet was Mount Chocorua which Mother, in her ignorance of the Hudson River School, equated with Japan's sacred mountain, styling it "The Fujiyama of America."

From the houses we usually occupied, we could look down on a valley enlivened with two linked lakes, such "mirrors of the sky" as were prized by the Hudson River painters. Beyond, thick woods formed a gradually rising pedestal for a long easterly ridge that rose to its own rounded top, a softer echo of the mountain peak behind. Above this foothill and shaped in harmony with it, a shoulder of the mountain advanced in a graceful curve until it rose sharply to Chocorua's sheer, conical peak, which dominated the entire wooded and watered panorama not only because of its height but because it was bare, white stone.

The view became part of my blood, although I was not certain, when I was small, that the mountain was altogether benign. There was a season when I was afraid that a bear would leap in from the peak that was so visible from my window.

*

It would have meant nothing to Mother had she been told that in the 1830s an artist named Thomas Cole, on a painting trip through

then wild New Hampshire, had so fallen in love with Mount Chocorua, that he placed it in landscapes he painted one after another,
even showing it presiding over his rendition of the Garden of Eden.
Although the Hudson River School that Cole had founded had been
the most popular school in all American art history, it was smashed
from correct esthetic taste by hammer blows of succeeding generations of French-inspired painters. But the taste in scenery the school
had inspired remained dominant among the American people, inspiring Mother to root her son in the very center of one of the White
Mountain views most admired by the Hudson River School artists.

It was decades after Mount Chocorua had begun its indoctrination
of the infant Flexner that my book *That Wilder Image* (1962) played
its important role in lifting American admiration for the Hudson
River School toward the heights which still prevail as I write these
lines.

*

During the for me emancipating year of 1918–1919, the influence of
Mount Chocorua received a major reinforcement. My family had
never bought in New Hampshire, which was too far away for Father
to join us during weekends. But the heartland of the Hudson River
School was accessible to New York City. Mother wrote, "If I am
destined to reach any sort of paradise in another world, it will be
gazing at blue shadows on mountains." She bought a house in the
most picturesque reach of the entire Hudson: the Highlands, where
for some twenty-five miles the water passes in a narrow channel
through a spur of the Appalachian Mountains. At the northern gate
of the Highlands stood its tallest, most imposing mountain, Storm
King. It rose sheerly from the water to about fifteen hundred feet.
Facing Storm King from the east bank mounted a declivity, "too
precipitous to sustain vegetation," called Breakneck. Mother had
found on the face of Breakneck a plateau several hundred yards deep
and about the same distance over the river. Here stood a cottage,
"old," as I put it in my poem "Near Cold Spring," "and secluded and
queer." It was Hudson River Carpenter's Gothic, gabled, erratically
shingled, with occasional mullioned windows. Father described our
house as "quaint," but it had a strong and benign character, and we
came to love it.

All we knew of the history of the house was that its name, Rock Neath, had been suggested by George Pope Morris, the author of a then famous poem, "Woodsman, Spare That Tree." Our information did not extend to the fact that the tree in question, referred to as "the most famous vegetable in the world," had stood almost directly downriver.

Morris was the dominant figure in New York's leading literary group, known as "The Knickerbocker Poets." The walls of Rock Neath once rang to the voices of William Cullen Bryant, James Kirke Paulding, Fitz-Greene Halleck, Nathaniel Parker Willis, and others. A spiritualist could argue that some emanation remained behind from these poets, since at Rock Neath I abandoned my obsession with the horrors of war to turn to nature verse.

Was my historical sense also excited? Rock Neath was the first old house I had ever come to know. And I was conscious that the surrounding countryside was rich in history. In fact, I could hardly have been in a spot that teemed more with the intangible emanations of the American past than this commanding area of the Hudson River. Many of my books were to hover over it: *Steamboats Come True*, *The Traitor and the Spy*, works on George Washington and Alexander Hamilton.

*

Our view from Rock Neath, although grander, was very confined as compared with the deep vistas we saw from our various Chocorua lawns. When they had painted their tutelary river as it passed dramatically through the Highlands, the landscapists of the Hudson River School, who reveled in distances, sighted obliquely up or down the waterway, usually up from West Point some ten miles below us. We looked due west, directly over the river at the craggy and wooded mass of Storm King as it rose almost perpendicularly, it seemed to the sky. Of the river, we could see, as we leaned to stare downward, only a narrow strip along the western shore. However, its presence at the bottom of the declivity prevented the mountain—it was less than half a mile away—from psychologically seeming to crowd in. Storm King was a looming presence at night, and during the day we could view, in every variation of light, cliffs and glens, declivities and watercourses, vertical constellations of scenery rarely subjected to the foot of man.

The different view, that which was so famous, which moved tens of thousands of travelers on river boats, could be made mine by the five minutes' walk down our steep driveway to the road that clung closely to the river's shore. Now Route 9D, it is infested with gasoline-guzzling monsters that speed by as if chased by demons. Then it was hummocked and sandy (I remember it as pale, almost white), so narrow that when two vehicles met (which was rarely) one had to draw up in a ditch. The railroad track, which the road crossed and recrossed according to the dictates of geography, lay flat in sun or shade until there suddenly appeared and disappeared a windowed comet which emitted the wild cry which for generations of Americans connoted adventure in strange places.

As daily, hour after hour, month after month, I wandered deep down in the Highlands on the Hudson shore, I could easily imagine that I was floating in a small boat on the water. Washington Irving remembered, "What a time of intense delight was that first sail through the Highlands. I sat on the deck as we slowly tided along at the foot of those stern mountains and gazed with wonder and admiration at the cliffs impending far above me, crowned with forests, with eagles sailing and screaming around them; or beheld rock and tree and sky reflected in the glassy stream. And how solemn and thrilling the scene was as we anchored at night at the foot of these mountains, and everything grew dark and mysterious, and I heard the plaintive note of the whippoorwill, or was startled now and then by the sudden leap and heavy splash of the sturgeon."

*

Our possession of Rock Neath, however significant it was to my landscape sensibility, spanned only two years. In September 1921, Father noted in his diary, "Not satisfactory as full-time summer place." The closeness to New York, although it served weekends, subjected Father to continual bother during his vacation. And being on a river shore almost at the bottom of a deep canyon made Rock Neath humid and hot. Father felt we could not afford two country locations. "What to do?" We sold Rock Neath* and resumed renting at Chocorua, where the family summered, with only short breaks, for many years.

*

Henry James, who had sometimes stayed at Chocorua with his brother, William (whose house the Flexners for two summers occupied), described the brightness of American light as an affliction for Americans returning home from years in Europe. But Henry James's view of our native land was not mine. Every sunlit scene that comes back most vividly among my memories of Chocorua is enhanced by the clearness of the air: trout streams shining between glowing white rocks that had been smoothed by freshets; deep gorges where I dived from grass-grown heights into water as clear and cold as ice; overgrown fields where butterflies glistened among the sharply defined petals of wildflowers; other mountains, seen from our own mountain top, their shaggy sides enlivened by the movement of sun and shadow, and, farther down, lowlands where tiny plumes of smoke were illuminated like clouds as they rose from chimneys small as pinheads; lakes where we swam and fished in air as clear as crystal.

---

*After our departure, Rock Neath was greatly damaged in a fire. Then Route 9D filled the air overhead with a viaduct.

8

UGLY DUCKLING TO SWAN

*

UNCLE Abe had inadvertently opened to Alan, Breading, and me an entrancing playground by planning the Lincoln School as a self-contained microcosm of the larger world. The school day would be long, and "homework" would be done not at home but during study periods. Avoiding antiques like Latin and Greek, the curriculum would be concerned with contemporary living. There would be a student government that would supplement courses in civics. There would be well-equipped workshops for carpentry or printing, etc. Under the inspiration of able teachers, the students would find their school life so exciting that all other experience palled beside it. Uncle Abe had no respect for parents: there was no parent–teacher association. Nor did home environments appeal to him as a possible source of education. The school would open at eight in the morning and not close until five in the evening.

This "ideal" became much more achievable when the school was moved from Sixty-sixth Street and Park Avenue, in the part of town where most of the students lived, to West 123rd Street, contiguous to Columbia and Teachers College, but for almost all the students a considerable trip. My magic chariot was a Fifth Avenue bus that rattled uptown to 110th Street, then west to Broadway, and on to within a block-or-two's walk through a shabby immigrant neighborhood to the large red brick schoolhouse, facing Morningside Park, Rockefeller money had built.

Each morning as I was about to leave home, I telephoned Alan who lived farther up Madison Avenue. He would get on the same bus. We were waiting at the school door when it was opened. Breading having appeared, we spent eight or nine hours, until we were locked out, mostly in high jinks.

Another of Uncle Abe's theories emancipated us: the freedom of children to express themselves should not be interfered with. This had worked to my great despite when I was the dregs. But now Alan, Breading, and I were using the freedom at Lincoln to amuse ourselves. I was hauled before the authorities for making uncouth noises in singing class, but never for my activities in establishing our own underground government. Our objectives were simple: as lower classmen to harass the efforts of the upper classmen to use the student government to keep order; and when we became upper classmen, to get fun out of running things our own way.

A caper we engaged in when lower classmen: there was a "Deportment Committee" through which the graver of our schoolmates were supposed to establish some kind of order. As a safety measure, no one was supposed to sit on the sill of a window when it was open. Breading was caught, reported by some sobersides, and summoned to appear before the committee. Alan and I went along. When we announced that we had been retained by Breading as his lawyers, the committee, pleased by this amplification of legal procedure, agreed. We got them to define that the purpose of the ruling was to keep the accused from falling out. Arguing that he would not fall out if he kept his feet on the floor, we secured a ruling that having your feet on the floor was an adequate defense. We then called in a host of witnesses. When the flustered chairman said that so many people could not have been so absolutely sure that Breading's feet were on the floor, we pointed to the size of his feet and had him wave them in the faces of the committee. By now the room was full of "witnesses." I forget how the case was decided, but remember that the incident kept the school amused for days.

Our civics teachers considered it essential to our education that all our formal meetings be conducted according to strict parliamentary procedures. The source, we discovered, was Robert's *Rules of Order* which we got out of the school library to find a whole magic bag of tricks. You could add to a motion an amendment that utterly changed its meaning; you could, when you had the floor, assign it to one of

[63]

your friends, thus fostering a filibuster; you could put motions "on the table"; you could stop discussion by yelling, "Question! Question!"; or you could bring everything to an instantaneous halt by "rising to a point of order," which had to be settled before the session could continue. The teachers might become livid, but what we demonstrated was how conscientiously we had studied parliamentary rules.

I described to my parents how we handled an election for class chairman. In the best Tammany Hall style, we did not nominate ourselves but a henchman. To a group of new boys in the class we managed to convey that if they wished to be accepted they should vote as we dictated. The girls helped things along by putting up a female candidate. They thus solidified the male vote but not that of their own sex as some of the prettier girls preferred to vote with the boys.

Why did we engage in these shenanigans? It was partly a mischievous thumbing our noses at authority; partly for the joy of maneuver and the excitement of the game; partly because of the interest supplied by studying the personalities of the fellow students whom we hoped to influence; and certainly because of pleasure inherent in the possession and wielding of power. Alan and Breading, of course, did not share my background as school pariah. To what extent were my drive enhanced and my pleasures increased by my consciousness of how far I had, in the school environment, risen?

It might be assumed that my memories would make me use my popularity to rescue students still outsiders. But this, alas, is not the way psychology normally works. Mother with her privileged background was much more concerned with organizations to help the poor than was Father who had been brought up poor. Having himself worked his way out, he saw no reason why others if they had the intelligence and determination could not do the same.

*

My high points were when the idealistic school authorities established a "Town Meeting": the whole high school brought together to consider some matter of general policy, such as whether the giving of formal marks should be abolished in favor of discussions between student and teacher. By now, diffidence had entirely vanished from me. I would rise and give impassioned orations. Since these were usually against the policy the management wished to put over, they were highly popular. I have periodically in later years met graduates of the Lincoln School who expatiated on their vivid and admiring memories of how, rising under my flaming red hair, I brought dull meetings to life with spirited speeches.

The final compliment was not intended as such. Dr. Otis W. Caldwell, the director of the school, made an appointment with Father to plead with him to curb his son, who, he complained, was undermining the discipline of the whole Lincoln School. Father's response was to say that the job was not his but Dr. Caldwell's. But the director could find no way within his own regimen to squelch me.

*

The Lincoln School's announced intention to experiment had made innovative teachers prick up their ears. The school was besieged with applications. Whether or not the projects accepted were in themselves sound—many a crackbrained idea was tried out on me—was of little importance beside the fact that the instructors possessed original minds and unusual abilities. Their methods sparked the imagination. Perhaps I learned most from those ideas that appeared to my juvenile intelligence unsound. I could stretch my brain in arguing with the teachers, such being the pedagogical theory of the school, and, indeed, I impressed the teachers who were pleased to have stimulated controversy and often to have convinced me.

The Lincoln School backed the experimental thinking I was learning from my father: accept nothing on the basis of authority, demand evidence, try to think every proposition anew in its own terms. This was so in keeping with what the school admired that, far now from being sent to the print shop to set type, I was encouraged to preen myself as the school's most brilliant pupil.

*

To prevent athletics from being over-emphasized by contests with other institutions, the Lincoln authorities divided the entire student body between two teams, the Oranges and the Blues. This was one of their conceptions that worked out very well. All the pupils became involved, since even the smallest matches observed the all-over divisions and thus were a call to all-over rivalry.

Alan and I were both Oranges, and he was always captain of whatever team we served on; thus, I always had an inside track. Basketball was the major winter sport and, in a manner that would seem comic today, I was, despite my small size, considered a valuable forward for the leading Orange team. To help things along, I bullied Father, despite his complaints about expense, to erect on our lawn in the country a basket for me to practice on.

As the deciding game of the next winter's season approached, I was laid up with influenza. Alan mourned publicly over the danger to the Orange prospects. I was able to attend school just in time. As I put on my playing shorts and shirt I felt wobbly, but as I ran out with the others there were cheers. The ball was put in play, I found a good position a little to the left of the basket, the ball was thrown to me, and I fainted. This was the most conventionally dramatic event of my entire lifetime.

However problematical was my importance as a basketball player, I did have an incontrovertible role in the twice-yearly track meets that, to the excitement of all the students, established the ultimate supremacy of either the Oranges or the Blues. In each event, first place won five points. I regularly brought in five points. Despite the shortness of my legs, I had become the fastest sprinter in the school. This was, I suppose, because the schoolyard was short and I have always been able to summon my nervous energy for a burst.

Although these bits of athletic prowess helped round out my reputation, there was another, much brighter feather in my cap: writing poetry. When, at the close of my junior year, I was elected by the entire student body president of the Student Council, I preferred another office that was in the same way offered: editor-in-chief of the school publication, *Lincoln Lore*, which was grandly subtitled, *A Magazine of Literature*.

9

A YOUNG POET

*

WHEN I was in the eighth grade, there appeared at the Lincoln School a new English teacher. Hughes Mearns was a shortish, stocky, very effervescent man, his body in continual motion while the large eyeglasses on his flat face enhanced the evangelism in his eyes. He had come—although this we were not told—to conduct an experiment of which my class was to be the focus, although Mearns intended to inspire the whole school and reform the teaching of writing everywhere.

He espoused the romantic doctrines that the "instinctive" emotions of children were, at their best, "so right and sure, so beautiful and wise." They were being crushed by established pedagogy. Yet "the hope of civilization" lay in releasing "the beautiful religion of the child," which was "the true faith." His method would be to foster "the astonishing revelations of the inner self" which would come to children through the writing of verse that would truly express their inner feelings. Whether the verse was good or bad as poetry, it would nonetheless be salutary, but he hoped to inspire enough impressive poetry to demonstrate his gifts as a teacher and the literary importance of juvenile self-expression.

Mearns's classroom technique exactly suited my predilections. The students were encouraged to read whatever poetry they pleased, select for themselves what excited them, and, having brought their findings to school, read them to the class. Mearns himself read aloud and revealed histrionic gifts. Matters of poetic technique were hotly debated and made a source for further study. I remember in particular an examination of the sonnet form in all its variations and possibilities.

Although the great verse of the past was appreciated, Mearns turned our attention particularly to contemporary verse, mostly American. This created immediacy. Taught by him to think of ourselves as practicing poets, we felt part of the movement we were studying. It also gave us encouragement since most of the poets publishing at that moment were not, as Keats or Swinburne would have been, so far from our own points of view and potentialities that a dream of rivaling them would be absurd.

Having discovered for myself, in the magazine where it was originally published, "Stopping By Woods on a Snowy Evening," I felt a particular closeness to Robert Frost, and was enchanted when he came to one of our classes and was complimentary. I also greatly admired Edna St. Vincent Millay, moved (I fear) as much by the explicit (for those days) sexuality as by the beauty of her poetry. Our whole class went to hear her read, and I was gratified to see that she was a very attractive woman. Sara Teasdale's quiet verse I found enchanting. Mearns did not lead us in avant-garde directions, but my family subscribed to the *Dial* and I discovered for myself e. e. cummings.

*

Mearns's most brilliant inspiration was never to assign verse as a classroom exercise. He wished the initiative to rise in the child himself. A pupil with a poem was urged to seek out Mearns privately. He was always appreciative and could, as I was often to experience, chatter with enthusiasm, waving his hands. He objected to anything modeled on reading rather than expressive of the child's own experiences and feelings. Symbolic of our movement was our scorn for poets who enthused about nightingales in American landscapes, there being none on this continent.

To prime the pump at the start of his endeavor, Mearns had to ferret out pupils who were already writing poems "bound away in secret notebooks or hoarded in private drawers." Getting these treasures brought to school required tact, he noted, and the winning of confidence. As an example of his success, he cited his experience with me: "A boy permits me to tell the story of his earliest efforts, how he brought me a small volume of verses that were like *The Young Visitors*, so bad that they were good. The war had made a terrible impression upon him; he wrote of battle and blood with a seriousness that was almost comic.

"My advice was to keep them one year, and then to show them to me. I forget now how I made that suggestion reasonable without offense. I told him to keep on writing, however. Then one day he gave me 'City Nights.'*

"When the distinctive poem arrived we always made a ceremony. . . . The occasions were rare, for we were careful not to give the honor to any but the best, and therefore we were able to put a right thrill into it. At those times, as I looked on the suddenly stilled and alert faces, I often thought of the boy Agathon receiving the prize for tragic poetry in the presence of those thirty thousand Hellenes. . . . The news would spread quickly down the halls, sometimes overtaking the astonished poet."

Mearns had presented "City Nights" to an older class; I was stopped in the hall by a girl full of excitement. So charismatic was the teacher that the excitement spread until it surrounded me. For many of my twelve years I had been writing verse as a private enterprise. Now a poem of mine was famous in my daily environment. To this day, I feel the thrill. Indeed, I sometimes date my career as a professional writer from "City Nights."

Years later, I remarked to a group of *New York Times* editors that being published in their newspaper was like being published in my high school magazine. *Times* worthies being not lacking in self-importance, my remark was not well received. They were slightly mollified when I explained that in both cases what you had written was seen by your entire world.

Mearns's arrangement that the school publication *Lincoln Lore* be subtitled *A Magazine of Literature* at first annoyed pupils who wished to have a normal school paper with jokes and gossip and emphasis

---

*When the lights of the city are bright and they gleam
And the moon looks down on the level street,
I always dream the self-same dream
Of hills that are wide and of woods that are green
And of places where two brooks meet.

on athletics. They could not understand, Mearns remembered, "what it was that set a small group of us going so excitedly." He was determined to make them understand, and he handled things so well that he got the whole school excited about poetry. To be published in *Lincoln Lore* came to be considered as much of an achievement as athletic prowess.

*

Mearns's objective required his persuading the whole student body of the importance of the Lincoln School Literary Renaissance. He explained, "We never praised outright until we found the superior thing, . . . then we cheered and spread the news afar. The staff as a whole joined in the exultation; and the Director of the School— instinctively aware of his part in the plot [sic]—was never too busy to learn the good news and to share in the rejoicing."

Reaching beyond the school, Mearns induced William Stanley Braithwaite to index *Lincoln Lore* in his annual *Anthology of Magazine Verse*. Mearns told us of enthusiastic reactions by various well-known literary figures. He boasted of bringing to his most gifted poets (I was included) "something of the voice of fame," adding piously, "we do not know of anything but good that came out of this frank and sincere appreciation."

Under Mearns's hypnotic influence, in so smiling an environment, I came to consider the major poets of the past my predecessors. When, after time had passed, I was driven by literary sterility to the edge—if not beyond—of a nervous breakdown, I came to hate Hughes Mearns.

*

Taking advantage of the fact that verse is so much shorter than prose, I shall reprint here three selections from my Lincoln School years:

In the Hours of Darkness

When the night is cloudy
And mists hand on the hill,
There are ghostly footsteps

And voices, thin and shrill;
Nothing will your looking
Show you in the dark
If the door is opened,
But harken, harken, hark!

In the hours of darkness
Thronging from their camp
Dark and ghostly goblins
Flicker by the lamp;
Listen to their laughter
As they flicker by the lamp!

When the rain is falling
And the night is bleak,
Something moves the knocker
And makes the hinges creak;
Sometimes on the window
A waving shadow falls;
Sometimes clammy whispers
Echo through the halls.

They lure you with sweet voices
When you should be in bed;
Something creaks behind you,
Something creaks ahead,
Something gazes at you
From out behind a tree,
But if you look around you
Nothing you will see.

In the hours of darkness
Thronging from their camp
Dark and ghostly goblins
Flicker by the lamp;
Listen to their laughter
As they flicker by the lamp!

Age 13 to 14, 1921–1922

(These verses, written when I was thirteen, have been among the
most published of my works. They travel in tandem, in anthologies

or the parts of anthologies aimed at children, in tandem with James Whitcomb Riley's "An' the Gobble-uns 'll git you / Ef you don't watch out")

Sunset and Moonrise

The clouds that spurred across the sky
Were puffed with redolent wonder
And nearby
The hills were golden under.
He said, "Goodbye."

Just the last few rays in a sunset scene
And the clouds grown gray in the gap between,
He shook hands, stuttered, and turned away,
Not quite sure what he ought to say,
And the higher hills had now turned gray.

She thought:
"Soon the moon will rise and bring
Peace more lovely, and wondering,
More dreamful than the sun has ever brought;
The moon will drive the shadows far away,
And make the night more lovely than the day;
(He has gone without a word—was there nothing he could say?)
The night shall be more lovely than the day!"

She stood still, straight and silent, and the cold
Black closed around and held her in its hold,
But soon the sky grew softer, and the night
Stepped back and left her in the moon's thin light.

It burst the massive shadows of the dark
But formed some trailing tendrils of its own
To crawl from out beneath the trees and mark
Which way its slim light shone.
It roused the sullen stupor of the sky
And made the night seem twice as high
As it had seemed before:

With blanched white face began to change
All things massy into something strange,
It took the ponderous mysteries of the black
And then with wistful hands it gave them back
More subtle, yet more searching than before.

Again he came through the moonlight scene
Sure of his welcome, tall, serene
And laughing.

She heard him come and break the charm
Of wistfulness the moon had gently brought;
His crunching footsteps burst the lovely calm;
And yet his advent was the thing she sought!
She felt his light and power begin
To clutch her hard and then sink in.
An impulse snatched her and she fled,
Leaving his shadow motionless, a blurring gray;
She fled, and laughed to see the moon still bright above her head,
Making the night more lovely than the day.

Age 15–16, 1923–1924

Vagabond

A dim, dank night and the road ahead,
Passing through latticed woods, was a shining thread
That tied him to the real,
For the wind in the trees was a crumpling tread,
But the road beneath his heel
Was a tangible thing that he could feel
While the wind with its whimpering fled.

Mystery hung in the clustered boughs that gagged the sky
And the pulling black where numerous dreams had seemed to
  solidify.

And then—a throbbing note on the road behind
And a light like a man who had lost his mind.

[73]

And each shadow-cupped slim leaf
Stood out in obscene relief.
He stepped aside and let it pass,
This thing that broke the chain of fears he loved.
He watched the night again become a mass.

The mosses caressed the trees that pressed
Their darkness down.

He walked ahead and began to feel
That his feet were sore from the bruising stone,
And laughter rung in his ears like steel
For they all had laughed when he set out alone.

Discouraged, he stopped, and the night became
Huge, blank, oppressive. The stillness was a frame
Vast and black that towered over all,
And on its top he crouched, giddy, small—
One movement and the height would fall!

His footsteps smashed, and the immense
Structure of silence toppled, fell,
But then it sprang up and became more dense
Each footbeat made its hugeness swell.

He still walked on and felt how long the road would wind
Before it brought him to a journey's end.
What was the use forever to ascend
A hill that only was a mirage of the mind?
                    Age 15–16, 1923–1924

Shortly after my graduation from the Lincoln School, Mearns published *Creative Youth* (1925), a panegyric to what he considered his
triumphant experiment. Included was an anthology of the children's
verse, in which my contributions were featured. The poet Louis Un-
termeyer praised my works as "sensitive designs." This characterization did not seem to me apt, but I felt by instinct what I have later
learned from experience: "Never quarrel with a favorable review."

   Thus launched into the world, my juvenile poems have lived a life
of their own, mostly cited as models by teachers of writing. It was

after some two generations had lapsed that a selection of my poems, including later examples, was published by the Stonehouse Press in a slim volume entitled *Poems of the Twenties*. Despite a laudatory introduction written by the distinguished poet William Jay Smith, they set no rivers on fire.

10

Transatlantic Adventures

*

During my senior year at the Lincoln School, my parents were engaged in an extensive trip abroad. The possibility existed for me to join them at mid-year since my marks would then be sufficient to ensure my entrance to Harvard without an examination. To take advantage of this situation would mean abandoning at its very apex the triumphant role at the school which I had achieved after so bad a beginning. But it has always been a characteristic of my temperament to look ahead. It was agreed that I should ship on a Mediterranean cruise and join my parents in Egypt.

Egyptian art proved to be too far beyond my experience for me to see the pyramids and the Sphinx as more than exotic literary symbols; nor was my boyish appreciation wide enough to keep me from regarding the celebrated Santa Sophia in Constantinople as an anticlimax. But I wrote home to my classmates, "Athens is wonderful. All the praises you have heard of the beauty of the Acropolis and the Parthenon are insufficient. It seems hardly possible that such grace can be achieved in heavy marble. . . . Despite my non-classical education at Lincoln, I must admit that the most beautiful things I have seen so far are in Greece."

Only "so far." The Renaissance art at Venice struck me as a revelation. It kindled in my mind the love for painting that has flamed there ever since. Father noted that I was perpetually buying photographs of the pictures I most admired. "Quite positive in his opinions."

On to Rome. "He is developing," Father recorded, "an inclination to moon about galleries alone." We motored from Rome to Florence during four of the most blissful days I have ever spent. Father's diary laments automobile breakdowns and periods of rain, but of these discouragements I have no recollection. I was enchanted by the walled hill towns. The cathedral at Orvieto, its façade bright with mosaics, glows in my memory as almost supernatural splendor.

Perugia: I reveled in distinguishing between the paintings of Pinturicchio and Perugino, and was thrilled to recognize Perugino's influence on Raphael. Siena and Giotto! Unexpectedly we swung, when almost at Florence, into the narrow streets of San Gimignano, over which the hostile towers of rival families rose in romantic competition. And always on both sides of the open road the hill towns that seemed an ever-renewing bouquet of fortresses.

Florence! Florence has been built into my life. The impact of the Uffizi and also the Pitti was overwhelming. And a few miles outside the city there awaited a more personal excitement which became a major force in my career. With my parents, I stayed at I Tatti, the villa of the famous art historian Bernard Berenson, whose wife, Mariechen, was Mother's first cousin and long-time friend.

On the walls of the sumptuous mansion I glimpsed, as the butler showed us to our rooms, a succession of great paintings. It was with a high heart that I began to unpack.

Then there arose a sound of rushing water. A knock on the door and a maid appeared to announce, intellibly enough in Italian, that my bath was ready. I was still young enough to resent having anyone tell me to take a bath, but I felt grimy and agreed.

No sooner was I dry and back in my bedroom than rushing water again sounded. Another knock on the door; a different maid but the same announcement. I tried to tell her in my halting Italian that there had been a mix-up. My bath had already been run. I had taken it. She listened uncomprehendingly, repeated her announcement, and, with a look that implied "you dirty pig," departed.

What to do? I had no intention of taking another bath, but the water was in the tub, unctuously, accusingly waiting. I felt like a complete fool as I tiptoed out in the elegant hall, shut the bathroom door behind me, and surreptitiously pulled out the plug. Back again in my room, I could not help straining my ears apprehensively for another gurgle of flowing water. But what I heard was the luncheon gong.

I was still somewhat flustered when in a large crowded drawing room I for the first time met Cousin Bernard. He was a small, delicately featured man with a soft white beard. Obviously proud of his tiny, manicured hands, he moved them when he talked with precise self-conscious gestures. Surrounded by an admiring group of very stylish middle-aged ladies, he accorded me no more than a handshake.

Finally, bored with sitting silent and unnoticed, I rose to look at the pictures on the walls. They were so beautiful that, as I stared, I forgot the company. Once, as I turned to move from one masterpiece to the next, I thought I saw Berenson's eye upon me, but, if so, it returned instantly to the ambassador's wife who was grinning at him.

Lunch in a large ornate room was then more populous than my mother's grandest dinner parties. I was seated near enough to BB to eavesdrop on his ritualistic flirtation with a striking brunette, whose middle-aged face was so expertly made up to appear young that it presented a disturbing double image. She seemed to have a facial tic, but I could not be altogether sure, since every time her mouth began to pull out of shape she would absorb the movement in a dazzling smile.

No one paid the least attention to me. Eventually, the human spectacle palled, and I became conscious that I had been sitting for more than an hour clodlike in the middle of chatter. Mother's favorite story of how she had silenced my brother in the presence of Bertrand Russell arose in my mind, trailing irritation. I resolved that I would speak up, although it seemed certain that I would be immediately squelched. When reading Solomon Reinach's account of Italian painting, I had been skeptical about a statement that I had found there. I would ask Cousin Bernard.

Into a momentary pause, I launched my voice: "Is it true that there are only three existing paintings by Cimabue?"

Berenson's mouth had been opening to speak to the lady by his side, and his little hand had been preparing a gesture, but with the quickness of a cat he dropped his hand and turned his head to face me. "You got that statement from Reinach, didn't you?"

"Yes."

"Reinach got it from me, but I've changed my mind." He was suddenly chuckling. "It's the most ridiculous statement I ever heard."

As the party filed back toward the sitting-room, Cousin Bernard appeared at my side. "These people will be going home soon. Nickie"—he nodded in the direction of his handsome companion-secretary—"is expert at shooing them out. Don't you go anywhere. I've told Nickie. I have a plan."

When we were alone with the sweet-smiling Nickie, Berenson explained that it was time for his rest, but then he would take his afternoon walk. Would I come along? He would show me some fine views of Florence. He seemed genuinely pleased when I assented.

"While I rest"—and he was already leading the way—"you might like to read here in the library. I noticed you looking hard at my Piero—at least *I* call it a Piero. It does present problems." He was pulling books from a shelf. "You might like to see what I say about it. And also what the fools"—the word was altogether cheerful—"write who disagree with me. You've got a fresh, unspoiled eye; at least, I had when I was your age. Tell me later what you think."

When I looked up from the volumes he had handed me, he had vanished, it seemed miraculously, since no means of exit was visible. I was in an unbroken circle of books, tier on tier rising to where high windows intervened. When he came to get me an hour later, a section of the bookcase swung back. It was so delicately cantilevered that it moved at a touch.

How well I remember that library where day after day I read as he rested! How well I remember our daily walks! Berenson could be a prickly companion for pompous adults. I can still see him standing on his toes, looking like an angry bantam rooster, beside the huge column of flesh that was an English general. The general had said that a good beating never hurt any man. Screaming with rage, Berenson might well have physically assaulted his gigantic adversary had not Nickie intervened. But with me he was all joy and gentleness.

As I look back on it now, I see that, chameleon-like, he took on himself my youth. Although his shiny car with its immaculately respectful Italian chauffeur usually let us out where the walk was downhill and met us again before the road turned sharply upward, how jauntily he strutted down the slope, how gaily he leapt on rocks to secure a better outlook, how boyishly he swung his cane! He was not really old, only sixty, but to me he seemed frail. He would have been deeply hurt had he known that the contrast between his capers and those of my usual adolescent companions gave me, perhaps because I came to love him, my first deep sense of the tragic physical weakening that comes with passing years. But there was nothing weak about his talk—that was pure excitement.

I remember that he tickled me up by saying that my Italian was so execrable that I should instantly get an Italian mistress; it was the only way to learn a language, and he himself had had—this statement was accompanied by a little histrionic gesture—several mistresses by the time he was seventeen. As a politely bred American boy, I would have been confused and embarrassed by an Italian mistress, but I was complimented by BB's suggestion.

Of art we talked by the hour. He took me sometimes to the galleries in Florence, and never expressed an opinion until he had heard mine. If we disagreed, we would argue. He never talked on a level on which I could not follow him, or spoke with any note of authority. If I was usually convinced in the end, that was because he had won in a fair debate. For his part, he seemed interested by my untutored reactions, eager to absorb what little I could teach him. He had me write out for him my favorite sonnet by Edna St. Vincent Millay, and he seemed edified by my demonstration that certain angels, in I have forgotten what picture, were doing a dance step that I had learned in New York. But sometimes our debates became heated, and then visitors to the Uffizi or the Pitti would be horrified to hear a boy shout at the great Bernard Berenson, "You're crazy!" and to have the great BB shout the insult right back.

This unorthodox introduction to art-historical study was to have a major effect on my career. An early indication of this was my decision at Harvard that, having been taught by Berenson and being in a position to go back to him, it would be pointless for me to take any of the art-historical courses the university offered. Thus, as I wrote my many books on the history of American painting, I was a maverick. This was from a practical point of view a very unwise decision since, although I was to write many books on the history of American painting I was not indoctrinated, or even informed, about the shibboleths of academic art scholars.

*

On to London, where Mother eagerly brought me together with her own literary mentor, Logan Pearsall Smith. He had been copiously informed by the female correspondents who kept family communications open that on the American branch a young writer was beginning to leaf out. If he had been actually inflicted with anything I had written, he was never to mention it to me. He could have been nothing but put off by my crude if energetic effusions. For my part, I read his most famous book, *Trivia*, with a feeling that I was being unfairly treated. It was nice to have a literary cousin whose name made my English teachers gasp—but why did he have to write epigrams and prose poems that seemed to me drops of elderly vitriol or artificial garlands of delicately withered flowers?

However, there was no doubt that Cousin Logan was a much-admired writer, and, for all my brashness, I knew I had much to learn. It was with a nervous hope that I could bridge the gap between myself and the author of *Trivia* that I accompanied my mother through springtime London to the family settlement on St. Leonard's Terrace.

Mother had paid the cabby and was now standing on the sidewalk, her face alight with happy memories. Finally, observing my anxious look, she smiled with a mingling of affection and amusement. "I'm sure you'll get on with Logan," she said. "After all, you're both writers."

Thus complimented, it was with a certain confidence that I awaited the opening of the door and then followed the maid down a narrow hall to a drawing room where I saw a sight that delighted me: my first Englishman with a monocle! He proved, on introduction, not to be Cousin Logan but his disciple Gaythorne-Hardy. Cousin Logan had not yet made his entrance.

We had been received by Cousin Alys, who shared the house with her brother. The divorced first wife of Bertrand Russell was a large woman, still handsome, dowdy in the ineffable manner which contributes so much to the impressiveness of British matrons. She had twin passions: charitable work and the family. She and Mother were soon deep in discussions of some distant relatives about whom I had never heard. The man with the monocle, motionless as if stuffed, showed no desire to recognize my presence.

Eventually, there was a shuffling sound and in came an elderly man who I realized must be Cousin Logan. He was taller than I had expected from the delicacy of his writings. However, he was stooped and peered nearsightedly through glasses. Giving me a limp hand, he said in the impeccable British accent that had got him appointed a monitor of pronunciation over the BBC, "I understand that you wish to be a writer."

"That's right," I replied, beaming.

"I hope you will not produce best sellers."

"Why not?"

"No good writer has ever produced a best seller."

This was too much for my modern education. "What about Byron?" I asked. "And, of course, Dickens?"

"Byron and Dickens were not good writers."

At this, the man with the monocle suddenly came to life. He laughed heartily, as at something devilishly clever. Logan simpered. I observed them with amazement, for once completely tongue-tied.

*

All the more because my mother was disappointed, I was not happy about my failure to get together with Logan. However, he was not the family literary connection in whom I was most interested.

Cousin Ray, Logan's and Alys's niece, was married to the brother of the biographer Lytton Strachey. Although I had no foresight of what would be his influence on me when I became a biographer, Strachey's prose style—clear, simple, yet capable of all emotion—came to me as a perfection I would like some day to reach. Ray explained that Strachey was very shy, and that he would never knowingly allow himself to meet a teen-aged admirer. But, she added that, as he was staying at her house, she would slip me in unannounced to breakfast.

I arrived in the early morning to be seated with my cousins at a table with one chair still vacant. Eggs and toast were tasteless as I waited. At last, an amazingly perpendicular figure—tall, narrow, emaciated, drooping a red beard—appeared in the doorway, clad only in trousers and an undershirt. Startled eyes fixed on me. A high, almost falsetto voice cried, "I see you have company!" And Lytton Strachey vanished, never again to be seen by me.

*

Alys was an inveterate lecturer on "good causes." Eager to impress me, she took me along on a train trip to a girls' school where she was to deliver an address. We strode—she was an energetic walker— from the rural station to an ornate gate in a high fence. A watchman stopped us: no male visitors were permitted! Alys replied that she was the lecturer and she intended to have her cousin hear her. As Alys was trying to push by the watchman, enter a woman who would have been an impressive fullback on any football field. She announced herself as the headmistress, and said that since His Majesty had been the Prince of Wales there had never been a male visitor in the school. Alys replied that the rule was silly and that she would not leave her cousin outside. It became a battle of Titanesses from which I would have quailed had I not witnessed Aunt Carey on the warpath. The two combatants were equal in determination and conviction of their own consequence, but my cousin had the edge: the lecture had been scheduled, the girls and guests were already in the assembly room. And Alys was threatening to take the next train back to London.

A compromise was reached: after the meeting had begun, a senior prefect would smuggle me in surreptitiously through a back window, through which I would withdraw again as Cousin Alys was being applauded. But even the most masterly strategy can be frustrated by an overlooked detail. Directly beyond the window, invisible to me as I climbed over the sill, lurked a spindly chair. I knocked it over with a crash. All the girls turned as one girl, and, seeing a boy entangled with a chair, they giggled in chorus.

Had I been Wodehouse's Bertie Wooster, I would have burned with embarrassment, but Bertie's redoubtable aunts did not include a president of Bryn Mawr who had for years made him trail after her into female classrooms where he was the only male and all the girls had stood up as we entered. Already highly amused at the whole situation, I laughed harder than the girls, further incited by the furious glances aimed at me by the headmistress from the platform. Cousin Alys merely rapped for order and went on with her lecture.

As we returned together to London, she did not consider the incident worth mentioning.

*

During my six months' trip abroad, my affairs had been boiling at home. I was officially admitted to Harvard, "a weight off his mind," Father noted, "as quietly (I think) he had feared some failure on the school's part to see him through." On the basis of the three issues I had edited before sailing, *Lincoln Lore* had won a national prize as a school literary magazine. And Mearns's *Creative Youth* had been published.

I I

HARVARD

*

MY four years at Harvard, from the ages of seventeen to twenty-one, presided over the change from boyhood to manhood. Not given to boasting—my father saw to that—I never mention in social situations the books I have published, the prizes and honors I have won, but I do not hesitate to state that I am a Harvard man. This seems to me as basic as stating that I was born in New York City.

Harvard furnished me, during those transition years, with a solid and inspiring environment, but without impeding in any serious way my individual freedom. Other institutions are inclined to sneer at what they call "Harvard indifference." It is true that a student could disappear for a month or more without any official notice being taken. A student should not get in trouble with the police. You could flunk out or be put on probation for inadequacies in your studies, but for the most part you could do what you pleased. The whole atmosphere welcomed individualism, freedom of thinking as long as it was not utterly crackbrained. The pressures of the oldest college in America, and the greatest, was for excellence, however achieved.

*

New to me was living altogether with males. Had I gone to boarding school this would not have been new. Had I been much younger this situation would not have existed. In my day, the surest way of getting expelled was to be caught with a woman in your room. True, an occasional female graduate student could be seen passing through the Yard (Harvard's campus) but I do not remember any women in my classes. I enjoyed the relaxed informality of living altogether with my own kind. Perhaps my companions also had childhood memories of being bossed around, to the insult of our emerging sense of manhood, by women.

From my sophomore through my senior years, I traveled from one dormitory to another with seven other boys. We were a random selection who had come together at the end of our freshman year; only one, Jack Phillips, remained my close friend. Perhaps the lack of singularity contributed to our relationship as a group. We resolved that chess, with all its tempting complications, would interfere with our studies, and established our game as checkers. We became very skillful. This had for me an unforeseeable advantage. When, after my sophomore year, I bicycled through France, I discovered that the husbands of the landladies of the village boarding houses where we stopped believed they were checkers players. I would challenge them for twice the bill or nothing, and usually they were putty in my hands.

Our male world was far from monastic. Harvard was surrounded with young women. Radcliffe and other women's colleges; debutante parties in Boston; in Cambridge a series of dances attended mostly by professors' daughters. And then there was heavily populated Boston, a short subway ride away, and also our environs in Cambridge.

All the Lincoln School boys had pitied the girls who, fired at an earlier age by Nature, looked at us emotionally. But at Harvard I passed the divide, starting my realization of how different one from another such relationships can be!

Cambridge had, with its long cultural tradition, attracted an intellectual population of its own. Among those attracted was a couple, whose name you might well recognize, who had played a major role in the great days of Greenwich Village. They had a fascinating daughter, a few years younger than I, alive with wild ideas and with energy, who was the first girl I believed I loved. She wanted me to initiate her into sexual intercourse. This, following the theories of her father, she considered a major rite, so important to a woman that were it butchered it would damage her whole life. As for me, I had not yet "gone the whole hog" and, attractive as I found my companion, was frightened by the responsibility. This contretemps was so harrowing that I was not so much jealous as relieved when she told me that some older man had successfully carried her through the initiation. But far from pursuing the path he had opened, I fell out of love.

Another romance was sparked by Harvard's failure to supply dining facilities beyond the freshman year. This sent us out to restaurants. At one we often frequented, there suddenly appeared a young waitress whose black hair and eyes were in stunning contrast with the blondest of complexions. As she put a lump of sugar in my coffee, she whispered into my ear the refrain from a popular song, "I can't give you anything but love, baby." This was far too intriguing not to follow up.

When completely revealed, the contrast in her coloring was even more dramatic. Sexually she was voracious but also fastidious. I was more experienced by then, but if I attempted anything beyond the basic relationship, she was outraged. In conversation I had to be very careful since she found shocking what a debutante would find amusing. Concerning herself, she confided to me only a name and that she had come from French Canada. I was subsequently to discover that she had lived in a cheap boarding house, but I picked her up at the restaurant when it closed. Concerning me she showed no interest beyond what was obvious: I went to Harvard. She would not let me give her even the smallest present or take her to a movie.

One evening, she was not there when the restaurant closed. The management told me she had, without notice, failed to appear. I made a little search from what information they could give me, but could discover nothing. She had moved on without leaving a clue. I could only hope that the world would be kind to her.

*

In great contrast with the situation at the Lincoln School, I found, during my four years at Harvard among my fellow undergraduates, no literary companionship. There was, it is true, a traditional literary magazine, the *Advocate*. Its self-perpetuating board of editors was filled by inheritance with boys from the principal preparatory schools. In those environments, dominated by athletics, they had been regarded as semi-effeminate freaks, and had responded by determining to show how much more genteel literature was than football. They went in for mulled wine ceremoniously drunk by candlelight. They did publish two or three of the poems I submitted but then, in returning another, they enclosed the sheet that had gone from editor to editor for comments. The comments were all supercilious and snide, cooked up I presumed to impress each other, and enclosed, I assumed, to squelch me. I submitted no more writings to the *Advocate*.

As a sophomore, I tried to bring together a group interested in writing. It seemed a good start when I corralled two impressive members. One was Conrad Aiken, an excellent poet who was about to win a Pulitzer Prize, and had been appointed at Harvard as poet-in-residence. The other was Lincoln Kirstein, the son of a wealthy department store owner, who had spent several years in Paris associating with avant-garde celebrities. As a freshman, considerably older than his classmates, he had founded *The Hound and Horn*, a magazine intended to fill the gap left by the demise of the *Dial*, which Marianne Moore had edited. The other members were whatever undergraduates I had been able to sieve out.

Aiken, by attending, was carrying out his job at Harvard but felt no obligation to go beyond being present and looking bored. Kirstein, on the contrary, felt it his duty to educate us: he lectured without stopping about his contacts in Paris and how important they were. My lack of enthusiasm made him, when our paths crossed again some years later, remember me as a "stuck-up kid." I don't remember that the group ever met again.

I did have a poem I wanted to get into *The Hound and Horn*. Lincoln grandly referred me to his managing editor. When I visited the editor in his college dormitory, I found myself in the kind of situation women complain about. He expressed himself as much more interested in me than in my poem. After I quickly departed, he returned the poem.

I continued writing poetry, but lacking the Lincoln School's electric atmosphere and Mearns's evangelical backing, I was less prolific. My major poem was a long—a hundred lines—effort called "Monk," dealing with religious doubts, which principally impresses me today because of its elaborate rhyme schemes. However, it did win one of two honorable mentions in an all-college poetry contest. My shorter works were much better, and I was proud to publish a selection in my 1991 anthology.

Eagerly, I took what composition courses Harvard offered. Foster Damon, my instructor in the freshman course, came to regard me as a star pupil and invited me around to his house. Although he put none of his own energies behind my writing as Mearns had done, our discussions were elevating. He was the first professional writer—himself a poet and an expert on William Blake—I had ever encountered.

There was no sophomore composition course. The course for juniors had been given for decades by "Tubby" Meynadeer, whose figure was signaled by his nickname and whose lack of fire was demonstrated by his having never risen above instructor. It may have been because of his inertia that he agreed to my unconventional request that I be allowed to submit portions of a novel as my weekly themes. These he accepted with no further comment than that he found interest in their depiction of the younger generation. At the end of the year he awarded me a B, which was a double irritation because it barred me from what was designated "group one" where you were allowed only half a B under 3 A's.

*

Although I entitled my novel "Dogs Shall Eat Jezebel," I lacked the experience to depict a bona fide Jezebel; nor had I ever known a dog capable of eating one. The plight of my heroine might have been a "women's lib" homily concerning the education of women.

The setting was the overlapping worlds of the Boston debutantes and the graduates of socially correct boarding schools now at Harvard. There are two major characters: Jerry, one of the leading debutantes of her year; and Bo Willard, a lower-class saxophone player in a band that played for society dances.

Jerry is a true fascinator, high-spirited and bright. The trouble is that, having gone to the most correct finishing school in Boston, she is basically uneducated. She has no resources beyond the wealth and social position to which she was born except a peppy allure that overwhelms her male contemporaries and makes her the belle of every ball.

Her preordained companions are the most socially correct Harvard undergraduates. My spiteful depiction of them sparks my plot. With a much brighter mind than theirs, easily able to dominate them, Jerry becomes bored with their chatter and admiration. Her success at the dances become routine. She yearns for variety, some new excitement, but can visualize it only in terms of a different kind of man.

I supply her with a mathematical whiz, available because he does appear at some dances. Although he is despised by her habitual admirers as a "greasy grind"—there is a disgusting rumor that he gets all A's—she invites him to one of her weekly tea parties. His clumsy embarrassment and the cruel mockery directed at him by her other guests enrage and humiliate Jerry. She realizes that this respectable road to escape is not open to her.

The great inspiration of Jerry's life is jazz, and at the Antipodes Club, her favorite cabaret, Bo Willard, the saxophonist, is the Great God Pan. By expertly maneuvering out of sight of her escorts, she makes a date with him.

I avoided normal plot devices. Bo is not a virile seducer like Lady Chatterley's gardener, or a calculating schemer, or a natural philosopher, or a political radical. He is a good-natured, simple son of the people, set up by his naïveté to be the victim of my novel. He is, of course, endlessly complimented by the interest of the fascinating, rich, and socially correct Jerry. He tries to find the manners to please her, and resolves to make himself worthy to marry her, not doubting that her family will accept him if he achieves his ambition of having a jazz band of his own.

Bo wishes to protect the purity of his future bride. And Jerry is not enough of a rebel to break so basic a taboo. Yet she enjoys the sense of danger. Although they go only so far in their lovemaking, they go that far with the deepest passion they dare permit themselves.

There is, however, an ever-present, actual danger in Jerry's situation. For men to associate with lower-class women is acceptable, a subject for boasting in male circles and considered an alternative vastly preferable to seducing "nice girls." But for "nice girls," clandestine assignations with "lower-class" men is a heinous violation of the code. If Jerry's activity is discovered, her whole social world will turn against her. Her Harvard swains, ruling that she had besmirched herself, will discard all the admiration that is the fuel for her resplendent career. And her family! They will surely not drive her out into the proverbial snowstorm, but they will surely take drastic steps:

most probably annihilate all her Boston triumphs by banishing her to some very strictly chaperoned refuge in Europe. And there would be a blot on her reputation she might never be able to erase.

Jerry refuses to allow Bo anywhere near her house, or let him take her to any place frequented by her set. He accepts this with some resentment, but is on the whole not sorry to wait until, having a band of his own, he will be welcomed into her world. The affair continues until Jerry's birthday when her mother decides to arrange for her a surprise party.

Anxious to please her daughter, the mother hires the band from Jerry's favorite haunt, the Antipodes Club. Bo sets out with his fellow musicians unconscious of where they are going. Finding himself in Jerry's house, displayed on the wrong side of the social barrier, he concludes, not knowing that Jerry has not been informed, that she is purposely humiliating him. Making a belated appearance to be surprised by cries of "Happy Birthday!" Jerry is delighted until she looks up to see Bo glowering in a fury at her from the improvised bandstand.

She recognizes the urgent necessity to explain, but how is she to reach him? She cannot, without casting to the winds all discretion, walk up on the platform to whisper in his ear. Her getting one of her admirers to carry a cryptic message, plus Bo's inability to hide his anger, raises suspicions. As she tries to be her usually peppy self on the dance floor, Jerry hears, or thinks she hears, whispering all around her.

I had got almost this far by the end of my junior year. I intended to finish the novel in English 5, the senior composition course that had been made legendary by the magic of Charles Townsend Copeland. Copey had retired but he still held court in his top-floor rooms over the Harvard Yard. An old-fashioned lamp in his window would indicate that he was at home to his undergraduate friends. I would climb the stairs to be greeted by a tiny histrionic man who enjoyed playing the role of the oldest relic from times past. His walls and tables were covered with mementos. He loved to hold forth about the glories of that famous actress of his youth, Minnie Maddern Fiske.

When, as an old lady, Mrs. Fiske appeared in a Shakespearean comedy in Boston, I went in honor of Copeland. Although actually on the verge of death, she appeared as the ingenue, hobbling across the stage flirtatiously manipulating a fan. This seemed to me comic until I looked around at the audience. Mostly men, they were the actress's contemporaries, and every wrinkled old face revealed affectionate pleasure. They were all not seeing her as the decrepit figure on the stage but picturing the actress they had loved when they were all young together. An interloper from my own generation, I felt out of place and departed deeply moved.

Copeland's joy in the past as a living thing gave him no use for arty pupils or namby-pamby writers. Most of his disciples—I was to run into many as a newspaper man in New York—were virile, active in the contemporary world. About whom he talked so movingly as to elicit tears was his favorite pupil, John Reed, the flashing journalist and poet who wrote *Ten Days That Shook the World* and who, because of his support of the Communist revolution, was buried in the Kremlin.

Celebrated for his gift of reading aloud, Copeland honored and educated me by reading to me from some of the manuscripts I showed him. Jarring notes stood out as did effective passages. This training encouraged my natural tendency to write for the reader's ear.

*

Copeland's retirement from English 5 proved for me a tragedy. My instructor became Robert Hillyer.

Hillyer had entered Harvard from a correct boarding school and was now honorary editor of the *Advocate*. A prolific poet—he was to win a Pulitzer prize—he was praised for never allowing the slightest hint to enter his stanzas that he lived in the twentieth century. Here is a quatrain picked at random from his *Collected Verse* (1934):

> The Swordsman by the Quiet gate
> Is pacing at his wonted post
> Wherefore no wind can agitate
> The pond that holds the lily's ghost.

In all innocence, I submitted to the devotee of the lily's ghost a chapter from "Dogs Shall Eat Jezebel" which contained the following passage:

"That evening the Antipodes Club was going full blast. The orchestra played indifferent tunes, favorites that in a season would be forgotten, but many a heart beat high and many a body thrilled to their rhythm. Tunes plaintive with the sadness of a wistful child; tunes gay as ear-rings, as trinkets, as silver shoes; tunes brutal as brightly rouged lips. Through it all there was rhythm: the rhythm of life, quickly and carelessly turning all to a dance.

"Here, in the temple of youth, the only sin was not to care for living. So long as your eyes shone with desire and your limbs moved with joy you were beautiful. The marble sculptured beauty the poets sing would not be lovely here. Strong limbs that dance with a will, minds that are drunk with the animal joy of living and loving, the music sings to these its hymnal, to these who worship the brutal rhythm, the mad rhythm, the tragic rhythm of joy."

Hillyer's reaction to such passages: "Perhaps true to life, but to a part of life so futile and meaningless that a report of it is sure to lack interest." Obviously, no more segments of my novel could be used as class themes. As a senior plugging for honors, I could not find outside my studies time to continue "Dogs Shall Eat Jiezebel," and then the world swept me in other directions.

*

The unfinished manuscript was, of course, no more than a trial run. However, my elderly eyes are impressed by how my youthful self avoided one of the most destructive pitfalls to beginners: wandering off into byways. There is not an episode in "Dogs Shall Eat Jezebel" that fails to further the story. I made modified use of Aristotle's three dramatic unities: space (social Boston and its Harvard adjunct), time (only a month or so), and action (social comedy that does not deviate into farce on one side or deep emotion on the other). Although there is no lack of poetic prose, there is no sentimentality.

From reading Percy Lubbock's *The Craft of Fiction*, I had imbibed a technique that I have frequently found useful as a biographer. The writer takes a firm stance looking over his protagonist's shoulder, hearing only what he hears, seeing only what he sees. Most scenes in "Dogs Shall Eat Jezebel" are written exclusively from the point of view of one participant, although the setting is particularized, and the action presented as far as possible as dialogue.

To get inside the minds of my characters, I followed Virginia Woolf's method of coalescing streams of consciousness into successive, interweaving formulations. Thus, I tried to show the mental conflicts and vacillations which led to action, often halfhearted, which in turn created new situations to be faced in equal confusion.

*

I did not take Hillyer's persecution lying down. So much so that Hillyer complained to Copeland that I was disrupting his class. He asked his predecessor to intervene. Copey's sole comment to me was, "Gentlemen do not make trouble." However, I considered myself a writer.

The prep-school boys had flocked to study with their representative. For the first time I had an opportunity to be in person condescended to by editors of the *Advocate* and their ilk. Hillyer was proud to have them in his class, and perpetually read aloud with admiration the stories they wrote. I began to notice a sameness. The hero had gone to one of the best schools where he had been an outcast because, revolted by athletics, he spent his time wandering along a river bank or through a flowery field, murmuring verses. Yet he shed an aura that made his classmates secretly admire him. When they all got to Harvard, the hero, who edited the *Advocate*, occasionally heard with distaste of his classmates' exploits on the football field. On graduation, he set up as a poet and wrote verses too exquisite for popular recognition. Eventually, the vulgarity of the world became more than he could bear and, and at some esthetically perfect moment, he committed suicide.

In a story I submitted to Hillyer, the hero was a pug-ugly who loved to box and wrestle but was sent to a school like Lincoln where everyone was writing poetry. They despised him because, as they discussed the sonnet form, he practiced with a punching bag. Yet somehow they respected him. (If they didn't, he'd punch them in the breadbasket). At Harvard, as captain of the football team, he heard vaguely of their exploits on the *Advocate*. And when he returned to his high school for his tenth class reunion, he found himself truly unique. All the others had, at exquisitely perfect moments, committed suicide.

That Hillyer was far from pleased with this effort goes without saying. He gave me for the course "C−," much the lowest mark I received during all my four years at Harvard. After I had become a successful author, I ran into him at a literary party and wondered whether he would apologize. Far from it. He minced up to me and said, "I am proud to have been the first to recognize your talents and to have given you an A." The S.O.B.!

*

Participation in organized athletics was required of all freshman. When I informed the track coach that I had been the best sprinter in my high school, he looked at my short legs, smiled, and assigned me to cross-country. Not relishing the prospect of grinding along mile after mile, I rebelliously entered myself in the dash at the all-college "Fall Handicaps." Again smiling at my legs, the coach gave me a considerable handicap. No other runner, not even the great Al Miller, passed me. I was given a gold medal featuring a wingèd foot, and had my picture in a Boston newspaper.

I have always particularly relished achievement outside my usual beat. I dearly loved that gold medal. However, when I showed it to my best girl she could not have been less interested. Thus, I began my long, long experience in the futility of trying to impress artistic women with non-artistic achievements.

Enrolled in the freshman track team, I got great satisfaction in sitting with the muscle boys, under the eyes of the whole freshman class, at the "training table" where we were served food, mostly red meat, that was supposed to enhance our energy. And I spent one of the most amusing afternoons of my life at the pep talk we were given before our contest with the Yale freshmen.

The problem to be overcome by our head coach, Eddie Farrell, was that in published statistics in newspapers—speed for runners, height for jumpers, distance for hammer throwers—we were out-classed. After each specialty coach had finished his instructions, Farrell commanded him out of the room, slamming and locking the door behind him. When finally we were alone with him, he leapt to his feet in a fury, shouting that we were "yellow," a bunch of cowards afraid we would be beaten because of a lot of damn fool figures. He ticked each of us off one by one. Then he became sentimental. There wasn't an American boy who would not be proud to be in our shoes tomorrow. Ten thousand men of Harvard would be running or throwing behind us. The freshman sitting next to me said that he could feel the presence of those ten thousand Harvard men.

P.S. We were clobbered.

*

This was the end of my athletic career. I preferred the Harvard Dramatic Club, which made me break "training" by staying up late at night. True, I entered ignominiously as a member of the properties department. Furthermore, I was not allowed, when my turn came, to manage this aspect of the production because of the rule (I do not remember how that was explained to me) that, although Jews might be members, they were forbidden positions from which they could admit further Jews.

Father, while preparing me for discrimination, had urged me not to regard it as a wall, but as a hurdle to be leapt. My interest in the theater was plenty great enough to make me accept the situation and thoroughly enjoy my membership in the Dramatic Club. There, I learned my first lessons in dramatic production since the club was living up to an important tradition, being a continuation of the "47 Workshop" which, before the professor, George Pierce Baker, had been lured to Yale, had trained Eugene O'Neill, among others.

I remember best what was the first production in America of James Elroy Flecker's poetic play *Hassan*, from which I had memorized passages in high school. Laid in Istanbul, it was replete with romance, lust, and cruelty. I was allowed to play the keeper of the gate. As the curtain rose on the first act, I stood alone on the stage wearing only a skimpy loincloth. The audience burst into applause. I was as amazed as I was pleased. I had not realized that I had so impressive a physique. But, after a euphoric moment, I realized that they were in fact applauding the scenery.

*

My predecessors from the Lincoln School handed on to me leadership in the Harvard Liberal Club. I did stump Massachusetts around Harvard (although too young to vote) in "The Brown Derby Brigade," a group of students thus accoutered supporting Al Smith (who, as governor of New York had been an associate of my father's) for president against Herbert Hoover. However, I much preferred the Dramatic to the Liberal Club. This did not prevent my being run for

Liberal Club president at the end of my sophomore year. Fortunately, I was defeated, as I was not interested enough to do the job well. But, I was elected secretary, in charge of procuring speakers. Thus, I was enabled to spend a day with Clarence Darrow, the lawyer who defended John Scopes during his trial for teaching evolution: a rumpled, benevolent, outgoing, elderly man symbolized in my memory by a rain of gray ashes from recurring cigars on his generous front. I got to know, to my subsequent profit, when I was a reporter and then a government official, the perennial Socialist candidate, Norman Thomas, whose political conceptions foreshadowed the New Deal. Wishing to present all views, I dug out a Communist speaker, although Communism was illegal in Massachusetts.

Shortly thereafter, there appeared in my dormitory room a young man dressed so meticulously as a collegiate gentleman that I assumed he must have some connection with Princeton. Once seated, he started a conversation about college football. His information was accurate, but I detected a hollowness in his enthusiasm that was un-Princetonian. I was becoming restive when he abruptly changed the subject. He was empowered to inform me that I had been granted a great honor and opportunity by the government of the Soviet Union. Distressed at the slanders about Communism promulgated in American institutions by the enemies of the people, the government was inviting leading undergraduates from leading universities to visit Russia at the government's expense so that the truth could be revealed to them. We would be accorded special honors and privileges! I had been selected to represent Harvard!

What would have been the effect on my career had I accepted? Instead, I spent the summer with a classmate bicycling in France.

*

During all my time at Harvard, I did almost disgracefully well at examinations. Having been modernly educated and admitted by certificate, I had never faced an examination until my freshman mid-years. What might well have been a disadvantage worked in my favor. My friends, having for years been menaced by periodic examinations, viewed them with a combination of resentment and dread. Novelty enabled me to enjoy the challenge. Furthermore, I had the gift of gab with my pencil. I usually filled three of the blue-bound blank books supplied during examinations while my neighbors had difficulty filling one. Once, having attended few lectures and done no preparation for a course, I had to rely on my roommate's notes. I got a better grade than he did. An explanation is that, if I did not know the direct answer, I would write around it, thus indicating a broader understanding than if I had come up with the specific facts. This went down well at Harvard.

Every year I received an honorary Harvard College Scholarship, and I was always on the Dean's List, which carried with it the only practical privilege earned by high grades: I could lengthen vacations, cutting my last class before and my first after, without getting into trouble. There was a great luxury in dashing through the countryside between Boston and New York on trains that were from a Harvard point of view almost my private vehicles, since almost all other undergraduates were trapped at Cambridge in their usual round.

*

It seemed to me at the beginning that the Harvard professors were less exciting than my teachers at the Lincoln School, who had been chosen because they were zealots for new ideas. The Harvard professors, I assumed, must have become bored from repeating their courses year after year. But I came to realize that what I had called stuffiness was maturity, an accumulation of depth in a lifetime.

The worst offender from my Lincoln School attitude was James Robinson, an expert on Anglo-Saxon and Middle English, whose lectures on Chaucer went to a considerable extent into the exact derivation and meaning of words. Robinson did call our attention to the risqué parts of *The Canterbury Tales* by refusing to assign them. Of him and the sources he loved to cite, I wrote:

> Old Robinson grow contemplative
> On an Anglo-Saxon dative
> Made by romance plurals merry
> Quotes from Manly and Lounsbury
> And, by leaving out what coarses,
> Present a maiden's view of Chaucer.

But under his teaching I became a passionate devotee of Chaucer.

I was inspired by the oratory with which Kirsopp Lake expounded the Bible: he was able to move undergraduates crowding a large lecture hall to actual tears when he described Christ on the Cross crying out, "My God, My God, why hast thou deserted me?" He set me to a passionate study of the Bible as a work of literature.

Every undergraduate had to pass an examination in the Bible. Shortly after I had taken mine, a diminutive elderly man in the garb of a minister hurried into my dormitory room, took both my hands, and stared ecstatically into my face. In twenty years of reading the examinations, he had never come across a paper as good as mine! He wanted me to tell him about the religious family in which I had been raised, of how I had read the Bible over and over from childhood. I made up the best story that on the spur of the moment I could. It would have been cruel to admit that I was a devotee not of religion but of great writing, and that my fascination with the Bible had been enhanced by its being new to me.

The professor who most deeply influenced my thinking was anything but an orator. His head always tilting to the left, Irving Babbitt never looked at the class as he read without emphasis from his notes and the books stacked around him. When a bell indicated the end of the period, he would finish his sentence but not his line of thought, gather up the pile on his desk, and walk out. The next lecture would begin without prologue at the exact spot where he had ended.

The brand of "humanism" Babbitt taught was at that time subjecting him to violent attack for questioning, in a manner considered to smack of fascism, fundamental assumptions of American life. I was fascinated because he challenged the shibboleths on which my Lincoln School education had been grounded. He denied that man was naturally good; that the innocence of a child babbled invaluable insight; that inspiration was more important than accumulated wisdom; that progress advanced with history; that the golden age lay not in the past but in the future. Thus, Babbitt opened to my view the historical and cultural importance of the classicism that denied the romantic assumptions which I had been taught to accept as revealed truths. It became clear to me that there were profound values in both systems, and I began to realize that the change of emphasis from one to the other which accompanied the decline of aristocracies and the rise of the middle class was one of the tremendous currents in human development.

This realization was to become of the greatest importance to my biographical and historical writings. Envisioning the American experiment in terms of advancing positions in the slow, inevitable shift from classicism to romanticism brought a broader view and deeper understanding. To take a major example: a basic explanation of the greatness of our Founding Fathers, including Washington. Their position in the transition, just when the balance was truly beginning to shift, enabled them to be simultaneously classicists and romantics, to bring together, with no inner sense of conflict, a totality of human nature, the backward and the forward view.

*

Entering my senior year, looking ahead to my graduation, I resolved to try for high honors, a degree either *magna cum laude* or *summa cum laude*. I would have to pass brilliantly the divisional examinations, covering the whole field of English literature, that were given to all English majors; I would have to write an impressive thesis, and, if I got that far, pass an oral examination, again on all English literature. Preparation should, I felt, engage all my efforts, but what about the courses I was routinely taking? There was a provision that if you did achieve high or highest honors, you would be excused from your routine examinations. I decided to neglect my courses, although accepting a risk of not graduating at all.

When the divisional examination I had prepared for so passionately was put before me, I felt crippled by the pedantic questions that permitted nothing but bare factual answers. This inspired me, although I had achieved the high mark I needed, to write a diatribe which was published in the *Harvard Crimson* denouncing the examination for having "no question longer than twenty minutes, and all these little problems deal with trivialities. . . . Upon such unimportant massing of fact the English Department places its emphasis."

Fortunately for my immediate ambitions, this expression of a point of view to which I would have said "Amen" during my entire career was published as an unsigned editorial.

*

My disgust at Hillyer's trying to shield the muses from modern times helped spark my desire to have my honors thesis consider what should be the subject matter of poetry in a machine age. The proposal was slapped down by the English faculty as inadequately scholarly. My tutor then dug up a half-forgotten poet who in the nineteenth century had sometimes written about machines, and my subject became "The Influence of Industrialism on Ebenezer Elliot." This made the English Department purr.

My divisional score and my thesis being judged adequate, I was summoned for an oral examination. I found some dozen of the English professors awaiting me. They were justified in questioning me about any aspect of English literature, and sometimes I was stumped. How I longed for those blue-covered examination books in which I could write an extensive circle around a question! Sitting outside a closed door to await the verdict, I was haunted by the course examinations in individual courses that I might have to take and for which I had not prepared.

Called back at last, I was informed that I had been awarded a degree *magna cum laude*. My immediate reply elicited a laugh: did this mean (it did) that I was excused from my final examinations?

There must have been some discussion as to whether I was to receive a *summa*, as one of the professors came away with the impression that this was what I had been awarded. A *summa* from Harvard, nationally recognized as the greatest honor an American undergraduate could receive, would surely have been useful in warding off attacks when in my books on biography and history I invaded, without a Ph.D., fields marked off as purely academic preserves. However, my *magna* indicated that I had done better at my studies than ninety-four per cent of my class.

*

I found three extra uses for my honors thesis. I submitted the whole rigmarole to Babbitt as a term paper. His comment: "Probably better than anything that Ebenezer Elliott ever wrote." Extracting some five pages in which I wrote down my own conclusions, I submitted them to Hillyer who read them out to his class as an abomination. I also submitted my argument to a competition that was open to all seniors for the two short speeches annually delivered at the august university commencement as the contribution from the College. My essay being chosen must have given Hillyer the pip—and it set the professors of diction upon me.

They were horrified to discover that I made the sound of an R in the wrong place in my mouth.*

In what I assume was an anguished discussion as to whether they should try to retrain my R so that I would not disgrace them, they had to conclude that they did not have time to achieve so radical a change. But they felt a greater need to have me in every way perfect according to their standards. They rehearsed me relentlessly before recording machines.

*

The Harvard commencement was the most portentous event in all American academe, representing all the faculties of what was the oldest and considered, although reluctantly, the greatest of American universities. The ceremony began with a procession that was heavy with dignitaries receiving honorary degrees, brightly colored with hundreds of caps and gowns awarded to members of the faculties from all over the world. Close to the front, as I had to mount to the stage, I came along looking like a mouse (and feeling like one) in my ordinary black undergraduate's cap and gown. From the platform I saw several thousand heads filling a wide amphitheater surrounded by low hills. I had been so aggressively trained by the elocution department that my voice had seemed hoarse the night before, but as I left my friends to step into the procession, it had seemed normal. However, the elocutionists had not warned me about the booby trap that was to assail me as soon as I began to speak into the highly amplified microphone.

My first words had set out satisfactorily, but they would not stay away. Almost instantly they reappeared to interrupt what I was now

---

*Mother had recognized that I had a weak R and had made me say over and over "around the rock the ragged robin ran," etc. This achieved enough of a result that my lack of a true R has never got in my way in speaking English—it is recognized only by experts—but it does interfere with my French.

trying to enunciate. The shock was great, and even after I had realized that I was hearing echoes coming from the surrounding hills, I remained disturbed. But I managed not to disgrace myself before the largest live audience I was ever to address.

*

The university authorities did not limit themselves to allowing me to address the great ceremony. They printed my entire essay on permanent paper (when I unearthed the release more than fifty years later it was in mint condition) as number 112 of all documents that had thus been sent out in the almost six months of 1929. How my speech was received outside of Boston I could not know, but it was published in the three major Boston newspapers: the *Transcript*, the *Globe*, and the *Traveller*, which ran my picture on its front page.

Here are three extracts:

"If poets nowadays try to write as if the industrial revolution never existed, they are doomed to failure. A man's life is more made up of the myriad insignificant minutes he has lived than the few hours he remembers. A thousand trivial events have combined to make him what he is: the beat of his feet on the pavement during random walks; the shine of an electric light over his shoulder; the rumble of a street car which he did not notice as he studied. These innumerable trivialities, rising inevitably round him, each one making a tiny impress on his consciousness, force him to be a man of his period. Though he wishes to be a man of the Middle Ages, though he steeps himself in the literature and culture of past centuries, no matter: even as he reads of Tristan and Iseult the horn of a passing truck colors his mind. . . .

"Great poetry must have reference to the great movements of its time. When kings ruled the world in power as well as name, tragedy could deal only with the fall of kings. A complete study of either Shakespeare or Chaucer would give a better idea of his time than many a history book, as no important elements would be found missing. The flowers of the fields are still beautiful, but since they are not a part of the dominant movement of modern times, no poet can make from pure descriptions of them truly great verse. His work, however finely wrought, would represent only a minor phase of life; it would not be universal. . . .

[103]

"A poet may not content himself with describing machines, for the machines of one generation are different from those of the next. An ode to a 1920 airplane would be out of date in 1929. Authors may no more forget that such machines exist for men than that the men they write about are living in a machine age, traveling in automobiles, talking over the telephone, lighting their houses with electric lights. Poets must see the essence of life through the accident of their own time, but their emphasis must nonetheless be on the essence. Then their work will be immortal. No one fights nowadays with a sword for a weapon, and a shield and a breastplate for defense, but Homer is still read and admired."

*

This argument presaged, although somewhat crudely, the controversies I was to get into years later with academics whose "disciplines" required that art be studied altogether in artistic terms. It was, indeed, at the very moment when I wrote it, heresy that would make professors of literature in lesser institutions rave and almost faint away. That Harvard should so honor and widely disseminate under its official aegis such an essay by an undergraduate seems amazing, and certainly it encouraged me to proceed on what was to be my maverick's path.

12

HERALD TRIBUNE

*

WHATEVER may have been the other effects of the parental ambition that had made me always a year younger than my classmates, at the time of my graduation from Harvard it proved a major boon. Had I followed the norm, I should have been seeking a job after the stock market crash of October 1929. But I emerged during the previous spring into a society confident that the boon would go on forever. My problem was not to find a job but to decide among possibilities.

I intended, of course, to pursue my goal of being a writer. Mother wanted me to do what I might well have been forced to do in the 1930s. Her long discipleship to Logan Pearsall Smith had persuaded her that contact with the vulgar world diffused the creative spirit. The family would put up the money and I would live in a "garret"— the old-fashioned word appealed to Mother—and spin out beauty. Had my primary drive still been to be a poet, I might have listened, but I was now thinking as a novelist, which meant finding a job that combined writing with experiencing the world. My decision hurt Mother's feelings, all the more because I was backed from the other side of the family division by Father. A writer I might become, but no longer under Mother's intimate tutelage.

Following my then primary concern with poetry and the novel, I had not competed to get on the *Harvard Crimson*. But now, I suspected that newspaper reporting would most right the lopsidedness of my upbringing. However, I was glad to consider what advice my parents could procure for me.

Father knew Ivy Lee, the inventor of "public relations," who was using every kind of publication to shape the images of his clients, conspicuously the Rockefellers. He proved to be of impressive presence, jovial without any true joviality. The hand he stretched out was so soft that my hand sunk into his palm as if caught in a quagmire. At first, Lee encouraged my propensity for newspaper work, but suddenly he offered me a job. He would introduce me to a young assistant who would explain the advantages of working with him.

I followed him down a hall to the office of an intense man of about thirty. He was very obsequious, but as soon as Lee left us alone together his face began working with fury. "Don't come here!" he whispered. "Mr. Lee takes all the credit for what I do, so that no one outside these walls knows my name. Lee would never give me a recommendation for any other job. He's got me trapped."

Back in Lee's office, I said that, although it was hard to resist his assistant's enthusiasms, I still preferred newspaper work. Lee replied that the newspaper that would best suit my needs was the *Herald Tribune*. Although I could not expect a regular job or any pay, he was such a great friend of the owners and could probably squeeze me in as an apprentice. It would be a tricky business, and I would, he warned, queer everything if I made any other overture to the *Tribune*.

*

The other of my parents' friends relevant to writing was a publisher, Harrison Smith. He received me with informal friendliness, said be would be glad to give me a job, but that I would do better, as a future novelist, on a newspaper. The *Herald Tribune*, of course. The city editor, Stanley Walker, was a drinking companion of his. He might see Walker any day but, to make things doubly sure, he would give me a note.

Remembering Lee's warning, I tried to dissuade Smith, but I was smart enough not to mention my reason—I suspected that Smith, like all liberals, hated Lee as the prime defender of "malefactors of great wealth." Smith assumed I was being modest, said he was delighted, wrote the letter, and handed it to me. I went off with it in my pocket, feeling somewhat like the Ancient Mariner with the albatross dangling around his neck.

What to do? Trained by my institutional father to admire elevated contacts, I did not realize that it would have spelled disaster to be forced on Walker from above at the behest of the hated Lee. I considered that Lee's offer should be protected from the prior approaches he had warned me against. But supposing Smith did talk to Walker and it came out that I had not delivered the letter?

My father must not have been available to advise me, as he would surely not have countenanced the strategy I decided on. I was going to Wyoming for a summer vacation, and would present my letter a few hours before the train left. All the more because that would be lunch time, Walker would probably be unavailable. So I would re-pocket my letter and skedaddle, able to write Harrison Smith from Wyoming that I had tried.

The she-dragon—I got to know her well—who manned the door to the city room, said that this was a very inconvenient time for Mr. Walker (it was, indeed, when he gave out the day assignments) and that I should come back in a couple of hours. I replied that I would be on a train for Wyoming, grabbed the letter, and made for the door. She called me back, reclaimed the letter, and said that at least she could give it to Mr. Walker. She soon returned to say that Mr. Walker would see me.

I met a slight man with sharp features, intense in contradiction to a very relaxed bearing. He expressed an understanding that I wanted a job on the *Tribune*. Grasping at what I saw as a way out, I said I was not sure. I had been offered jobs in publishing and public relations and had not made up my mind what I wanted to do. Walker's face showed no reaction that I could perceive, but he must have been surprised. To get a job on the *Tribune* was among the highest ambitions of journalists all across the United States, and here was this puppy! However, he did not throw me out. He asked mildly when, if I so decided, I would like to start, and when I would make up my mind.

In a flash I realized that I should throw Ivy Lee out the window, but, of course, I could not instantly change my ground. I said I would be back from Wyoming by the first of September and would know my mind in a few weeks. Walker replied that I should write him if I wanted a job, and he would see what he could do. I wrote without giveaway haste and received a reply that I report on September 1st. I was to receive what was then a good starting salary, twenty-five dollars a week. With great satisfaction, I reported to Lee that I had done it for myself, not as an apprentice but as a regular reporter being paid!

I have been inclined to attribute this miraculous result to a demonstration of how ignorance, clumsiness, and naïveté can sometimes achieve wonders. A job at the *Tribune* was in such tremendous demand that I must have stood out from the endless seekers Walker interviewed by being skittish about whether I preferred the *Tribune*. That Harrison Smith had in his letter dwelt on my being my father's son I refused to take into consideration. In any case, I have never been granted by the world greater good fortune.

*

It was with considerable tribulation that I returned to the *Herald Tribune* building that I had left so lightheartedly, and again found my way to the city room that was now to become my habitat. The she-dragon recognized me (she had that gift), and let me through the door. I found myself in a tremendous room, almost as deep as a city block, with a bare floor and walls, populated by separated clusters of desks. Facing the central cluster was a little colony of desks, with Walker sitting in the center. Walker rose (for the first and last time) to greet me, then handed me over to an assistant.

I was led to the cluster of some thirty-five desks facing Walker. The reporters were huddled so close together that I had difficulty squeezing through to the desk that I was told was assigned to me.

On every desk there sat a battered typewriter which, as I discovered, would respond, although grudgingly, to sharp blows delivered according to the newspaperman's traditional "hunt and punch" method. Any sissy who defied convention by using the touch system must have had difficulties. Even more out of place would have been any delicate soul who could write only in quiet. You were not acclimated until you could compose your story while your neighbors were arguing, often drunkenly, across your typewriter. One of the boons given me by my newspaper experience is the ability to write anywhere—a hotel lobby, a railroad station—impervious to all interruptions that have no personal reference to me.

I was at first puzzled by the intimate conjunction of the desks, unnecessary because there was vacant space on the broad city-room floor. It was, I came to conclude, an inheritance from old newspaper days. Walker had no use for that modern invention, schools of journalism, which he believed taught a lot of folderol. Reporters learned on the job and from each other, and their interaction created the personality of the newspaper.

In his book *City Editor* Walker explained that he hired a beginner on the assumption that he "has some sympathy for the roaring comedy and the tragic foolishness of the human race, that he has a restless and searching mind, that he soaks up smells and information and significant trivia . . .—that is to say, . . . he shows a clear talent for newspaper work.

"Such a young man will find, for all the occasional dreary interludes, that he has been plumped down in the midst of the liveliest and most amusing of worlds. It is, for him, like attending some fabulous university where the humanities are studied to the accompaniment of ribald laughter, the incessant splutter of an orchestra of typewriters, the occasional clinking of glasses, and the gyrations of some of the strangest performers ever set loose by a capricious and allegedly all-wise Creator."

Walker liked to extol to us youngsters charismatic newspapermen, prima donnas of the printed page, whose own personalities often outshone hard news, particularly Gene Fowler and Joel Sayre: both— "Fowler, the playful Hamlet who could bend an icepick double with one hand and for whose safety scores of prizefighters, wrestlers and underworld characters would have given their lives, and Sayre, the puckish ribcrusher from the jungle who can sing old songs for twelve hours without repeating—were, and are, excellent learned reporters, but their value to a paper in what might be called a priestly capacity would be incalculable. As balloon-prickers, daubers of stuffed shirts and philosophical pranksters such men are worth any dozen efficiency experts. There are few things so soul-cleansing as the sound of the seat of a chair giving way when the synod is in full cry."

Sayre was on the *Trib* briefly in my time, and we established a friendship that continued after we had both moved elsewhere. My first signed review for the *Herald Tribune Book Review* (where I was treated with great kindness from the beginning) was highly appreciative (more so than I really felt) of Fowler's novel *Trumpet in the Dust*.

*

I had hardly found my seat on that first day when I was called on to extricate myself from the squeeze to be introduced to a tall debonair reporter in his early thirties who combined the breeziness of Texas with an Irishman's blarney. He was suitably known as Tex O'Reilly. I was to go out with him on a story to learn the ropes.

We covered "The Seventy-Third Annual Scottish Games" at Ulmer Park, in Brooklyn. (I still have the official program along with the clippings of almost every story I wrote.) It proved to be a combined fair and track meet, loud with bagpipes, embellished with kilts and sporrans. As we were departing, Tex asked me what I thought should be the lead?

"What," I asked, "is a lead?"

Tex came to a halt and stared at me. "My God! You've got a job on the *Tribune* and don't know what a lead is?"

Tex explained that the lead opens a story with that aspect which the reporter considers most newsworthy and interesting. The lead is supposed to catch the reader's interest, and it also determines, to a considerable extent, the progression of the rest of the piece.

From that moment to this, some sixty years later, I have been a devotee of leads. I state it differently now, saying that once—it may take days of worrying—I have established the right beginning for a short piece the rest falls into place. This goes for essays, speeches, contributions to magazines, chapters of books, or sub-sections of chapters. For the books themselves, I reverse the process. Having reread the completed manuscript, I extract the gist, which I publish as a foreword.

On that fertile first day as a newspaperman, I received another lesson that also cast a long shadow before me. While Tex wrote his story for publication, I wrote mine for Walker to criticize. I described a sword dance as "fascinating." Walker objected that the adjective achieved nothing: I should describe the dance in a manner that fascinated. How often has that sword dance admonished me when in a fit of laziness I have labeled something rather than trying to bring it to life.

*

After I had been on the *Tribune* about three weeks, Walker gave me my first assignment beyond the altogether routine. John Erskine was a Columbia professor, a best-selling author, and a big wheel in New York's politely cultural circles. His teen-aged son had, under Erskine's aegis, organized in Erskine's barn an art show for himself and the other teen-agers in Wilton, Connecticut. I was to cover the show. I set out jubilantly, not conscious that there was any catch.

I was to be met at the Wilton station by a member of the Erskine family, but, as the other arrivals were wafted away, no one spoke to me. A middle-aged lady had been staring forlornly around and, when we two were alone on the platform, she walked with obvious annoyance up to me.

"You aren't from the *Herald Tribune*, are you?"

I acknowledged that I was.

"Are you one of the art critics?"' She was obviously displeased by my appearance as a twenty-one-year-old.

In informing her that I was a news reporter, I felt it wiser not to add that this was the first story that had been entrusted to me.

"My husband definitely told them to send an art critic. Did you study the history of art at college?"

I considered dropping the name of Berenson, and decided not to. "No.

"I suppose since you are here there is nothing we can do."

She led me to her car and soon we were in her parlor. I was introduced to a gangly youth as the impressario of the show and the principal contributor. His manner was sullen, as if he thought people were putting things over on him. But when the mother complained that I was not an art critic but a reporter, his whole attitude changed. "You hunt gangsters?"

I felt I had dashed enough hopes for one day, so I nodded assent.

He had just seen the movie *Front Page*, which was then exciting everyone, and assumed that like Hildey Johnson I spent my time outwitting the police by hiding murderers in rolltop desks. Having said my adventures had been somewhat different, I made up a lurid tale that satisfied. Thus I began developing a method I had often to repeat if I were not to disappoint addicts of *Front Page*—particularly pretty girls.

On entering the art show, the first thing I saw was a large cardboard key with "The Key to the Heart of Wilton" inscribed on it. Mrs. Erskine held me there to explain that it had been given to her husband because of his many kindnesses to the villagers. I was thus confirmed in my growing suspicion that Walker had sent his greenest and youngest reporter as a response to Erskine's pretentious demand for an art critic. This pleased me very much as it indicated in my new environment a free-swinging style toward sacred cows that suited my predilections. Had I not been brought up with a plethora of sacred cows? And my knowledge of the species enabled me to write a story that would please Erskine while amusing other people.

*

Although I had no personal association with the members of the rewrite desk, they became the most practical instructors in writing I have ever had. Every story passed through their hands. Experienced reporters could count on minimal revisions, as the *Tribune*, much more than some periodicals with much greater literary pretensions, cherished diversity. Walker had been safe in hiring me despite my inexperience because nothing I wrote would get into the paper without attention from the rewrite desk. And he expected me to learn the trade from studying their emendations.

The first of the *Tribune*'s four daily editions was intended for the suburbs, but a few copies went to selected city newsstands. The nearest to my apartment in Greenwich Village was at Seventh Avenue and Fourteenth Street. I would wait at about midnight for a truck to come roaring down the almost empty avenue and throw off a bale of newspapers. This in itself was exciting to me, made me feel, as the bale presumably contained something of mine, more a part of the city's life than I had ever felt before. As I struggled to go through the newspaper while standing, my hands trembled in eagerness and anxiety to discover whether my story had been printed and how the copy desk had changed it. Back in my apartment, I compared the copy I had kept with the copy that had been printed in order to puzzle out the reason for each change.

It did not take many weeks before the changes became less drastic and I began to feel that some of them were random rather than improvements. However, the influence of the copy desk reigned over me during my entire newspaper career—and thereafter.

The gift of the copy desk was the direct utilitarian prose which is as basic to rational expression as walking is to animal propulsion. Furthermore, and this was a great advantage of working not on a rural newspaper but on a great metropolitan daily, there was so much news to be fitted into the paper that brevity was taught and insisted upon. When, on midsummer Sundays and similar empty days, a lack of news allowed us to be expansive, it was so delightful a privilege that we worked doubly hard to achieve an effective result.

Some college writing courses assign a theme a day. I wrote one or two stories a day, but on how different a basis! To see my compositions appear almost instantly in print and to know that they were going out to several hundred thousand people encouraged me to hone and harden and raise my standards. And I was cheek by jowl with fellow professionals who expressed pleasure when I made a happy stroke, and groaned at an unhappy one.

It took about two months for the copy desk to begin letting me flirt my tail in my own way. I was allowed thus to describe the famous, annual Macy's Thanksgiving Day parade:

"The gigantic balloons, designed by Tony Sarg, illustrator, to represent whales and sultans and comic strip characters, started the march. But at Columbus Square a gale twisted the neck of a twenty-foot turkey that had hoped to survive Thanksgiving. For three blocks he got thinner and thinner, and when the crowd looked for him at Fifty-sixth Street, he just was not there. Later, one of the Katzenjammer Kids and the wild and wholly whale suffered the same fate. The figures which got to Herald Square received a long drink of helium at which they promptly stood on their heads, jumped into the sky, and rode like mad on a high wind."

The city staff was much more important to the *Tribune* than to the *Times*. With its greater assets and far-flung correspondents, the *Times* could cover national and international news much more thoroughly, but in the metropolitan areas the *Tribune* beat them hollow. The *Times* reporters we worked beside were usually some twenty years older than we were. They were better informed but bored by what was for them repetition. We were interested, even excited. Add that the *Times* dictated a dry, institutional style. Our other morning competitor, the *World* (which was dying on its feet) favored a bookish style. We wished to practice newspaper prose in the old tradition at its highest level.

*

Six days a week, at 1:30 on every afternoon, I lined up with my fellow reporters to approach the city editor then on duty who would inform me of my afternoon assignment. It would not concern crime, police news, fires, stories purely political (except during elections) or purely financial. Beyond that, anything that was happening in New York (particularly Manhattan) was within my beat. Only sometimes was there continuity between one day and another (or, indeed, the morning and evening of the same day). I covered meetings of every description, interviewed all kinds of people, was often sent to Harlem to report on issues there, covered news breaks in art, theater, or publishing, attended riots, viewed the pleasures of the rich and occasionally the plight of the unemployed. Not having had any advance knowledge of what I would be immersed in an hour later brought a sense of adventure.

Like a hero of romance, I wielded a magic weapon. As a red-headed youngster of twenty-one to twenty-three, I was in a position to exert, by what I would write, the power of a great newspaper. Even the mighty, not only politicians and publicists but presidents of colleges and banks, industrialists, and ministers of the gospel, indeed, almost anyone who played or wanted to play a public role, were more or less at my beck and always anxious to make a good impression.

*

There were days when the *Tribune* was short of copy, particularly midsummer Sundays when nothing was happening in the city and a full Monday newspaper had to be filled. The outcome was for me either torture or delight. Torture when I was given an assignment that involved consultations almost impossible because everyone was out of town: I would hour after hour call again on the telephone hoping that some bigwig, who sometimes never did, had got back home. Delight because the gaping space opened the possibility of being assigned, or thinking up for myself, a feature story. Spared the responsibilities and imperatives of hard news, I could write concerning whatever I found amusing as long as it could be presented as a report of what was happening in New York. The older newspaper tradition that survived on the *Tribune* came in very handy: the effect of the feature story was considered its justification. The trick was to portray ascertainable or at least believable action against a New York background humorously conceived and stated. In giving the writer such leeway, this violated the hard-nosed definitions of news. *The New York Times* almost never achieved a successful feature story.

*

Our location just off Times Square—which in our columns we always referred to as Longacre Square—put us at the heart of New York's theatrical life. The excitement and gaiety contributed to the *Tribune*'s spirit. Were we not putting on our own daily performance for the city and the suburbs that spread around us?

The work hours of reporters on a morning paper precluded ordinary social engagements. We were given our assignments at 1:30 in the afternoon, which made luncheon engagements impossible. Since we often also had night assignments, we could not know in advance when we would be set free. A reporter who did not have a family to return to was thus cast loose in the city, too keyed up from his recent labors to go quietly to bed. The conventional girls we knew either were out with other men or had turned in for the night. There were two alternative recourses: drink, or actresses who would be released in a similar mood at about the same time. We insisted that the *Times* went in for liquor, the *Tribune* for girls, a generalization that the *Times* tried to reverse on us. Actually, it was a matter of predilection and age. Next door to the *Tribune* was a speakeasy, Blake's, where the veteran reporters—newspapermen were traditionally heavy drinkers—congregated. In the late evening, Blake's resounded. Somewhat excluded from the inner circle by being not much given to drinking, I had was the theater beat which would almost always, if the hour was right, supply companionship. We got to know girls in various shows who, if they themselves were tied up, could supply volunteers. We all wanted to blow off steam at some noisy and necessarily cheap place. Chorus girls were not in our sphere, and the actresses tended to take themselves very seriously, as artists, and be full of philosophical quirks. Going on to bed together was sometimes a possibility but rarely the primary intention.

I had several run-ins with the New York Society for the Suppression of Vice, which concerned itself with closing burlesque theaters, cleaning up fiction, etc. I once caught several august "civic leaders," who had intended to be there anonymously, at a session discussing how much flesh could emerge from around women's bathing suits. I was besieged in a telephone booth as I informed the city desk while holding the door shut with my back.

J. S. Sumner, the secretary of the Society, would say but little to me as he doubted my soundness on the subject of vice. However, there bloomed in the city room a very pretty crossword puzzle editor. I liked to take her out on assignments, and one hot summer afternoon, when little news was coming in, I asked her what she would like to do. She said she had always wanted to meet Mr. Sumner. Soon Sumner was ushering her ceremoniously to a chair beside his desk, as I unceremoniously retired to the back of the room, copypaper in hand. She led him on with coos of admiration, and he poured his heart out. One of his admissions was that he did not interfere with the pleasures of the rich since the need was to raise the level of bestial lower classes. Quite a nice story it made, and I hope it taught Sumner to keep his eyes off pretty girls.

*

All of his young reporters being in their own minds incipient novelists, Walker used periodically to amuse himself by assigning one or another to ferret out a great writer—"there's a rumor that Hemingway is in town"—for an interview. Although the writer was almost never found, the reporter felt complimented. My turn came: "Dreiser is just back from a trip across the United States. Find out what he found out."

Of course, he was not in the phone book, but somehow I discovered his address on West Fifty-seventh Street. I managed to persuade the doorman to let me get him on the house phone. After he had denounced the *Tribune* as a fascist newspaper and told me that I had driven out of his mind the best idea for a novel he had had in years, Dreiser added that, since the damage was done, I might as well come up.

I was ushered in to an elegantly furnished sitting room filled with sunlight. Behind a desk sat Dreiser. He fumbled with papers for some ten minutes before he suddenly rose, pulling himself to his considerable height, and exclaimed, "All newspaper interviews are stupid. I will bet you ten dollars that you can't get into your newspaper what I will say."

I knew enough about Dreiser to foresee that he would come out with blasts against American capitalism and political institutions that the editors of my Republican sheet would consider Communist propaganda. But I took the bet.

Dreiser then enthusiastically orated for an hour and a half. The government of America had abdicated to the trusts. Business interests dictated what teachers could teach. The citizens had been made into "trudging asses." "There is hardly such a thing as an individual left in America."

When I asked him whether such things would kill American literature, he rose in his chair in excitement. "They have already practically done so." All modern fiction was trivial junk. But hope remained. "The life of America today, fast verging as it is on social tragedy, should lend itself to satire and irony. Perhaps we might have a literature of despair like that of Dostoevski. Conditions are in many ways similar to those in Russia before the Revolution."

As I looked around, I was glad to see an ironical setting that might serve as an anodyne for the *Tribune* editors. Dreiser was spouting about the misery forced by capitalism on the American people from the parlor of an elaborately decorated duplex apartment. A silky wolfhound lay curled at his feet. Wandering in and out was a seductive young blonde in a negligee. Finally, Dreiser ran out of steam, and I returned to the *Tribune* to write my story.

What should I do about the bet? The "nose for news" I was developing told me that, if used as the lead, the bet would add to the interview tremendous punch. I could end with asking for the ten dollars. But the punch enlarged the challenge to the *Tribune*'s willingness to publish an obviously newsworthy story that was contrary to their editorial policies. Of course, the editors could throw the whole thing into the scrap basket. Me too?

On the next morning, the story could not be found in the paper. Also the day thereafter. On the third day, there it was, almost exactly as I had written it, the only major change being that they had removed the young blonde in a sexy negligee. (The *Tribune* considered itself a "family newspaper.") On the editorial page there was a lengthy blast denouncing what Dreiser had said, and getting much mileage from the duplex and the wolfhound.

I later heard that the discussions of the editors had been as profound as was the issue. I do not believe it was held against me that I had presented them with such a quandary, since the outcome put the *Tribune* in a most favorable light as a free newspaper, and the story was a great hit, being quoted in newspapers and magazines all over the nation and even abroad. (It appears in Dreiser biographies.)

*

On another story I tried to go too far. Had I not been stopped, I might have detonated a major explosion in New York City history, setting several years in advance the investigation that, under Judge Samuel Seabury, destroyed Tammany Hall.

In December 1929 I was given what seemed a routine assignment: a testimonial dinner staged by the Tammany Commissioner of Public Works for a former police commissioner now general manager of the Fox Film Corporation. As soon as I entered a banquet suite at the Ambassador Hotel, I was faced with something amazing: a table on which lay seven or eight revolvers. It was presided over by two police captains in full uniform, grinning their heads off. A large sign read: "Park your gats here." As each new group of Tammany guests saw the display, they burst into laughter, all the more if one of the police lieutenants pretended to frisk one of them.

This, I realized, was Tammany Hall thumbing its nose at the reformers by making a joke of a recent scandal: at a testimonial dinner to a magistrate and important leader in the Bronx, Albert H. Vitale had been held up by masked gunmen. Vitale's ability to get all the money back within two hours had revealed a close connection between Tammany Hall and organized crime.

A reporter for the City News Bureau, well known for his political connections, greeted me, and said that, although censorship naturally was far from anyone's mind, it was assumed that I would use discretion. On the dinner table there was before every guest full quarts of imported Scotch and rye. This seemed to me suitable, if lavish, hospitality since Prohibition was by then a dead letter in New York. But the law against gambling was another matter.

We emerged from dinner into an elaborate casino set up in one of the hotel rooms. The Tammany leaders, including many holders of public office, crowded around, and the stakes were very high. Mayor Walker had just been criticized for raising his salary by $40,000: I saw him lose that much at the roulette table. The higher Catholic clergy was well represented: among them was Father Duffy, the war hero after whom a part of Times Square, complete with his statue, was to be and still is named.

There were reporters from the other papers present, wandering around tipsily and taking part in the gambling. In those years a light drinker, I was not tipsy, and I felt there was another thumbing of the nose—at the New York press—in our being invited there. I took inconspicuous notes, stored more in memory, and went back to the city room. I had hardly started to tell the night city editor when he closed the subject firmly, "You were there as a guest." So much for any crusading on the part of the New York press at the start of the Depression!

Actually, I became fond of Mayor Jimmy Walker. In the evenings, he would make a round of semi-public occasions before he joined his mistress, Betty Compton, at the Central Park Casino. I remember his entrance into the Astor Ballroom where many women were congregated for some cause or other. Flags were hanging from the balcony. At the sight of him, the women all drew in their breaths, making the flags wave. He would come to a meeting unprepared, ask a reporter what it was all about, and then make by far the best speech of the evening.

I also have a personal memory. I was sent to City Hall toward evening to ask Walker about some insignificant matter. As always, he kept me waiting long beyond the appointed time. I greeted him by saying, "Mr. Mayor, you've ruined me." When he asked why, I said that the best-looking girl in Greenwich Village was getting madder and madder. He replied, "Take my car." I was lent for the evening the mayor's limousine complete with chauffeur and the other fixings. In telling this story, as I have often done, I add as a final flourish, "It's amazing what going with a siren through red lights does to a woman's virtue."

*

The financial department strutted their grandeur by not being open on the city-room floor like the rest of us, but enclosed by a balustrade resembling the banister along a Victorian stairway. Not deigning to acknowledge the presence of hobbledehoy reporters, they sat meditating gravely or whispering to each other. Thus we were amused when, on October 29, 1929, they began leaping around and shouting as if someone had thrown a nest of hornets into their sanctuary. I was told that there had been a tremendous crash on the stock exchange, but the stock exchange meant nothing to me and I continued laughing.

Although I was soon informed that a very serious blow had been given to America's financial system, the true gravity of the situation swam only slowly into my ken. My parents were not involved; nor were any of their circle, who either held permanent jobs in solid institutions or, if financiers, had not been plungers like those whose final plunge was out a Wall Street window. Some of my classmates did lose their jobs, but their parents had not been overwhelmed.

My own job was not endangered: newspapers were slow responders to the Depression. The effect in the city room was to impede salary raises—I did get up to thirty dollars a week—but I was not altogether dependent on my earnings, and the plateau of low pay played to my advantage. It was a strange aspect of the Depression that, although it became almost impossible once you became unemployed to get a new job, those who had held on to jobs could without too much difficulty move on to others. The more experienced reporters filtered out for better pay from over my head, opening to me earlier opportunities to cover front-page stories. I became, indeed, so happy at the *Tribune* that when I was called in by the city editor of the *Times* I turned down his offer of a job there. I felt that, although I would be better paid, my freedom to write as I pleased would be much curtailed. However, I was stupid not to let the matter hang until I had used it to get more money from the *Tribune*.

*

The crash of 1929 had not been a guillotine, beheading the "Roaring Twenties." As bankruptcy among the rich and poverty among the poor rose slowly and in irregular waves, the old frenzy continued, taking on perhaps a more hectic tone. I had become a newspaper man for the purpose of seeing life, and the most glamorous life around me I wished to see. The necessary money I did not have, but I had my open sesame, a press card with its magic inscription: *"Herald Tribune."* And I believed that a city-room reporter should know as much about New York as he could.

Surprisingly, I had been given no instructions, as far as I can remember, concerning ethical behavior required of a reporter who would be open to so many temptations. I made up my own rules. Of course, I took no bribes, but I saw no objection to gaining access to interesting places where I could not on my own have penetrated. I went to expensive night clubs, my favorite being Mayor Jimmy Walker's Central Park Casino. I never took along a girl or scrounged a meal, but felt free to ignore cover charges and to welcome drinks on the house.

Invariably, I was enthusiastically received. I might prove a useful contact, and a red-headed reporter in his early twenties caught the eye. Helen Morgan was famous for singing blues sitting on a piano. I once sat on the piano beside her.

*

Except for an occasional harrowing story selected for "human interest," the *Tribune* did not find news in the individual rigors of the unemployed. I did cover several "Communist riots." The real bash was in Union Square. By this time, I had come to realize the dynamics of the situation. The police commissioner, Grover Whalen, wished to rise politically as a battler against Communism, and his cops enjoyed beating up radicals. The Communist leadership wished to attract attention, and their followers, like many zealots, were not overly averse to martyrdom. It was to the interest of both sides to stage a riot. The Communists, by calling a meeting contrary to police regulations, in effect sent an invitation (although not engraved) to Whalen, which he enthusiastically accepted.

The riots were for me far from pleasant assignments. Despite the press card in my hat, I was in danger of getting clubbed. One huge policeman did, indeed, appear before me like a blue-coated wall. He raised his nightstick over his head for a strong downward blow, then saw my card, and, with disgust on his features, withered away.

The scenario was as follows. The Communists, half the police-men's size and many of them looking underfed, had no weapons and no muscle, yet they could dodge quickly. They mocked the policemen who chased after them with clubs. Every so often one was brought down and hassled off to a patrol wagon. I followed conspicuously, noting down the numbers of the worst club-wielders, hoping this would deter them, although I knew the *Tribune* would not take sides by publishing the numbers.

*

After I had for a year and a half worked for the *Tribune*, I felt that inner urge that makes birds migrate. It seems to be part of my nature that when I have succeeded at something I want to move on. I had curtailed the leadership I had established at the Lincoln School by departing at mid-year. I was again and again to abandon a subject once I had, to my satisfaction and to public approval, completed a book about it.

There were particular reasons for my wanting to leave the *Tribune*. My nervous setup remained that of a sprinter, but the *Tribune* sched-ule was suited to a long-distance runner. Six days a week! If I wanted a free weekend, I had to make it up by working without a break for thirteen days. A minimum each day of seven hours with time out for dinner; the maximum for as long as the city editors wished, often eleven hours. Sometimes more. And I had to be perpetually ready to deal with new situations. I did not then know that I was building up to real trouble that was to plague me for much of my lifetime, but increasingly tight nerves created symptoms that induced Father to send me to a stomach specialist. Being of the school that diagnosed physical ailments altogether in physical terms, he was of no help. But I was becoming more and more conscious of being dangerously overstrained.

Looming large was my overall objective of writing novels. I had become a reporter to gain experience that would broaden what I realized had been a limited contact with the world. This I had copi-ously achieved. My contacts had become so wide that I could not go to the theater, could hardly walk the streets, without being spoken to by people I had got to know on one assignment or another. Yet I remembered that on my first appearing in the city room, Alva Johnson, the *Tribune*'s chief feature writer, had walked up to me and said, "What are you doing here? Get out as fast as you can." In reply to my look of amazement, he explained that he never wrote a story that his clippings would not reveal he had written before. This was, I now realized, because, although a reporter saw endless action, he was almost never allowed a glimpse of the underlying motivations that made one happening very different from another. I had been given an almost miraculous opportunity to see innumerable situations but little help toward understanding the motivations and the characters of the actors.

Furthermore, my own typewriter was lying fallow in my rooms, used only for writing an occasional letter. Was it not about time for me to get back to consulting my own muse?

*

I was offered a job which, although it paid better than the *Tribune*, was represented to me as being only half-time. Having not yet learned that no significant job can really be part-time, I saw myself as having the cake and eating it too. And the cake was a very alluring one: a pioneering post in the New York City government where I was assured I would be allowed much autonomy. The position—Executive Secretary of the Noise Abatement Commission of the New York City Board of Health—offered, indeed, such possibilities that, a year later, when I was twenty-four, my biography was to appear in *Who's Who in Government*. And I would not be reporting what other people were doing, but myself doing things that were reported.

*

My decision to take the job may or may not have been wise, but the way I severed relations with the *Tribune* was stupid in the extreme. The villain in this situation was modesty. As I slashed around New York doing, without pushing the rules too far, pretty much what I pleased, I realized that I was on the whole satisfying my editors, but I did not realize how much I was being regarded as a seven-day wonder. Walker, in particular, was preening himself on my being a signal example of his skill in judging youths and bringing them up from scratch as newspapermen.

Not viewing myself as an asset the paper would really be sorry to lose, I went quietly up to Walker one afternoon as he sat at his desk and informed him I was leaving. To my surprise, he lost his seemingly imperturbable nonchalance, showing anger. In trying to explain, I made the mistake of revealing that my intention had never been to make a newspaper career but rather to gather impressions that would serve me as a novelist. Walker replied, "You were not hired as a gatherer of impressions." This induced me to ask whether or not I had earned my salary during my time on the *Tribune*. He could not deny that I had. He then upbraided me for never having asked, when dissatisfied, for a raise. I said proudly (and stupidly) that I would never ask for a raise. All in all, an unfortunate confrontation, and my fault.

The managing editor, who had hardly ever spoken to me before, accused me of disloyalty. And so, as a twenty-three-year-old with limited practical knowledge, I ended one of the happiest and most fruitful times of my life unhappily.

*

The *Herald Tribune* city room, as presided over by Stanley Walker, is pictured in the lore of New York journalism as a magical time. I was much complimented when an extensive history of the *Herald Tribune* was published in 1986 (*The Paper*, by Richard Kluger). My exploits were given top billing in his account of Walker's staff. This may have been because I had become well known as an author, but it made me wonder whether, if the Newspaper Guild had existed in my day to regulate working hours, I could have learned to pace myself and made an impressive career in journalism. Did I have the charisma to become a celebrated reporter, perhaps the anchor on a national television show? But I doubt that I would have been happier.

13

SILENCING NEW YORK

*

As Executive Secretary of the Noise Abatement Commission, New York City Board of Health, my new job was to bring quiet to New York City and, by extension, through propaganda and example, to cities all over the United States. There was no other such municipal commission anywhere in America to rival or stand beside us. And I soon discovered that I was, in my new home ground, the Board of Health, an utter and resented freak, my appointment having been made possible only because the commission, being foundation-financed, was immune to civil service legislation.

As second in command of my agency, I was assigned on the executive floor a privileged desk by a window. The entire floor, occupying almost a whole block, was without partitions and filled with desks that received increasingly less light the farther away from the windows. Veteran bureaucrats, more than twice my age—civil service promotion being by seniority—viewed from semi-darkness this twenty-three-year-old basking in daylight. And the infant was soon breaking all rules. Being outside the bureaucratic network that trammeled all my neighbors, I was, as a veteran maverick, soon going my own way, even speaking, under the aegis of the Department of Health, in my own voice to the press and over the radio.

A desire to squelch me became manifest enough for me to amuse myself with an analogy from one of the clichés of Wild West melodrama. Pioneers are surrounded in the wilderness by a pack of wolves, wolves who are afraid of the campfire. As long as the settlers can keep the fire burning they are safe, but their fuel is getting lower and lower, although they are throwing in their packs and their saddles. As the flames sink, the circle of wolves draws closer and closer. If the fire were to go out!

My protection was the belief that I had the ear of the Commissioner of Health, Shirley W. Wynne. Should any evidence appear that this was not the case, my position would instantly become untenable. And I was far from sure that it was the case.

Edward F. Brown, the director of the Noise Abatement Commission, was a deputy commissioner of health, but he was also a foundation-supported outsider, and I did not know how close he was to Wynne. The only other employee of the commission was my secretary, Miss Finkelstein, a wizened child of the slums who felt for me hero-worship and bothered my conscience by being so able that, if the world had allowed her the psychology of command, she could have done my job perhaps better than I did.

The opposition was led by the power behind the throne, one of those spinsters who gain from secondary positions great control in organizations by being efficient and altogether dedicated, having no other interest than the organizations while their male superiors have wandering thoughts. (Wynne's secretary was extremely handsome.) This dragon (whose name I have forgotten) had disliked me because when I was a reporter I had made a date with one of her pretty secretaries. Now she threw what roadblocks she could in my path—I had difficulty getting my press releases mimeographed—and then she determined to demonstrate to all that I had no power.

When I was away from the office, Miss Finkelstein phoned me in great perturbation. Two porters had appeared with orders to carry my desk away from its window into a dark corner. Miss Finkelstein had sat on the desk until they went away. She was dashing back to sit once more. But action higher up was definitely required.

I felt like a fool when I put in an emergency call to Brown on such a seemingly trivial matter as the moving of a desk. But Brown well understood the functioning of bureaucracy. He hurried to Wynne's office. The dragon was given orders. Miss Finkelstein was able to descend from the desk, which remained in its position by the window, demonstrating that I was not to be fiddled with.

*

The basic conception around which the Noise Abatement Commission had been organized was that city noise could be abated only through the wish and the cooperation of so high a proportion of the population that, in addition to refusing themselves to be sources of unnecessary racket, they would bring effective pressure on their neighbors. Laws could be enforceable only through popular support. Furthermore, most noise, being generated by ordinary citizens as they pursued routinely their business or pleasure, was beyond any effective reach of the law. Thus, the basic function of the Noise Abatement Commission would have to be public education.

Toward that end, the commission had been brilliantly planned. Attaching it to the Board of Health had been a major stroke as it gave it impressive auspices. We could claim to be the first municipal noise abatement commission in the world. And the Board, appointed by Wynne in October 1929, was made up of citizens with great weight in the community.

The commission had been divided into five committees: 1. The Effect of Noise on Human Beings; 2. Noise Measurement Survey; 3. Practical Application of Remedies; 4. Building Code and Construction; 5. Finance. "Thorough studies" were not yet intended, so read the report, "since we were convinced that the noisy condition of the city constituted a kind of emergency situation, calling for a speedy survey of the most preventable and diminishable noises in order that New Yorkers may as soon as possible begin to enjoy the fruits of the Commission's efforts." In less than a year the report was published in a handsome paperback volume. *City Noise* presented evidence from many sources, including the commission's own experiments and surveys, to demonstrate a frightening effect from noise on city dwellers and to outline possible practical remedies. At this point, the various committees into which the Board had been divided ceased to function. All activities were handed over, with only distant supervision, to Brown.

*

My boss was some twenty years my senior. He was very generous to me, pushing me forward when he might have gathered in credit for himself. Insofar as I ever achieved any education in team play, it came from Brown. I remember particularly that he criticized the business letters I wrote as being too abrupt, saying that it is just as easy and more effective to be courteous. I am reminded of this advice when I receive imperative letters from people who wish favors, particularly Ph.D. students desiring me to do their research for them.

As deputy commissioner of health, Brown had a city automobile complete with chauffeur in which he took me on some evenings to places my budget could not reach. We were often joined by a lanky friend of his with reddish hair called Harry, who was also engaged in "good works," being director of the Tuberculosis and Health Association. He left a particular mark in my memory because his face, conspicuously distorted with tension and anxiety, did not relax as he got more and more drunk but drew even tighter until the effect was terrifying. After Harry Hopkins had become so powerful an adviser to Roosevelt in the New Deal and re-creating the world after World War II, I wondered whether he had stopped drinking or had just loosened up.

*

Brown had proved to be too busy in other directions to pay much attention to Noise Abatement. I did have to consult him on major decisions, and he gave me rulings, but I quickly discovered that should he veto what I wanted to do, I had merely to rephrase the question and bring it up again and he might agree to my going ahead.

My function involved an intertwining of the local and the national: seeking amelioration of conditions in New York City on the one hand, and through newspapers and radio spreading the gospel, using our New York experience as a news peg, across the nation. This second objective was made easier by our being in New York, at the nexus of American communication facilities. Newspaper stories, if the leads were contrived to make them seem spot news, were natural attention-getters since they dealt with nuisances that impinged on everyone and I had easy access to the municipal radio station, WNYC.

*

To prepare our local ground, law clerks had, before my arrival, combed the two fat volumes, *City Ordinances* and the *Sanitary Code*, to identify laws relevant to noise abatement. Since laws were passed at every session and almost never repealed, statutes existed in the thousands. Hundreds could be applied to noise problems. By just opening the books at random, I found laws that the lawyers had missed. But all this accumulation was of little value since the basic issue was what laws the authorities chose to enforce. Although the police commissioner was a member of our commission and we were supposed to be an arm of the Health Department that administered the Sanitary Code, it was usually useless for me to cite a law and ask that it be applied.

The choice between enforcing or not enforcing "nuisance laws" was (and still is) based on an evaluation of public opinion. Thus, the efforts to build up opposition to noise were also efforts toward law enforcement. But there were situations that did not follow this rule.

On the face of it, no violation should have been easier to eradicate than the then ubiquitous blaring of loud speakers outside record stores. The nuisance was moored to one spot, and a subject of much neighborhood outrage. Yet, letter after letter to my contact at the Police Department produced no result.

I finally had recourse to my adviser whom I had met when he visited Harvard and I had consulted when puzzled on the *Tribune*, Norman Thomas. He explained that the local police were undoubtedly collecting money for protection. If they received the poking up I wished sent from headquarters, they would show the documents to demonstrate that they were being hassled, and up the price of protection. The only way such a law could be enforced was to have a special squad, unconnected with the local precinct, dispatched from headquarters. If I suggested to Brown that we ask the police commissioner, as a member of our board, to appoint a special squad of "fly cops" (as they were called in the force) to enforce the noise laws, I was surely told not to be so naïve.

*

The publicity we received stirred up a storm of complaining letters that broke on my desk. They were answered over my signature by Miss Finkelstein, who came to know the formulas so well that I had to dictate only two or three letters a day. In any complaint concerning neighbors, we urged conciliatory conversation. Beyond that, the commission having no administrative powers, we would inform the writer that we were referring the letter to the police department for violation of the Municipal Code; to the Health Department for the Sanitary Code; to the relevant city agency for transportation or building noises, etc. There was no point in my trying to follow up. If I received (as was often the case) an angry communication that nothing had been done, we would just repeat the referral.

Sometimes I would intervene myself. I remember particularly the time that the Doctors Hospital, on York Avenue and Ninetieth Street, complained of loud bangings in the night that disturbed their patients. Since they had been unable to determine the cause of the bangings, I decided to post two policemen on the hospital roof. They were to meet me at my flat.

A choir singer with impressive lung power lived below me. On the appointed night, she emitted a tremendous scream. When she had opened her door in response to a knock, she saw that the entire stairwell, three floors down to the street and overflowing out the front door, was crowded with policemen. A burly sergeant asked, "Where's Flexner?" She had always suspected I was up to no good, but had not suspected that I was so violent a criminal that it would take some fifty cops to arrest me. Almost fainting, she pointed up the stairs.

When the next day I met her in the stairwell, visibly not in prison, she almost fainted again. I did not explain that through a misunderstanding I had been sent not two cops but two platoons of cops. I subsequently enjoyed the awe with which she viewed me and the sound of her closing, whenever I appeared, the multiple locks she had had fastened to her door.

*

The most extensive operations I undertook were surveys of the noise hazards suffered by schools and hospitals throughout the city. Questionnaires were mailed to the principals of 846 public schools, ninety-three per cent of whom replied, and to the superintendents of hospitals, of whom seventy-nine per cent replied. Forty-four per cent of the schools reported that noise interfered appreciably with the teaching of the children and their development, from which I concluded that future prospects of 447,000 children were damaged by noise. Of the hospitals that answered, eighty per cent were surrounded with din sufficient to retard appreciably the recovery of patients," while fifty per cent regarded the effect as "really serious." Since most of the complaints specified traffic, especially heavy trucks, the laws concerning "school streets" and "hospital streets" would, if enforced, handle these problems. I did not hesitate to give the police department a sharp lecture on their laxness. I went on to urge the police to investigate the possibility of completely closing, during school hours, 318 streets which I specified.

We forwarded the specific complaints recorded on the questionnaires to the agency, mostly the police department, that had legal jurisdiction. The entire report, with more of my perfervid prose concerning the hazards to humanity of noise pollution, was distributed nationally in releases and widely printed. In New York, admonitory editorials appeared in the many newspapers with which the city was then graced.

*

I inherited as coadjutors a branch of the Bell Telephone Laboratories, Electrical Research Products, which had developed a machine for measuring the intensity of sound waves and a unit of measurement for which they had invented the word "decibel." The young engineers who handled the equipment were agreeable if extremely serious-minded, and we traveled (I almost wrote junketed) around New York taking measurements and setting up experiments.

One spring day, we established ourselves on York Avenue and Seventieth Street in front of a public school to study vehicles that had just passed three hospitals and a public library. If a truck was particularly noisy, traffic policemen would command it to draw up in front of the noise meter. The trucks were then minutely examined by three mechanics lent by the Mack and General Motors truck companies.

"The average noise made by these trucks," I wrote in my report, "was equivalent to an elevated train heard from the street. . . . The noisiest truck made the same din as a steam-operated pile driver." The mechanics discovered that "eighty-six per cent of the trucks examined had loose fenders; seventy-one per cent rattling motor hoods, badly adjusted motors, and loose shackle bolts; fifty-seven per cent loose sides; forty-three per cent loose tail boards, loose running boards, squeaky brakes; twenty-nine per cent loose license plates, rear end drives, tool boxes and head lamps, chattering brake shoes, faulty brake mechanisms, faulty bodies, and rim squeaks; fourteen per cent noisy rear doors, loads, transmissions, loose radiators, spare tires, and side boards extending over the body." Just for fun, we stopped a passing motorcycle, which produced some of the highest noise readings of the day.

Tests on passenger cars, although less dramatic, also revealed a direct correlation between condition and noise. This induced me to write that drivers of badly maintained vehicles were endangering not only the health of the community but also their own by moving in carriers of contagion, as if Typhoid Mary were sitting beside them.

Much apprehension was expressed about the fate of the city after "progress" brought flocks of airplanes overhead. A preview was offered when the army air force made a display over New York: 597 planes flew in twenty minutes over the city. On the roof of the Fiske Building, my colleagues and I were taking aim with our noise-measuring apparatus.

"Even on a normal day," I wrote, "the roof of the Fiske Building is not a very quiet place. At eleven A.M., the roar rising from the busy streets below was forty-six decibels, and by three P.M. when the planes came, it had jumped to fifty-one. A tri-motor transport plane pushing through the fog of sound at an altitude of 2,500 feet only raised the noise level four decibels and a bi-motor bomber over the river a mile away only raised it three. Thirty-two bombers, at an approximate distance of a mile and an altitude of 2,500 feet made a racket of eighty-five decibels, being just as noisy as one truck in bad condition passing down the street. The highest reading of the afternoon, eighty-five decibels, was made by thirty pursuit planes at about half a mile and an altitude of about 3,000 feet. The noise was no greater, however, than that which is experienced twice daily by passengers in an express subway train. The average noise level while the planes were passing by was only sixty-two decibels, about the equivalent of church bells heard from the street."

For once I was optimistic. Airplanes were being improved, I noted, with reduction of sound in mind, and they could be kept high above

Dr. Simon Flexner and Helen Thomas Flexner, and their sons, William Welch Flexner and (at right) James Thomas Flexner.

At left: Helen Thomas Flexner; pastel by Adele Herter. Below: Dr. Simon Flexner in his office at the Rockefeller Institute for Medical Research.

The author in a baby carriage, with brother William, outside New York's Central Park. See page 16.

"Rock Neath," the Flexner family's Carpenter's Gothic house on the east bank of the Hudson River, facing Storm King Mountain.

Mount Chocorua, New Hampshire, as seen from a house rented by the Flexner family. Such views as this, and from "Rock Neath" (above), helped inspire the author's interest in the Hudson River School of painting.

1957 Degrees Conferred
at Harvard Graduati

JOHN PHILIP COOKE

JAMES C. T. FLEXNE

ALLSTON BURR

GOV. FRANKLIN D. RC

Newspaper clipping on the 1929 Harvard commencent, at which the author and Governor Roosevelt spoke.

Agnes Halsey Flexner, the author's first wife, with Topsy.

Beatrice Hudson Flexner, the author's second wife, at her piano.

Painting of the author by Joseph Hirsch, 1971.

the city. If landing fields were kept far enough away, the air age would, I prophesied correctly, create no real noise problem for New York City.

Steamships seemed to be another matter. The lower Hudson was then full of traffic, and the deep hoots of ocean liners bothered the West Side from the Battery to the Fifties. Steamship owners pointed out that their vessels had to shout across miles of ocean. When it was suggested that less resonant whistles could be used within the confines of the river, the reply was that safety required that big ships make big sounds. My observation that large dogs could scare away the smaller just as well with low growls as with barks was brushed aside as frivolous.

Efforts to get automobile manufacturers to install less clamorous horns met similar opposition. A General Motors executive stated that a car going sixty miles an hour had to be heard many miles away. When it was suggested that perhaps they didn't go that fast in New York, the executives turned the table on us by stating that, if we reduced the din in New York so far that weak horns could be heard, they would think about installing some weaker horns.

I did succeed in applying a childhood dream. When a kid (it was possible then), I used to run after fire engines in the hope of seeing a fire. What was my dismay when after I had thus exhausted myself, the engines ended up at their firehouse. I persuaded the fire commissioner to order that a distinction be made. Sirens were to be blown only on the way to a fire.

*

We do not need to be reminded today that important painters of New York City streets were known as the Ash Can School. When coal furnaces were universal, metal ash cans that could receive glowing embers punctuated the streets. During their daily dumping into garbage trucks, the reiterated bangings were among the most unpopular sounds. I resolved to vanquish this multitude of dragons by setting up a tournament that would reveal a modern St. George. I wrote the 113 principal manufacturers of ash, garbage, and milk cans requesting them to develop semi-noiseless apparatus to be demonstrated at a competition "held in a public place, in the presence of city officials and representatives of the press." It would show householders that they themselves could silence their ash cans. To bring publicity to triumph, a jury would designate the winning ash can.

Only five manufacturers submitted entries, but that was enough. On June 29, the lunchtime crowds near City Hall Park were delighted to see the square in front of the Health Department cordoned off by the police. Eagerly they gathered in droves, joggling, certain they would see something exciting. For the moment, they could only see men setting up peculiar-looking apparatus.

Then hope was encouraged: the police were separating the crowd to make an entrance. What fascination would follow? But, alas! There appeared only a truckload of battered ash cans followed by a beaten-up old garbage truck.

From out of the truck stepped a man of such muscular development that, had he not worn a sanitation worker's uniform, he might have been Hercules. While the machinery recorded, he banged the battered cans on the pavement, emptied them into the battered truck, and dropped them on the pavement in the noisy routine with which every New Yorker was familiar.

The crowd was beginning to move on when a dreamlike cast of characters appeared. New and undented garbage cans garnished with rubber, and such a spotless Department of Sanitation truck as seemed a figment of a dream. It even had rubber pads on the shelves against which cans would strike while being emptied.

Nunzio Parrino, the Herculean garbage man, glared at these objects with all the hostility of a warrior threatened with being disarmed. He went after that prissy truck and those prissy cans. All the cans were insulated with rubber around the bottom. Under Parrino's ministrations two of the bottoms flew off into the air like rogue bicycle tires, disqualifying their cans. Although the other contestants managed to hold, Nunzio gleefully banged them down on unpadded spots. Then he made a delightful discovery. If a can were dropped when empty, it would bounce like a rubber ball, making it fall on its side with a clamor even the noisiest of the old-fashioned cans could not rival. The noise was indeed so great that it brought dozens to the windows of the Department of Health and of the Supreme Court Building across the street. As for the rubber linings on the truck, they were also completely frustrated.

The four judges were William Schroeder, chairman of the Sanitation Commission, Charles S. Hand, Sanitation Commissioner, Brown, and me. There was only one possible verdict: complete failure. I had to guard my features to repress any glint of amusement, and perhaps Brown had the same need, but the two sanitation commissioners gloried in looks of triumph.

Never underestimate garbage collectors! After coal furnaces had been replaced by oil, there was no more need for metal ash cans. They were replaced by noiseless plastic bags. But has the Department of Sanitation been foiled? Of course not! They have placed in each truck a paddlewheel-like compressor that joins with the engine that runs it filling whole blocks, for ten or fifteen minutes at a time, with insane screams.

*

After some six months, Brown told me he was going to resign and would recommend that I succeed him as director of the commission. To my parents I jubilated "I shall be my own boss, and shall have a lot of fun." Fun! I wrote nothing about serving my fellow citizens and the public health.

Whatever hopes I may have had of quieting New York, or even seriously denting the problem, had quickly vanished. I concluded that "no other power on earth than five million people can say 'hush,' to six million." And, despite all my activity and the public notice engendered, the commission, although it remedied an abuse here and there, had not even begun to build an effective constituency.

Being my father's son, I was unimpressed by the hand-to-mouth research the commission had done during its first year concerning the dire effect of noise on physical and mental health. I did make use of their pronouncements to concoct macabre stories that pleased my literary instincts, but I could not believe that city noise did actually addle brains. Down history, the world's great intellectual centers have been cities, and noise has always characterized city living. Athens with its chariots and orators; medieval cities, featuring within echoing walls armored men and horses that clanked like ash cans. And there has always been that great noise-maker, the human voice, so much more essential in its louder tones for advertising, spreading news, etc., among populations who could not read. No one would willingly be a city dweller unless he had tolerance, even taste, for racket.

Furthermore, my experience on the commission had convinced me that noise as a social phenomenon could not be measured by decibels or judged by moral imperatives. Noise is accurately defined as a sound that the individual hearer finds disturbing. A singer practicing her scales by an open window is driven to a frenzy by the hoots of children playing below. To insist that communal noise, forced willy-nilly on all, should, particularly near schools and hospitals, be kept to a minimum was the true function of the commission. I had been fighting for it energetically, but not with any passion. Being more interested in understanding people's predelictions than changing them, I have never had the instincts of a reformer.

But I did relish the possibilities opened to me by my job for exerting power and doing amusing things. There was a resemblance to my high jinks at the Lincoln School, although my stage was infinitely wider, and my objective was not making mischief but carrying but what was almost universally regarded as a worthy task.

The fly in the ointment had been the complete collapse of my original theory that, having shifted to "a half-time job," I would be able to occupy the other half at my typewriter. I discovered that the activities of the commission so occupied my attention that I could not keep my thoughts concentrated on literary creation. I was, there-fore, far from upset when the noise commissioners, finally meeting together, decided that the commission had achieved everything it could, particularly as abating noise cost money and the nation was sinking ever deeper into a depression. It was for me a withdrawal of temptation. I would get back on my main track as a writer.

14

FRIENDSHIPS

*

DURING my years with the *Herald Tribune* and the Noise Abatement Commission, I roomed in New York City with John Goldsmith Phillips, Jr., who had been my best friend at Harvard and remained my best friend until he retired, after many years at the Metropolitan Museum, where he had filled in for a while as an acting director. This association, joined with my ability to help because the museum had no curator knowledgeable concerning American painting, made me regard the Metropolitan as almost a home away from home.

Jack and I had rented an apartment on Charles Street in Greenwich Village. It was up four flights. This reflected my passion for top floors based on a dislike for footsteps or loud radios overhead. The long stairway proved to have another practical use. When on some mornings we would set out down the stairs we would come on the snoozing figure of a friend, or several, prone on a landing. They obviously had set out drunkenly to call on us but had found our stairs too many.

A source of amusement, fortunately known to only a few cognoscenti, was offered by the fireboxes at the opposite ends of our Charles Street block. Each was connected with a different firehouse. If revelers pulled the alarms simultaneously there would ensue the enchanting spectacle of fire engines rushing at each other down the narrow street from opposite directions. I never took part in setting up this caper, and was annoyed when I tried to sleep by the augmenting bells and sirens and then dramatic squeaking of brakes, but it did seem to me that this gave our block superiority over its Village neighbors.

*

The Village of my era was no longer the mecca of advanced artists and writers. Nor had the tourists and bourgeoisie yet moved in. Journalists set the tone, and the Village institution was the speakeasy.

These speakeasies responded to the darkness of the times by serving, in the most downright manner, the grimmer aspects of drinking. The brightest object might well be an old brass spittoon which had, in memory of bygone days, been kept polished by the bartender. The bartender would not be a soul who would sympathize if you complained of your wife's tantrums or your girlfriend's infidelities. He looked as if he had a pistol in his pocket and probably had. The long reflecting glasses over the bars were filthy, reflecting us back to ourselves as smudged and sordid. A group of men—this was no haunt for women—could be hilarious there in each other's company, but if you drank by yourself, the effect could be suicidal.

*

The alliance between stomach trouble and over-strain which had made me doubt my future in journalism did not vanish when I joined the Noise Abatement Commission, although it no longer seemed created by my job. It manifested itself during wakeful, sometimes horrifying nights. Medical care was needed.

Loyal to the Hopkins where he had first spread his wings, Father believed that illness was best treated in Baltimore, and, as ill luck would have it, there was an elderly stomach specialist, Julius Friedenwald, who had been Uncle Abe's best friend when they were both undergraduates at the Hopkins some half-century before.

Friedenwald was one of those physicians who acknowledge for the brain no more than a distant, bowing acquaintance with the body. Having once noted, "he is nervous at times," he pursued that direction no further. Although I knew very well that my nerves were playing a major role, I gladly accepted Friedenwald's approach as I much preferred to blame my troubles on my body, which I regarded as merely a tool, than on my brain, which I regarded as my true self. I was therefore "terribly depressed" when, as I was returning to New York from a healthy vacation, "the old stomach started to misbehave the moment the train pulled into Grand Central Station."

Friedenwald advised that, through "intermediate feedings," I should keep my gastric juices occupied. I was given medicine to take before and after each meal, and was to regulate my diet "according to the list given to the patient." On the list: "ALCOHOLIC BEVERAGES, NONE."

Drinking being so basic to life in Greenwich Village, I ignored this prohibition until a particularly extended succession of midnight horrors and nausea made me decide that nothing else could be as bad. Although I had none of the alcoholic's withdrawal symptoms, the result was catastrophic.

I would set out for a party in high spirits. As I quaffed soda water while the others were having drinks, all would be well for a time, and then it gradually would come upon me that I was in a madhouse. Incoherent gabble surrounded me, and the most inane witticisms enlisted shrieks of laughter. As I stood there glumly, the hostess would come to me with concern: was I feeling sick? One, I remember, said that if she had invited someone to her party whom I could not stand, it was not intended, and she was sorry. I felt forced to stay home in a solitude that left me a helpless prey to my nerves.

My career as a teetotaler was brief.

*

After I left the *Tribune*, Jack and I moved to the respectable East Seventies, more convenient to his Museum and an easy subway ride to the Noise Abatement Commission. No longer held down by peculiar hours, I was free to be widely convivial. Old friends were headed by Breading from the Lincoln School; Jack from Harvard; and Ben Robertson, a suave and warm South Carolinian from the *Tribune*. Jack contributed the younger curators at the Metropolitan Museum, particularly James Rorimer, a future director, and younger curators from the American Museum of Natural History. Our exotic was a one-eyed Parsee, Nassily Heeramaneck, who was a great expert on Indian art, representing in America a major international firm of dealers.

The only older member of our group that I can remember was Joseph Brummer, a scholarly dealer in Renaissance art. He was well known in Chinatown and stood us gourmet dinners there. I particularly admired him for having the greatest boulevardier among dogs

I have ever known. In the winters we would encounter his chow wandering relaxedly blocks away from his Fifty-seventh Street establishment, and in the summers we would come upon the chow in Paris, alone and nonchalant on the Rue de la Paix.

Our group of bachelors chased and were chased by women. If one of us gave a party, women might be invited, but they were almost never included in our evenings out together. We dined in Yorkville or Chinatown, went to the movies, or lounged in each others' apartments in jocoseness and good humor. We never discussed our escapades or affairs with women, although we freely sought advice and even consolation concerning our professional activities.

15

WANDERING

*

As the Noise Abatement Commission died out, my track record would undoubtedly (despite the Depression) have enabled me to get a good job. But I was more concerned with furthering my career as a writer. I agreed with my parents that my experience was too limited to America, my trips abroad having been short and as a tourist. My parents agreed to back me on a trip to Europe of whatever length seemed advisable. The theory was that in the fructifying atmosphere I would be more inspired than I had been at home, and, having no other employment, would speed ahead with my writing. I was foolish enough to state that, after so many years and with such an opportunity, if I did not finish a novel I would never be able to.

*

During mid-May 1932, aged twenty-six, I sailed with a high heart on the French liner *Lafayette*. I had a preordained companion, Aunt Lucy having brought me together with a socially correct highbrow from Bryn Mawr who was to sail on the same ship. However, on board I met a demure-looking brunette who, when I asked what college she went to, answered George White's Scandals, a Broadway jazz extravaganza. When I laughed at what I assumed was a sally of wit, she was visibly offended. So, when she added that she was traveling with a dinosaur, I was careful to show no surprise. I merely asked her whether they shared the same stateroom. She said no. The dinosaur was traveling in the ship's hold. It was some thirty feet from the tip of its nose to the tip of its tail, and was attended by its personal mechanic experienced in doctoring its mobile anatomy. At each of the major European music halls where she was booked, five or six stagehands could be recruited to serve the dinosaur's less complicated needs.

I quickly learned from fellow passengers that I had met a celebrity. The extreme agility and suppleness required for acrobatic dancing made it an art that could hardly be practiced beyond the age of twenty-six. At twenty, Lucille Page was America's most famous acrobatic dancer.

I was to watch Lucille's act in both the London Palladium and the Paris Odeon. Lightning flashed in the upper scenery and there were earthquake rumblings. Then the dinosaur entered slowly, revealing his great length yard by yard. Hearts contracted to see in the monster's gruesome mouth the prone figure of a girl, her arms and legs and long hair hanging from its jaws. The monster paused for a few moments of prehistorical meditation, and then extended its fifteen-foot neck out over the audience, swinging Lucille, in a skimpy tiger skin, just beyond reach of the people in the front rows. The beast then deposited Lucille onto the stage. She executed with amazing grace the awe-inspiring contortions of her dance, was picked up again, swung again over the audience, and then carried offstage to thunderous applause.

On shipboard, Lucille was unassuming, gentle, and humorous. She was traveling with her mother, a robust vaudevillian with a gargantuan laugh. The mother was attended by a retired comedian whose face seemed to consist altogether of dark glasses and a grin. Making a fourth in a group that found everything funny, I sailed across the ocean with more sustained hilarity than I have ever again enjoyed.

Feeling guilty about the Bryn Mawr girl to whom I had been so portentiously introduced, I asked if I might escort her to the ship's show. (Lucille, being in the cast, was unavailable.) Frances, who had been eyeing me reproachfully, was placated as this was the voyage's gala occasion. We were seated at a table far back where we could see almost nothing. I was inwardly upset (I had never seen Lucille dance), but a beckoning hand was raised in the very front, and the word "Jimmie" reverberated the ship's saloon as it had once over the vaudeville theaters of America. I gathered up Bryn Mawr. We were soon sitting at the edge of the platform with Mrs. Page and her friend. Frances did not seem to be too pleased with the appearance of her companions, but she was glad to be in front.

The first indication of trouble was when Lucille appeared on stage. Frances endoubtedly recognized her as the girl I had been going around with, but Lucille had seemed respectable enough if giggly. Now, in her skimpy tiger skin, she was the provocative performer. What seemed to have particularly upset Frances was the routine in which Lucille coyly covered her eyes while executing bumps and grinds, as if shielding her sight from what the lower part of her body was doing.

Frances was obviously relieved when the act was over. However, when Lucille returned to the stage for applause, she was held there by the master of ceremonies. "While we applaud this little lady," he cried, "we must doubly applaud her mother, one of the greatest figures in vaudeville, who has given eight children to the stage. Mrs. Page!"

The spotlight turned on our table, and before Frances's horrified eyes, the woman sitting next to her rose, threw kisses, spread out both her arms, one of which barely missed Frances's hair, and then, as the applause continued, pulled up her skirts and went into a little dance.

The instant the spotlight no longer illuminated our table, Frances mumbled something about a headache and fled. Mrs. Page's reaction was a burst of hilarious laughter. "That's quite a fancy dame you had there," she commented, slapping me good-naturedly between the shoulder blades. And soon Lucille appeared to roost comfortably beside me in the chair that had been so stiffly vacated.

Lucille and I continued to see each other after we were back in New York. One evening, she confided to me her bitterest memory. As a young adolescent, she had been deeply religious, finding Sunday School the apex of each week. But she was already performing, and one week, to her great regret, she had to appear on a Sunday, missing Sunday School. When asked, the following week, to justify her absence, she explained, confident of sympathy. Instead, the teachers expressed horror that she had danced on a public stage and double horror that she had thus profaned the Sabbath. She was expelled.

When she told me that she had thus been driven from religion, tears stood in her eyes.

But tears were not at home in Lucille's eyes. By the time we went on to a nightclub she was her old cheery self. After a roll of drums, there appeared on the dance floor a somewhat chubby acrobatic dancer. She was in no way comparable to Lucille, who was observing her with passionate attention. The instant the act was over, Lucille sprang from her chair and hurried to speak to the performer. I followed. Lucille praised her dance, made some suggestions, and said that she was lucky not to be, like most acrobatic dancers, too thin. The girl was at first puzzled, but when Lucille identified herself, she almost swooned with pleasure. It was as if Albert Einstein had come to praise a beginning physicist.

I now sometimes see Frances at a cocktail party, but I have heard nothing of Lucille in fifty years. If any reader of this book knows her now, please tell her that I remember her as one of the most admirable people I have ever known.

*

On my arrival in London, I taxied to the family settlement on St. Leonard's Terrace. I was to stay, until I could find "diggings" on my own, with Aunt Grace whose house abutted on its twin occupied by Alys Russell and Logan. I found that my relations were eager to serve my ends by introducing me around. In particular, Alys's exertions to find me companions of my own age succeeded. The letters of introduction I had brought with me were also fruitful, and the people I met introduced me to others. Aunt Grace wrote Mother: "Jim has really had an awfully good time. Everyone likes him. He is gay and jolly, and clever." Hardly more than a week after I had been in London, I had an engagement for every night.

Alas, I did not get on with Logan any better than I had before. He had become unstable mentally, given to asking jumbles of questions, never allowing listeners time to answer. I did succeed in getting him to recommend to me what he considered the best book recently published by a young Englishman. It was an autobiographical account of a delicate youth who found peace and philosophical musing in the countryside associating politely with sunsets, quaint peasants, and twittering birds: a sort of Etonian Walden.

I tried to hide my reaction from Logan, but he took a strong dislike to me which was to be reflected in Italy by the Berensons' not inviting me around when he was to be there.

*

The only girl with whom I had dates that I remember was the daughter of Logan's great friend, the celebrated critic and essayist Desmond McCarthy. I described Rachel to my parents as "Pretty in a very English way but not intriguing looking, intellectual to a fault (I think) but gay and energetic." By then I had moved to "digs" of my own in a house run by former top servants where my meals were served in my room if I wished. One evening I took Rachel there. The former butler was so concerned about the honor of his house that he kept knocking on my door every fifteen minutes or so with trumped-up questions: what time did I wish to be awakened the following morning; he had forgotten to ask what I wanted for breakfast; would I have my lunch there; he had forgotten to ask me what I wanted for lunch; etc. Both Rachel and I, our intentions being altogether respectable, found this highly amusing and speculated about what he would dream up to ask next.

Rachel was to marry Lord David Cecil, whose lives of Cowper and Lord Melbourne are among the biographies I most admire. Decades after we had last met, I was seated next to her at a dinner given by Mrs. Vincent Astor for Lord David before he addressed the Morgan Library in New York. Sure that she would without the least embarrassment answer in the affirmative whatever was the fact, and hoping to guess the fact, I asked her whether she remembered our association before she was married. She said yes, but I deduced she did not remember. How could she have?

*

Although Logan and his close friend Desmond McCarthy were leading figures in the Chelsea Group of writers (which went back beyond Henry James), the family had infiltrated to the heart of the newer Bloomsbury group through the marriages of Mary Berenson's two daughters by a previous marriage: Ray to Oliver Strachey, Lytton's brother, and Karen to Adrian Stephen, the brother of Virginia Woolf. In her diaries and letters, so often supercilious and scornful, Woolf was particularly hostile to Ray. Concerning Ray's death in 1940, Woolf wrote, "That very large woman with a shock of grey hair and a bruised mouth, that monster . . . is suddenly gone. . . . Disappointed, courageous, and without what? Imagination?"

Ray had published many books as leaden as they were serious and been parliamentary secretary to Lady Astor. I found her altogether disagreeable, exuding an invisible cloud of hostile superiority. She had stayed with us in New York, making Father (who had a sensitive nose) complain to Mother that she never washed. By way of paying back this hospitality, Ray asked me for dinner, giving me a full dose of that insolent rudeness which is the dark side of British upper-class manners. I was allowed in and fed, but completely ignored as she conversed with her husband.

Concerning her sister-in-law Karen, Virginia Woolf wrote, "Never, never have I known so odd a character. . . . She is hearty, good humored, and right minded. The poor devil interests me for having tried to live with Adrian [Woolf's brother], for being inarticulately aware of her obtuseness. . . . Dumb, twisted, gnarled, stockish, baffled—still she comes."

The novelist particularly scorned my cousin's efforts to cheer herself up with bright clothes which "almost wrenched my eyes from their sockets. A skirt barred with red and yellows of the vilest kind, and a pea-green blouse on top, with a gaudy handkerchief in her hair. . . . The effect is like some debauched parrot who has been maltreated by the street boys, but she doesn't know it, and half suspects it, poor fool."

In contrast to Ray, who had been idolized by her mother as an emerging powerful "Whitall Woman," Karen was from birth disliked by her mother because of her resemblance to the father whom Mary Berenson had deserted. Although she loved parties, Karen had been from childhood almost completely deaf. An operation, which only partially restored her hearing, permanently disfigured one side of her face. She had become a doctor, although she could hardly hear through a stethoscope, and then became one of the earliest psychoanalysts. Karen was looked down on by those who had been personally analyzed by Freud; she had been analyzed only by a disciple and was sometimes guilty of doubting an idea of the master's. However, she had given the first lectures on psychoanalysis at Oxford. To me she was charming: downright, intelligent, and warm. I did meet her husband, from whom she was partially separated. The brother of Virginia Woolf was, as I remember, stringy and seedy, one of those Englishmen whose offhanded indifference could be due to shyness or rudeness—probably both.

*

I had a letter to that famous presider over literary salons, Lady Colfax, of whom it was said that the dimple on her chin was actually her navel, her face having been lifted so often. She was very cordial the first time I went to one of her parties, and introduced me around. Subsequently, she would, having shaken my hand upon my arrival, hand me into the air. I would then hang around the bar waiting for some guest to get intoxicated enough to break the British taboo against speaking to strangers.

During the first evening I was introduced to an attractive middle-aged lady who complained that the novel she was writing was giving her trouble. When, as I was offering her advice, I noticed an amused twinkle in her eye, I interrupted myself to say that I had not caught her name. She replied that I had been given her married name, but she wrote under her maiden name, Margaret Kennedy. The author of *The Constant Nymph*!

I decided that I would offer no more advice to Lady Colfax's guests. My next literary lady was Mrs. Belloc Lowndes, the sister of Hilaire Belloc who had written an endlessly successful best seller about Jack the Ripper. She was a cross between a Mack truck and Aunt Carey, having the bulk force of the first and some of the panache of the second. Aunt Grace wrote Mother that I had asked her how she wrote her novels. "She was delighted and told him she loved him and liked him better than any American she had known for a long time." I had not confided to Aunt Grace that when I had gone to Mrs. Lowndes's house for tea I had had to struggle physically to keep from being dragged upstairs.

*

Through letters from Uncle Abe, I met several ministers in the Tory government. I attended a luncheon at which the Home Secretary sponsored the debut of a new kind of kipper that was to add to the prosperity of the British Empire. What happened to the Empire I do not know, but, after I got home, my Yankee stomach reacted in the most unpleasant manner.

And then there was the time when a cabinet minister came up to me after he had emerged from a discussion of the Irish problem. "Flexner," he said, "you look like a progressive young man. How would you like us to make you a present of Ireland?" I replied that the honor would be too great.

Again through Uncle Abe, I was invited to lunch by Lord Astor. My New Yorker's provinciality, which kept me from realizing that London, as a big city also, would have traffic jams, got me to Lord Astor's very late. My embarrassment at finding a consortium of elderly Conservative statesmen waiting with ill-concealed impatience was so great that I was utterly extinguished during the luncheon, and did not try to carry my acquaintance with Lord Astor any further.

*

My contacts, on the other end of political spectrum, were more relaxed until they led to the greatest emotional crisis of my life. At the home of one of Alys's young connections, I met Robert Fraser and his wife, Betty, whom I described in a letter to my parents as "prominent in the Labour Party, both having run for Parliament." He was a reporter on the *Daily Herald*, an Australian by birth. She was more intelligent and attractive than he. With the speed of a thunderclap we became close companions. I was soon able to write, "I must know all the members of the Labour Party by this time. I keep getting invited to parties, very often by people I have hardly met, where the discussion is all very communist and socialist. I can't gather whether the Frasers, who are friendly with everybody, engineer the invitations, or whether the socialists are just very friendly."

The group with whom I became so conversant were predominantly graduates of the London School of Economics and mostly, like the Frasers, in their late twenties or entering their thirties. They constituted the "intellectual wing" which played in the Labour Party a role utterly disproportionate to its numbers. At party conventions, the trade union leaders cast the votes of their entire memberships, which could run to tens of thousands. The intellectuals' constituencies were political clubs that enabled them to cast votes only by the hundreds.

They were powerful because of the trouncing union labor had received when they had called a general strike in 1926. The nation rose against them, demonstrating that organized labor could not on its own achieve national power. The intellectuals served as window dressing, and, even more important, supplied the party with ideas that had more of a national appeal than primarily trade union concerns.

There was another ingredient of which, as an equalitarian American, I became conscious. The class system was so strong in England that the blue-collar workers were glad to have among their political leaders men and women who were ladies and gentlemen.

Probably because it was used to signal connection with an elite school or college, the necktie was (as amazingly it still is today) in England a puissant symbol. Gentlemen would not be seen without a necktie, but workingmen resented its presence. I was amused to see how my Labour friends handled this situation. As they walked toward a party meeting, they could be seen wearing neckties, but within a block or two of the hall they indicated solidarity by putting their ties in their pockets. This visible compromise was accepted.

Wandering New York in the 1930s, I had heard much left-wing palaver: angry, denunciatory, and doctrinaire. Prefabricated ideologies were expounded, and clashed against each other. In comparison to the discussions at the social gatherings of my Labour friends, this might have been the arguing of adolescents at a sandlot baseball game. The talk I now heard was always serious but never combative, and to my American ears amazingly well informed. At home, we paid no attention in those days to the rest of the world, of which we were in fact almost utterly ignorant. The discussions I now heard wrestled with such questions as how it would be possible to establish an international minimum wage. Even altogether visionary issues—when and how to create an ideal society—were discussed in practical terms as became persons who were not, like American ideologists of the left, howling in a void, but were leaders of a party that had ruled England and might well do so again. The presiding genius of the group was Herbert Morrison, chairman of the London County Council (which governed the city) and well along a road that might lead to his being prime minister. I remember him as always serious, with an air of indomitable efficiency.

At the gatherings, I managed to hold on by keeping my mouth shut most of the time, while what inanities I did produce were blamed on my being an American. I was only really caught out when Betty Fraser arranged for me to interview Morrison—I was supposed to be preparing a profound article on the Labour Party for the American press—and I asked such superficial questions that he complained to Betty about having had his time wasted. She repeated the criticism to me with some asperity, but our friendship was not affected.

In describing to my parents the parties given by the Labourites, I wrote that sometimes "my weak American mind would welcome a little talk about clothes and how much liquor was drunk last night." However, I was influenced into resolving to study Communism—I might go to Russia—because "in order to write intelligently these days you have to know what communism means." Nothing came of this or of an effort to learn economics, which I abandoned when the textbook I had been given did not offer insights to the world around me, but engaged in a complicated examination of what was the basic nature of money.

The Labour Party girls I met were not amusing dates. When I held forth, to one of the least frumpy, on the difference between English and American jazz, she looked at me with bewilderment and finally said, "Oh, I see. You like to dance?" I did not meet, until after I had returned from three summer months on the continent, that very different Labour Party girl who was to overwhelm me.

*

My first stop was Paris, where I joined my former classmate at the Lincoln School, Breading, who was living on the Left Bank, studying and practicing sculpture. The friends he had made in the studios and life classes were a polyglot group of aspiring artists—not a French person among them—who, although they considered themselves "movers and shakers," were a century behind my Labour Party friends. They were living out "La vie bohème" as defined in Murger's novel (1848) and Puccini's opera. Even when I was in my teens, one of the dramatic scenes—Rodolfo throws the manuscript of his epic poem into the dying fire to add a little heat—struck me as a proof of superficiality: a true artist would rather have set fire to the house than to his manuscript.

However much I could have relished the thought that my bottom was pressing at the Café de Dôme or the Deux Maggots on chairs that might have sustained the bottom of Hemingway, Hemingway expatriotism lay a generation in the past. To the now elderly Gertrude Stein I had no access. But I did have a letter to Glenway Wescott, whose receptions were then considered the height of American literary life in Paris.

Having established a great reputation with novels laid in his native Minnesota, Wescott had come abroad for more culture and had developed, instead of increased creativity, a graciousness of manner—the opposite of Hemingway's roughness—that made him remain one of the most agreeable inhabitants of the American literary scene. Years later, I was amazed to have him remember happily our early association when I had been a young man of no importance. However, a letter that I have just unearthed reveals that he had talked his heart out to me, explaining his drop in literary output on everything except what I silently guessed was the real reason: he had, in completely uprooting himself from the Minnesota soil that had contributed strength to his early work, put down no roots elsewhere. Had I seen in this an object lesson for me?

My own efforts to write a novel were going badly. "I have just passed page 110 which should be a little more than a third. I hoped to get the first draft done by Fall, but that seems unlikely now. It is discouragingly slow work, partly because I am learning my technique as I go along. However, it holds my own interest and I still think it has the possibility of turning out very well."

*

Despairing of getting much writing done in Paris, I went to the French Riviera to visit Aunt Carey, who had rented an elegant villa on Cap Martin, a headland which commanded the bays of Menton and Monte Carlo. Having known her only while she was still active as president of Bryn Mawr, I expected to be managed every minute. What was my amazement to have the seventy-four-year-old martinet and feminist behave toward me almost flirtatiously, as if between a girl and a boy. Although she always dressed for dinner, she would not let me wear a coat in the hot evenings. Vociferously a violent teetotaler, she worked out for every evening a reason for celebra-

tion—some poet's birthday or the anniversary of the publication of
a classic—which required that we share a bottle of wine. Then she
wrote Mother complaining of the cost of always having wine for me
at dinner.

She did not object to my taking the bus every day to swim on
the beach at Monte Carlo. "Everybody," I noted, "wears practically
nothing. . . . I find that familiarity breeds contempt with the human
figure. So few look well. However, it gives a pleasant, relaxed
atmosphere."

I wrote Mother and Father that Carey was in much better form
than at Bryn Mawr. "She still has decided opinions on every subject,
but this time she is willing to discuss them in a friendly spirit, rather
than lay down the law. She is also becoming a parlor socialist, disap-
proving of all the things she enjoyed during her life-time. Of course,
the world is still going to the dogs due to drink. She is convinced the
women will be able to throw the shot as far as men, once they get a
proper chance to be physically fit. Childbirth is not a great experience
in a woman's life: that is a man's sentimental idea, and before long,
all embryoes will be grown in bottles, as is proper. The Catholics are
undermining the world with a considerable help from the Germans,
the Negroes, and the Japanese. Wars are over and done with because
the world war was really a war to end wars. By crushing the German
military machine that foolishness was put aside.

"I should say that, despite these statements, she is still perfectly in
control of her faculties. She just loves putting things strongly; it is
her game. She feels a little thrill solving the world's problems in one
sentence, and of course you can't do that unless you follow extremes.
But when you argue with her, she comes quickly to a sensible point
of view. She is full of energy."

We agreed when we parted that we had never known each other
before. I had found an aunt and she had found a nephew. She was
almost to a day fifty years my senior.

*

In Milan, I was determined to see a ceiling painting by Tiepolo (then,
as still, one of my favorite painters) that was hidden away in the
Court of Appeals. "My Italian was not up to asking for it. I walked
blithely into the building and whenever I met anybody I smiled my

best social smile, pointed at the ceiling, and said the one word, 'Tie-polo.' Most people looked at me pityingly, one man who looked like a judge began fingering in the law book to find the statutes on commitment for insanity, but occasionally I would find an intelligent gleam in a face of a person and he would explain copiously in Italian and then point a direction which I would follow blindly. Thus I traipsed through court rooms and offices smiling my inane smile, until finally I got to an office marked in gold letters, CHIEF JUSTICE. In it was sitting a dour individual with handlebar whiskers. I pointed at the ceiling and whispered ingratiatingly, 'Tiepolo.' The old boy began to shout and rushed out of the room—for the cops, I imagined. But he returned in a minute with a key and led me into the next room where was the fresco. He was very pleased. He would have kissed me on both cheeks if I had not avoided him. It seems very few people come to see his lovely fresco. And lovely it was."

This episode, quoted from a letter home, I quickly forgot, but I have not forgotten what happened one afternoon in Switzerland. I was on a mountain top which I had reached in a funicular: a narrow, open car pulled almost perpendicularly upward by a cable attached to a pulley on the summit. Going up had made me queasy, and when the time came to go down again I found I was no more able to face the descent than I had been able to cross that horrible beam when a small boy at the Lincoln School. Then it had been a matter of not continuing to be a coward in the eyes of my schoolmates. Now I was trapped. I had to go down if I were not to stay on the top of the mountain forever.

Back and forth I walked behind the little funicular station, watching the car plunge and come up again and plunge again. Trying to quiet my anxiety with statistics, I estimated how many thousand trips the little car must have made safely every year. How many years? And what about the hundreds of other funiculars that operated without mishap all over Switzerland? I wished to make the sum as large as I could, but I was too upset to carry through the multiplications. Not that it would have made any difference. No aspect of rationality could have had any effect on my terror.

I must have found the fortitude at last since I am not still up on that mountain, but the experience remained shattering. Would my devils be forever with me?

16

PASSION

*

BACK at London early in October 1932, I settled down for an extended stay in Chelsea by subletting a furnished flat in what was grandly called Beaufort Mansions, an old, block-long line of heavy masonry buildings, each with its own entry, three flights of stairs, and one flat on each floor. Mine was on the top. There was no exit to the roof and no fire escape. Inside my flat, the electricity had originally been connected to three fuses, but wires must have broken in the walls since everything had been hitched with black tire-tape to a single fuse. However, fears are selective. Remembering that while fire engines were perpetually dancing around in New York, you never seemed to see any in London, I signed the lease without further concern.

I was very comfortably settled: a long living room with a small table for dining at the far end from the coal grate, a bedroom, a kitchen, and a bathroom inhabited by a fiery metal contraption which seemed haunted by the reincarnation of a super-temperamental opera singer. The "geyser" was attached to the bathtub. You lit a gas jet which heated a copper coil. Steam would explode upward and sometimes hot water would flow downward into the bathtub.

A maid came with the flat. Appearing in mid-afternoon, she cleaned up and cooked dinner. Promising to follow its dictates, she posted Dr. Friedenwald's diet sheet in the kitchen, a great comfort to me as stomach upsets had been my traveling companions.

*

My English friends, who had kept in touch with me by letter, greeted me with enthusiasm, particularly the Frasers. They invited me to the Labour Party "blow" which preceded the opening of Parliament. I was not surprised to find the celebrators dowdy. Some of the men looked distinguished, but the girls were (as I wrote home) "awful." I was wondering whether to brave the lifeless English jazz to dance with any of the serious-minded freaks when a door opened and there appeared a girl who would have lighted up the most glittering ballroom. She carried herself as if used to making a sensation and pleased me by having exactly my coloring: red hair of the same tint and the same, although larger, brown eyes. I made for her like a parched Arab for an oasis.

The Frasers watched with much disapproval. The girl's name, they told me, was Mari (Welsh for Mary, pronounced Mahri) Stevenson. She was the daughter of Bob's boss, the editor of the *Daily Herald*, and had led her parents a dreadful dance. She was notorious for making men fall in love with her and then treating them badly. I would, they warned, be an utter fool to give into her charms. But how could I remain immune?

In Max Beerbohm's ironic novel *Zuleika Dobson*, the fascinating heroine incites all the undergraduates at Oxford to drown themselves for unrequited love, and is last seen setting out for Cambridge. This fantasy had seemed too far from possibility, but that was before I had met Mari. I was to see her set a whole group of men on fire.

She was not a classic beauty. However, on her my coloring was startling. Energy and excitement seemed to flow from her. She was conspicuous among British girls of her age (twenty) in dressing not as "a good sort" but up to her looks. However, her clothes were never flamboyant, or particularly in fashion, or physically revealing. Although her appeal was obviously sexual, there was no flaunting of sexuality. Her aura included innocence that stirred up emotion. And emotion, as Mother's Aunt Hannah wrote, is more contagious than the most contagious disease in the universe.

There was nothing surprising about my falling in love with Mari. The amazement was that she fell in love with me. Passion overcame us unexpectedly as we were having a presumably quiet drink in my flat. Not then knowing much about her, I started to say "the next time," but halted to say, "there won't be a next time."

"Did you say that," she asked with the intuition she possessed, "for you or me?"

"For you," I replied.

"Of course," she said embracing me, "there will be a next time." And so the roller coaster took off.

*

Mari was too tempestuous and catastrophic to go down the years with a circle of companions. Disappointed suitors do not make good friends; nor do out-rivaled women. But Mari did have one longtime intimate: a soft-spoken, plain, intelligent girl of her own age who loved and admired her without jealousy. Peg was terrified (as she was later to confide to me) when Mari told her that she had "after holding out so long" gone to bed with a man. Surely her friend had been victimized by the smooth wiles of an experienced middle-aged seducer! It was with many misgivings that Peg accompanied Mari to my flat. What was her relief to have the door opened by a smiling young man. Pleased to feel that this new connection would not separate her from her friend, she became my strong partisan. However, she remained puzzled as to why, when so many had failed, I had been chosen. Concluding that I must have set myself off from Mari's flood of admirers by refusing to let her walk over me, she warned me that I would lose Mari if I ever let her get the upper hand. This warning, which I kept much in mind, played an equivocal role in my love affair.

Not sent to college, Mari was much concerned with Labour Party politics. She also enjoyed exerting her power over male admirers. She told me with much mirth of joining an evangelical sect and persuading her suitors to accept the humiliation of being baptized by total immersion in white robes while old ladies sang. Then, annoyed by their making her wear stuffing under her own white robe, she renounced the sect, leaving her suitors to realize what fools they had made of themselves.

At one point, she had run away from home, supporting herself by working in cafeterias and moving so cleverly that it took months for her father, with all his political resources, to find her. Told that her mother was sick, she agreed to go home.

Shortly before my appearance, she was seeing off on the train a

White Russian émigré who lived in Paris. He suddenly proposed marriage and she impulsively accepted. The train departed. Since then she had not seen him, as her father had used his pull with the government to close for him England's borders.* But she was still presumably engaged. Having written him breaking off the engagement, she assured me that, should he somehow get to London, he would, as a former officer in the Imperial Guards, shoot me and then himself. I objected that that would be silly: it would make more sense for him to shoot her. That, she replied, would be contrary to the rules of chivalry.

Again and again, as Mari and I entered my flat together, the telephone would be ringing. I would pick up the receiver to encounter complete silence. Mari was sure that her father was not responsible, as violent action was more his style. The Russian? It seemed inconceivable that he would induce somebody—a compatriot?—to watch and indicate thus obliquely that he knew what was going on. But what other explanation was there? In my normal environment, I would have been greatly perturbed by these mysterious calls, but they chimed naturally with the excitement into which I had been thrown. One evening, just after Mari had left, the phone rang and a voice did answer. It was a deep voice with a guttural accent that said something unintelligible, and then clicked off. I thought to myself, "I am going to have a visitor." So unusual was my state of mind that when the doorbell rang I walked down the hall without a qualm and opened the door. I was actually disappointed to see only a delivery boy.

The phone calls, which persisted as long as we were both in London, were never explained.

*

On the front of Mari's neck was a gentle swelling, and her large brown eyes glowed all the more brightly because they protruded in their sockets. My beloved was hyperthyroid, which went far toward accounting for the exciting and disturbing intensity of her behavior.

---

*Although the *Daily Herald* was the Labour Party organ, it had the largest circulation in England, which gave Stevenson clout with the Tory government and its secret service. This was to become a menace to my love affair.

Her mother was also hyperthyroid, so much so that she was operated on, although without much effect in toning her down. To their combined explosiveness was added the ebullience of the Welsh temperament. The maids were all so Welsh that they spoke only Gaelic.

Her father, however, was a Scot with a dark temperament. He would not sit down to dinner without having at his elbow the pint of whiskey which, on top of his other potations, he emptied during the meal. As the liquor sank in, he became increasingly morose. Extreme behavior was in the Stevenson household so much the norm that it was hardly noticed. On Christmas, Mari's little brother, who had been given a tricycle, disappeared. Although it was observed that he had vanished, no one paid much attention until the phone rang. No one was particularly surprised at the information that the child had pedaled halfway across London to show his acquisition to his best friend.

On that Christmas, although the Stevensons did not approve of or really trust our friendship, Mari was allowed to invite me to their house at Highgate. I noticed at once how her father perpetually kept her on his knee as if to demonstrate to me his possession. The guests were the true aristocracy of the Labour Party including the highest official, James Middleton, who was national secretary, and George Lansbury, the grand old man, still a passionate pacifist. I listened with them to the broadcast of the king's Christmas message (written, of course, by the Tory ministry). As the august audience heckled and laughed, I decided to join in with a negative comment. As a group, they denounced my Yankee impudence.

*

Despite her much greater volatility of temperament, Mari and I had much in common. Our similarity of appearance, which enabled us to pass when prudent as brother and sister, was a bond, although we teased each other by saying that our love was not love at all but narcissism. We both had quick wits and tongues with which we could amuse each other. Welsh ebullience chimed with my Yankee breeziness and set us apart from the staid Englishmen around us. As revealed by the speed with which I had been adopted into inner Labour Party circles, I shared to some extent her ability to charm strangers. Although I was obviously no male Zuleika Dobson, we shared confidence in our ability to get on with the opposite sex. We both had deep wells of anxiety under the bright exteriors that facilitated our having a good time together.

Mari's self-confidence vanished only in relation to sex, concerning which she was at the beginning very shy. I analyzed that being assaulted by drives which she found it very difficult to control, she dreaded the effects of the most compelling emotion of all. This did not prevent her from exploding as I had never before known passion to explode, but when each storm subsided, she felt not completion but suffered from fear. Her modesty was such that when we first spent the night together and the time had come for sleep, I had to be resolute in dissuading her from climbing into her pajamas.

Someone had frightened her with stories of bursting condoms. She examined the drugstore where I bought mine to convince herself of its solidity and reputability. To be found pregnant outside of wedlock when she was not even engaged would be the most humiliating demonstration that she had allowed herself to be conquered by a man. And what her father would have done can be hardly imagined. Mari did not hesitate to tell me that we ought to get married. If there was conventional morality behind this desire, she never admitted it. She said it had never occurred to her in her wildest imagination that a man who became her lover would not be all the more eager to have her for a wife. And, since she herself loved passionately, she could not bear the thought that I was cynically using her as a plaything.

She had worked out our future. We would marry so secretly that her father could not intervene, and once we were married he would not prevent her from going with me to the United States. I would continue my writing and she would vitalize the American Socialist Party. In common with her Labour Party colleagues, Mari believed that the two major American parties could do nothing toward reforming the government, being loose conglomerations signifying nothing. A third party was needed. If the Socialist Party could be so energized that it would attract several million votes, it would have enough prestige to attract the progressive wings of both the Republican and the Democratic parties.

If I was not slated to be personally involved, I could have enjoyed the thought of Mari trying to reform the American Socialist Party. She was surely a firebrand, but her fire did not foster tact. (Most of my Labour Party friends disliked her.) I could not see the always controlled Norman Thomas taking this uncontrollable missionary from England into his inner circle. And the American Socialist rank and file, mostly unpropertied immigrants from Central Europe and Russia, would have been unable to believe their eyes.

And then, of course, there was the question of what marriage with Mari would be like. The very nature of the fascination I felt so strongly would have made her for me an impossibly destructive wife. Our basic difference was that when the break between controlled and uncontrolled behavior came, I did my best to draw back and she went jubilantly forward. And she was much too highly keyed ever to be restful. I could not visualize her accommodating herself to a domestic hearth. Nor could I believe that, swung by cyclonic emotions, she could be in the long run a faithful wife. To walk on the wild side was not part of my upbringing or my temperament. Nor did I, at that season of my life, have any intention of getting married.

However, all that would be necessary for immediate harmony was to propose and be accepted. Although she herself had broken two engagements, I did not feel I would be justified in getting engaged to her without the intention of marriage. The intention of marriage had been there in both of the previous situations. And certainly I would be dishonorable to encourage a woman I truly loved to continue sexual relations by an insincere promise.

And then there was the practical question of how I could most effectively, for the foreseeable future, serve my passionate desire to hold on to the woman I loved. I remembered the warning Peg had given me about keeping the upper hand. Proposing in response to her desire might well boomerang. Thus, honor and expediency seemed to be on the same side. While continuing to express the passion I felt, I avoided any commitment on the matter of marriage. Mari accepted this without any cooling of ardor. It could be assumed that the matter was in abeyance, to be worked out as our relationship matured.

*

With the new year, Father Stevenson decided that the time had come to break up the friendship (which had existed for two and a half months) between Mari and me. He arranged for her to have a job with some altruistic British organization working in cooperation with the League of Nations, and shipped her off to Geneva. He could not prevent me, with my American passport, from following her, but we agreed that it would be discreet for me to wait until after she had a chance to rent a flat of her own. We could then be together while I officially resided with a newspaper friend from the old days, Johnny Whitaker, the *Tribune*'s Geneva correspondent.

Our separation was extremely uneasy for us both, neither Mari nor I being sure of the other. I still carry the visual image of a long-awaited letter from her dropping through the mailbox in my door, and she became so tense that it took the appearance of a passionate letter from me to release belated proof that she was not pregnant.

Mari had identified a secluded inn in the mountains where we could go for a secret weekend. Taking the night train from London, I should arrive at Geneva on a Friday morning. She would meet me and take me to her flat, where I would leave my heavy luggage while she went back to her office. I would toward evening take a taxi to the station and she would meet me on the train platform. Then on Monday morning I would arrive with my bags at Johnny's flat. This maneuver was not only for respectability but to frustrate her father's spies. (She induced me to burn all her letters before I left London.) We could not foresee that I might stir up an altogether different set of spies.

During the trip to Geneva from London, I was physically sick in my anxiety lest she might not be on the platform when we reached Geneva. She was not on the platform. Some fifteen minutes later she appeared in a great rush. It had been hard, she explained, for her to escape from her office. She hurried me and my bags to her flat and, having promised not to be late for our train, vanished.

When the time had come for me to set out to meet her, it looked as if I would not make the train. As I stood on the street corner holding my overnight bag and hers, I could not get a taxi, and I was too unfamiliar with the city to know how else I could get to the station. Finally, an occupied taxi stopped. A man leaned out from the back seat and said in meticulous English with a German accent, "I presume you wish to go to the railroad station. May I have the privilege of giving you a lift?" I leapt.

The man was middle-aged, of a military bearing, and, if I remem-

ber correctly, wore heavy-rimmed tortoiseshell glasses. Having sur-
veyed me closely, he said, "I believe that you are an American?"

I acknowledged that I was.

"I don't believe I have ever seen you before." (He had picked me
up within the geographical orbit of the League.)

I replied that I also did not remember having seen him.

"What are you doing in Geneva?"

"Nothing in particular."

"Where are you going?"

"Paris."

"What train are you taking?"

Having replied that there were many trains and I would take
whichever was convenient, I asked him who he was and what he was
doing in Geneva.

He clicked his heels together on the floor of the taxi and enunciated: "General von Blomberg." Realizing that my companion was
Hitler's Minister of Defense, I could not help smiling, which did not
please him. I had long dreamed of being a central character in a novel
of international intrigue. Would German spies follow us around on
our unofficial honeymoon? Would they become entangled with Stevenson's English spies? And what of the Swiss gendarmerie? The start
of a new European war? Mari, like Helen of Troy, would make a
perfect inspirer of such a conflagration.

The general did not get out at the station and Mari was for once
on time. As I sat beside her in the train compartment, able to look
at her and touch her, setting out together on our first private adventure, all anxieties and dangers for the moment past, I felt such happiness as I had never on any other occasion known. I still see the roads
covered with snow that took us to the little inn, warm and welcoming, wedged in a narrow valley between high mountains. I remember
brandy and hot water, with which we toasted our arrival, as the
most ambrosial drink I had ever tasted. Thirty-six hours of bliss and
then we were on the train back to Geneva. It was almost as if the
wheels as they turned were churning up an evil spell. As the world
came closer, we found ourselves, to our dismay, irresistibly squab-
bling. It was an angry couple that disembarked at Geneva.

I find among my papers a letter from Mari's dear friend Peg:
"Thanks so much for your little note and the news about Mari. I

think you are both quite mad. One would expect whole rapture from sinners week-ending in a mountain village. But they say it is 'nice,' both of them, and talk about tomorrow. You must learn the wisdom of today. However, romantically I will imagine that you are too pleased for words about being together again."

*

When I emerged from Johnny's flat to be introduced to Mari's new friends, I discovered, much more to my dismay than to my admiration, that she had succeeded, in the few weeks during which we had been separated, in casting her Zuleika Dobson spell, mostly over young Englishmen associated in one capacity or another with the League. She was also being followed around by a silent, dark, and frightening Russian diplomat. A glowing twenty-year-old appearing in that narrow society of disillusioned idealists—the League was clearly dying—was like a ray of sunshine in a coal hole. Naturally, her crowd of admirers were not pleased by the appearance of a young American with whom their newly acquired darling was clearly involved. The question of what exactly was my role in her life and heart became a matter of great concern, and was to a considerable extent answered by a dramatic happening.

Mari and I normally came together after she had finished her day's work. That she would never be sure of exactly when she would get off, and was in any case flighty about getting anywhere on time, gave a practical use to the romantic symbol of possession: giving your lover your door key. I would wait for her in her apartment. Spurred on by anxiety, I was always early, and she was always late. Thus, one late afternoon I took it for granted that her apartment would be empty. Having inserted the key and turned the lock, I opened the door to see Mari serving tea to a group of her English admirers. They all stared. I should, of course, have walked nonchalantly over to Mari, handed her the key, and thanked her for her thoughtfulness in lending it to me in case she should be late. But I did not think of that, or maybe I was, subconsciously, establishing my right. In any case, I put the key back in my pocket.

Mari was pink with embarrassment. The followings were motionless with shock. Although international Geneva went in for every kind of vice, it was horrifying to have the pure and beautiful blossom they all adored brought down to the common earth—and by an American interloper. Every breast seething with dismay and jealousy, the upper-class English do-gooders departed in a crowd.

Mari, who when the stakes were down relished a gambler's excitement, did not upbraid me that night. She was indeed somewhat amused. But on the following night she informed me that she had explained to her friends that we were engaged. Obviously, I would back her up with our friends, but within our relationship I was unwilling to be driven. I asked, "Are you engaged?"

"No," she replied.

In being so downright, I was following Peg's advice, and I may well have taken the wisest course. Since I had only reinforced what we both already knew, Mari took no offense. And the physical aspect of our relationship went on without impediment. It was indeed enhanced as she shed her shyness and her obsessive fear of becoming pregnant. I remember saying to her that I had felt her body coming alive in my arms, and when she replied, "I'm not sure I thank you for that," it was with a loving smile.

When we went out together independently of her claque, we had very happy times. It is a bittersweet memory how gleefully, after we had in our amorous ardor won a waltzing contest at a nightclub, we made use of the prize, a bottle of champagne, to toast ourselves and our love. We could not know that this was the only public achievement that we would ever share together.

*

Geneva was no backdrop for happiness. The already staggering League was being dealt death blows, perhaps not altogether coincidentally by the two nations that were to be the principal adversaries of the United States during World War II. Hitler, who had just consolidated his power in Germany, smashed, through my taxi-mate von Blomberg, the disarmament conference. And Japan, by marching through Manchuria, challenged the League's ability to do anything effective toward preserving peace. When the League did nothing beyond passing resolutions, the Japanese delegation went to Geneva's premier whorehouse, the Moulin Rouge, to celebrate. There they met the Chinese delegation who had gone there to slake their wounds. A fight started, and the efforts of the naked girls to separate combatants were Geneva's only active steps toward peacemaking. The disillusion-ment in the League community was the more shattering because, as a group, they were former idealists who had once really believed that, after "the war to end all wars," the international organization would establish lasting peace.

I wrote my parents that in Geneva "no one believes anything any-more, either in the world of politics or in personal affairs. Peace and brotherhood of man are meaningless words and so is love, but you have conferences and go to bed nonetheless with the proper words on your mouth. But all the participants know it is only kidding. You have to have something to keep you amused and so you apply the technique of intrigue to everything, and set out elaborately to spy into the national and personal affairs of everybody. All the interna-tional colony is keyed to the most frightful pace; no one ever gets any sleep or peace of mind; everybody is busy picking up exclusive news stories, or getting a member of the German delegation so drunk he'll spill something; or making love to someone else's wife, or just going places and doing things because it is a habit you can't stop. Of course, the crop of nervous breakdowns is bumper and almost every-one is in the most frightful neurotic state. The jangling of nerves is the national anthem of Geneva."

My official host, Johnny Whitaker, was the only friend I had in Geneva other than Mari. Concerning the tribulations of my love affair he was far from being a help. An experienced seducer, he be-lieved that the only satisfactory relationships were with women who were also experienced. His doctrine was that no one but a fool would get mixed up with a woman who would get over-involved and make trouble, by, for instance, calling you on the telephone to announce that she had left a note for you and taken poison. Insofar as I confided in him, I got kidded.

Johnny's sexual philosophy and exploits were well known in Ge-neva and he was the only aspect of my past Mari had ever encoun-tered. Following my long-established policy of keeping my family out of my personal affairs, I had never introduced her to Aunt Grace. All Mari had known of my life and behavior in America was what I had told her. Was Johnny typical? Was my normal society made up of libertines, and was she another of the routine victims?

This conclusion was, of course, eagerly insisted on by Mari's English claque. They preferred to believe that she had in her innocence been duped by a rotter who, when he was tired of having his wicked way, would desert her, while they themelves would remain staunch and true. They treated me with extremes of insolence for which the British upper-class character at its worst is notorious.

If Mari remonstrated with them, she got nowhere. She did, in bringing us together, try to heal the breach, but it was hopeless. Since she was unwilling to discard either me or her claque, the only solution was to keep us apart. Her job belonged to the claque. Her flat was my sanctuary, where she would join me in the late afternoons or evenings and we would spend the nights together. But she became more and more tardy for our appointments, and there was no way for me to seek her out as my anxieties rose.

Life in Geneva became for me a nightmare. Both Johnny and Mari were busy during the day, and I was in no mental state to go on with my writing. Having no occupation, unable to sit still, I walked the streets worrying about when, if ever, Mari would appear for our evening rendezvous. I leaned forlornly over a bridge to watch diving ducks go down under the water, come up, and go down again in what seemed to me an endless rigmarole of frustration. Wandering hour by hour in that "capital of nerve jangling," I felt that I might, as I had always feared, lose my hold and sink into undefinable chaos.

I yearned to be in touch with Mari but felt I could phone her at her office (where she had never invited me) only once a day. Sometimes, to my utter humiliation, I could not resist calling a second time, using a falsetto voice until I got through to her, so that whichever of her scornful associates who answered the phone would not know that I was calling again. My behavior, I realized, could hardly sustain in her mind the image of a strong man I wanted always to present to her, but in my weakness I could not help myself.

To Peg, the only confidant I had concerning Mari, I wrote of my despair. She answered, "I hope you have decided to stay in Geneva. And even if you don't like it, you can hide yourself in a back alley and write something big and earn a place with the immortals. (There are a lot of them nowadays but very few with red hair, Jim.) And soon it will be spring (one has always to say that and it happens to be true) and you and Mari can take yourselves off to the ends of the earth where Père S. cannot follow you, with all the cash and influence in the world. . . . Stay with Mari! You won't ever find another like her!"

The night came when she went out on a formal date with one of her claque. Ivan Power seemed to me the most objectionable of them all. He was the son of an extremely rich real estate magnate who had become a public benefactor and been created a baronet by a Conservative government a few years before. Heir to so new an elevation in an aristocratic group so traditional, Ivan was snobbery incarnate. To my objections, Mari replied that she would not stay out late.

However, as I waited in her flat, the hours passed one after another, the streets of Geneva becoming quiet with the small hours of the morning, until my mixture of anxiety and rage and jealousy made me fear that I had indeed gone insane. Then the familiar footsteps on the stairs, the key turning in the lock, and Mari walked in. She was smiling with the afterglow of an agreeable evening. The contrast of her smug mood with my wild state of mind filled me with such fury that I grabbed from her bureau her framed picture of me, smashed it on the floor, drove my hand into the broken glass, extracted the photograph, and, with bleeding fingers, tore it into bits which I threw into her face. She stood there dumbfounded as I walked out of the door, slammed it behind me, and ran headlong down the stairs. On the way to Johnny's flat, I stopped at the station and bought a ticket to Italy.

*

Mari called me on the telephone the next morning. She had been so shocked and desolated, she said, that she could not bare to face her emotions alone. One of her British admirers living overhead, she had gone upstairs to his flat. Fully clothed, she had found some comfort by sleeping beside him in his bed. Since in telling of her hurt, she was clearly seeking reconciliation, she was obviously not implying physical infidelity; nor did I suspect it. But there was in her story the implication that, if I went away, she could find a haven with friends who hated me. I told her I had bought tickets and told her the time of the train.

Mari was there to see me off. After we were on the train alone in a vacant compartment, we stood facing each other without movement, staring at each other numbly. A cry of "All aboard" broke the silence.

Then Mari said in a low voice, without emphasis, without joy or sorrow, "If you want me to, I will go with you.

The words hardly penetrated me. I had no answer.

She leapt off the train and was gone.

*

My first reaction, after my mind had started going again, was the anger that is an essential concomitant of every sundered love affair. She had made demands on me that I could not meet; had been more and more attentive to followers who were my enemies; was alien to my fundamental needs. But underneath this rage was a deeply wounding realization of my own inadequacy. It would have been much easier for me had she spurned me there on the train, made out that I was a good riddance, expatiated on her new friends. A heart broken by a tempestuous love affair quickly heals and is looked back on with pleasure. But to be made to doubt oneself!

Had not Peg been right in urging me to hold on to Mari for I would never again find anyone like her? And had not Mari wanted to stay with me even in that last quick moment on the train? There surely were men who would have swept her away, taken her to America, married her, eager for the excitement, willing to take the chances, confident of their strength to stand up to the consequences whatever they might be. But I had been afraid, driving from me the most fascinating woman I had ever seen or would ever again see. Why had I been unable to put on wings to match hers and fly with her through the fierce storm clouds of ultimate romance?

Although reason, if listened to, could tell me nothing except that tying my life to Mari's would have ended in disaster, the memory of my failure of nerve remained with me as a source of depression. Concerning any permanent effect on her emotions, I felt no worry or guilt, confident that so resplendent a creature, looking down from her temperamental heights, would see me only as a speck left behind as her life streamed on. But when, it was two years later, we came together, I found that she had remained as haunted as I had been.

17

COMPASS SPIN

*

I spent three months in Florence, staying at the Pensione Annalens, which had during a generation been the stopping place for Americans interested in art.

One afternoon, I was met at the threshold by cacophony. A bearded old man was sitting at the piano. Holding a short ruler in each hand, he was pressing down contiguous groups of keys. As I paused with curiosity, a voice called "Daddy," and there appeared an attractive brunette who surprised me even more. She blushed when she saw me, and neither of us knew what to say. The old man put down his rulers, rose, and said in a courtly manner, "May I present my daughter, Edith Ives?"

By now the young lady and I had regained our composure. Although we had never met, we were already familiar with each other. Over New York City backyards we had seen each other's bedroom windows.

I asked around, but none of our fellow boarders, even those who professed a great knowledge of music, had heard of this man who played the piano with rulers. (The reputation of Charles Ives had not yet passed beyond a small elite.) Edie was not much of a help. Stating that her father had just retired from a successful career in insurance, she considered his music an eccentricity. With much mirth, she informed me that he was writing a symphony which would require so many instruments that the orchestra would fill the body of the theater, the audience being restricted to the stage. When the Iveses moved on in a week or so, Edie asked and I agreed that we would get together again in New York.

Florence seemed like heaven after my anguish in Geneva. The Annalena which occupied an upper storey of a huge old palazzo had along its front a long porch overlooking the Boboli Gardens and the Pitti Palace. Here I sat at my typewriter as I plugged away at my novel. The coming and going of guests supplied a variety of company. But the true bonanza was a trolley line that ran beyond the outskirts of the city and would pause a short walk from I Tatti.

The Berensons summoned me there several times a week. I would arrive in time for lunch where, as of old, there was a small party. Then, as I had when in my teens, I would read in the library while BB had his rest, before we went for a walk together, followed by his automobile. Then there was a large dinner party before I took the streetcar back to Florence.

A perpetual in-and-out flow of the great world! To my parents, I described an Austrian diplomat, Count Coudenhofe-Kalergi, who was the leader of a pan-European movement aimed at uniting all Europe into a single nation. "His mother was Japanese, and he was married to a retired famous actress who was all a retired actress should be: full of temperament and exaggerated gestures and energy and disdain for the lesser orders of men. The count has just been to see Mussolini for Austria's Chancellor Dollfuss. He is a violent anti-Hitlerite. He says Hitler has done much for Austria by uniting the whole world against Germany. There is, however, much danger that the Hitlerites will take possession of Austria, but he thinks it can be staved off. He seemed in favor of an international boycott of Germany (although he did not say so in as many words). He said that this would not mean war or Communism, but that Germany would break up into little states again. Nobody knows, he admitted, how well-armed Germany really is, but he thinks not well enough to withstand France at the moment, although it will be in a few years if nothing intervenes. He says he thinks Japan will conquer all China and put the Japanese emperor on both thrones, then proclaiming a far eastern Monroe Doctrine. His wife's comment on Hitlerism was that she thought since the war men had become so small that only small men and small ideas can reach them. Her disdain was classic."

The retired actress had a daughter whom I invited to an open-air concert that evening. A dark-haired, sensational beauty, she was truculently conscious of her allure. When a man stared at her, she would direct toward him the gesture traditionally used to ward off the "evil eye." This was in Italy a great insult (I was nervous lest some man assault me as her escort), but the men accepted it because she was so handsome. As I observed her, tears pressed against my eyes at the realization of how vulnerable by contrast Mari had been.

I was naturally much interested in Jefferson Fletcher, professor of Italian literature at Columbia, and chairman of the committee of three which selects the Pulitzer Prize—winning novel each year. I walked back to town with him and discovered all the things a novel must do to win ye greate prize. First and foremost, I gathered, there must be no nice young American girls seduced. If the scene is laid in China, like *The Good Earth,* or among Indians, like *Laughing Boy,* a polite seduction or so may be permitted, but a nice American girl, that's something else again. As the august chairman said, the kind of people he knows don't seduce nice young girls, so obviously when there is a seduction, it is just box-office appeal. Dos Passos he doesn't like at all, because if you are writing in the English language, why not write in the English language, which argument seems irrefutable, don't you think?

"However, I am making him out a fool, which he is not. He just has very old-fashioned ideas. As I am getting more and more old-fashioned in my ideas about the novel, I was able to agree with him a good deal of the time. For instance, I am sympathetic with his regret that the story element has so dropped out of the novel and with his feeling that characters should be normal people and not freaks or perverts. The only real trouble with his point of view is, I think, that he judges what are normal people in terms of his generation. He still lives in the world of Edith Wharton where a girl is forever ruined if she is seen coming out of the house of a married man when his wife is away.

"He was just as nice to me as he could be, listening to my opinions and ideas with interest (I was careful to couch them in very mild terms), asking me to come see him when I got back to New York, and promising to read my novel, when (and *if*) published, with great care. I gave him an outline of the plot, thinking it might get him interested in the old thing. Of course, if that problem child ever does get launched in the world, it won't have a ghost of a chance of the Pulitzer or any prize (a precocious young writer is one thing I'm not) but it never is bad to make a good connection."

*

BB did not, as on my previous visit, accompany me to the art galleries, probably for me an advantage as I could look around for myself. I had taken no courses in art history; nor had my reading been more than cursory. I was not concerned with those lines of influence with which academics play cat's cradle. Of iconography in the Germanic sense I had no inkling. My sources were the pictures themselves and the labels beneath them. My objective was to become so familiar with the paintings of the artists I was interested in that when I encountered further works I would be able to recognize them as I would recognize a friend on the street.

With the passage of time, I found what seemed to me inconsistencies in the attributions I read on the labels. I would hurry to BB, and we would have discussions that added much to my education. His sympathy with what I was doing was a demonstration that, as he had grown older and more experienced, he had come to feel less tied to scholastic and iconographical minutiae, placing more emphasis in attribution on the personality of the artist as revealed by the total picture. His judgments were, of course, based on vast erudition. I lacked the erudition, yet my efforts were an invaluable preparation for writing on and in America, where so much of the best work was based more on the character of the painter and his total environment than on past artistic traditions or learned tomes. BB was thus training me, although with no such intention, to be the rebel I came to be considered when, after I had successfully published several books on American painting, academics, bearing their "methodology" with them from outside, belatedly condescended to enter the field.

*

I was having in many ways a broadening and exciting time in Europe, yet the fundamental mood of my letters home was, despite sprightly incidents and bursts of youthful high spirits, discouraged. This darkness seemed to my backward-looking eye inexplicable until I realized that when I wrote my parents my mind was automatically drawn to problems and hopes I had taken with me across the ocean. These concerned my health and my writing.

My reports concerning "the old guts," though not devastating, were far from encouraging. If I violated Friedenwald's diet, I was instantly punished. And there were unexplained upsets. I reported home that I lost at least a day of writing every week because I felt too bad.

I had brought with me a manuscript which I intended to finish abroad. Hardly two weeks after my arrival, I reported: "This morning I completely tore the old novel apart and am building it up a new way which I think will be better. But, unfortunately, I will have to discard what I have written so far. . . . The novel as I had originally planned it was really two stories tied together rather flimsily. I have cut one story out, reducing the characters from thirteen to six. My plot [now] centers around a boy of medium ability who wanted to be a great poet. It is the reporter and the model and the communist that I took out."

Although as the months went on there were spurts of optimism, I was not writing fluently and well. Often finding myself blocked, I backtracked, starting helplessly over. After I had returned to London from my trip to the Continent, I reported: "My writing still lingers. I seem to have got terribly worried about form and am spending hours thinking and experimenting, which doesn't swell the number of pages written. I am becoming increasingly convinced that this work will have to be regarded as part of my post-graduate education and not as a professional thing in itself. Which means I shall return from Europe not having accomplished what I wished to do: namely, convince myself one way or the other whether I could go on with serious writing. I have not convinced myself that I cannot write, as I feel that I am learning a vast amount and as long as you are still learning there is still hope. Only when you have gone as far as you can, is there any logical cause for giving up. . . .

"I feel that only recently am I beginning to see writing as an art and realize the possibilities within form and style. The result, of course, is to make you realize how far you have to go. But I suppose literature is as difficult as bacteriology so you must expect as long an apprenticeship. Anyway, a more sophisticated point of view in-creases the interest of trying it."

The validity of my concern is checkable today. Already influenced by my lifelong nervousness concerning the safety of my manuscripts, I had, as I went along, mailed Father at the Rockefeller Institute carbon copies. The envelopes, much disintegrated by time, still hold in brown cobwebs the text in perfect condition. I must have splurged on expensive paper. This unfinished novel proves to be as far inferior to my unfinished college novel as it is more ambitious in intention. Although there are effective scenes and chapters, the manuscript as a whole can be best described as a mess.

I had failed to catch the subtlety with which Virginia Woolf united the past and present together within an unbroken flow of conscious-ness. As a preparatory maneuver, I had written a profile of each character up to the moment of his or her appearance in the novel. Perhaps presaging my future career as a biographer, these sketches turned out so well that I was inclined to incorporate them in my text. This involved following the introduction of a character with a flashback, sometimes lengthy, which halted the movement of the chapter. The static effect was increased by my failing to present the personal philosophies I had evolved for my actors in terms of action. I had recourse to long speeches which took on the tone of essays rather than talk. I was so bemused that I inserted metaphors which I considered effective but which, for the presumed speaker, were out of character. The narrative flow which, ever since I put pencil to paper, had been my valuable gift was blocked.

Under the influence of Aldous Huxley's *Crome Yellow*, I set up a large cast of characters, but I did not follow Huxley into tying them together in a single place and time by interlocking action. My settings were unparticularized parts of New York; my characters criss-crossed seemingly at random.

In Florence, after some further six months of struggling, I aban-doned the novel on which I had spent most of my working time since I had been in Europe. It was, I wrote, "an abject lesson in what not to try to do. Its subject matter was too neurotic, deadly serious, and complicated. . . ." It would suit my style better to write chronologi-cally, and with a great many short scenes.

Determined not to become too downhearted, I was annoyed by

Mother's suggestion that I accept the situation and devote my energies to perfecting my French. That would be admitting defeat! I had started a new novel on an altogether new plan, and I believed it was going well.

Yet the question loomed, my European trip having proved from a writing point of view so unfruitful, whether, so I wrote my parents, I should not join them at Chocorua where there were no distractions to lure me from my desk. And surely I ought not to lose touch with America, "which must, after all, be the subject matter of whatever I shall write." But Europe still held me. It seemed foolish not to go back to London and revive the friendships I had made there. After that, I concluded to my parents, "Who knows?"

*

My immediate plans were determined by cousins of Mary Berenson's on the Smith side: Mrs. Wilson Smith and her daughter, Kim. They were planning a motor trip to Venice and, the mother wishing company for the girl, invited me to come along.

This trip would enable me to see the Giottos at Padua and the great art at Venice, but most specifically exciting in anticipation were two novel attractions about which BB was himself excited. There was to be at Ferrara a special exhibition of Ferrarize art—pictures gathered from all over the world which would for the first time permit a real definition of that school; and then we would be able to hunt out the still almost unknown fresco that BB and Aldous Huxley were hailing with the greatest enthusiasm.

Such is the copy-cattishness of man that I was fascinated by the Ferrarize pictures because they were a revelation to my betters, although they were no more of a revelation to me than almost everything else. I developed such a sense of personal friendship for Cosima Tura that I still never see one of his crabbed pictures without wanting to offer it a friendly handshake.

It was not easy to find the masterpiece of which BB had told us. No one by the roadsides seemed to know the way to that decayed Renaissance center, Burgo San Sepulcro, and when we did finally reach the old town, no one there seemed to have heard of a *Resurrection* by a painter called Piero della Francesca. Night was falling and, in a community unprepared for visitors, we had to do the best we could with wretched accommodations over a bar.

The next morning we set out to find the fresco. It took a long time before we found our way into the huge but unfrequented entrance hall to an old palazzo. High up to the left on a bare brick wall a fresco was visible, but it was so dwarfed by its surroundings that it was only after a second look that I fastened my gaze on one of the greatest pictures I had ever seen: Piero's *Resurrection*.

*

The Smiths and I got on so well that they invited me to continue with them in their automobile from Venice over the Alps to Paris. We spent several nights en route, one of them in Switzerland, high up on the bank of a river that flowed in a deep gorge perpendicularly across our view. I was lured out by pale moonlight which, in that rarefied atmosphere, gently softened distances without blurring details. The far shore of the river, rising steeply to the left and right as far as the eye could see, was turreted and richly wooded. It was alive with waterfalls, emerging at different heights, some dropping all the way to the river that flowed below, others re-entering the forests from which they had appeared. All glowed in the soft light which Tennyson described as "downward smoke."

The scene, as seductive as the most luxuriant of women, called to me, as the sirens called to Ulysses, to leap into enchantment, swim through magic seas, abandon forever my voyage home. Yet I knew in my heart that this beauty, this moonlight, this enchantment, were alien, as dangerous to what I wished to achieve as a sickle that cuts a vine stem from its roots. The choice had finally to be made: would I become an expatriot in body or mind, or would I hesitate no longer, would I go home? If I lingered, I might well be overwhelmed, alienated from the American world where I had been born, that was my own.

I resolved that, on reaching Paris, I would book my passage home. And this immediately I did.

*

That evening spent on the bluff overlooking that Alpine valley has remained in my memory as among the determining happenings in my life. Forced, as I am writing this chapter, to find an explanation, I have realized that the menace was the overall quality of light, the all-encompassing atmosphere that bathed the extensive valley. I had previously written my parents that I had been blocked in my writing by the absence of "the alcoholic drafts of our native air." This was exactly opposite to the attitude of those Americans who became artistic expatriots. The sculptor William Wentworth Story, fresh from Italy, complained that at home "every leaf is intensely defined against the sky," and Henry James, repelled by "a brilliance, a crudity which allows perfect liberty of self-assertion to every individual object in landscape," quoted with approval Story's conclusion that "the heart turns to stone."

But the great success of Thomas Cole, the father of the Hudson River School (whom I was to do so much to rediscover), was due, according to William Cullen Bryant, to the delight of his fellow Americans at the "opportunity of contemplating pictures which carried the eye over scenes of wild grandeur particular to our country ... and into the depths of skies bright with the hues of our own climate, skies such as few but Cole could ever paint, and through the transparent abysses of which you might send an arrow out of sight."

Bryant also wrote a sonnet, "To Cole, the Painter, Departing for Europe":

Thine eyes shall see the light of distant skies:
Yet, Cole! thy heart shall bear to Europe's strand
A living image of our own bright land,
Such as upon thy glorious canvas lies.
Lone lakes—savannahs where the bison roves—
Rocks rich with summer garlands—solemn streams—
Skies where the desert eagle wheels and screams—
Spring bloom and autumn blaze of boundless groves.

Fair scenes shall greet thee where thou goest—fair
But different—everywhere the trace of men.
Paths, homes, graves, ruins, from the lowest glen
To where life shrinks from the fierce Alpine air.
Gaze on them, till the tears shall dim thy sight,
But keep that earlier, wilder image bright.

When I had fled home, I had hardly heard of the Hudson River School, of Cole, or of Bryant. It was decades later that I took the titles of the second and third volumes of my history of American painting from Bryant's sonnet: *The Light of Distant Skies*; *That Wilder Image*.

18

HOME AGAIN

*

My transatlantic liner docked in New York on July 1, 1933. As a dramatic introduction to what had occurred during my absence, friends rushed me to the newly opened Radio City Music Hall. The "grand lobby" was long enough to accommodate a sixty-yard dash, the whole space lighted by two chandeliers, each reputed to weigh two tons. Their refulgence was sent in every direction by gold-framed mirrors which crowded all four walls.

The auditorium, I was told, seated 6,200 people. Rising upward and outward from the huge proscenium arch, the egg-shaped ceiling was broken into perpendicular bands that were painted and illuminated to give the effect of a sunburst or Northern Lights at their most intense. I had already been told of the great capacity of the stage and wings since Joan Woodruff, a modern dancer I had got to know on the boat, had been in the performance that had inaugurated the Music Hall. She told me that she was standing beside the impresario when a sweating stage manager rushed up to say, "I'm sorry, Mr. Roxie, but we can't find those two grand pianos."

Just off a transatlantic liner, should I have reacted with disgust to the Radio City Music Hall? I found it "very impressive." Today it is admired as a masterpiece of the "Art Deco" style. The words Art Deco had not been coined in 1933, but I reveled in this stunning outburst of energy. I was back home.

*

My old roommate Jack Phillips having got married, I rented an apartment on the top floor of a walk-up on Sixteenth Street at Lexington, only two blocks from where I was born. Two of Manhattan's three subway systems met at the nearby subway station, bringing the whole city almost to my doorstep, and streetcars ran both ways on Lexington Avenue. It was a way of life for young bachelors to employ women who came in one or two half-days a week to clean and tidy up. I never heard of this slipping over into a sexual encounter, yet there existed a particular kind of intimacy with these women who dealt with our personal effects and, although they usually did not last long, filled the age-old female role.

One of Ben Robertson's cleaning women presented the perfect excuse for not showing up: "I was taken unexpectedly drunk." My closest approach to this was with the only pretty cleaner I ever had. She explained to me the advantage of having a husband who worked in the post office department. Since his hours were determined by law, she always knew when it was safe for her to be with her lover. But I had reason to doubt whether she would appear on schedule to work for me. Finally, I told her that if she ever missed another day, I would fire her. She thereupon missed ten days, arriving as perky as ever. I reminded her: "Linda, you remember what I said!" At which she looked at me as if I were the most unreasonable man in the world, and asked, "How could I come in when I was in jail?" (She and her boyfriend had had the bad taste to ram into the rear end of a police car.) I could do nothing but admit to having been most unreasonable. Of why Linda vanished I have no memory.

One of the strangest characters I ever got to know was a West Indian cleaning woman who, on first entering my door, told me proudly that she was a witch. Her dog and cat wore clothes and had perfect table manners. Naturally, I hired her. When she later explained that she was a devout Catholic, expert at casting spells, I asked how these two went together. Her explanation was altogether lucid. Voodoo came from the Devil and was therefore imperfect. Thus, a spell cast according to voodoo was only temporary and had perpetually to be "freshened."

Catholic spells were permanent. The mechanics were simple. You had to have candles—the cheapest would do. You needed to know what psalms fitted what spell. You quoted them with the right gestures—and it was done.

For my witch, all the objects in my rooms had personalities. I would find a slip of paper stuck in the handle of the ice box: "Dear Mr. and Mrs. Icebox, If you don't stop reaching out and tearing my dress, I will sue you for malicious mischief. Mrs. Marlborough Purvis."

Or I would find a note addressed to me: "Mr. Flexner, Some things you want to look feeble. Others you want to look well. Please let me know which needs the medicine. I thought you need the ash tray feeble looking. Please do you need this thing looking intelligent. Please let me know and I will schooled it with some Babbit."

To one of my African sculptures, she wrote: "Ay, Mr., you looks like one of the monsters that drive Pharaoh off his throne at the time of the plague. My name is Louise. What's yours? That face of yours looks like the one that help to swallow Pharaoh and his army in the red sea, tell me if it's you. Pleased to meet cha."

Sometimes there was an essay. "Communism is like when Lucifer, Mr. John the devil, was thrown out of heaven. He fall in the pig pen and even try to convince the pigs of the most delicious manner of his kingdom. Then, as he gradually gain their confidence the pigs finally find themselves deserted by all, but worst of all they couldn't get the Seven days Adventist to eat their pork, so right away the pigs, hogs I mean, sow and all, decided to declare war on Satan as the 7th day Adventist disbound them. Wasn't the hogs fault. Lucifer fell there and ever since his reputation is known to be awful bad. But with all of that he isn't a bit disheartened. He is trying on."

The witch was the most conscientious of all the part-time maids I had, and she operated successfully in the world. Whenever she wanted anything, she would write directly to the Mayor, which, as I had discovered at the Noise Abatement Commission, was an effective tactic, since a note referred down from the Mayor's office was likely to be attended to.

*

It did not take me long to learn that "the composer named Ives" who had played the piano at the Annalena with a ruler was considered by the most musically sophisticated friends the greatest American avant-garde composer. I was told that his period of creativity had come to an end in the 1920s, when he had had a serious illness. He had also abandoned a successful business career. Although he was still only fifty-nine (he was to live for another twenty-one years), he had become very much of a recluse. Almost nobody was allowed into his home. Naturally, I was made the more eager to renew my acquaintance with that charming brunette, his daughter.

When, on being telephoned, Edie asked me to come around, I expected to find, in the home of an icon of modernism, abstract paintings and sculpture with perhaps some advanced music playing. Received by a maid in an old-fashioned uniform, I found myself in a Victorian vestibule. I was concluding that I was in the wrong house when Edie appeared.

She led me into a drawing room at least two generations in the past. Mr. and Mrs. Ives received me with formal courtesy, but the composer seemed to be nervous and jumpy, while his wife seemed almost completely withdrawn.

This did not mean that I was not allowed in again. Edie was permitted to have me around whenever she pleased. I even came to meals. Once as I was lunching with the family, Ives opened a letter enclosing a clipping from an indiscreet disciple who had, despite his dislike of publicity, discussed him in an interview. The composer was so upset that he got his beard in the soup. No one seemed to notice. Ives wrung out his beard as you would wring out a washcloth, and the luncheon proceeded.

In his country place at Pound Ridge, Connecticut, Ives was a different man: he allowed himself to relax. Wearing a wine-colored velvet smoking-jacket, he received me with what could be considered an approach to cordiality. He led me out over a considerable estate to show me his horses, cows, and pigs. I got the impression that he very much enjoyed being a country squire.

Back in New York, when his music was to be played and a central box was reverently assigned to him, he would refuse to go. Edie told me somewhat scornfully that he felt degraded when an audience did not, as of old, get up to leave but sat there applauding. On several occasions, I escorted Edie and her mother. As the enthusiastic audience turned their faces toward the composer's box, they must have been disconcerted to see not a venerable bearded figure but a young redhead. I considered rising and bowing, but thought better of it.

Edie told me, after I had known her for some time, that she was an adopted child: the Iveses had first seen her sitting on the floor eating a dirty piece of bread. She gave no further details, and I have subsequently come to wonder how much she herself knew.

I later discovered that Edie was the youngest child of a poor family occupying a gate house on the Iveses' country estate. The baby was very sick, and Mrs. Ives, who had been a trained nurse, took her home to cure her. Adoption was not intended. But the composer and his wife could not bear to return the child to a sordid environment. The natural parents then preyed on them, with demands for money and such threats to recapture Edie that it was considered necessary to hire security guards. Reminiscences of Ives's associates tell us that not until the matter had somehow been finally quieted did the composer settle down to considering Edie his daughter.

The Iveses (they had been in their mid-forties when they had taken in the baby) seem never to have been able to adjust themselves to the needs of a young girl. Edie told me that when her first menstrual period came, she was upset. No one had prepared her for this strange phenomenon. She asked Mrs. Ives, and was told (so Edie said) that it was a piece of Eve's apple coming out.

Edie's chance to escape had been when she was sent to Farmington, a large girls' boarding school, where Mrs. Ives had gone, but this only made matters worse. I learned that she had been exiled by the more energetic and well-adjusted girls, since I knew several of her former classmates who expressed wonder that I could find anything to interest me in such a "pill." Edie's failure to get on seems to have discouraged her adoptive parents who let her hang around the house on the assumption that she was "sickly." (She never seemed sickly to me.) In any case, all the household attention centered on Ives, who was considered so hypersensitive that he had to be sheltered from everything that might upset him.

Although Edie never said so, it became clear to me that she was very unhappy and deeply resented her adoptive parents, although she lacked the "get up and git" to rebel. She told me as a funny story on herself that she had decided to drown herself in the bathtub but refrained at the thought that her naked body would then become visible.

The fluke of Edie's and my meeting in Florence was welcomed. Her elders did everything to encourage the relationship. I could come and go as I pleased. There was no restraint on where I might take

her or on how late I would bring her home. Finding her gentleness
and melancholy charm an attractive change from other girls—and
pleased with the Ives connection—I took her out periodically, but I
had no designs concerning her of any description. It was not very
long before I got frightened, all the more because I was being referred
to as "Edie's young man."

Surely the composer, however self-centered and protected, could
not help worrying sometimes about his isolated, melancholy adopted
daughter, and what about Mrs. Ives? I feared that I was being envisioned as that godsend, a son-in-law, who would take responsibility
for Edie off their hands. However, I was less concerned with their
reactions than Edie's. She gave signs of becoming in her loneliness
too fond of me. To stop dating her seemed cruel, but surely it would
be crueler to get in more deeply if I did not want to follow—in
whatever direction—through.

I never saw Edie or her adoptive parents again. I know that several
years after we had parted she had married, and she had a son. By
the time that I was asked to contribute to an oral history book about
Charles Ives,* Edie was dead. The custodians of the papers at Yale
have refused to confirm or deny the rumor that she committed
suicide.

*

The platonic friendship that grew up, shortly after my return from
Europe with a handsome woman, Rhys Caparn, who had just returned from studying sculpture in Paris, came to be the closest friendship I have ever enjoyed. There was a limit to what I could confide
to my male friends, and I was glad not to incinerate my life with
another love affair. Despite modern heresies, romantic literature from
many centuries—Dante and Beatrice, Petrarch and Laura—cele-
brates love not disrupted by sessions in bed.

Rhys Caparn was extremely tall—her some six feet would now be
the equivalent of six and a half. During the 1930s, tall women, not
wishing to put men off by towering over them, went in for low heels
and a round-shouldered posture. Rhys preserved perfect posture over

---

*Charles Ives Remembered: An Oral History, ed. Vivian Perlis (New Haven: Yale
University Press, 1974).

heels proportionate to her stature. She dressed to the advantage of her narrow, gracefully molded figure. That, with my broad shoulders and strong build, I weighed about as much as she did kept me from feeling like a pygmy as her companion. Our congeniality was indeed enhanced by our being embarrassed neither by shortness nor by height.

Rhys's face was dominated by cool gray eyes. Her voice was rather low in pitch and intonation; her manner, gentle but by no means soft. She had not a touch of girlishness: I do not remember that she ever giggled. She was quite capable of disdain but always courteous in the manner of her southern aristocratic mother. Her indomitable spirit was like a hidden steel beam. She was one of the most intelligent people I have ever known and solid within herself.

That she was an attractive woman and I a man underlay our entire climate of behavior. Yet neither tried to dominate the other. Having no overlapping finances, feeling no need for sexual jealousy, we had nothing to squabble about. We were a team, closer than many married couples. It was a great bond between us that, although in arts so different that there was no possibility for rivalry, we were engaged in the same endeavor: to extend our skills and output in preparation for invading, in the near future, the professional tournaments of our crafts. The novel I had started in Florence was proceeding apace; Rhys was scheduling exhibitions of her sculpture. We advised together, sharing each other's triumphs and disappointments.

*

Rhys had become a pupil and then a favorite disciple of the internationally famous Ukranian sculptor Alexander Archipenko. During the formative years of Modernism in Paris, Archipenko had pioneered application of cubist conceptions to sculpture. His two major inventions demonstrated that concave surfaces could be substituted for what was convex in nature, and that plastic shapes could with effect be pierced with circular apertures. He was an originator of what came to be called "negative form."

The inventive phase of his career was behind him when he taught Rhys, but his fundamental approach suited precisely her temperamental needs. He regarded sculpting the human nude not as an end but as a point of departure for making a liberated work of art. By preserving the rhythm and implications of nature, the artist profited from mental association with humanity and traditional subject matter, while following her own sensibility and preference for form. Rhys was thus enabled to express the human figure, exerting her own insight, skill, and charm, without becoming involved in anatomical detail, which somewhat repelled her.

This could be an invitation to superficiality, but Rhys was both profound and serious. Archipenko, himself a craftsman, encouraged her to have in her studio equipment for casting her clay figures in plaster. I enjoyed watching the efficiency with which she went about it. Indeed, her studio in the West Fifties comes back in my memory as one of the happiest places I have ever known.

We found refreshment in joking together about the creations we were so passionately pursuing. When Rhys had a show, we felt it necessary to have a title for each sculpture, although in the making she had been concerned only with the evolution of form. We enjoyed suggesting the wildest and silliest of names (which, of course, we did not use).

Rhys had her first exhibition at the Delphic Studios on Fifty-seventh Street in November 1933. Together we transported and installed her sculpture. Among them was a portrait of me. During the opening reception, Rhys welcomed my backing her up in a manner that must have been conspicuous. I was encouraged to feel that I was playing a real part in her occasion, in which my emotions were much involved.

Archipenko wrote for the catalog: "The idealism of Rhys Caparn and her love for the spiritual permit her to create a new form of sculpture, without her losing the ability to sculpt in a naturalistic form when she so desires. She passed through careful and profound academical studies, but her inventive mind guides her to a new conception of sculpture. Rhys Caparn is one of those rare artists who create lyrical poetry of pure form. The lines of her statuettes remind one more of a quiet melody than the anatomical lines of the human body. Her art is purely feminine in sentiment. . . . Rhys Caparn is the first woman in America who had the courage enough to use the new combinations of form and line for self-expression."

This first exhibition was most appreciatively praised by the newspaper critics, but a second exhibition held thirteen months later was subjected to ridicule. The critic for the *Herald Tribune* amused himself by imagining with what consternation her abstract nudes would be viewed if used to decorate a barroom.

Rhys and I could sympathize with each other as my novel, by then finished and going out into the world, was bouncing back from publishers. It was only at a later date that I came to feel that in our mutual discouragement we had discouraged each other.

*

I came to know Archipenko through his desire to write an essay expressing his conviction that the release of creativity that characterized modern art would, if more generally applied, save the world. But he knew that his command of English was inadequate. Rhys enlisted me to help in my capacity as a writer.

Archipenko was middle-aged and blondish with a bristling black moustache. He was hardly taller than I was and even stockier. You would have taken him not for a sophisticated artist but as an artisan in some skilled trade. He was gentle in manner, ebullient, unpretentious, courteous, friendly, and almost shy.

The plan was that he would talk out his ideas to Rhys and me, while she interpreted from her knowledge of his thinking, and I inscribed in literary form. His words poured as from a millrace, but his confused English and his not being a cerebral man prevented us from following him far onto what seemed to be incoherent philosophical heights. When we attempted to echo his ideas back to him, he would frown and enunciate, "Noch! Noch! Noch!"

Archipenko eventually abandoned the project. Blaming his inadequate command of English, he felt an obligation to us for trying to help. His friendship with Rhys was compensatory; he invited me to attend his life class free of charge.

I went as a lark, and, as he prowled around among his students to see how they were doing with the female model, he saw on my paper only one form: it looked like a curvacious peaked hat drawn sideways. He said to me emphatically, "You cannot start with the brüst!"—an admonition which I will have carved over the door if I ever found an art school.

Archipenko explained that as soon as one sharp detail had been established, the entire composition was dictated. It was, therefore, necessary to build up the image gradually, organically. I recognized that this advice was essential for his type of abstraction, but I was only having fun. I did not outrage him by attending any more of his life classes, and when in later years I amused myself by drawing from the nude beside my artist friends, I always started with the "brüst," producing results that amused us all.

Feeling further obligated, Archipenko asked Rhys whether it would be all right if he gave me a drawing. She, of course, said yes, and as a result I possess a large drawing from his best Paris period. It is dated 1920. (See illustration.)

The picture, featuring two female nudes, can be taken by an unseeing eye as naturalistic: a "huntin' and fishin' man" we once had in for cocktails preened before the "naked women" like a mating bird for a full five minutes. But, in essence, the picture is a construction of solids and depths, where reality is implied to heighten legerdemain. Scrutiny brings the realization that major anatomical forms are missing: one of the women has no eyes; one has only a single arm; and each has only one leg. The ponderousness of the thigh, hips, and buttocks of the crouching woman, emphasized by a double black outline, should by all rights pull her over backwards out of the picture, but the composition holds so tight that the imagination cannot budge her. The total form is shaped like an elongated candle flame and despite the interior interplay of solids and voids seems weightless. As an almost humorous indication that the two women are not standing on their one leg apiece, Archipenko did not finish their toes.

*

Rhys caught the eyes of intelligent men everywhere, and she was particularly taken up by the inner circle of highly publicized foreign correspondents who wrote best-selling books about their exploits and their personalities. These were the prima donnas of my old trade as a newspaperman. I was jealous not for lovers' reasons but because I thought it unfair that a handsome young woman could enter stimulating circles from which I was barred as a young male.

Rhys told me that she was being particularly chased by Walter Duranty, famous for his dispatches to *The New York Times* from Russia. In the words of the *Dictionary of American Biography*, Duranty was recognized "as the sort of romantic foreign correspondent glamorized by Hollywood and envied by other journalists." He liked to be known as a great conquerer of women, but I had confidence that Rhys would not let herself be conquered unless she wanted to be, which seemed unlikely as I could not believe that she would be deeply interested by so flashy a personality. I saw no objection to Rhys's arranging that Duranty pick her up for some late evening party at my apartment.

It was about ten o'clock when there was a rapid clumping on my three flights of stairs—Duranty had lost a leg in a railroad accident and liked to show off how agile he could be with its artificial replacement. He came accompanied by a tall, willowy man, obviously quite drunk, whom I identified as Vincent (Jimmy) Sheehan, the author of the major best seller *Personal History*, an account of his dramatic newspaper career that features a marvelous woman. Rhys and I were playing chess.

When Rhys put on her coat, I stood to one side. The scene, so reminiscent of a tear-jerker in an old melodrama, was too much for Sheehan's sentimental heart: here was a young beauty preparing to go off with a notorious middle-aged seducer leaving forlorn, beside an unfinished chess game in his humble dwelling, the young man who worshiped her and was obviously her correct mate. Sheehan invited me to come along. Duranty's face registered extreme displeasure. Sheehan insisted. Rhys, usually unflappable, was flustered. But I had my understanding with her and stuck by it. Only after the three of them had departed, Sheehan expostulating apologies to the last, did I recognize in what a demeaning position I had been placed. My angry jealousy of Duranty was born.

Rhys came away from the evening determined to make peace between me and Duranty. And a necessity quickly arose. Duranty had a whole series of impressive occasions to which he wished to take Rhys on Christmas Eve, but as I was her dear friend, Christmas Eve in effect belonged to me. The obvious solution, which might also heal the previous wound, was to include me. Duranty undoubtedly bridled, but Rhys handled him.

And so we three set out in a taxi together. Duranty boasted almost without stopping. I was half-listening when I remembered something I had heard: nothing annoyed Walter Duranty more than being confused with another celebrity, Jimmy (Schnozzel) Durante, the beloved comedian risen from burlesque who drew laughter with his vulgar humor and his perpetual references to his own tremendous nose, his "schnozzle."

It did not take long, after we had reached our first party, for Walter Duranty to gather around him an admiring group, mostly women, to which he pontificated. But on the periphery, I found a pert, petite blonde whom I quickly recognized as the accomplice I needed. After a few words from me, she inserted herself into Duranty's revering circle, used her obvious attractions to cut him out of the herd as expertly as if she were a trained sheep dog, and led him to a secluded corner where she squashed down beside him on one of those short sofas called love seats. Watching, I could see her register awe at his importance, gratitude for his paying attention to little her, and indications that she was completely overwhelmed. The sex light was shining in his eyes (I liked to think that he was scheming how to ditch Rhys and me) when he rose so precipitously that it could almost be said he jumped, and stalked away. She had breathed amorously that she particularly admired the artistic effect he had got from his schnozzle when it really was not quite so very large.

Anything that is worth doing is worth doing well. Although at subsequent parties I could find no collaborator as spunky as Doris (who became my good friend), nothing more was needed to keep the ball rolling than induce some girl to tell him how much she admired his performances on the stage. He never caught on to my complicity.*

The three of us were in yet another taxi. Perhaps because his self-importance had been having a rough time, he felt called on to practice ultimate condescension on me. Again dilating on his importance, he held forth on how useful the influence of one as great as he could be

---

*I was to play this trick again, this time in cahoots with Henry James's biographer, Leon Edel. Since most of the subscribers to the Book of the Month Club were women, there was pressure to select women writers. In the realm of history, Catherine Drinker Bowen was for many years the star. Then, enter Barbara Tuchman. Their temperaments were very different—Kitty, who happened to be my cousin, was "a big-hearted slugger." Barbara, who undoubtedly looked down on Kitty, was smug. She was to machinate to become an American candidate for a Nobel Prize.

At an occasion staged by the Society of American Historians, both Kitty and Barbara attracted admirers. Leon and I egged on various members of the Bowen group to join the Tuchman group, praise Barbara up to the skies, and then ask reverently, "What masterpiece are you going to give us next, Mrs. Bowen?"

in launching a beginning writer like me. He would put his magical push behind my career, acting as my Puss in Boots. The metaphor appealed to him. He repeated the phrase "Puss in Boots" three or four times.

Finally, I exploded. I told him he was a self-enchanted publicity hound, a phony, a four-flusher, and a hack, adding that I would rather have as a puss in boots an alley cat scrounging an honest living out of garbage cans. The passage of time has revealed that my summary of Duranty's character, based I must suppose on instinct as well as jealousy, was not far off the mark. Drew Middleton, a later *Times* correspondent in Moscow, tells me that Duranty, spurred on by the comforts and privileges he was granted as an official favorite, permitted himself to be hypnotized by Stalin. Sitting in his comfortable flat, surrounded with adoring women, he denied the great famine in the Ukraine. He defended the Moscow purge trials in the 1930s, thus, according to the *Dictionary of American Biography*, "misreporting the biggest story he ever covered."

Having reached the end of my tirade, wishing to avoid an anticlimax, I leapt out of the cab and disappeared down a street.

*

I had hardly gotten to my apartment before the phone rang. Rhys had been so upset that she had made Duranty take her directly home. Although we talked for an hour or more, I cannot remember the specifics of what we said for over-all hung a realization: we were very fond of each other and could not bear to lose each other, but the platonic nature of our relationship had reached the breaking point. We must either go ahead or go backward. We could not stand still.

The night's adventures and realizations did not occasion an explosive result. Rhys and I met as we had before, but we gradually moved into a sexual relationship, not as an outburst of passion but as a deepening of friendship.

However faithfully we had previously looked the other way, lack of consummation had inevitably stood between us, a wall Mother Nature herself had built. But once we passed over the wall we found ourselves in a landscape less bucolic: the declivities were steeper; the streams ran more strongly; storm clouds, even if they did not break, hung on the horizon. I had, to a greater or lesser degree, accepted cheerfully flirtation between Rhys and other men. Now that was impossible. And I now felt myself restricted, by both honor and taste, in my relations with other women, all of whom seemed to me so inferior to Rhys that to pursue or accept possibilities would be degrading.

The issue of fidelity or infidelity was never discussed between us, although we stopped teasing each other about smiling at other members of the opposite sex. I assumed that Rhys was being as faithful as I.

*

Although they had never met, Rhys's mother and my parents assumed that Rhys and I would eventually get married. We never mentioned the possibility to each other, although it seemed to be so clearly there. What was in the back of Rhys's mind I did not know. But for me there was a major impediment which, although I tried to drive it away, would not lie still. One happening is deeply engraved in my memory.

I was idling down Lexington Avenue as I passed the Unitarian Church and saw displayed there a placard: "On the last day, it will not be asked what you believed but what you loved." Suddenly my eyes were full of tears. What indeed did I love? Would I never free myself from Mari?

19

"ENTER AND POSSESS"

*

THE altogether new novel I had started in Florence had indeed escaped from the confusions that had plagued me during most of my European stay. I had got back to the fluency with which I had written my college novel. As in "Dogs Shall Eat Jezebel," my protagonists were women. Today this would seem affrontery in a mere male, but it seemed natural to me because my male friends never confided their intimate emotions to each other. I had got to know several women with much greater intimacy. Furthermore, I was moved and fascinated by the female sex. There was another advantage I did not recognize: I was prevented from getting bogged down with the somewhat morbid introspection that had plagued my writing efforts in Europe. My task was extroverted rather than introverted.

For some reason that I have never been able to analyze, I have been much taken, during much of my career, with action involving more than one major protagonist. In this novel, I decided to contrast the two major categories of women I had known: a privileged society girl with a free spirit outside the conventional world.

To establish some unity, I made the two girls half-sisters. Their common father had lived a conventional affluent life, but after his daughter Nancy had been born, he deserted his family to become a poet, fathering with a girl from Greenwich Village a daughter they called Carmen. Nancy was brought up in correct affluence by her grandfather and her mother; Carmen was set adrift by the death of both her parents. I entitled my book "Enter and Possess" since my youthful protagonists were emerging from girlhood to find their own destinies.

Nancy's was the social world that I had satirized in my college novel, but I now dealt with it much more sympathetically and at greater depth. Her environment adequately paralleled the world I knew to enable me to describe her tribulations with understanding generated by my own experiences. I saw Carmen as a free spirit, almost immune (as I would have loved to be) to irrational fears. Willing to throw everything away for love, she was in many ways a creation from my own imagination. Concerning her adventures, I wrote poetically, not, as with Nancy, analytically. The ending showed Nancy, whose family had lost their money in the stock market crash, marrying for security a middle-aged man she did not love; while Carmen was left emotionally destitute, having been deserted, as she foresaw she would be, by her dashing newspaperman lover.

I felt that the paths of my two heroines, which I pursued in alternating groups of chapters, were too far apart ever to merge. The dichotomy was enhanced in the telling by the technique, which I had first used in the college novel, of standing always at my protagonist's shoulder. I never indulged in the generalizations, the comments and comparisons, permitted to an "omniscient author."

Only once did I bring my protagonists together. Carmen was wandering a night club in her capacity as cigarette girl when an overheard name made her realize that an elegantly dressed customer who was there with a middle-aged man was her half-sister. Carmen observed with amused disdain Nancy's efforts to entrance her stuffy companion. Nancy, noticing that she was being stared at, concluded that the cigarette girl was studying her dress in the hope that she could run up on her sewing machine something like it. Adhering to my stylistic approach, I did not interweave the behavior and reactions of my two heroines but told them separately, each in her own sequence. I was foolishly pleased with this consistency, regarding it as a new departure.

Thus, I tried to hold my novel together by echo and counterpoint. In my inexperience, I did not realize how formidable a task I had set myself. I was, indeed, pleased with the total result, being particularly proud of my poetic rendition of Carmen's great love affair.

*

Ever since before I was old enough to read for myself, I, as a writer, had been preparing for this climactic moment. On August 23, 1934, aged twenty-six, I set out carrying a package addressed to Eugene Saxton, Editor-in-Chief, Harper and Brothers. Enclosed was a letter of recommendation signed by Margaret Ayer Barnes, a Harper author whose novel *Years of Grace* had won a Pulitzer Prize a few years before. My friend had told me that Saxton read a recommended manuscript on the day of its arrival. I would receive a verdict in reverse quickness to the extent of his interest.

Harper had its own small building on a side street. A receptionist sat beyond the door. My statement, "Please give this package to Mr. Saxton," had a most frightening sound. Was I not aiming a pistol at my own head?

*

Within forty-eight hours, as I leaned out of the door of my apartment, I heard the package thump on the table downstairs. Without daring to cut the string and see what message was inside, I carried the package upstairs and went out to a nearby cafeteria for breakfast. There I found a friend who was also circulating a first novel. When he asked me if I had heard anything, I said, "No." He accompanied me to my apartment. The phone rang: it was Mother asking whether there had been any news. I made a noncommittal answer. After my guest had gone, I wrote my parents, making the best of the situation. The letter Saxton had enclosed was "quite nice and shows that he did not think the work entirely hopeless, unless he was being just polite."

From Putnam's, which was next on my list, the novel came back, but this time a rift appeared in the gathering clouds. An editor named Henry Hart communicated great personal enthusiasm. Having failed to sell my novel to his own editorial board, he expressed eagerness to help me sell it elsewhere. To my parents I wrote, "He really appeared at the crucial moment as Perseus rescuing a poor, weeping Andr—, hell, you finish the name yourself."

It was through a letter from Hart that I had a session at Scribner's with that celebrated editor's editor Maxwell Perkins, whose triumphant manipulation of Thomas Wolfe (a gifted writer with no judgment whatsoever) has made him the patron saint of those editors who like to think of writers as plasticine figurines to be shaped by their own fingers. Editors with that point of view were always to enrage me, and my meeting with Perkins did nothing to start me off with a favorable opinion.

Perkins did not rise from his desk when I came in. From under the battered hat that as his trademark he wore indoors as well as out, he eyed me hostilely. "If Hart thinks so highly of your book, why doesn't he publish it himself? And what the hell have I got to say to you before I have had a chance to read your manuscript?" Placing my little bundle on a corner of his desk, I departed. He was to have the courtesy in his letter of refusal to explain that Scribner's had published a similar book three years before.

Next, Harrison Smith, who had got me my job on the *Tribune*. "I don't think he recognized me. However, he knew he had seen me elsewhere and was polite, asking me into his office. When I gave him the manuscript, he, of course, saw the name on it and asked me if I was still on the *Herald Tribune*. Without any prompting on my part, he said he would get the manuscript back to me in two weeks. We shall see."

A month passed as I anguishedly watched the mails. In those years, there were three deliveries a day. For individuals waiting in great anxiety for a communication from either a woman or a publisher, the one delivery of more recent times is kinder. I found it almost impossible to keep from hanging around all day, in frustration and anxiety, awaiting one delivery after another.

Eventually, a letter from Harrison Smith arrived: "I am afraid you will think we have kept 'Enter and Possess' a very long time. It took, however, a good deal of thought and several readings, which you may rightly interpret as a compliment if you wish. In my opinion, it is a well-written and a capable first novel, but . . . like many authors at the beginning of their careers, you have chosen an extremely difficult theme" with which it would have been astonishing if I had succeeded. "But you can draw characters when the conventions of formal plot permit you to do so, and you do not fall into the sin of being superficially clever." He felt the novel would be publishable by someone with different reactions, and hoped that if I had not already found a publisher, I would let him see my next manuscript.

After several more turndowns, I wrote to my parents: "Everyone seems to have taken it seriously, been interested in the characterization and writing which are after all the important part as far as future books are concerned. On the other hand, everyone seems to think that [in never allowing my heroines to meet] I picked a very difficult, nay, almost impossible, plot. This is not so discouraging as another criticism might be, for after all it is the thing that is most individual to this book and most easily correctible in another. In moments of clear thinking, I can see that whether or not I get this book published will make very little difference ten years from now if I keep on writing. By that time, it would just be a name on the page listing the author's other works. The important question is not whether it is published but whether it shows promise."

Whatever I might conclude in "moments of clear thinking," I was from day to day, from week to week, increasingly wounded by the world's reiterated repudiation of "Enter and Possess." When Dodd, of Dodd Mead, wrote me, "after all, first novels, from the point of view of the writer, often are, or more often should be, experiments in experience," I commented angrily that Mr. Dodd was "a fool." It was impossible for me, after my many years of apprenticeship, to consider myself a beginner. The augmenting failure of "Enter and Possess" seemed to me to mark a betrayal of my family inheritance and expectations, and ultimate failure in my lifelong ambition.

*

Watching me getting more and more frenzied, my friends came to the conclusion that I must be gotten off the roller coaster of submitting, being rejected, and submitting again. I should secure an agent who might be more successful than I had been and would, in any case, send out and get back. I was advised to go to Ray Everett at Curtis Brown.

Everett said to me that "Enter and Possess" would probably not be acceptable to any major publisher, but it could be published. There were second- and third-rate houses that had to scrounge for authors. One might bring out "Enter and Possess" in anticipation of better work to come. Such publication, he continued, would bring me no reputation and I would be trapped for the future in a minor league. Better to put the book aside in the hope that my next one would carry me into the majors. Having been born into "the big time," I did not for a moment consider asking Everett to sell to any publisher who would be willing to bring the book out.

I "went pronto to see Hart." He offered to introduce me to his favorite agents, Pinker and Morrison. Eric Pinker was the son of the major Edwardian agent in London who had handied Joseph Conrad, et al. While his brother continued in England, Eric had come to the United States and married Adrienne Morrison, the mother of the three "Bennett girls" who starred in many movies. Eric handled the literary side of the agency; Adrienne, the dramatic.

Henry showed me the letter in which he asserted that he was doing Pinker and Morrison a great favor. That this was a very fine book which Putnam would have published if business had been better; Pinker would have "a find." This letter produced a flutter in the dovecotes of Pinker and Morrison. They said they had rarely received so enthusiastic a letter, that old man Hart was not given to writing letters like that, and that what they were always looking for was a find.

"Miss Pindyck," so I continued to my parents, "the person to whom the letter was addressed, a very energetic, bright Jewess of not more than thirty-five, floored me, however, by first getting from me a list of the publishers to whom I had sent it—that I expected—and then asking me one by one what each had said. I hadn't the vaguest idea what to answer, as I didn't want to prejudice her against the book at the start and several of the publishers hadn't said very much anyway; so I'm afraid I gave her the impression of being unwilling to confide in her. However, I told her I would be glad to show her the letters if she wanted to see them. I dilated on Hal Smith's long epistle, told her that Scribner's had said that they had published a book somewhat like it three years before, and she asked me whether Mr. Saxton himself had written me from Harpers, to which question, thanks to Miss Bailey, I was able to answer yes. Finally, hard pressed, I told her that the consensus of opinion was that the writing and characters were better than the plot.

"Just now," so I continued to my parents, "within ten minutes, she called up to say that Mr. Pinker had seen the book and wanted to see me at 12 noon tomorrow. I will add a P.S. on the results of this interview."

"Saw old Pinker this morning. He is a very handsome, tall, and upstanding Englishman of about forty, dressed in a dark coat and double-breasted vest (waistcoat) over striped pants. He was very agreeable and I liked him although he gave the old book a terrible roasting. Having finished three quarters of an hour of criticism which showed he has read it with care, although he had missed a few things, he said that he always believed an agent should be frank with his client and that he would be glad to handle it, although he thought the chances that he could sell it a little worse than even. I think I shall let him. It involves signing a contract that I will let him handle all my writings, except for journalism, and give him 10% of all proceeds except for the first published novel on which he gets fifteen.

"The only objection I can see is that I might be able to find a more enthusiastic agent, one who would have more faith in the book. He made the usual criticisms about the two stories not meeting; said that the girls should have fallen in love with the same man, and when I replied I had avoided that as a cliché, he replied that I was young and optimistic and he was middle-aged and cynical, and that he knew there were only seven plots in the world, and if you started on a certain plot, you had to obey the rules if you wanted your book to sell. . . .

"On the other hand, he said he read hundreds of first novels and he regarded mine as an unusually promising one. Also, he is willing to handle it, which, as an agent's success depends on the faith publishers have in him and that faith is kept by not recommending trash, shows that he must have some interest. Also, I liked him, had faith in him because he seemed to be perfectly frank and told me exactly what he thought, and he might be very useful in helping me with my present book, which I imagine I could show him when I completed the first draft; his suggestions might be very useful. So I think I shall sign the contract; *en tout cas*, it gets the damn thing off my hands and I can get a certain satisfaction from telling my friends that I am being handled by one of the top notch agents in town."

Henry had objected on professional grounds to the contract—authors did not sign contracts with agents—but he gave in to my eagerness to sign. Although he did not discourage me with an explanation, he must have realized that Pinker's real interest was not in "Enter and Possess." His concern was with building the future by acquiring me as an author, and he did not wish to go ahead without making sure that I would not wander away. Pinker was, indeed, to protect the future by sending my manuscript only to first-rate publishers.

*

Handing the manuscript over to Pinker did establish a buffer between me and the happenings of every day, but my basic plight was not changed. The fundamental anxiety remained. The telephone took over from the mail as the instrument of suspense. Miss Pindyck intelligently discouraged me from perpetually calling her, but it was always my hope that a publisher would express real interest. Then my telephone would shrill. Every time the telephone rang, my heart took a jump, and when I came up the stairs from outside, I would have my key in my hand so that if the bell were ringing, I would not miss the call.

Jack Phillips was going to Spain to collect for the Metropolitan Museum. I had never been to Spain. And my Labour Party friends were urging me to come again to England: a general election was in the wind and excitement was rising. Bob Fraser was to run for Parliament from the city of York. Mari was also running but as a beginner, from some hopeless constituency.

Although I had not had any direct communication with Mari since I had returned to the United States, her friend Peggy had written me that she had married Ivan Power, the man with whom she had had the past-midnight-extending date that had in Geneva exploded our relationship. However paradoxical it may seem, instead of being upset, I was enchanted by the news. Now that Mari was safely tied down, it would be safe for me to see her again, and I had a vision of dissipating the passion that remained in my blood as a lightning rod dissipates. It might take some doing with Ivan Power, but if I appeared conspicuously as only a friend, I might be accepted as such in her circle. I imagined comfortable occasions that would bring my relationship with Mari down to a level of ordinary living, removing the curse.

In New York, Pinker would presumably keep sending out my manuscript. And I would come home to my friendship with Rhys.

20

ON THE BRINK

*

WHEN Jack and I first reached there in May 1935, Spain proved to be not a happy place in which to gather strength. The Prado is, of course, a marvelous museum, and I received on the esthetic side much sustenance: Titian, Velásquez, El Greco, Goya. Goya fitted in best with my state of mind—too well. Downstairs, somewhat segregated in a basement gallery, were his wild drawings and etchings of torture, sadism, morbidity, and the blackest black magic. Fascinated, considering these his best work, I found myself again and again going down the stairs into this world of horror. Later, after darkness closed in on me, I wished I had never seen these pictures.

Jack's and my social life in Madrid was grounded on his position at the Metropolitan Museum. Art historians and dealers felt it would be advantageous to entertain us, but deep resentment brought to the occasions a rasping note. When, after generations of neglect, El Greco had swum into the center of modern taste, Spain, off on its peninsula, was slow to catch on. American museums, including the Metropolitan, had "abducted"—at low prices—what our hosts considered part of Spain's national treasure.

A further grimness was added to our social evenings because our hosts were living in a state of terror. They were, as liberals, identified with the republican government that had overthrown the monarchy, but they were horrified by the atrocities being carried out under its name. Tales of convents being sacked and nuns raped! Unless the atrocities could be stopped—and they saw no way of stopping them—there would be a counter-revolution, and they dreaded being caught in the holocaust.

I myself was so far from good health that a doctor put me on a strict diet of eggs and milk; so worried about the fate of my novel in New York that I hardly dared pick up my mail from home. Although Franco's invasion was still a year away, I felt menace in the air I breathed. I resembled the Irish terrier of my boyhood who, although he had never seen a lion or a tiger, reacted with terror when brought within smelling distance of the Central Park Zoo. Never have I felt so great a need to escape from anywhere. Convinced that I would never get well so long as I stayed in Spain, I left Jack at Barcelona and set out for London.

I had planned to stop over in Paris, that city of public places which is a balm to the soul of the traveler, but when the train pulled up in the station I could not bring myself to face even so mild an adventure. I took the next train to London.

*

I was received enthusiastically by my Labour Party friends. In response to my first phone call, Betty Fraser, recognizing my voice, said she was giving a dinner party and, if I ran out and caught a bus, I could get there in time. Since I had been away for more than two years, I could only listen in silence to the intimate discussion of strategy for the expected general election, but at dinner I felt I ought to say something, and asked the stranger to my right who, if Labour won, would be the prime minister. All the chatter ceased as if cut with a knife.

Suavely he said, "Lansbury," naming the superannuated leader they all intended to sidetrack. It did not take me long to discover that I had asked Hugh Dalton, who was a major contender.

Despite my faux pas, I continued to be gathered in, even accompanying the Frasers on a campaign trip to the city of York, where he was running for Parliament. I was having so good and interesting a time that I might have returned home with a regained balance had I not resolved to close an aching emptiness by gathering Mari back into my life—but not as a flashing, destructive lover. I yearned to transmute, as the healing body transmutes an infection into healthy flesh, our dark love into friendship. Although I had in Geneva hated

Ivan Power, now her husband, and he had hated me, I hoped some-how to become with them a family friend. This was much more than a gesture. There was a deep wound in my psyche that needed to be healed.

*

When I finally found the fortitude to make an approach, on the envelope of my letter addressed to "Mrs. Ivan Power," I inscribed my name and address in large letters. This was intended to demon-strate that I was not seeking to re-enter Mari's life surreptitiously.

When Mari called me on the telephone, almost before expressing pleasure at my being near again, she asked why I had been such a damned fool as to write my name on that envelope. Fortunately, she had gotten hold of the letter before her husband could see it. We made a date to meet for lunch.

I was at the restaurant ahead of time, although I knew she was always late. As, eventually, she weaved toward me between the tables of other diners, I saw again the face I had so often seen in visions. But she was differently dressed, more expensively and more in style. We were too enthralled to be together for any other emotion than pleasure. We caught up on each other's news. I told her that I had finished a novel, and dilated on my trouble in getting it published. She made no mention of her marriage, but told me that she was running for Parliament in one of the districts impossible for a Labour victory which were assigned to beginners as try-outs and experience. Then we joked and teased with the old intimacy.

The restaurant was emptying out. As we did not want to walk the streets or go to the movies, I suggested that we go to my room in my "bed and breakfast" lodging house in Bayswater. The door of my cramped bedroom closed behind us.

Mari walked over to the mirror over the narrow bureau and combed out her hair: she had just come from the hairdresser. The beautiful red locks gathered as of old around the face I had so loved.

Mari had been carrying a package. She had, she said, bought a present for her husband. Out of the box came the most diaphanous of nightgowns. Holding it before her, she demonstrated, by putting her hand behind one surface, how utterly transparent it was. Did I think that her husband would be pleased? Not then but only much later in retrospect have I wondered what Mari (if she herself knew) intended by bringing so seductive a garment to our first rendezvous. My mind was so set on not reviving our old affair, on joining her family circle, that I felt she was taunting me by showing that another man had complete access to her body. I commented, I will admit bitterly, that her husband would undoubtedly be very pleased. She looped up the nightgown and crammed it back into its box.

All relaxation that had been between us vanished. She looked at her watch and said she did not know it was so late: she would have to run. I made no effort to stop her. But we did set a place and time to meet the following day.

Having in common many happy memories, much true congeniality, and the habit of sharing confidences, Mari and I could spend happy times together as long as shadows stood unobtrusive in the background. We never again went to my room. She avoided all references to her husband except as an impediment to our meeting. Although I told her of my tribulations with "Enter and Possess," I did not mention Rhys.

*

Sitting at a small table on a balcony that looked down on the bustle of a busy restaurant, we were chatting comfortably about this and that when Mari, without any transition or warning, stared into my eyes and said, "I am willing, if you want, to go back with you to America."

I was stunned. Whether or not she would have gone through with it, that Mari could seriously consider such a possibility—she had been married only six months and by deserting her candidacy she would have finished herself forever with the Labour Party—revealed again that extremity, that wildness, that made so menacing our love. As in that dramatic moment on the railway train in Geneva, I could not find my voice. This time, she attempted a little chatter before she departed.

*

Although I was conscious that if I could not control my emotions and my sexual desire for the most sexually desirable woman I had ever known I would be building for myself catastrophe, I could not keep from continuing to get together with Mari, though I was glad to see my sailing date approaching. It was still more than a week away when Mari told me that she and her husband were giving a large cocktail party. She offered to tell him that she had heard a rumor that I was in London, and try to persuade him that, despite old Geneva memories, it would be polite to send me an invitation. She must have been surprised at my enthusiasm.

Perhaps, after all, I would achieve what I had longed for! I might be able to disarm the situation, reassure her husband, please her friends, and thus gather my relationship with Mari into the normal flow of our existence. Although when I next saw Mari she reported that her husband had been unwilling, I so continued to express eagerness that she said she would work on him. No result by the day before the party which was in turn the day before I would sail for America. If Ivan finally relented, she would telephone me that evening or on the day of her party in time for me to get there.

At my boarding house, the telephone occupied its own little closet on the ground floor. This was contiguous to a lounge of sorts. After parting from Mari, I gobbled some supper and then sat in the lounge until it was so late that there was no more possible hope that she would call that night. I hardly slept, and in the morning I was back in the lounge well before Mari was likely to be awake. It was a continuous vigil, hour after hour. I was, of course, inured to anxious waiting, but my tension rose and rose until I feared I had actually lost control. My imagination did not extend to what I would then do, but the feeling of probability! I stayed in the lounge long after Mari would have begun greeting her guests.

When I had finally abandoned the last shred of hope, I found myself irresistibly drawn out onto the street, although I was terrified of what I might do when I got there. I had hardly reached the curb when an automobile slid to a stop beside me. Looking up in dread, I saw smiling down on me a Labour couple who were my friends. They said they were driving to a restaurant in the country for dinner. Wouldn't I hop in and come along? Never again in all my life have I felt more grateful.

*

Mari and I had not even considered the possibility of her coming to see me off on the boat train. No replay of our Geneva parting! Waiting until her husband had surely gone off to his office, I would call Mari on the telephone to say goodbye.

This dictated a tight schedule. I started trying to reach her from the closet in the boarding house while a taxi waited for me. As we advanced toward the railroad station, I made the driver stop, after every few blocks, by a telephone booth on the street. I must have become frenzied, because as I dialed and dialed, there was every kind of result. There were busy signals, and rings that were not answered. Also, alien voices denied ever having heard of Mrs. Power. I almost missed my train by dropping my bags in the station and calling again. The answering voice said there was no such number.

Down decades of my life, this sequence has acted itself out again and again in nightmares. To escape a horror never defined, I am faced with the absolute necessity of putting through a phone call. There is no lack of telephones in the alien, mist-like environment through which I wander, but an unrelenting succession of confusions prevents me from ever getting through.

*

I got on the boat in a very ragged state of mind, and the trip was anything but propitious. I found also assigned to my stateroom a youngish man in the woolen business. He admired the suits I had bought in London, but had a fixation on his hair. Engaging in the ship's festivities until the small hours, every half hour or so he would appear in our stateroom, turn on the lights, comb his hair before the mirror, and depart only soon to return. I found myself getting haggard from lack of sleep.

On shipboard, there was a young woman of the greatest exhibitionism and vulgarity. I was viewing her with disapproval when an Englishman said she was typical of all American women. In a burst of patriotic rage, I asked him to "step outside." Looking down on me from a considerable height, he said, "I think I ought to tell you that I was middle-weight boxing champion at Oxford." This pulled me up with a shock. What in the world was the matter with me? I had never boxed. I had never struck anyone in anger. What would I have done had the Englishman, champion or no champion, "stepped outside"?

I was only too conscious that things were not going well with me. But, I could look forward to nesting in my cozy apartment. It was possible that some communcation had missed me, and I would discover that Pinker had sold "Enter and Possess." And I hoped with all my being that I would find Rhys in New York.

*

Rhys! the temperate and wise, a brilliant sculptor who would further my lifelong desire to be a writer, whose love for me like mine for her had grown slowly, strongly, as an oak tree grows. By no means an alternative for Mari, Rhys was an altogether different breed, to be relied on and trusted till the last breath. Had not a beneficent providence ordained that I should marry Rhys?

21

HORROR

*

"A non-writing writer
is a monster inviting madness."
—FRANZ KAFKA

I had sublet my apartment to Rhys's sister, but she was supposed to
have departed. After I had carried my bags upstairs, I found her still
in possession. She was terribly sorry but she had been unable to find
any other space to stay. She could not pay the rent, but I should not
worry. She would eventually pay up, even if only in installments.
And she regretted that her cat had smashed the large Chinese lamp
that had been the centerpiece of my living room.

There was nothing for me to do but carry my bags down the stairs
again and direct a taxi to the Harvard Club where I knew there was
a honeycomb of small rooms for recent graduates. To someone in a
more tranquil state of mind, the room to which I was assigned would,
I suppose, have been adequate. It was narrow and dark, and the
window opened onto a wall only a few feet away. To me it seemed
like a cell in a prison—or an insane asylum.

Downstairs to a telephone booth! I looked up Pinker and Morrison
in the directory. The phone rang and a voice answered. I asked to
speak to Mr. Pinker. He was away on vacation. I asked to speak to
Miss Pindyck. She was away on vacation. I asked who I could speak
to. The voice replied that she was speaking. So I gave my name
and asked the voice what the situation was concerning "Enter and

Possess." She had never heard of my manuscript and seemed to doubt that it ever existed. I demanded that she find it. She said in a resentful tone that if I would hold on, she would do her best. I fed coin after coin into the machine. Eventually, she reappeared to say she had succeeded in finding my book in a pile of manuscripts which were no longer being circulated and which the authors had carelessly failed to pick up. If I cared to, I could come and get it.

*

If only Rhys should prove to be in town. Every successive ring of her phone induced anxiety, and then she answered! I was to come right over. My heart leapt. I was on the way to my true haven of peace.

Rhys greeted me with a kiss, but it was a stranger's kiss. She was in such a state of excitement as I had never seen before. She told me that she was about to be married. This was a blow but not annihilating—had I not looked forward to friendship with Mari and her husband—and Rhys had been a hundred times more of a friend than Mari ever was. The annihilating blow came when she named her fiancé: Johannes Steel! This was the alias of a man who (rightly or wrongly) was notorious as a charlatan and an imposter in the circles in which I moved.

A refugee from Hitler's Germany, Steel had made use of the dislocation to hide his identity. He never disclosed his real name, although Rhys said she knew it. Under this cloak, he attributed to himself sensational adventures as a foreign agent for the German republic and a subsequent super-audacious and super-dangerous escape from a Nazi prison camp. The editors of the *New York Post* used as a circulation builder banner headlines screaming "JOHANNES STEEL SAYS"—and reported his claim that he controlled a personal spy network that extended even into the highest echelons of Hitler's government. Although he could assert that he had prophesied Hitler's "blood purge," there was no way to ascertain whether his other floods of "inside information" had any validity beyond his imagination.

Rhys had introduced me to Steel before I went abroad. I had seen a large, Germanic egg-shaped face that looked stupid because he had kept it blank: no lines, no facial expression. But his speech was entirely different. He spoke so volubly with such energy that the words tumbled over each other. Everything was black or white: J. P. Morgan had financed Hitler. His boasting achieved heights that made Walter Duranty's self-satisfaction seem the whisperings of a shy maiden. His manipulations were determining the fate of Europe. Hitler, he assured me, would by now have been assassinated had not the American Jewish community, whom he excoriated for being so pusillanimous, refused to give him the necessary million dollars.

That Steel's power over Rhys was sexual I instantly assumed. Having known Mari as I had done, I realized that my relationship with Rhys had been less exciting than life-enhancing. Yet I had fought off Mari's attractions in order to be faithful to my own lights, my ambitions as a writer, and to Rhys. My reaction, she later wrote me, stunned her into silence. But eventually, for the first time in our long friendship, she lost her temper. Her reiterated statement that she did not care what I thought seemed to be the ultimate denial of our relationship. As in the nightmares of my childhood, a major foundation of my life crumbled into emptiness.

*

Some escape was necessary. I believed that one of my oldest friends, Breading Furst, from Lincoln School days, might be in town. I was only able to reach one of his friends who said that if I would come over to see him, he would tell me the news about Breading.

On my arrival, he told me that Breading had gone insane and was locked up in the mental ward at Bellevue Hospital. My informant was a hunchback who took pleasure in the misfortunes of others. With relish, he launched into a long account of what had happened.

Breading had been at some endowed artists' colony in the Middle West. He became more and more unruly, hostile, would not stop talking, and smashed things. Finally, he was expelled. Another member of the colony decided to leave with him, and tried to control him so that his behavior would not become conspicuous. As gruesome detail after detail of Breading's demented behavior was revealed in the unctuous voice of the hunchback, I had a horrible feeling that it was I who had lost control. I felt myself screaming out in a movie theater, laughing without being able to stop, insulting strangers until a heavy hand on my shoulder presaged my being locked up as insane. I felt a desperate need to hide from the hunchback that I too was going mad. I hardly dared move, and it took me a long time, as the gloating voice went on, to feel enough in command of myself to look at my watch, express surprise that it was so late, and walk with exaggerated stateliness out the door.

*

Only with the greatest difficulty was I able to undertake the journey to my family at Chocorua: an all-day train ride, including a change of stations at Boston. With every turn of the railroad wheels I feared I would give way to some act that would alert my fellow passengers to my madness. I was horrified when an elderly, former secretary of Father's sat down beside me. She felt privileged to ask me personal questions and repeated stories about my cute behavior as a child. The greater my resentment rose, the greater I felt my danger. Finally, she departed.

Back in the family nest, I said nothing to my parents of my fear that I was insane. To put the possibility into words would have transmuted dread into fact. My parents must have observed that I was in a very unhealthy state of mind, but for them to ask questions would have been to break a long-established pattern. And, as the familiar atmosphere gathered around me, my terror, without vanishing, became quiescent.

After my return to New York, a nervous breakdown, much more profound than what I had experienced at the beginning of the Lincoln School, overcame me. Leading the attack and constantly reinforcing it was a conviction that I was failing utterly in my lifelong ambition—the only true ambition I had ever had—to be a writer. This failure did not strike like a bullet. It was rather like falling, minute after minute, hour after hour, month after month, in darkness down a narrow abyss as I clawed perpetually, ineffectually, increasingly without hope, at the grimy walls for a handhold or a foothold. And at the bottom of the abyss lay madness.

*

From many months of labor and despair, only one packet of manuscript remains: two opening chapters, forty-five pages, of a novel. There were indications that I seem to have intended what could be described as an introspective *Dr. Jekyll and Mr. Hyde*. The two protagonists were to personify the most conspicuously opposite facets of my own behavior. One was a reporter, dashing, energetic, exerting an easy charisma which made achieving popularity effortless. The other was a miserable worm of a frustrated writer, afraid of the world, torn by neuroses. In delineating the frustrated writer, I tried to give expression to my own nervous torments. If this was intended as exorcism, it had an opposite effect. I was induced to feel even more that I was toppling over.

I could not stay in my own apartment. A bank was being noisily built next door. Every day I went to my parents' apartment where an empty bedroom was assigned to me and my typewriter. I would start each morning with at least a glimmer of hope, putting a sheet into the machine, and sometimes I would achieve a sentence or two that did not repel me. However, I felt the wording could be improved. I attempted one change and then another until my paper looked as if a raven with inked feet had walked over it.

The result of this method being despair, I tried an alternate method. I would read out loud the passable first sentences as an incantation to summon up more effective prose. The further prose failing to come, I would read the decoy over and over until, as I complained in a letter, "the essence ran out of it, the diction became wooden, the meaning uninteresting and conventional. I watched this with the horror of a lover seeing his elfin bride at cockcrow turn into a witch." In anguish, I tore the paper, throwing the pieces on top of many others in the scrap basket.

Before an hour had passed, I became unable to write anything at all. And it was only ten o'clock in the morning. I had before me a day to kill! I tried to read the newspaper but could not keep my mind on my reading. The paper, I knew, contained a crossword puzzle. I tried to forget about the puzzle. To have recourse to such a toy, when I should be proceeding with the writing that was the purpose of my life, would be an abysm of degradation. With trembling hands, I located the puzzle in the newspaper, only to discover that I could not concentrate my mind to find words that fitted the spaces.

All my friends were at work. But, I had the whole city with which to amuse myself: museums and libraries, and art galleries and movies, streets and parks. But I was usually too upset to leave my parents' apartment. And when I did . . .

My habitual fear of heights had expanded to not daring to go up in elevators or look out of upper windows. Claustrophobia would not let me go to the Museum of Modern Art where they used movable partitions to make viewers weave through labyrinths. Theaters were the worst. You were trapped in a row of occupied seats. It was the object of a play or a movie to excite emotion, and I was afraid of emotion lest it become more than my control could handle.

At home, although the building noises stopped with late afternoon, I was the most beleaguered of all. I had to sleep, but once I was asleep all conscious control was gone. I would suffer from nightmares and awaken into an overwhelming atmosphere of doom. This was usually accompanied with nausea. To give way to vomiting seemed to me a dangerous surrender, although, if I did vomit, my tension relaxed and I could sleep.

Sometimes I found the fortitude to make dates with my old friends in the hope of escaping from my evil spell if only for a few hours. But, as the day approached, I became increasingly terrified lest the mask I intended to wear should slip. But, if I could keep from calling up at the last minute with an excuse, if I did finally go, I found myself transmuted into my other protagonist in the novel that was not getting written. Miraculously, I was again the person I had been during so many of my earlier years. My friends asked me how I managed always to be so cheery. Did I never have any troubles? The result was that when I successfully forced myself to go out, I almost always enjoyed myself, but this did not keep me from another day of apprehension before my next appointment.

People did tell me that I was losing weight, but this was not among my worries until I went to pick up a dancer friend, Joan Woodruff, in her studio. She gave classes in a large room lined with mirrors that extended down to the floor. I was aghast to see in one mirror after another that the clothes which had fitted me a few months before now hung around my body as if I were a scarecrow.

*

That I was so clearly physically ailing disturbed Father. We agreed that I should not consult a "nervous doctor." Father, not believing that psychiatry was a science, had almost completely banned it from his Institute. And I felt that my defense against madness was to keep doors to my brain locked. I did not want any outsider prying them open. In January 1936, five months after my disastrous return from England, Father arranged for me to enter the Union Memorial Hospital in Baltimore for an exhaustive examination concentrating on the digestive tract.

Although I spent several nights in the hospital and was much pummeled around and poked and x-rayed, no significant discovery was made. The contribution to my cure—and it was a very major one— was nine spoken words. A Dr. Austrian, who was not one of the physicians to whom I was entrusted, said to me as it were casually, "Don't get the idea that you are going mad." I was too apprehensive to ask for elucidation, and Dr. Austrian walked away.

But, for the first time in all my months of despair, the dread word had been spoken, and not as a shout of catastrophe! This was in itself not enough, but the darkness became less black.

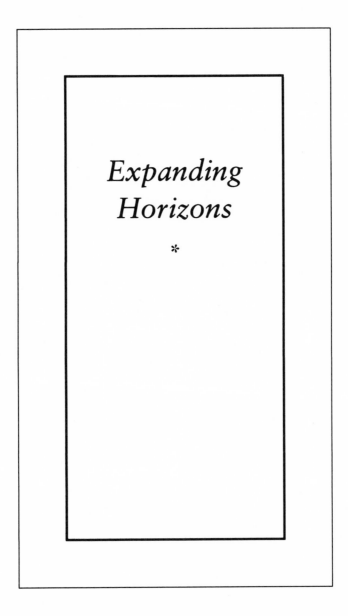

Expanding Horizons

*

22

RESCUE

*

SOON after my return to New York from the hospital in Baltimore my father handed me a history of American medicine by H. E. Sigerist. The author had, before launching into his "systematic discussion," presented short biographies of pre-Civil War medical pioneers. Three to six pages long, they described exciting adventures. Having just been reading Lytton Strachey's *Eminent Victorians*, Father was inspired to wonder whether I could not escape from my writer's block by telling in linked chapters the lives of the first American scientists who had made important discoveries or built more solid foundations for the practice of medicine. Like a drowning man reaching for a floating log, I grasped at the idea.

In my eagerness, I accepted, without further investigation, the individuals Sigerist had named as of superior scientific importance. My concern was literary: would these lives singly and as a group be exciting to read about and enable me to pursue my artistic aims as a writer? A quick preliminary survey including other sources indicated that Father had pointed my way to a gold mine.

Every one of my potential protagonists was aglow with lights and somber with shades, while the historical landscapes they had inhabited were as various as the vastness of the continent and the unregulated idiosyncrasy of American society could supply. Their adventures could add up to a rough mosaic of America, from the Revolutionary to the Civil War generations.

But how was I to fashion this into a book? Since I had hardly ever read a biography for its own sake, it stood to reason that now, when my desperate need was to get my literary feet on some ground that would not crumble from under me, I would seek great biographies to use as models, and look up manuals on the form. But my drive to get going was too great. I turned only to Father's inspiration, Strachey's volume, *Eminent Victorians*.

I remembered, of course, my one personal contact with Strachey, when he had turned his back on me to disappear down a corridor. Now he was no more helpful. *Eminent Victorians* raised a question whether the hodgepodge of biographies I was contemplating could be gathered into a coherent book. Strachey's four protagonists had all belonged to the same class in the same English generation. My presumptive protagonists were seven, with no further link than having been the earliest Americans who had made important contributions to scientific medicine. My time span would be from 1735 to 1878; geography extended from the eastern seaboard, both north and south, to the early settlements on the Ohio and farther to the Indian country on the Great Lakes. My characters came from widely various social backgrounds, were violently inconsistent in behavior, and were for the most part unconscious of each other's existence.

Strachey had based his short lives on the tremendous biographies of his subjects that had been published during the Victorian period, his irony being sparked by the opposition between his own values and those of his sources. He wore colored eyeglasses through which all his protagonists took on balancing hues. But, as I was discovering, I would find no standard, extensive lives of any of my protagonists to rely on and disagree with. As for colored eyeglasses, I had no use for them. I wanted to see each of my heroes in his own light.

These comparisons with Strachey would have frightened me more had I not been fleeing the much greater terror induced by my dreadful excursions into my own psyche. And what I intended had resemblances to what I had done in my more distant past happily and successfully: newspaper work.

As a reporter covering an assignment, my task had been to reach the physical scene, look around, witness what action was going on at the moment, observe the actors, and extract what information I could from the guarded answers to what questions I was capable of asking. The realization of the superficiality of results had encouraged me to abandon my career as a general news reporter.

But I would now travel another road which, although it offered no hands to shake, no voices to hear, presented possibilities for human understanding, broader, and perhaps in that sense deeper, than personal contact could achieve.

Even best friends, wives, colleagues, are limited in their knowledge by their positions in an individual's life, but a biographer can view, should the documents exist, his protagonist's beginning years and follow the growing man wherever the tides of circumstance, achievement, and personality may carry him.

Of course, the biographer going into the past cannot see his subject, but there are paintings, photographs, written descriptions, sometimes preserved clothes, hats, coats, shoes. The biographer cannot hear his subject speak, but letters are speech solidified, preserving the rhythm and even the intonation of voice. Letters convey to the reader intimacies that are in ordinary social intercourse hidden, and can even propel the biographer over the threshold into the bridal chamber. If the subject soliloquizes in diaries as if behind closed doors, the biographer can look invisibly over his shoulder.

Concerning the subject's world, the biographer can know many things the protagonist himself could not have known. What his friends and enemies wrote behind his back. Forces hidden from him that molded his possibilities, advanced or retarded his ambitions. The biographer even has the advantage, which has to be handled skillfully so as not to distort the contemporary record, of knowing how things will work out.

I had since I was a child suffered from the fear that the world I envisioned around me did not actually exist outside my own brain and senses. The characters I had dealt with in my attempts at fiction were solecism personified as they had existence only in my brain. The persons I now intended to write about had existed altogether independently from me. Yet through the magic of the written word, I could hope to get closer to them than to anyone I had ever encountered in "real life." And insights I had gained through experiences in real life would, I hoped, clarify my understanding of their behavior.

*

The necessary research changed my day-to-day life with the rapidity and finality of a magic spell. Now, when I awoke early in the morning, I did not, foreseeing a sterile day, mourn that I had not slept to a later hour. I leapt from my bed full of energy. I regretted only that the days were not longer.

As I resurrected people and worlds from documents, my attention was riveted, there was no place for my own troubles, but I was not separated off from the troubles of men and of the world. I was able to sublimate my own joys and sorrows in the joys and sorrows of others, making them more universal and thus, in a large sense, the fuel of art.

*

When I closed behind me the doors of my ordinary living, I was free as a bird escaped from a cage. Escape from introspection and anxiety was facilitated by my working in impersonal environments. Public transportation took me to the steps of a library. There, what my physical eyes had never seen claimed sovereignty in my brain, opening vistas to be investigated and comprehended. I became so absorbed when working in libraries that the movement of people around me, some pausing to gossip, was agreeable, a warm touch, a breathing spell. But a telephone call regarding my intimate personal affairs would instantly shatter the mood.

It became my lifelong habit to establish the library most apposite to whatever book I was writing as my home away from home. I have never been repulsed. Rather, the other way around. A consciousness that I was working hard and achieving results encouraged librarians to make exceptions for me. I dedicated one of my books (*Steamboats*) as I should undoubtedly have dedicated them all: "To the librarians, whose unsung efforts and unfailing co-operation play so important a part in the preparation of such books as this."

*

Doctors carried me most often to the New York Academy of Medicine on Fifth Avenue and 103rd Street. The whole third floor of the large building was occupied by a reference library for practitioners. On busy days, it was like a railroad station. I could pass through quickly to a narrow circular stairway, which I climbed with rising spirits. Eagerly I opened the door to the academy's rare book room. An effort had been made to create the atmosphere of a gentleman's library: maple bookcases with decoration incised on the risers were topped, close to the ceiling, with carved fretwork. Here, fortunately for me, were not only collectors' items but the academy's holdings on medical history.

Here I inaugurated my lifetime education by librarians. That such instruction was called for after my *magna cum laude* from Harvard may seem odd, but assistance by librarians is much more to the point than lucubration by professors. Professors mold thinking. The librarian shows you how to carry out most effectively your own intentions and needs.

In the rare book room of the Academy of Medicine, my instructors were two. The academy's head librarian, Dr. Archibald Malloch, a Canadian of most impressive British mannerisms, would, as he was passing by and I was taking notes, look over my shoulder. One of his many suggestions remains in my mind because my first reaction to it was so silly: I should note not only the title, etc., of my source but the page number. Since I intended a bibliography rather than source references, why, I thought, should I bother? Having come to realize the innumerable reasons why I might want to find a source again, I now jot down not only a page number but indicate on my cards every subsequent turning of a page.

Dr. Malloch also served me as auspices. In those years you had to have credentials to get into almost any library except the New York Public Library (where I was to argue, many years later, as a member of the Board of Trustees, to keep the doors freely open to all). I had become a more or less permanent guest of the New-York Historical Society when they found my original admission application of almost exactly a half-century before. It was signed by Malloch and, to the amusement of all, filed under "undesirables." I can only assume that, in the headlong speed with which I was working, I tried to hurry the elderly employees in what was then almost a private club. In any case, on the fiftieth anniversary of this non-triumphant appearance, the Society gave me a party. Asked to speak, I pointed the moral: "If you ever let an undesirable in, you'll never get rid of him."

*

Miss Gertrude Annan, who was in charge of the rare book room at the Academy of Medicine, was one of those irreplaceable librarians who not is only familiar with everything in her own collections but remembers every additional bit of information concerning the historical figures who have become in effect her charges. There was certainly no other individual in the world who could have been equally helpful to me as Miss Annan, who came to feel a strong personal interest in my book.

*

The nature of the research that lay before me was much affected by the refusal, despite the rising importance of science in contemporary life, of academic historians to accept the history of science into their pantheon. Long after my *Doctors* had been published, Dr. Richard H. Shyrock, a professor at the University of Pennsylvania whose main interest was medical history, was not allowed to besmirch the curriculum by giving a course in so unacceptable a subject.

Concerning my seven doctors, there existed only one moderately recent (twenty years), if second-rate, biography by a professional. This neglect rather attracted me: it suited my enthusiasm not to work primarily in carefully tended gardens, but to explore for wild flowers in field and thicket. I found perpetual excitement in this free-swinging research, never knowing from day to day what I would find: sometimes nothing at all, sometimes a dribble, sometimes a spring freshet, occasionally an explosion.

My objective fell into three overlapping categories: to define and explain achievements; to dramatize habitats; and to delineate personal actions and character. The first of these, which might seem the most difficult, was actually the easiest as it had been the objective of all those who had, like Sigerist, previously written about my characters. And if I was puzzled, Father could explain.

The environments of my protagonists could rarely be visualized through physical visits: so much had been changed. However, a great deal could be determined from printed sources, mostly local histories. Usually I could find enough detail to place my subject in the *mise-en-scène*, showing how his environments inspired, gave opportunities, speeded, or hindered. From a literary point of view, backgrounds made two contributions: they emphasized the American focus that supplied me with my unifying theme and gave me opportunities for descriptions, dramatic or poetic or both: the rigors of the wilderness; the drama of the fur trade; the horrors of the yellow fever epidemic in Philadelphia; the American Revolution seen from the unusual perspective of hospitals and the diseases that killed more American soldiers than did British military might.

Daniel Drake, whose family had been the lowest of homesteaders, most of whose contribution was to found medical schools for the new cities rising in Ohio and Kentucky, favored me with extensive autobiographical writings. When I had to fill in around the barest biographical details, I was frank with the reader: "Since [Ephraim] McDowell's childhood was lived among great events in the history of Kentucky, we may find many clues from which to resurrect the early influences that molded him into a great man."

*

McDowell was to launch on the greatest act of physical bravery presented in my volume. Called in backwoods Kentucky to help a woman who could not give birth to a child, he forded flooding rivers to find that she was not actually pregnant but swelled by an ovarian tumor. In all recorded annals of medicine this was a death sentence, but McDowell saw no reason why, with extreme precautions, the tumor could not be removed. He squired on horseback the woman to his village of Danville, but when word got out of the atrocity he intended, the preacher denounced him from the pulpit. A lynch mob gathered in front of his house as he engaged in the operation, determined to hang him for murder if the patient died. But she lived, as did several other women on whom McDowell operated. However, it took a long time for the medical profession to accept such an overturning of what had been universally accepted fact.

*

The most picturesque background engendered my weirdest scientific tale. William Beaumont, a bombastic military surgeon, was stationed at Fort Mackinac, the border outpost in Indian country which was the headquarters of the American Fur Company.

"June 1822," I wrote, "like every other June brought its flood of voyageurs and Indians to the shores of Mackinac. The silence of the long winter had been shattered by the shouts of many thousand men paddling in from the wilderness for their brief season of pleasure. Again the beach had become a fantastic parade ground. Indian braves in bright paint walked with grave and conscious pride, the strings of wampum heavy round their throats. And the French Canadians, those brown imps of the forest, were not to be outdone for grandeur; what money they could spare from liquor went for canes, and scarves, and gleaming jackets. The only soberly tinted citizens were the clerks of the fur company who appraised pelts by the thousands and grudgingly paid out a third of their value. Other clerks hustled behind the counters of the company store, taking the money back in exorbitant payment for trifles. But what if the voyageurs and the Indians were cheated; they were happy to have their hands on goods and liquor again.

"The store was a joyous place. It was crowded to suffocation with men buying and men boasting. Here the voyageurs strutted, telling of unbelievable loads they had carried over portages, of rare pelts they had snared. Or the tone would change to horror and they would frighten each other with tales of vengeful *manitous* or dead Indians come back to reclaim their scalps. Suddenly a man gestured with too wild exuberance; the shotgun in his hand went off. And Alexis St. Martin, the nineteen-year-old voyageur who stood within three feet of him, fell to the floor, his stomach blown open. His shirt caught fire and burnt until it was quenched by the flow of blood. A shout went up for Dr. Beaumont."

Beaumont believed that there was no hope of saving St. Martin, part of whose stomach was hanging out through a puncture "large enough to receive my forefinger." St. Martin survived, but the hole did not heal, becoming through Beaumont's inspired experimentation the open sesame through which the human race first ascertained the true nature of digestion. The top-lofty army doctor and the Canadian he treated as a servant and who had to put up with experiments he felt defamed his manhood came to hate each other. They separated and came together, but they were tied, like an unhappy married couple, by Beaumont's need and St. Martin's inability to find a better way to make a living.

*

In this my first such book I already demonstrated my propensity to obey subject matter rather than adhere to a consistent format. The greatest of early America discoveries was anesthesia. But this was not the contribution of a single protagonist. The two major discoverers, Crawford W. Long of Georgia and Thomas W. C. Morton of Massachusetts, knew nothing of each other, and there was a third major contender, Horace Wells, who had known Morton and who has remained the favorite son of Connecticut and the dental profession. A fourth dragged behind. Thus, I found myself, although my emphasis was still biographical, writing as my last chapter a short history of this boon to mankind, much as I was to do later, although then in a full book, concerning the invention of the steamboat.

How romantic was my approach is revealed by this opening of my last chapter, "The Death of Pain":

"A strange story this. The story of a discovery waiting for half a century almost found, a discovery of overwhelming importance knocking continually at the doors of the scientific great, begging to be taken in, only to be turned away until at last, like the angel of an old fable, it knocked at the humbler doorways of the inconspicuous and found a home. And astoundingly this great boon to mankind was a scourge to its inventors; of the four men who claimed the discovery in the great ether controversy that raged during the last half of the nineteenth century, two died hopelessly mad, one by his own hand, and a third starved, had a series of nervous breakdowns, and was finally killed by a stroke due to the pamphlet of one of his opponents. Only the fourth lived to an old age, and even he was embittered by a sense of injustice."

*

I could not foresee such passages as I galloped ahead with research. When I was not too absorbed in my discoveries, the realization pushed into my brain that a sword of Damocles was hanging over my head. Research, I remembered, was, although essential, only a means to an end. What was for me infinitely more important: to overcome my writer's block, to complete a book that would justify my life so far, be worthy of my background, my training, my previous experience, and my literary ambition. Half a loaf would not be enough. Had I not refused to attempt an easy way out for "Enter and Possess" by considering a second-rate publisher?

*

Ever since my compass needle had swung from fiction to biography, ever since I had found sanctuary in libraries, I had not opened the door to the spare room in my parents' apartment where I had anguished, month after month, in my sterility. The typewriter that had been the companion and the instrument of my despair remained there untouched. I did have in my own rooms another typewriter on which I banged out letters. But I felt that before really launching out on my new literary endeavor, I would have to brave the dragon of sterility in his lair.

Having found the resolution to pass through the door so long unopened, having thrown open a window to dispel the long stagnant air, I blew away accumulated dust and removed the cover from the typewriter that had for so long been my enemy. I carried my machine to a larger table so that I could lay beside it some reassuring reference cards. Then I pressed my finger on the keys.

It was almost as if I had applied dynamite to a dam. Words I had not premeditated, aptly expressive, forming into sentences and the sentences into paragraphs, poured out onto the paper that kept rushing across and then jumping upward. My fingers seemed to be moving automatically.

This was the most exciting happening of all my life—and the most determining. I have had bad interludes, but never again, for more than sixty years, have I been crushed by writer's block.

23

CATASTROPHE

*

I was some way along in my experiment with biography when a mysterious letter appeared in my mail: a London postmark but no return address; the word "private" underlined in red ink; and the address headed, "J.H., C/o Messrs. James Flexner." When I opened the envelope, there fell out a letter on my own stationery addressed to Mari. There was also a letter on her husband's business stationery which read, "I very much regret to inform you that Mrs. Power died suddenly yesterday. I enclose a newspaper clipping related to this. As you omitted to sign the letter returned herewith (I had used my monograph for JTF], I regret that I cannot return it personally. If you care to write to Mr. Ivan Power, c/o this office, I will see that your letter is delivered. Yours truly, D. S. Jones, secretary."

The clipping had to be unwrapped as it was topped with a headline that had been run across a whole newspaper page: "LABOUR'S YOUNGEST WOMAN CANDIDATE DIES AT TWENTY-THREE." The article, which filled the first column, contained a subhead: "MRS. MARI POWER." Then, "Throughout the night four doctors fought for her life and her husband, Mr. Ivan Power, was on call all the time."

The *Star* reported that Mari had outdistanced all previous Labour candidates in the solid Tory constituency to which she had been assigned to try her wings as a campaigner. There was a photograph of Mari which, as always, did not do her justice as the camera failed to catch the vitality that exploded into her charisma.

That the secretary had come upon my letter so soon seemed to indicate that Mari had it with her wherever she was when she died. I found this possibility terrifying. The newspaper having not given the cause of death, it suddenly came over me that she had died in childbirth and that the fault was mine since she had been bearing my child. This dread overwhelmed any realization that, whatever may have been our emotions, we had not, during my stay in England, had the necessary physical relationship. It required the impersonal testimony of the calendar—we had been separated considerably longer than nine months—to dispel the hallucinations into which Mari's death had plunged me. I was then assailed by a different cause of terror: wild irrationality into which Mari's death had thrown me. As time passed, my sorrow became tinged with a sense of relief: Mari's irrevocable departure had left me more free to reach out for the new horizons opening before me.

24

DOCTORS ON HORSEBACK

*

JACK Phillips had stored somewhere in his brain a reservoir of effective titles. But like many valuable facilities, it had to be carefully tapped. If you asked Jack when he was sober, he was his usual taciturn self. If you asked him when he had too much to drink, he was just silly. But at the right moment, he came up with *Doctors on Horseback*.

After it was clear that my writing was going well, I got in touch with Miss Pindyck at the Pinker Agency. She told me, after I had described what I was doing, that I needed to submit—this saved publishers' time—one complete short biography along with synopses of the others. She said she would speak to Pinker. It was encouraging when he made an appointment with me for the next day, but after my dashing there he kept me waiting for more than an hour.

Immaculately dressed as always in his black suit and gray waistcoat, Pinker with no apology offered me a seat. But when I began describing *Doctors on Horseback*, "for the first time in my knowledge," so I wrote my parents, "he showed great enthusiasm. He thought the idea for the book was swell, and expressed little doubt that he could get it published. He decided on Harpers as then parts of it could be serialized in *Harper's Magazine*. . . . He is playing with the idea of trying to sell it to Harpers without any sample chapter at all, nothing but the summaries. He wants me to prepare all the summaries at once and send them to him. Then, if an occasion offers, by which he means that if some time he is having lunch with someone at Harpers and they seem in a good mood, he may spring the summaries on them. Otherwise, he'll wait for a sample section. He says he needs only one."

In continuing my report, I teased Mother, who liked to insist that no literary writer should besmirch himself through association with Hollywood, by telling her that I had discussed with Pinker "movie possibilities. Why not follow up Pasteur with an American? . . . He thinks we could shake Hollywood down for some cash, despite the fact that the material is accessible to anyone. The only danger he sees is that someone might get ahead of me. I suppose the only thing you can do about that is pray."

*

Everything continued to go so easily and fast that early in 1937, about a year after I had begun to work on *Doctors on Horseback*, the completed chapter—I had chosen McDowell as the most melo-dramatic—and the five summaries of the others were in Pinker's hands. If he ever made his effort with Harpers, I have no memory or record of it. I don't suppose that I was notified until later of the book's first turndown by Houghton Mifflin, who were later to be my publisher. This information, had I received it, would certainly have left a scar in my memory. My memory zeroes in on the ringing of a telephone. Miss Pindyck's voice. Viking Press wanted *Doctors on Horseback*. She had made an appointment for me with an editor named Marshall Best.

*

I dressed with great attention: newly pressed suit and carefully chosen necktie examined in a bright light for spots. As I walked toward the address of Viking Press, I searched my mind for jubilation, but found myself depressed. It seemed unbearable that on so world-shaking an errand I should still be dodging pedestrians, blocked as usual by lights that released traffic to dash idiotically across my way.

As I entered the offices of Viking Press, my overall anxiety was submerged by a specific fear. I felt that I could not bear to be kept waiting as I had been at Pinker's, and was much relieved to be quickly directed to a door down a hallway which was labeled MARSHALL BEST. I knocked. A voice said, "Come in." The man sitting behind a desk reading some papers raised his head. After a quick glance he returned to his reading. There was nothing I could do but stand in the doorway. I stood there. It seemed a very long time before Best pushed aside his pile of papers and rose. Sitting he had seemed tall, but as he stood up he shrank. His legs, I concluded, must be very short.

He motioned me to a chair. I assumed that he would say something nice about my manuscript, but he asked some routine questions about myself. At last, he said that Viking Press might be willing to publish *Doctors*. However, it would be no more than a marginal publication. I should warn my agent not to force Viking to abandon the project by making expensive demands. Then he closed the interview by standing up again.

I had taken his warning so much to heart that I could hardly wait— all the elevators were going up, not down—to reach the lobby and find a telephone booth. I insisted on speaking to Pinker himself. I pleaded with him not to let the marvelous opportunity get away. He did not exactly laugh at me, but he seemed amused.

*

The contract was signed in March 1937, after I had been actually working on *Doctors* for a little more than a year. Publication was scheduled for October, seven months later, although five of the six sections of the manuscript were still incomplete, and illustrations were to come. I banged on my typewriter jubilantly and worried about what Viking was doing. On July 29, I wrote my parents: "Saw Best this afternoon. He was very agreeable, but what he had to say wasn't too good. As far as I can make out, they haven't touched the section they already have. . . . He hopes to get everything off to the printer the beginning of next week but I have no faith he will do it. . . . He has not read Beaumont yet."

Having applied my old newspaper approach of a lead, I had brought with me a "Foreword" so short that Best could read it as I watched:

"The early doctors of America fought on two frontiers: riding the wilderness of a new continent, they explored the mysteries of the human body.

[231]

"During the eighteenth century they labored to cure the sick on a strip of sea-coast separated by months of ocean from the nearest medical professor and the source of drugs. Gradually, painfully, they groped towards medical institutions of their own, but the work was only started when shots rang out at Lexington. Then the doctors of America marched with an under-fed, ill-equipped army. Treating thousands of sick and wounded who were crowded into barns, often without drugs and instruments, they aided thirteen colonies to defeat an empire. No sooner had peace brought into being an independent nation than another call came: they climbed across mountain passes and drifted down unknown rivers; they struggled abreast of the pioneers. The settler in the most isolated log cabin could count on the ministrations of a doctor who had hanging from his saddle beside the bags of medicine a musket and an ax. When cities sprang up where forests had been, these men labored to make them healthy, fighting sometimes against new diseases the Old World had not known.

"As they took part in every adventure that built a continent-spanning nation, America's pioneer physicians met a higher adventure than the darkest forests, the fiercest Indian wars, could offer. The world of medicine was also a wilderness only half explored whose mysteries challenged the mind. Laboratory technique was in its infancy. People had died of fevers for untold centuries, but no one knew why fevers came and there were a dozen theories of how to cure them. Foreseeing infections in every wound, surgeons limited themselves to simple operations on the extremities of the body, and never expected to cut without giving pain. Although the circulation of the blood had been discovered, no one understood the processes by which a wound healed, or the nature of digestion, or the cell structure of living matter.

"Much of medical practice was a blind stumbling through darkness, yet the challenge of disease was always there, more insistent to the doctors on horseback than the challenge of the wilderness. Listening to the breathing of sick men, they did not hear the noises of the forest. And in the settlements of a new nation there appeared doctors of genius, explorers who, without laboratories or instruments of precision or even any formal training, made great discoveries that helped usher in the age of modern medical science. The modern physician, with all his varied resources, follows the trails these half-forgotten pioneers have blazed."

Best put down the paper and looked at me in amazement: "I never expected anything like this!" As it turned out, these few paragraphs contributed tremendously to the public reception of *Doctors on Horseback*. Reviewers echoed the romantic tone and built their reviews around the conception of the "two frontiers," which was greatly to widen the appeal of the book.

However, the powers at Viking ordered what was for a house of such voltage a minimum printing—3,500 copies—and allowed themselves to get so far behind that they had finished books an unsatisfactory two weeks before publication date.

*

Publication date was October 11, 1937. Although anyone with the least experience would have laughed at us, Agnes Halsey, who was to become my wife, and I were waiting at a newsstand where, as I knew from experience, the first printings of the *Times* and the *Tribune* hit the street. I was remembering back to my days as a reporter when what I wrote would appear at once or not at all. I did not consider that the reviews each newspaper ran on Wednesdays and Saturdays totaled only a few hundred out of the thousands of books published each year. And, even if *Doctors* ended up in this tiny minority, the chance that the daily reviewer would leap to meet the publication date was almost nil.

In any case, there I was, now not a reporter but an author, now with a young woman by my side, waiting as of old for the trucks to come rushing down the almost empty midnight street. Now there was infinitely more in the balance: not only a day's work but two years', and looming behind, like an endless mountain range, the hopes, ambitions, and labors of my whole lifetime.

The *Times* truck came first. The bale that contained my so fragile hopes came flying from the still-moving vehicle. I watched as the newsstand attendant walked leisurely to where it lay on the sidewalk, and leaned over to read the headlines, before he carried the bundle onto the counter in front of his shack. I thought he would never cut the binding cord, but he eventually did. We grabbed the paper at the top of the pile.

It was easier to juggle the newspaper now that we had two pairs of hands. But the result was disappointment. A book review, yes, but not of *Doctors*.

More waiting. The *Tribune* truck. Again a newspaper to juggle and behold: a review of *Doctors* by Lewis Gannett whom I had known on the newspaper. The start was a little snide, but all right: The author has set out "to tell heroic sagas . . . but the facts seem to have got the better of him. Instead of writing a Sunday School story, he has produced a chronicle of some of the most cantankerous petty bickerers in American history." Gannett admitted that this added "immensely to the interest of the book," but later on he wrote, "Perhaps he has been led on by the drama of conflict to neglect the dramas of achievement. There is more than a touch of the tabloid in his treatment of some of these conflicts."

"MORE THAN A TOUCH OF TABLOID!"* These six words shouted down in my and Aggie's minds all the rest of the review. I had been accused of cheapness and vulgarity! Trying to bear as best we could this utter destruction of my career, we returned sadly to my apartment.

Bright and early the next morning, my phone rang. It was Marshall Best: "Congratulations on that fine review!"

"What?" I replied in amazement. "Did you like it?"

*

Eleven days later. As on all mornings, I walked around the corner to a dark little restaurant where I ate breakfast from a counter. The regulars included an epileptic who periodically screamed and frothed at the mouth. On that Friday morning, the quiet was broken by a scream. Everyone looked around for the epileptic, but it was I who had screamed.

I had found in the *Times* a review of *Doctors* by Charles Poore. It was such an enthusiastic rave as rarely troubles the sober surface of

---

*For younger readers, it should be explained that "tabloid" was then the term applied to newspapers that featured the cheapest and most vulgar sensationalism.

the *Times*. In the first paragraph, Poore placed me on a par with Hemingway and Sinclair Lewis.*

Poore kept inserting praises for *Doctors* in his columns as the august reviews came in from the Sunday book-review sections. The *Tribune* assigned a literary reviewer, Mary Ross: "Mr. Flexner writes the all-too-rare kind of biography which has both the concreteness and vigor of fiction and the ring of authenticity." The *Times* preferred a medical historian, Dr. Saul Jarcho: "It is abundantly clear that in all parts of the book the evidence has been selected with care and evaluated with precision. Innumerable interesting details, resurrected from obscurity, are incorporated in a fluent and brilliant narrative."

Although my style was often called journalistic, Gannett's crack about tabloids was never repeated. The staid London *Times Literary Supplement* wrote that the book would be a joy to all admirers of biography.

Much was written about historical importance. According to the *Dallas Morning News*, *Doctors* "made a contribution of lasting value to the interpretation of the [American] frontier." The *Beaumont Texas Journal* saw it somewhat differently: "The stories of these pioneers in medicine rival in romance and daring the more familiar history of Indian battles and other hardships of the country's pioneers." From the *London Spectator*, D. W. Brogan, the English writer most admired for books on American society, urged his readers to seek in *Doctors* broad insights into American life. Then Brogan matched Poore's Hemingway and Lewis by according my style "Plutarchian charm."

Most satisfactory to me was a short note from Bernard Berenson: "I feel impelled to write and congratulate you on your 'Doctors on Horseback.' It's one of the most delightfully entertaining, in-

---

*Lewis had just published his medical novel *Arrowsmith*. In a good many of the reviews of *Doctors*, the two books were compared not to my disadvantage.

There was a further coincidental connection. The institution where Lewis's protagonist worked was based on Father's Rockefeller Institute, a critical approach having been supplied by Lewis's adviser, Paul De Kruif, whom Father had fired from the Institute for various misdeeds. De Kruif had himself written *Microbe Hunters*, like *Doctors*, a group of short biographies of medical scientists, although none was American. Whenever *Microbe Hunters* was mentioned in my reviews, it was to point out that it was less accurate. However, its sale had been much greater.

forming, and suggestive books that I have read for some time and as coming from America for a long time, in fact since Faulkner's 'Pylon.'

"You have mastered the difficult art of narrating while depicting and interpreting, and you can be delicately ironical with no touch of archness, and happily you are never condescending. Your English is of its kind faultless. I am happy, truly happy to see that you have worked and attained. I wish you joy.

*

"My life," so I wrote my parents, "has been largely concerned with the book. A walk up Fifth Avenue showed that Scribner's had five copies in the window, nicely balancing the same number as Hemingway's new novel, and that Brentano's had a pyramid of them in its window."

Mother, who wished to send copies to various of her friends, had given me money to buy them in bookstores. The intention was to enhance the general sale: we neither of us foresaw a more specific use. Even after all these years when I wish to see whether a store has in stock one of my books, I find it clumsy to go beyond scanning the shelves by asking a clerk whether they have the book, and then, if it is produced, not buying it. To explain that I am the author just increases the embarrassment. But with Mother's order to execute, I could ask for the book and then engage the clerk in conversation. I was so pleased that almost all had heard of *Doctors* that I used Mother's orders sparingly so as to string out the pleasure.

Now, when I went to literary parties, I no longer needed to be apologetic. "People I meet around are beginning to have heard about the book and to know it got good reviews. I mean people who had never heard of me before. . . . I actually ran into a complete stranger who had bought a copy."

I began to experience a phenomenon which still disturbs me. An author looks forward, when a book is successful, to being rewarded by pleasing his friends, but the friends are often displeased because of envy. Many of my companions were trying to get well started in the arts, and they felt the triumph of *Doctors* denigrated their efforts. Rhys and Steel treated my success with resentment.

To my parents, I reported: "I discovered yesterday one of the tricks used to keep those queer animals, authors, from growling too much.

Best's secretary called me up and with sugary tones told me the Viks were submitting the book for the Pulitzer Prize. I expressed myself as moved almost to tears, although my guess is they submit every book on their list. It don't cost 'em nothing, and you can never tell what a bunch of cockeyed judges might do."

The impressive but not extraordinary success of *Doctors* rapidly became in my mind a satisfaction rather than a jubilation. I had, I felt, reached a shoulder on the mountain that I had been so long climbing, a starting point, I hoped, for a higher climb. I had achieved only a hint of the eminence that from my birth I had been expected to achieve—and my father still loomed above me.

After a party given in celebration of *Doctors on Horseback*, I wrote my parents that I had had a good time, but was glad to see ahead no further distractions to keep me from getting started on my next book.

*

Doctors on Horseback has been my lifelong companion. Edition has followed edition. Although a motion picture sale to MGM never eventuated in a film, it contributed considerably to my exchequer. During World War II copies designed to fit in the pockets of uniforms were supplied in the "Armed Services edition" to all military, marine, and naval installations everywhere. It is, as I write this, still or again in print.

25

AMERICA'S OLD MASTERS

*

BENEATH all the excitements churned up by the publication of *Doctors*, I had felt the daily lack of the mainstays that helped me keep my life on an even keel: my sanctuaries, the libraries, and that talisman, my typewriter. It was time for me to get back to work. •

Investigating the various environments in which my doctors moved, I had come to realize that a wide range of aspects of the American past were crying for investigations. Settlement, wars, politics, government, and economics were being examined and taught. But, with the partial exception of literature, the other categories of American achievement had been ruled outside their academic palisade. Why not make *Doctors* the first in a series that would blaze trails in one neglected field after another?

I hardly realized, and in any case did not care, that according to established scholarly conceptions what I intended was heresy, presumption, and insanity. Heresy because a scholar was required to occupy a single field of study, hardly looking over the surrounding fences. Presumption because scholars should not invade each other's fields. Insanity because I lacked formal training in any of the directions I intended to explore. But all the fields would be integral parts of the same American landscape, and I was concerned with human nature displaying itself as it interwove with high achievement.

I had come to *Doctors* cold and found no insurmountable difficulties. True, I had then had Father's help, but I was eager to get out from under Father's shadow. And I liked to contend that the best way to learn about a subject was to write a book about it.

The obvious direction might seem to be short biographies of early American writers, but I instinctively shied away from narrowing my gap between biography and autobiography. It would have been impossible for me to exclude from my accounts of other writers my own eccentricities and stylistic preferences. And if I started identifying myself with my subjects, the result would be disastrous not only for the book but also for my peace of mind.

My next interest was painting, and in that direction disadvantages would turn to advantages. Without any overlapping, similar creativity would apply. I have always regarded it as an advantage over conventional art scholars (a conclusion with which they passionately disagree) that my methods for understanding and judgment were primarily creative rather than analytical.

*

When I was preparing *Doctors on Horseback*, I had come to the conclusion (rare then and still not adequately followed) that illustrations for historical works should be more than embellishment: they should be as authentic as documented quotations. But finding life portraits of all my seven doctors had not been easy. I eventually heard of a library devoted to collecting on a scholarly basis photographs of authentic paintings.

The Frick Art Reference Library, which backed onto the Frick Collection, looked, with its marble façade, like an oversized townhouse. Some fuss was made about letting me in, but, after the small elevator had carried me to the reading room, my needs immediately attracted the attention of Hannah Johnson, the tall, nice-looking young woman sitting behind a desk. Soon I had before me photographs of portraits of my doctors, attached to gray mounts which had typed on their backs information concerning the pictures themselves and where negatives could be found for reproduction.

I found two portraits of Dr. Shippen: a battered original by Stuart and a seemingly exact copy that would reproduce better. When I tried to order a print of the copy, Hannah Johnson firmly informed me that you never used any sort of copy when the original was available. This principle I have never violated. I was further impressed when my phone rang at home. Miss Johnson had found a small mistake in the information she had given, and had done some sleuthing to dig me out.

*

My first act on seriously considering a book about early American painters was to hurry to Hannah. She assured me that no book existed that would make mine an also-ran. And she knew of no such book in preparation. By the time I went down in the little elevator, my mind was made up.

*

Since I had not yet identified my cast of characters, or defined the scope of my book, it was fortunate that in the new position to which *Doctors* had raised me, I could seek a publisher's contract without submitting an outline or even a summary, by merely stating the subject I wished to pursue.

Pinker was far from enthusiastic, but, being unable to dissuade me, he said he would try to brazen it through with Viking and might well succeed as "they would not want you to get away." He made a luncheon date for himself and me with Best and Harold Ginzberg, the president of Viking.

"Pink," I wrote my parents, "in a most perfidious manner, dropped out of the luncheon. Ginzberg did all the talking. . . . He came at me entirely on a basis of business. He did not doubt that the book would be a good book, but he felt it would sell less well than the doctors: he obviously wanted to follow the *Docs'* success with another medical book. He did not push this, however, when I pointed out that I would be irrevocably set down as a science writer. He then said that the doctors had appealed to a special audience and that now I wanted to write a book that would appeal to a different one. I was sacrifising the start I had got with *Docs*, and, in addition, the field of people interested in painters was much smaller than the field of people interested in doctors. I replied that I regarded both books as studies of American history, and that I felt that many people were interested in painting. He also said that he thought it a mistake to repeat the same technique in a second book: people would ask whether my next book would be on early American plumbers. However, if I was willing to accept the financial sacrifice, Viking would be glad to give me a contract. I should think the matter over carefully and let him know."

I had no struggle with temptation. There were few things I wanted less than seeming, as a medical writer, to be hanging onto Father's coattails. Having eschewed expensive tastes, I was immune to financial pressure. A falldown in sales from *Doctors* was irrelevant as long as there was no falldown in quality. Above all, I needed to preserve, at the highest possible level, the concern, the esthetic excitement, that had, as if with the wings of an eagle, lifted me from the depth of despair. No compromise could be risked.

When I wrote Ginzberg that I would go ahead, he replied that he was not surprised, "for it became more and more apparent that you have the book close to your heart."

*

It was now necessary to select my protagonists. In *Doctors* I had roamed widely through time and geography. I was willing to accept an equally wide span. A start in the Revolutionary generation seemed dictated, since little that was authentic had been determined about earlier artists (a gap I was to fill in a later book). I considered proceeding as far as to include Chester Harding, who had flourished after the Civil War. He appealed to me as being highly picturesque. However, my fledgling experience with *Doctors* had indicated that there is no important career which, if understood, could not be revealed as dramatic. Thus, I might make the quality of the paintings my only touchstone, and it soon dawned on me that Nature had set up a much tighter format than had been possible for *Doctors*.

Four interrelated painters, all born on the eastern seaboard between 1738 and 1755, had brought to American painting a greater international reputation than was to be repeated until the twentieth century by the Abstract Impressionists. The creations of my painters furthermore preceded the emergence of American literature (Cooper and Irving) by more than a generation. It seemed natural to bring together, under the title *America's Old Masters*, Benjamin West, John Singleton Copley, Charles Willson Peale, and Gilbert Stuart.

That they all knew one another and sometimes worked side by side would present to an historian the necessity to weave their stories together. This I was to do when I undertook my history of American painting. But now I adhered to my format of short biographies. When my characters fraternized or cooperated, each would be shown in his own biographical section playing his role according to his own predilections and personality. This enlivened events with several points of view. It was, indeed, a throwback to a form I had used in "Enter and Possess."

*

Unlike the history of medicine, art history was accepted by academe as a respectable subject. But American art was firmly excluded, being considered by definition so inferior to the European as unworthy of attention. There was not, when I wrote *Masters*, in any learned institution a professorship devoted to American art. This was to open to me a greater opportunity than I could foresee. My book came to be credited with an important role in sparking a major cultural shift: the leap of the appreciation of the art of the American past into a stratosphere of popular enthusiasm.

*

My story began with Pennsylvania-born Benjamin West, who, almost altogether self-taught, became a professional artist when in his teens, producing canvases of real merit. In 1739, when he was twenty-one, his neighbors paid his way to Italy. The earliest American painter to study abroad so impressed the connoisseurs in Rome that he was called "The American Raphael." He carried to England the neoclassicism that was to sweep through France and all Europe; became the favorite painter and a close friend of George III's, although he never hid his sympathy with the rebels during the American Revolution; succeeded Sir Joshua Reynolds as president of the Royal Academy; was an innovator of styles that were successively to dominate Europe for half a century; became a teacher of most successful American and English painters of the next generation. He was internationally considered the greatest living painter; became outmoded after his death; and, by the time I started on *America's Old Masters*, was generally regarded as little more than an historical curiosity. This lack of interest was encouraged by the fact that in our nationalistic world no nation claimed West: the English dismissed him as an

American, and the Americans, since he had made his career in England, denounced him as an unpatriotic English artist.

Basking in his heyday, West had turned out hundreds of pictures, many of them inferior works run up by his pupils. The canvases visible in the cellar of the Metropolitan Museum were miserable daubs which I found disheartening. However, I was rescued at Philadelphia, which had been and remained proud of its native son. Since, purely by chance, I had begun my study on the two-hundredth anniversary of West's birth, I was able to examine a special memorial exhibition at the Pennsylvania Museum, the result of wide borrowing that included his best-known paintings in England. Beyond all that, the local environs contained an almost complete representation of the portraits West had painted as a youth before he went abroad. An invaluable monograph concerning these paintings had just been published by that absolutely reliable scholar of early American painting, William Sawitzky (of whom much more later). Although this was the only important recent publication on West, his celebrity during his own lifetime had generated a mass of sources.

*

West, the born leader, mild, kind, charismatic, and relaxedly prolific, was in terms of character almost exactly opposite to Copley, who stayed in his native Boston long after West had sailed abroad. Inhabiting an environment with few and very inferior sources for artistic inspiration, Copley slowly, timidly, doggedly, painstakingly taught himself to create much better pictures than any he had ever seen. Finally, he found the courage to induce a sea captain to drop off one of his portraits at Reynolds's studio. Reynolds was amazed by his strange work, so different and so strong. Both he and West wrote Copley that if he hurried abroad, before he became too hardened in his provincial style, he would be one of the greatest painters in the world. But too timid to brave the ocean and the roads in Europe, which he was sure crawled with bandits, Copley stayed home to create the first major American works of art in any medium.

To escape from the American Revolution—he had in an amazing moment of courage tried to stop the Boston Tea Party—Copley finally sailed to Europe. Overwhelmed by the artistic richness now revealed to him, he achieved, in his forties, what must have been one of the most astounding about-faces in the history of art. He abandoned the tight, understated intellectual style he had invented for himself in Boston, for what was almost its opposite: coloristic, fluent, flamboyant rather than laconic. He became adept enough to compete with, and in some ways transcend, the leaders of the eighteenth-century artistic movement that made London briefly the center of the European painting world.

However, Copley could never make his peace with his new environment. He fought with his benefactor West, with the members of the Royal Academy to which he had been quickly elected, built around himself a flaming palisade of grievances, lost his ability to paint, and died a neglected, embittered old man.

*

Concerning Copley there was, except for his early years, voluminous material. By a fluke of history, a copious archive of his correspondence with his half-brother had been salted away among the papers confiscated by the British government during the Revolution. Later family letters have also been published, although sometimes in bowdlerized form. And much can be found in the British publications of his time.

Since Copley had been born in the same year as West, I again profited from a two-hundredth anniversary. The Boston Museum of Fine Arts, which had just published a catalogue of Copley's American paintings, staged an exhibition that, fortunately for me, included English works.

The fly in the ointment came when I was introduced to Benjamin Roland, the only professor at Harvard who would sometimes condescend to look at American pictures. He was also the only person I ever ran into who grew as a decoration shoebrushes of black hair from his nostrils. He treated me, as a non-academic writer, with a condescension that I considered funny. I would have laughed from the other side of my mouth had I realized how much trouble he was to make for me when he reproduced himself by nurturing the first Ph.D's who finally specialized in American art.

*

Concerning my third painter, Charles Willson Peale, little was known. However, a descendent had a voluminous archive of Peale's papers. Had I been told that Charles Coleman Sellers, a published author, was preparing a biography of his ancestor, I would have felt queasy about interfering. In my ignorance, I wrote asking to consult the manuscripts. His reply was the most generous I have ever in my long life received. Not only did he invite me to stay at his home, but he stated that, as he had classified the papers for his biography, he could easily find for me any document I wanted.

Thus began my first friendship with another student of American art. Sellers knew no more about other workers in the field than I did, but the great-grandfather we were both writing about haunted his house.

When Peale's first child died in 1772, his wife asked him to preserve the child's likeness. He responded by painting the infant lying in death, its lifeless arms held to its sides by a broad ribbon. His wife objected that this was too gruesome, so he sewed on more canvas, and added a lifesize portrait of her weeping beside the corpse, the useless medicines on a table beside her. When he saw it in 1776, John Adams wrote, "This picture struck me prodigiously." It is indeed a striking picture.

In the painter's house, it had hung in the dining room covered with a curtain that was drawn back on the anniversary of the child's death. In the Sellers's house, the picture hung in an equivalent position behind the same curtain to be drawn back on the same date. Since their farmhouse where the manuscripts and paintings were stored was not fireproof, Sellers and his wife never went away from the house at the same time.

Charles was a little older than I, tall and slight, with a blondish cast, warm but never effusive, the general impression being gentleness, diffidence, and intelligence. As time passed, my wife and I would visit the Sellerses, taking along our Irish terrier. They had a large dog. In the goodness of his heart, Sellers tried putting the dogs' dinners side by side so that they could eat in convivial fellowship. Of course, his bigger dog gobbled, pushed my terrier aside, and ate the other dinner. Sellers was overcome with embarrassment and abject in apology. I did not dare trivialize the matter by saying, "Dogs will be dogs."

The dearth of interest in American art was such that Sellers could for the time being find no publisher, although his works on Peale were to be much admired. He resolved to print the volume himself, offering copies by subscription. This enabled me to pay back my obligation. My book, backed by a powerful publisher, would go out in the world, and I could plug his book in my pages. We remained friends for years.

*

Peale exemplified the ingenuity developed in pioneer civilizations where every community had to manufacture its own needs: he made a fine watch and painted a fine portrait. However so transcendent was his genius, so versatile his mind, that he associated naturally with Washington, who became his friend, as did Hamilton and Jefferson. During the two years he had spent with West in London, he had engaged in so many occupations that, while adding some sophistication to his portrait style, he never broke with the Colonial methods of seeing. His work, with its charm and validity, indicated ways in which American painting might have developed had the Revolution not reshuffled the cards.

Having been a soldier and radical leader, Peale established his own museum of natural history where he worked out display techniques that were to be rediscovered in the twentieth century; he achieved various inventions; he dug up and put together the first mastodon skeleton seen since the Ice Age. And everything he did included verve and eccentricity so that he was a biographer's dream.

*

Gilbert Stuart had been a juvenile delinquent as a boy and an alcoholic when a man. He started painting as a youth in his native Newport, Rhode Island. A period as apprentice to a traveling Scots painter of conventional British skills made no dent on his practice. The portraits he created during his teens would be recognized, were it not for his subsequent career, as masterpieces of American Folk Art. Having been unseated by the Revolution, he determined, when in London, to make the British accept his primitive style rather than give in to their graces. But the art of the major portraitists was seductive, and, as he refused to follow, he lost his own ability to paint.

[246]

Finally, he wrote a piteous letter to Benjamin West, who took him in and recognizing his genius accepted him, despite the uproar he created in the quiet painting room, as a major assistant.

Stuart so absorbed the skills of the great British portrait school that he came to be considered a possible successor to the aging Reynolds. However, he did not follow Reynolds into renditions of grace and rank. He emphasized the Revolutionary attitude that what was most important about a human being was personality. He was said to "nail the face on the canvas." However, he was so brilliant a colorist, particularly at achieving flesh tones, and he had toward human character so broad and uncensorial an insight that his likenesses rarely offended. (Every successful person is pleased to be himself.)

It was not patriotism but debts piled up by extravagance that made him, in 1793, return to America after eighteen years abroad. He took advantage of the more equalitarian attitudes of his homeland to abandon altogether elegance of costume or setting, showing only a face against a plain background with only enough body to establish position. Thus, in his best portraits of Washington there is nothing beyond the face to reveal power and greatness.

Dissipation continued to wrack Stuart. When he died, his family, whom he had fought for years, bought a vacant place in a vault owned by a tradesman and then lost their record of where the great painter was buried.

*

Jack, being familiar with the shibboleths of art scholars, persuaded me to define my intentions so as to forestall wrath.

Under his guidance, I wrote:

"Dedicated to history not art criticism, to biography not the evaluation of pictures, this book attempts to tell the story of four amazing lives. In discussing the achievements of these men, we shall try to show how their paintings succeeded or failed in the eyes of their contemporaries and according to the standards of their own school, leaving to writers more skilled in such matters the evaluation of their work according to some universal principle of esthetics. It is not our object to make judgements but to resurrect from obscurity the men behind the canvases which gave American art its first stature in the world."

*

Old Masters appeared in 1939. Critical reception, although on a much smaller scale, was comparable with that of *Doctors*. Nothing could be more splashy than the comment by the distinguished biographer Marquis James: "The best book of its kind in existence." The surprise previously expressed at such an emergence of an altogether unknown young author was replaced by my being identified as the author of *Doctors on Horseback*. The paragraph Jack had persuaded me to include stood me in good stead as a lightning rod. The *Times* and the *Tribune* assigned their top art critics—Edward Alden Jewel and Royal Cortissoz—to write extensive reviews. It was stated that "Such critical comment as does enter his plan is shrewd and always pertinent." Berenson weighed in with, "You intended to present your painters first and last as human beings, as men among men, and you have succeeded to perfection, showing their art by the way." As with *Doctors*, the book was praised for its contribution to American history.

But what of the genealogists and antiquarians obscurely proceeding down their restricted paths when a book by a complete outsider landed in their preserve with a considerable beating of wings? They were sharpening their pencils for the kill when the towering scholar in the field, William Sawitzky, endorsed the book. And no one dared go against his word.

*

America's Old Masters was so far ahead of its time that it soon went out of print. For a quarter of a century, the book was available only in libraries and from secondhand bookshops. Then, in 1967, Dover Publications, smelling the growing interest, agreed to a paperback. They encouraged me to make revisions but, since they were to print an offset from the original edition, each change had to occupy, in order not to upset pagination, exactly the same amount of space as the passage deleted. Tricky but not hamstringing.

I corrected factual statements no longer valid and ameliorated gaucheries which had stemmed from my own naïveté or from misleading sources. However, whenever possible, I was tolerant of my old text, feeling that the youthful author who was once me had a right to self-expression without his older self intervening like a schoolmarm. Indeed, I could not have meddled greatly without destroying.

*

Come 1980, Doubleday took over *Old Masters* in a deluxe edition with color plates. This drew from John Russell, the art critic of *The New York Times* the following review:

"It is not every writer on art who is invited to republish—with no more than incidental changes—a book that first appeared in 1939. Nor can James Thomas Flexner be said to have pioneered a methodology that has been taken up with acclamation by academic art historians. On the contrary: He goes his own way, now as then. But he brought to these studies of Benjamin West, John Singleton Copley, Charles Willson Peale and Gilbert Stuart a knowledge of American political history that few historians of art can rival—and, with that, a gift of narrative, a delight in the human comedy and a generosity of spirit that do not turn up every day in art history. One could also adduce a quality of belief. Mr. Flexner believed in these painters at a time when they found few to praise them. His estimate of their achievement may lack rigor, by the standards of the 1980's, but he brought them alive as human beings. If this is 'anecdotal history,' it is not for that reason to be despised. John Aubrey's 'Brief Lives' are anecdotal history, too, and we never stop learning from them."

The Doubleday edition gave way to a paperback published by McGraw-Hill, which eventually faded. Dover Publications picked it up again in 1994. And so, *Old Masters*, flirting its tail, is trotting along toward the twenty-first century.

26

MARRIAGE

*

DURING the autumn of 1937—this was as *Doctors on Horseback* was being published—I became much interested in Agnes Halsey, whom I had known for some years ever since she had been an undergraduate at Bryn Mawr. She was a handsome, upstanding, buxom young woman, about my equal in height but some three or four years my junior. Dr. Carrel, who was concerned with what people ate, asked her what her father had raised her on. She replied, "Roast beef." Carrel said, "I thought so."

Agnes's father, Charles B. Halsey, had become rich as a real estate operator. He had owned two Rolls Royces, but had as a matter of gentlemanly honor not followed the usual precaution of incorporating each real estate venture separately so that the failure of one would not pull down the others. As a result of his idealism, he had been wiped out by the great Depression. Suffering from a vast sense of injustice, he had become an alcoholic. Perhaps I should have paid more attention to Agnes's conviction that if allowed to take her father by herself to some secluded spot and where she was in no way interfered with, she would have cured him of his alcoholism.

Agnes's education, presided over by her staunch, steadfast mother, was much in my world: the Brearley School, then presided over by my first cousin Millicent Carey McIntosh; and then Bryn Mawr, so much a creation of Aunt Carey's. At Bryn Mawr's presentations of Gilbert and Sullivan operas, Agnes had been the star, and it was ruled that she had potentialities of becoming a great coloratura. After graduation, she was given a fellowship in a music school. But it lasted only a year since she had no interior drive to music. She was, for better or worse, to make a career out of taking care of me.

During the early autumn of 1939, the year that *America's Old Masters* was published, Agnes and I were married in my family's house at Chocorua.

*

Agnes had the perspicacity and tolerance not to interfere with the research and writing which supplied to me, as previously, with a safe haven from my nervous troubles. But they had not been a total panacea. My traumas had been restricted rather than extinguished. They pounced in the morning if I could not get away fast enough, and I found them lurking when I came home in the late afternoons. I had nonetheless been operating pretty well, keeping my difficulties well hidden from the eyes of the world. Now Agnes's sympathy and love and eagerness to heal induced me to confide in her the maladies that I had kept sealed up lest releasing them might lead me to madness. To share without catastrophe was to me a great reassurance, and Agnes, from day to day, did her best to alleviate what might upset me. I might have felt humiliated by the dependence so developed had not my major energies and ambitions been directed to my writing, the part of my life that was elsewhere. As for Agnes, she was for the time being happy to carry on, gently and lovingly, and with considerable self-sacrifice, the mission she had chosen for herself.

During the summer before we were to be married, Agnes went to an acting school in upstate New York. The strength of my emotions is revealed by a letter I sent her from Chocorua, where I was staying with my parents.

"My beloved,

"I complain about missing you, I realize, with the dreary persistence of an old woman complaining about her rheumatism. Yet I must do so, for the ailment is the dominant fact of my life these days. Unless something untoward happens, I shall remember this summer as 'the summer in which I missed Aggie.' I have often been horrified by the one-track nature of my mind; if I feel something strongly, it swallows everything else. Thus, though I write religiously every day and am getting much done, that doesn't change my prevailing mood.

It hasn't quite been three weeks since you left, and there are more than five weeks more. I frankly don't see how I can bear them, though I suppose I shall. If only I could hibernate like a bear, I could go to sleep now and wake up on September 28 [the date of our marriage]! Not a day passes when I am not for an hour or so close to tears from loneliness. I can understand how people kill themselves for love. If anything were to come between us now, I would not want to live.

"I have got to work out some way of making life here without you bearable. I awaken in the morning with the dead feeling that there is no reason for getting up, since I shall not see you. But the morning is the best part of the day; I write and for a few hours forget to be lonely. But at last I am tired out and can write no more. Then I wait for the mail. If there is a letter from you, I read it many times and bask in the illusion that I am with you. However, it is an illusion and cannot last very long. Then comes the long afternoon; I go for walks, I read books, if I'm lucky I play tennis, but all the while I feel like a persistent pain the fact that you are far away. That is the worst time. In the evenings I feel the day is over; no more need to be sad that day, and I can settle down comfortably to a book. But I do not sleep well; I am troubled by dreams of you, frustrated dreams in which you run away and I cannot catch you. Then comes the morning and the dead feeling again."

*

After a honeymoon in an isolated forest cabin, Agnes and I settled down in our familiar New York City stamping ground, the East Sixties. I was engaged in an act of family duty. When Father had been retired as director of the Institute, he had been awarded a large grant by the Rockefeller Foundation to write a biography of his teacher and subsequently intimate colleague Dr. William Henry Welch. He set up an office in a far corner of what came to be called Flexner Hall, and hired an experienced researcher and a typist. All had gone well until the time came to create the written book. In his late seventies, never having undertaken such a task, Father found himself at a loss. I was drafted. The book was to be published under both our names.

Eager as I was to continue my own work, I welcomed the opportunity to pay back some of what had been done for me—my only chagrin being that Father felt it necessary to stipulate that on the title page his name should come first. Perhaps, if he had been working with Brother Bill, who always felt a drive to rival his male parent, this would have had to be stated, but I was hurt that Father did not take it for granted.

No ghost writer I, putting in salable flashy episodes. I toned down my literary style to fit the tone of the chapters that I was straightening out. Although it occupied me for about a year, I never have regarded *William Henry Welch and the Golden Age of American Medicine* as anything but Father's book. That I felt no literary pride was revealed by my assumption, when book critics polled by the *Saturday Review* gave the *Welch* second place in their nominations for the Pulitzer Prize in biography, that that was no more than a bow to Father's eminence. I was not disappointed when the volume the book critics put third won the Prize.

On reading *Welch* again after the passage of fifty years, when it is to be reprinted so that it can play a major role on the hundredth anniversary of the founding of Johns Hopkins Medical School, I feel that I had been somewhat swamped by the apparatus that enabled us, with no effort, to quote, in full, documents that, if I had had to copy them out myself, I would have greatly cut. However, the length of over five hundred pages is now in keeping with contemporary fashion and would have been commonplace for the Victorian biographies against which Strachey had revolted. We did indeed have to cover a great deal of ground. The ponderous title, *William Henry Welch and the Golden Age of American Medicine*, indicated that Welch had presided over the early growth of scientific medicine in the United States.

*

Freed from our mooring in New York City by the completion of *Welch*, Agnes and I decided to seek tranquillity by moving to the country. However, my professional needs forbade going too far from the publishing center of New York. And my resolve to proceed with my series on early American culture by bringing together short biographies meant that we would have to settle within striking distance of a first-class library. Harvard would be too far away. We had a choice of becoming parasites on Princeton or on Yale. College rivalries being what they were, Princeton would have been for a Harvard man an impossible choice. We would have to settle in the environs of New Haven.

The fashionable and lively country community close to and connected with Yale was Woodbridge. An old friend from the Chocorua days was a social leader there. He put Agnes and me up in his house, introduced us around, and urged us to rent a nearby home. This was an opening most people would have leapt at (I was later to regret that we had let it go by), but it did not present the bucolic quiet for which we were leaving New York.

We found on the opposite side of New Haven, the farthest from New York, an authentic seventeenth-century house that had been taken apart in Massachusetts and re-erected on a rural road. Our neighbors for some distance around were farmers in two categories: Italians who could make truck farming profitable because the women and children worked in the fields; and Yankees whose sole salable produce was milk, to be picked up by tank trucks. Local conversation was an endless argument about whether it was more economic to buy expensive pedigreed cows who gave more milk per head, or grade cows who cost less to begin with. Tiring of this issue, we found that for social life we had to drive the same ten miles to New Haven and Yale.

*

Although I was described in the *New Haven Register* as "Harvard man in the Yale woods," Agnes and I were eagerly received by the cultural faculty. Yale had no such hinterland as Harvard, which was surrounded by Cambridge and Boston and innumerable cultural institutions. Yale was isolated in a medium-sized industrial city with no cultural traditions or institutions. The industrialists' daughters occasionally married Yale football heroes or appealing esthetical graduate students, but there was the usual hostility between town and gown. The New Haven police delighted in ticketing professors' cars or arresting drunken undergraduates.

Our friends were almost without exception teachers in the humanities. They were well-bred and correctly cultured, in a manner that we at first found soothing, if not exciting. Each was by definition an expert in his field, but academic "discipline" required no encroaching on one another's territory. Almost never, for instance, was a student of American history or literature urged to visit the Yale Art Gallery where hung pictures they would have found significant. I do not remember any single occasion when a professor intruded by expanding on a subject where he was expert, thus starting a general discussion. There came to be, of course, much discussion of war news, but no one knew more than was in the papers.

By far the most common subject of discussion, everyone being concerned and interested, was parochial: the personalities and prospects of colleagues; who got or failed to get tenure, deservedly or undeservedly; budget allocations, etc., etc. There was much backbiting but little scandal, that being left to the more highflying inhabitants of Woodbridge. I found this interesting enough, as I often was familiar with the actors. It was as if I were sitting at the sidelines of a continuing tennis game where I knew most of the players.

One memory: a specialist on Impressionism and similar French schools decided to take up chess. He did not make any effort to play until he had prepared himself by studying all the manuals in the Sterling Library. When he finally decided he was ready, I was the first to be challenged. To his indignation, I checkmated him in three moves. His profound sources had failed to mention "the fool's mate." In more sour moments, I have considered this an allegory of much highfalutin' scholarship.

*

On December 7, 1941, Agnes and I staged a luncheon party. The principal excitement was that the librarian of Yale, Bernhard Knollenberg, being a tall man, banged his forehead full force against one of our seventeenth-century door jambs. He seemed to have knocked himself out, but proved to have no more than a bad bruise. After the guests had left, I lay down for a nap. Agnes, who had been listening to the radio, did not wake me, but when I arose told me that Japanese airplanes had attacked the American naval base at Pearl Harbor. The damage was reported as considerable. Feeling a need of company, we drove to a friend's house in New Haven where we listened to broadcasts that grew more and more terrifying. It finally became clear that the Pacific Fleet had been destroyed.

President Roosevelt's speech to Congress, which had to be a declaration of war was to come over the air at lunch time on the following day. Faculty friends invited me to a college dining room. It was crowded with undergraduates whose futures, quite possibly life spans, were to be determined. There was a radio on every table. There was almost complete silence until Roosevelt's mellifluous voice filled the air. The voice ceased and everyone walked out in silence.

*

What was to be my own role? With my disabilities, it seemed to be idiotic for me to try to enlist in the armed forces. However, when the draft laws were promulgated, I found that I was within the eligible age range. This in effect made the traumas I had for so long kept under wraps public property. It became necessary for me to find out for certain whether I would be useful as a soldier or would be deleterious to the cause, in the process destroying myself. I could no longer repudiate what had for so long been on the cards: consult a psychiatrist.

I got in touch with Dr. Austrian, who had so helped me years before by saying a few words. He arranged for me a privilege beyond price. I was taken on by Dr. Thomas A. C. Rennie, who had just come from Baltimore, as chief physician, to the Payne Whitney Clinic, the psychiatric branch of New York Hospital.

The immediate result was a dossier which Rennie mailed to my draft "induction board" on January 23, 1942. He himself wrote that I suffered from a "nervous condition of anxiety, tension, mood swings," adding that in "my capacity as induction board psychiatrist in the Baltimore area, I would have unqualifiedly rejected him."

Dr. Friedenwald's associate, Dr. Theodore H. Robinson, wrote that I had been under their care since November 24, 1931. "A thorough examination which included an x-ray examination revealed the fact that Mr. Flexner was affected with a duodenal ulcer and a spastic colon." It had been necessary for me to be under treatment ever since. The most recent x-ray examination, December 17, 1941, revealed that the ulcer had "apparently healed," but my colon remained "spastic and irritable" and it was necessary for me to continue "a strict ulcer diet."

Enclosed in the dossier was a statement Rennie had procured from one of America's most famous psychologists:

"TO WHOM IT MAY CONCERN:

"Mr. James T. Flexner, who is well-known through his book *Doctors on Horseback* and the biography of Dr. Welch, is afflicted with a condition of *psyasthenic obsessive fears* which hamper him greatly in the ordinary moves of practical life: the difficulty of breaking his routine, inability to go to theatres, difficulty of sleep, and special gastrointestinal involvements. He has a long history of gastrointestinal upsets and of a duodenal ulcer which has been treated intensively and for the prevention of any recurrence of which Mr. Flexner is still on a special diet. I consider him *unfit* for the demands of active military life and an attempt at service on regular duty *a definite hazard*. His actual talents can make him, however, very useful where he can have control of what is necessary for his self-protection. I therefore would recommend his being deferred from army service so that he can make himself useful along lines which permit the maintenance of the routine of life essential for fitness and for his welfare.

Respectfully yours,

(signed) ADOLF MEYER
Emeritus Professor of Psychiatry
The Johns Hopkins University"

A less apprehensive couple might well have foreseen the inevitable result, but day after day Agnes and I did not wait for the normal mail delivery to reach our road: every morning saw us at the post office. Eventually, as we came through the door, the postmaster (who had, of course, guessed our errand) handed me a very insignificant-looking postcard bearing the classification 4F: "ineligible for service."

Although I was greatly relieved, there was also humiliation: no man relishes being ruled too little of a man. I thus cherished Dr. Meyer's statement that I could be "very useful" if enabled to apply my own talents. I had already come up with the conception that I could spur on patriotism among recently arrived Americans from non-English backgrounds with publications demonstrating how their own natural and ethnic groups had helped shape the American society they were now being called on to defend. Although I traveled to Hartford, the Connecticut capital, and to Washington, I could not raise interest. My suggestion was at least a generation before its time.

I had to satisfy myself by preparing, through the Writers' War Board, articles desired by various wartime agencies. My most successful dealt with methods the Army Air Corps had developed for minimizing injuries during a crash. Don't become tense, but relax: drunks can fall down the cellar stairs without getting hurt. The most surprising advice was that, when you saw an accident coming, you should not try to protect yourself with outstretched hands, but press your head against some solid part of your endangered vehicle. A cracked skull is not serious compared to having your head swung so that the soft tissues of the brain is crushed against the inside of the skull. Useful for civilians as well as fliers, my article, which I titled "The Fine Art of Falling," was widely circulated, plagiarized, and anthologized.

*

Before America had entered the war, I had written to Esther Forbes, the biographer of Paul Revere, concerning my "deep and half instinctive feeling that in these days when European civilization is tearing itself apart, much of the torch of culture is being handed on to us, but we cannot carry it adequately merely on the basis of European traditions. . . . We must explore our own past to find other, stronger, roots."

Now, the three published books—Doctors, Old Masters, and Welch—were being gathered in by the governmental agencies that were entrusted with sustaining morale in our own fighting forces; with earning the respect of our allies, and then, after victory, the respect of the enemy countries that our forces occupied.

My lack of physical presence was overwhelmed tens of thousands of times by a paperback of Doctors distributed in the "Armed Services Editions" to all military, marine corps, and naval forces wherever stationed, in the United States and all over the world. I still, to this day, am periodically shown how much the book meant to men in active duty who were faced with extreme boredom which might at any moment switch over to extreme danger. Men I run into casually, far outside my normal world, say, "Flexner? Flexner!" and then suddenly brighten up: "Could you be the author of *Doctors on Horseback*?"

An edition was produced for soldiers who had not passed the fifth grade in school. An edition was distributed abroad in English: *The New York Times* stated that *Doctors* had been second in popularity following Charnwood's *Abraham Lincoln*. Excerpts from my books or from radio programs with which I had been involved were broadcast by the Armed Forces Radio Service. During the occupation of Germany, translations of *Old Masters* and *Welch* were subsidized by the Division of Public Affairs. There was no reason for me to skulk when women stopped me in the street to ask why I was not in uniform.

*

Wandering New York, I had come to regard psychiatrists as self-important blowhards—but not Dr. Rennie! He proved to be one of the most intelligent people I had ever met. And there was no hocus-pocus. I was not laid out on a couch. We sat in chairs and conversed. He accepted without raising any issue my desire to keep utterly secret, except for my parents and Agnes, that I was receiving psychiatric treatment. He would direct me out of his office the back way when someone who might recognize me was in his waiting room.

I came to realize that Dr. Rennie was doing successfully what I had to some extent and disastrously undertaken in the autobiographical sections in my uncompleted novels: break down the doors in my mind behind which noxious matter was festering. I do not remember that he stated his own conclusions toward what emerged, although the questions he asked, the interest he displayed, steered directions. The clichés one hears about Oedipus complexes, etc., were never present. Nor, so I believe, did he either over- or underemphasize the role of sex. In making these statements I have been less than positive since the amazing thing I have to report is that, although we must have spent some fifty forty-minute hours together, I have very little conscious memory of what transpired. I suppose that he raised trauma from their hiding places, sanitized them in the sunlight and open air, and then let them fall back again, not altogether cleansed but much less sources of contagion. I certainly did not want my experiences wiped out if only because they were the material on which my biographic writing fed.

*

It was a slow process. Despite my anxieties about traveling, I needed to make weekly train journeys to New York, which I found difficult although I usually had lunch with my parents. After a year or so in our rented antique, Agnes and I bought, with the money MGM had paid for *Doctors*, an unpretentious farmhouse with two barns, one big enough to hold several farm wagons, the other containing box-stalls. Owning our own land, we decided to return to nature by growing our own vegetables. In our ignorance, we had plowed an area two or three times too large. However, our incompetence at planting saved us from glut. All that came up were cucumbers, but these in such quantity that in the dark of night we deposited piles on neighboring porches.

I undertook carpentry and chicken farming, the two coming together in my major achievement. Needing a brooder for the day-old chicks I had bought, I fashioned an extensive shallow box, the interior kept warm with an electric light bulb, and at one end a porch separated off with a curtain. It was fun to turn the inner light off and the outer one on, and watch all the chickens flock out like theater audiences after the curtain had fallen.

Most ambitious was my effort to replace two rotting outside cellar doors. Since this required cutting boards on a large scale, I appealed to an old farmer down the road who possessed a circular saw. The saw was attached to a gasoline motor by a belt so designed that if the board being passed through was not exactly straight and the saw began to bind, the belt flew off. It was then necessary to unhitch the engine, re-center the board, reattach the belt, and restart the engine. The farmer being somewhat doddery with age, this routine was called for every minute or two. Becoming embarrassed, I wondered how to let the old farmer off, but without repining or making any comment he proceeded resolutely. Eventually, after a couple of hours, the boards were cut. And well cut! They proved to fit together perfectly.

This memory has been for me a parable, becoming more apposite to my life as the years have passed. When in writing this volume I have got tangled in a passage that would once have appeared on the page almost automatically, I remember the old farmer and take heart.

27

ANATOMY OF INVENTION

*

WELL before I had finished my stint on *William Henry Welch* and married Agnes, I had determined that I would, when once again on my own, proceed with my overall scheme of bringing together short biographies of individuals who had been pioneers in one or another branch of early American culture. Invention, made by the new problems of settling a new country the typical expression of American genius, was my obvious next step. Since my labors could be grounded in the facilities of the Sterling Library, this endeavor fitted in with Agnes's and my move from New York to the countryside near Yale.

*

For me to undertake a book on invention might well be considered rash, because I had never been particularly interested in machines. If an automobile I was driving gave out on the road, and I had made sure that I had not (as was so often the case) forgotten to fill the gas tank, my only panacea was to give the engine several smart kicks. Should this not suffice, I would call a garage.

However, I had no intention of making my book a mechanical treatise. I was concerned with what I understood better: the behavior of people and the growth of ideas. I assumed that with hard study I could master the relevant mechanical principles, and I had, as a neighbor and friend, Sidney Withington, the chief electrical engineer of the New York, New Haven, & Hartford Railroad, who was historically minded and proved an invaluable adviser. To have my own ignorance conquered by lucid explanations was an ideal preparation for conquering ignorance on the part of my readers. And the result satisfied the experts. No reviewer, even in the most technical journal, has ever shaken an admonitory finger at the mechanical explanations I eventually achieved.

My obvious first step was to identify the inventions and inventors that I would join in a group biography. But the further I got in my researches, the more it became obvious that, in the American Revolutionary generation, one invention was so overshadowing that no others could be included with it. I had no choice but to direct my book exclusively at the invention of the steamboat.

Since there were three major steamboat inventors and all were American, it seemed at first that I could continue my intention of a group biography, although I would merely interweave the lives rather than lay them side by side. And I had fascinating personalities to deal with.

The earliest of my major inventors, John Fitch, proved dangerously compelling for inclusion in a multicellular book. An archtypal wild man of genius, he was born to create what would not be accepted, to fight man and God for what he considered justice, and, in the end, to destroy himself. Even as Mercutio would have overwhelmed the artistic progression of *Romeo and Juliet* had Shakespeare not killed him off in Act Three, Fitch would have torn *Steamboats* apart had he not providentially been driven to the wall and then died in the middle of the action.

The second of my protagonists, Fitch's contemporary James Rumsey, was his rival and enemy. A backwoods gambler, suave and humorous where Fitch was torrential, Rumsey was also (but how differently!) self-destroyed. As these two losers, still wrestling with each other, faded into darkness, a new champion made his entrance, self-confident, radiating his own sunlight. Robert Fulton was born to succeed. Our story of anguished pioneering ends with an able and cynical hypocrite who carries away all the stakes. Robert Fulton became rich, socially elevated, and, down through the generations, famous. The question of whether he or Fitch, who had run one steamboat faster than the *Claremont* years earlier, should be considered the inventor forced me into speculations on the basic nature of invention.

By merging the lives of my protagonists into a single narrative rising to one climax, my change in plan had obvious artistic advantages. But it frighteningly widened my stage. The subject was no longer the summation of the achievements of selected individuals. It was the entire story of one of history's major developments.

The steamboat was not one of those inventions that is inspired by the existence of technology and that, with the help of advertising, creates its own need. For the dream of self-propulsion was surely as old as man. Navigators always imagined, with fear and longing, a boat that would sail against wind and current. And steam locomotion altered a fundamental human attribute.

Through centuries, human beings had learned to supplement their legs by using other natural forces: animals, or the wind, or the current of a stream. They had learned to apply these forces to advantage through sails and wheels and levers. But always the prime movers had been supplied by man's environment; he directed the energies they gave, but did not create them out of materials that were in themselves motionless. Preceding by years the introduction of the railroad or mechanical carriage, the steamboat was indeed something new under the sun. And when this invention had been accepted, a gap was made in the dike of human inertia and fear that let through the flood waters of the Industrial Revolution, those waters that buoyed up and engulfed man, and with which we are yet struggling.

*

Even from the strictly biographical point of view, complications quickly appeared as I commenced this volume. In my previous books, secondary characters were, because that was the very reason they were inserted, automatically attached to the large biographies. But now outsiders shouldered their way into the story: I had to include many biographical accounts, long or short, of individuals who had projected or actually built steamboats before the invention was completed. Some were Europeans, which forced me to step altogether beyond the boundaries of the United States.

The proliferation of steamboat inventors was made the more difficult to handle in a consistent narrative because for the most part the projectors had no connection with each other. Almost all were self-starters. Some did not even realize that the idea of a steamboat was not altogether original with them.

This made manifest what I had already sensed in my writing about painters: the prevalence of simultaneous invention. I was faced with a phenomenon that is not adequately recognized because it is so disruptive to an orderly analysis of events. The spotlights that shine on statesmen divide and shatter. In art history, the realization that painters can think alike independently of each other plays hob with the lines of influence that are of such great concern to art historians. And the conception undermines the conventional definition of an inventor as a towering genius struck by a unique revelation.

Simultaneous invention exists because similar environments engender similar combinations in widely separated minds. Environments thus became a compelling aspect of my story. And those I had to deal with implied the entire span of history.

There were the millennia when steamboats were magic and myth, and then the centuries when men could envision possible devices that society was not ready to activate. Finally, all the components of the steamboat existed: it was only necessary to combine them. One would foresee, after such seemingly endless expectation, a quick, triumphant surge. However, for twenty-five years of anguished effort, the combination was not effectively made. Why? That is the question which haunts the body of this volume.

Behind that question lurked further imponderables. What kinds of human temperaments operate at different stages in a line of progress? Why do humans repel changes that they have since the start of history desired? What is the nature of creativity, and why is it resisted?

*

By now, so it seemed, I had enlarged my subject to a point where it could not be handled. The difficulty was increased by my unwillingness to present the material in a scholarly compilation. Determined not to compromise literary form, eager to bring everything together into an ongoing narrative that would have esthetic unity and effect, I would undoubtedly have given up in despair had it not been for a conspicuous lack in my education.

Despite the best efforts of my teachers, I could never be taught to outline a piece of writing. To this day, I no more expect to plot the development of a book in advance than I make an effort to think out the literary techniques I will employ.

I do not believe that the world's most accomplished drafter of outlines could have plotted in advance the route I had to traverse in the book I entitled *Steamboats Come True*. Yet the problem worked itself out without too much difficulty in the writing. I was operating pretty much as George Washington did (so I was much later to discover) when, as a youth, he built the road that first carried wheels across the Allegheny Mountains. Knowing his objective, which was the Forks of the Ohio (now Pittsburgh), but having by no means plotted the intervening terrain, he launched into the wilderness. We both had upon occasion to make wild detours; we both sometimes lost our way and had to return to the last spot where we were sure of our direction. But I was luckier than Washington. My advance was not stopped by an army of Frenchmen and Indians.

*

Since the invention of the steam engine and the steamboat were of such importance to our machine age; since Fulton had become an international hero; since Fitch, to prove to himself that he was not insane, had written extensive manuscripts on his personal life and his invention; since books had been published in England and France as well as America, I was offered more source material for *Steamboats Come True* than for any of its predecessors.

The all-essential Fitch Papers, as the property of the Library Company of Philadelphia, would normally inhabit the cavernous spurious Greek temple which had so frightened me when I pursued the Benjamin Rush Papers there. But the Library Company, fearing that the Germans would bomb Philadelphia, had deposited the papers in a bank vault somewhere in rural Pennsylvania. I got the librarian to agree to get them temporarily exhumed for my use, but he was lazy and, although any danger of Germans bombing Pennsylvania had been reduced to almost nothing, he kept mumbling about security. Finally, I appealed to John Frederick Lewis, a good friend powerful in Philadelphia cultural circles and prone to starting explosions.

From my isolation with Agnes on the outskirts of New Haven, I would in the mornings hopefully keep my eye on our rural free delivery letter box that stood by the roadside. The mailman was always late, as he could not resist gossiping with all who came out to get their mail. Finally arriving one morning, he came out of his car to hand me several letters. He stood there watching as I shuffled them. On one I fastened with conspicuous eagerness. My reaction, after I had torn the envelope open, was so extreme that the mailman, who was craning over my shoulder, uttered a cry of surprise.

The letter, signed by the Library Company librarian, stated that several days before he had sent the Fitch archive to me by ordinary railroad express. Would I use the enclosed receipt to pick the box up at the New Haven railroad station. The librarian added, with what might well have been sarcasm, that I would undoubtedly find it more convenient to study the papers in my own house.

My own house, built of wood in the seventeenth century! The opposite of fireproof! Even more dangerous was the fact that the invaluable and irreplaceable papers had been dispatched without any safeguards. Pushing the mailman aside, I ran to my automobile and set out at full speed for Yale's Sterling Library. I stormed without knocking into the office of the university librarian, Bernhard Knollenberg. Knolly was used to my vagaries. He grinned at me until I blurted out my errand. Then, having spoken into his telephone for a moment, he leapt up and led me at a trot to the library parking lot where a panel truck was just arriving.

Our speed to the station was phenomenal but then—stagnation. It was a hot day and the expressman was lolling in his suspenders. He glanced languidly at the receipt I handed him, and said that he reckoned there must be a shipment somewhat like that somewhere. A lotta stuff had come in. "Just look at it!" He pointed over his shoulder to a large room awash with clumsily piled boxes. Perhaps, if we would come back in a couple of days . . .

It would have been useless for Knolly to try to pull his rank as university librarian, since in New Haven town and gown did not get on. So we assiduously plagued the expressman until he decided that he could protect his hot-weather relaxation only by getting rid of us. It was with considerable anxiety that Knolly and I watched him push and peer until at last he found the box. It seemed in no way damaged. But Knolly and I did not breathe easy until we had opened it in the library vault and found the papers undamaged. I, of course, made not the slightest use of my right to take them home. And Knolly saw to it that they were returned to the Library Company in the most professional way. Since then, they have to a considerable extent been published.

As for the book I called *Steamboats Come True*, it was to engage in its own extended voyage. Published by The Viking Press in 1944, it was subsequently brought out in paperback by Collier Books, and back in hardcover by Little, Brown, and then a deluxe edition bound in leather by the Easton Press, and then another paperback by the Fordham University Press, and then on toward the twenty-first century by being recorded for audio distribution by Books on Tape.

*

The more than three-millennial voyage, from temple magic at the dawn of written history to the establishment in the nineteenth century of practical steam locomotion, took me some four hundred pages. For those who have too much wit (or are too faint of heart) to follow my voyage, I can do no more, as I conclude this chapter, than reprint the last final page:

"Now that the whole story has been told, we still face the question of who was the inventor of the steamboat. The answer, of course, depends on what you mean by 'inventor.' Since applied science has triumphed so completely that it has become the core of our culture, the word has taken on a mystical significance: inventors are the saints of our materialistic philosophy. They are conceived in popular legend as great geniuses creating something out of nothing; semi-divine individuals who, like Prometheus bringing fire down from heaven, give the world a boon altogether new. There is no such inventor in the history of the steamboat; indeed it is safe to say that there has not been a single one in the history of the world.

"As we have seen, the steamboat evolved out of the consciousnesses of many men, out of a great shift in the whole status of mankind. Not one of the many historical influences that shape changes in civilization failed to have its impact on this development. Like a herd of buffalo stampeding across a prairie, mankind moves through time in a body, and all that can be said of any one individual is that he was half a step ahead.

"The term inventor then has a meaning only if taken in the sense of a man who was slightly in advance of the procession at the crucial moment when his civilization was already on the verge of the discovery he was about to make. Like the winner of a race, he is the first individual to step over the line that separates practical invention from improved application. Before him, the discovery was still a partially realized aspiration; after him, it is a reality so well established that its use is continual, without any break.

"The inventor is not necessarily the most original or the most able or the most admirable man entered in the race; he is more likely to be a follower than a leader, since leaders usually beat their brains out against a stone wall of inertia and prejudice. The inventor's eminence may be more a trick of chronology than anything else, due to his being active at the very moment when fruition became possible. Yet the facts of history cannot be changed. The poor devils before him, however brilliant, however worthy, went down as martyrs, because the times were not ready to receive and perfect their gift. Running a course made easier by the agony of his predecessors, the inventor crosses the finish line, triumphant and smiling.

"According to this definition, popular history is correct: Robert Fulton was the inventor of the steamboat. Whether this means he was the most creative and the most useful man connected with the invention, the reader may decide for himself."

The most expansive endorsement I ever received came from that brilliant and eccentric inventor Buckminster Fuller: "You may well take pleasure and pride in the reissue of James Thomas Flexner's *Steamboats Come True*. The only thing about it is the title may be inadequate. It is more than Steamboats coming true. It is the mysterious genius and initiative of humanity being realized in a most important way in respect of survival of our species in universe."

GOD BLESS BUCKY!

28

FIRST FLOWERS

*

IN 1944, as my steamboats puffed away from me to Viking, I felt an almost evangelical urge to reintroduce to the American people the American painting of the past. I resolved to write a history that would satisfy scholars and have a wider appeal. No effective general history of American painting had been published since I was born.

Since the Civil War, what publications there had been on American art had sought out and most valued the paintings that most resembled European models. I resolved to apply to art criticism my biographer's realization that it is the human being who does the deed, and that an artist was not a snake who could shed his skin. I was to explain:

"This book is dedicated to the proposition that artists, one with the rest of humanity, express the basic philosophical conceptions of their place and time. Like plants, painters are rooted by the falling of the seed into the soil of their own generation. The dreams of the mystic, the revolts of the reformer, although more exotic growths, suck their strength from the same subterranean springs and minerals that nurture the ordinary harvest in its even rows. Individual genius makes an important contribution to the strength of an artist's vision, but personality never functions in a vacuum. The objects seen, the thoughts expressed, are all determined by the environment in which a painter functioned. Therefore it should be possible to explain early American pictures in terms of American life, and to see the world of our forefathers through the pictures they left behind them."

*

Informed of what I wished to write, the Viking Press proved amenable. As I was to do years later when I started on my biography of Washington, I stupidly failed to foresee the scope of the task I had set myself. I signed a contract which specified a history of American painting in a single volume. I was still thinking in such large terms when Yale professor Ralph Gabriel told me of a new benefaction— he was on the advisory board—"Library of Congress Grant-in-Aid for Studies in the History of American Civilization." I drew up a prospectus which seemed adequate to my then intention despite the statement that they wanted to support works with "particular reference" to the nineteenth century. I stated that, although my book would start with the first known American paintings, it would "reach its climax between 1850 and 1900." On that basis, I received a prestigious grant: $2,000 with the probability of renewal.

By the time that the grant came through, my planning had been overturned by my realization that the subtitle of *America's Old Masters*, "First Artists of the New World," although it had then been accepted with no objections, was based on a whopping fallacy. Some three generations of American artists had preceded my "Old Masters." That this phenomenon had been examined only in little parts here and there thus challenged my taste for exploring. But going back not only to the early eighteenth but on to the seventeenth century was a violation of the focus of the grant I had just received. It also made entirely clear that my commitment in the Viking contract to a single-volume history could not be realized.

I had become so habituated to following my quests wherever they led me that I was not as upset as I should have been. To seek the approval of my editor at Viking would have allowed an outsider to shatter my concentration, and Viking had so far always agreed to whatever I wanted to do. In my quarterly reports to the Library of Congress, I assumed that the validity of my explanations would be accepted as justifying my following a variant course.

It was November 1945 when I reported that I had divided my intentions into two volumes. The first, which I was currently working on, would enter the wanted nineteenth century, going on from the 1660s to 1825. But on May 1, 1946, I reported that it had become "increasingly clear that the only logical break was at the end of the

colonial period." Previously, American painting had been characterized by semi-isolation from Europe. This was not true after the Revolution, which made as great a change in art as in politics. Since it
seemed wiser "to give in to history than to try to make history give
in to you," the first volume I was working on would extend from
1660 to 1776.

*

Gasoline rationing was the order of the day during World War II.
Having to drive around to see pictures, I appealed to my local rationing board, dropping the name of the Library of Congress. When
I received a slip labeled "special war work," I would have felt more
guilty had I not known that *Doctors* and various other of my writings
were active in war work.

While Agnes and I were away, her mother came to our house
near New Haven to take care of my cats, Topsy and also Bishop
Wilberforce.* Topsy was a good citizen, a "maîtress femme," but
Wilberforce was pixilated. He could not be trusted with catnip. He
once fell into my bathtub, sticking his claws into my bare flesh to
climb out. When Agnes and I returned from our trip, he expressed
his rage at having been deserted by aiming a blow at my face. Although he missed my eye, a claw cut a gash below it which made me
look as if I had been in a major fight. The whole right side of my
face was made black and blue by interior bleeding. I was thus disfigured when I entered a room also containing Professor Gabriel. As he
hurried toward me, I assumed that he was eager to ask me, as everyone did, what I had done to my face, but he proved to be in a rage.

---

*This name had a roll to it, and I liked to explain that if I ever needed to take up
a subscription it would be an advantage to put this name at the head of my list of
sponsors. There was also the fact that a major Connecticut highway had been named
after Governor Wilber Cross. We, of course, spoke of it as the Wilberforce Highway.
As bad luck would have it, I once found myself at a party with the former governor
himself. Not realizing that he was too far along in years to follow the joke, I told
him that we claimed that he had stolen the highway from our cat. He replied, almost
tearfully, "But, Mr. Flexner, they *did* name the highway after me." He then wandered
around the room pointing at me and saying indignantly, "That man says I stole my
highway from his cat."

I had disgraced him as my sponsor by willfully violating the clear stipulation concerning the nineteenth century!*

*

Agnes and I still had many good times together but, as the years passed, I (and she also) began to feel trapped by an intimacy so interwoven that there was no room for the mystery which is an essential element of romance. In growing restlessness, Agnes got us involved with a heavy drinking set in New Haven, who became so intoxicated on Saturday nights that they met on Sunday nights for a melancholy session at sobering up. I was walking my Irish terrier some miles down the wooded road on which we lived, when I came on an automobile motionless at an angle in a ditch. Going over to investigate, I saw that the front seat was occupied by a man and a woman so passionately clasped in each other's arms that they had not heard my footsteps in the fallen leaves. As I tiptoed away, I thought to myself with inner tears that all such passion was forever behind me.

In New York City, I was wandering aimlessly around Sutton Place when my eye was caught by two or three young men in evening clothes standing beside an automobile and staring up to a raised doorway. The door opened and there appeared, radiant in the light of a street lamp, a young woman who seemed to my entranced eyes the most beautiful I had ever seen. I stood there and stared, even after she had disappeared into the automobile and it had turned off onto York Avenue. Could she really have been? But I am getting ahead of myself.

*

Agnes and I had decided that country winters, followed by the mud of melting fields in March, were too oppressive, and we had sublet for the worst months in New York City. Then my growing dependence on the Frick Art Reference Library dictated putting up for rent

---

*I was not so dashed that, some time later. as I was about to advance with a second volume into the nineteenth century, I did not try to take advantage of the original statement. "The committee will be glad to consider a second application from you at the expiration of this grant." I received the curtest possible turndown from the Library of Congress.

our house in Connecticut and moving to New York. But finding a flat in New York was easier said than done. The city was in the grip of a severe housing shortage.

I walked the streets scanning the windows of such walk-ups as we could afford for indications that an apartment was being renovated. On Eighty-third Street near East End Avenue, I made a diagnosis. Mounting three flights, I found painters at work. Having secured from them the name and address of the landlord, I explored another run-down building and was eventually told that he was inspecting a boiler in the cellar. The boiler room was dark, but there were sounds within. Groping my way, I got hold of a coattail. I pulled, extracting a very indignant small man. He spluttered away until I divulged that my name was Flexner. A onetime inhabitant of a street through which Father had daily walked to the admiration of the community, he was enchanted to rent me the apartment at 538 East Eighty-third Street, which I was to inhabit until long after Agnes had departed.

*

My trip backward into the early generations of American painting was made possible by the Frick Art Reference Library and its creator, Helen Clay Frick. The daughter of the amasser of the Frick Collection had wanted, after her father's death, to carry on his interests not by infringing on his collection with her own purchases but in her own way. She fastened on the conception of creating a vast, scholarly library of photographs of paintings. She sought them from all over the Western world. Fortunately for me, she did not scorn American art, sending out photographing tours through state after state. Furthermore, she resolved to go in the opposite direction from her father who had gathered in what was accepted as the best. To use her own phrase, she collected "en masse." Had she applied any fashionable taste she would have dragged her photographers away from most of the unsophisticated portraits created in early America. In 1944, when I started on my history, the Frick had 38,000 reproductions of American painting. Add to this that the library housed almost every publication that would prove useful for my studies.*

---

*When in 1979 the Archives of American Art of the Smithsonian Institution celebrated its twenty-fifth anniversary by giving awards to pioneers like myself, I urged that Miss Frick be included. But to give an award to a multimillionairess, whose father had been a notorious union buster, was beyond their philosophy.

My perpetual presence at the Frick required legerdemain on the part of the staff. As creator and sole supporter, Miss Frick applied her dictatorial power to small matters as well as large, and the indulgences I sought were sure not to fit in. The front door of the library was locked by command until ten in the morning and again at four in the afternoon, although the staff was there from nine to five. The shorter period was incompatible with my drive and energy. A second problem was that the Frick supplied no facility for typing.

Fortunately, the head librarian had developed a technique. At some moment when the dictator's mind was well occupied with something else, Miss Manning would inconspicuously slip in a request and Miss Frick would agree seemingly without thinking. It is my guess that, being as intelligent as she was self-willed, Miss Frick was glad to have reasonable things done behind her back without forcing her to abandon a rule she had laid down. But one could never be sure.

Allowed to use the staff entrance and to occupy with my typewriter a cubicle officially reserved for staff use, I was warned that should I, as I arrived early, see Miss Frick's limousine drive up to the door, I should walk around the block. As long as the limousine was parked outside, I should be cautious, and in any case should always use the stairs between the reading room and the forbidden floor above, where I could secretly type. Miss Frick used the elevator. I saw her around— she was a small, birdlike, very energetic woman with white hair sticking out from under the hat she wore indoors as well as out— but I had only one run-in with her.

As I was correctly passing a floor devoted to stacks, the elevator door opened revealing Miss Frick and a party including Sir Osbert Sitwell. I offered to step off to make room. When Miss Frick nodded imperviously, Sir Osbert saw an opportunity to show that a British gentleman was more democratic than an American millionairess. He objected to displacing a scholar—Miss Frick's group could easily wait—and when Miss Frick only looked annoyed, he unctiously apologized to me. I was a little worried as I stepped out, but had faith that Miss Frick was too intelligent to blame me. That was the case.

The extent to which the Frick staff cooperated with me was revealed when they reclassified at my suggestion a whole file of their photograph catalogue. American portraits that could not be safely attributed to any artist were grouped together under "American School." Particularly for the earliest period, when almost no attribution was possible, this presented me with a sea of photographs to search through. Recognizing the problem, they refiled all the anonymous pictures under place of origin and in chronological spans. If I got wind of an important but unrecorded picture which my poor health made it impossible for me to visit, they would send out their photography team.

*

Early American portraits, however crude they might seem to later eyes, had been preserved by descendants for dynastic reasons. This was a quiet domestic process until at the end of the nineteenth century a frenzy developed among the white Anglo-Saxon Protestants to set themselves off from the new immigrants who were pouring in from eastern Europe. The best visible talismen were "ancestor portraits" even if they were not exactly of your own ancestors. A brisk market for such pictures was thus created, but how was it to be supplied?

It simplified the situation that almost no authentic criteria had been established for assigning seventeenth- and many eighteenth-century American portraits to any specific sitter or artist. It became an accepted rule that if an "ancestor portrait" was signed with the name of an artist who could be found in a provincial record, and was accompanied by a certificate from some presumptive member of an old family, its validity had been proved. Clever crooks who imported third-rate pictures that were dirt cheap abroad did not find these criteria too difficult to fake. Thus, there appeared on the market, along with authentic pictures, a mélange of European junk. The fakes not only had been bought by the snobbish but had been accepted by collectors and museum curators.

The cat had come out of the bag by first a paw and then a tail by the time I came along, but confusion had by no means subsided. How to separate the sheep from the goats? One problem was that, since absolute standards had not been established, anyone who published a positive negative was in danger of suit for libel from crooked dealers. Information was passed by non-actionable words of mouth, and fortunately I was given a head start by being in contact with those who were best informed.

My problems were greatly simplified by my complete unconcern with merchandising or defending purchases, or with any need to serve genealogical pressures. My basic task was determining whether the picture was not a phony import but an actual expression of the region where it was said to have been discovered. The specific identity of the sitter was usually of no importance to me. I could approximate date by costume. I did not need to identify an artist's name to bring together what I judged to be the output of the same hand. To identify the results I created appellations: the "Pollard Limner," the "De Peyster Marner," etc. I had reason to bless Berenson for encouraging me to rest attribution so much on "eye," since for the first sixty years of my study I usually had little more to go on. Even if an artist obligingly supplied a name and I had some biographical facts and even a key picture or two, to go further I relied again on eye. As for the thicket of frauds, it extended, although becoming increasingly penetrable, until beyond the time span of my present volume: the phony that finally blew the whistle was a fake Stuart *Washington*.

*

I was, of course, not alone in my labors. I was assisted by Louisa Dresser's magisterial catalogue of seventeenth-century New England painting, by less reliable publications of antiquarian genealogists, by dealers, and, above all, by my friendship with Sawitzky.

William (Vaseli) Sawitzky had been born in Latvia and trained as an ornithologist. Reaching America, he became fascinated with American art. By applying the scientific exactitude of his ornithological studies, he became the much-needed savior, viewed with admiration and awe by bewildered scholars, curators, and collectors. The Carnegie Foundation gave him a grant to clean out the Augean stable.

As will be recalled, he protected *America's Old Masters* from a developing mass of puny arrows. I had become a personal friend. In his late sixties, he was a fierce-looking man, with a very high forehead, an extensive lower face, and a jutting chin. His eyes glowed with unusual intensity because his movements were impeded by emphysema which forced him to stop every few steps and gasp for breath.

In 1942, Sawitzky brought out the first fruit of his grant, a book on West's pupil Matthew Pratt which corrected a wide range of mis-attributions. Tragically, this publication ran afoul of Alan Burroughs.

An x-ray expert attached to the Fogg Art Museum at Harvard, Burroughs had sold to the university press a book called *Limners and Likenesses*. However, the academic world was so isolated from the study of American painting that Burroughs was not informed, before his book was ready for distribution, that many of the paintings on which he had based his conclusions were in fact fakes.

Probably because American art seemed to them of no importance, the press refused to postpone the book for revision. His work thus scuttled, Burroughs was eager for revenge.

Using his academic connections to secure access to the august *Art Bulletin*, he scrutinized Sawitzky's text in a search for minor errors, and based a scathing review altogether on whatever he had been able to find. Instead of shrugging this nitpicking off as he made notes for future corrections, Sawitzky, as a perfectionist, felt deeply humiliated. He was driven to such checking and rechecking that he advanced with tragic slowness on what was to be his next publication, *Ralph Earl*.

It was the then accepted format, based on genealogical interest, that the discussion of every portrait had to be accompanied by a biography of the sitter. This got Sawitzky bogged down: Earl was prolific and many of his sitters obscure. I argued that his important contribution was attribution and discussion of the paintings—let the sitter-biographies go to Hades! But he felt that this would be an admission of defeat. This engendered a continual postponement which resulted in the withdrawal of his Carnegie grant.

However, Sawitzky was persuaded to give a course of fifteen lectures at the New-York Historical Society. Had a bomb been dropped in the auditorium, the whole generation of students of early American art would have been exterminated. However, in his perfectionism he refused to let his lectures be published. He died without revising them or finishing his book on Earl. His widow refused to release the lectures.

I was thus placed in a quandary. It would be impossible for me to separate off what I had learned from Sawitsky or contributed myself during our long conversations; or determine what I would have discovered for myself had Sawitzky not told me. And I had an obligation to make my book as informative as I could. All I could do, beyond specific source references, was to dwell in my text on the greatness of Sawitzky's influence and achievements, express gratitude for his assistance, and friendship. This I continued to do in my publications whenever an opportunity arose. When, in 1955, I dedicated my volume on Gilbert Stuart to Sawitzky's memory, his widow wrote me, "more than anyone else, including myself, you have kept the memory of his scholarship alive." I must have carried some sense of guilt or I would not have been so gratified.

*

I included a chapter in which I showed that the artists often advertised "painting in all its branches." But it was clear that, as artisans, they often meant not easel landscapes, genre, or historical painting, but signs, decorative paintings on fireboards, coaches, etc. Whatever less utilitarian canvases they did produce were not likely to have survived the ravages of housewives cleaning up attics who could see no reasons for cluttering things up with canvases that seemed of no interest and were shedding paint like chickens in molt. Yet I was able to find some very interesting pictures.

In the inventories of artists' estates, portraits were given by far the highest valuations. That this was the major concern offered a particularly direct insight into early American mores. Forced to please not only himself but also his sitters (to say nothing of their sisters and their cousins and their aunts), the portraitist was tied by a stout rope to the social demands of his generation. To see the physical peculiarities of our forebears would have been interesting, but it was even more interesting to learn from old canvases how they wished to be presented to the world.

*

Destiny began the panorama of American art with a portrait of such charm as was not to be achieved again on these shores for almost a century. *Mrs. Freake and Baby Mary* (ca. 1674) was an anachronism with a long tradition behind it, a hangover from medieval practice that still survived in the English backcountry from which the first settlers of Boston came. That neither weight nor depth is expressed creates the floating quality of a dream. A young mother, beautifully dressed in lace and an embroidered gown, looks at us gently from an uncharacterized face that might be the face of all mothers. The baby is a perfect little doll who never screams or sickens. Mother and baby reach out to each other in an allegory of happy motherhood.

But this static manner could not survive on the long seaboard where ships were perpetually landing people. Up and down the continent there appeared offshoots of the international court style inspired by Van Dyck. Since, in all Western European societies except Holland, a position in the world was determined by inherited rank, the emphasis was more on elegance of pose, costume, and setting than personal traits. One might expect that this would be repudiated by the American settlers who had crossed the ocean as individuals and were making their own way. But they had come to America to establish, not a novel society, but one differing from the old only by the opportunity for them themselves to rise to the top.

The portrait painters themselves, affected by the new environment, stood before sitters who had unconsciously responded to inner and outer forces not in keeping with the images they demanded. The quality of the pictures increased with lack of social pretension. This was not only because of confused sincerity and conviction, but also because the models for the international aristocratic style, available in the form of engravings, were much too complicated to be grateful for the artisan painters. By and large, the most successful portraits during the first century served not social but documentary ends. There is the fascinating rendition (1721) of Ann Pollard, who claimed to be over a hundred years old and to have been the very first settler of New England, because "as a romping girl," she had leapt from the ship onto Boston Neck. The whole canvas is an exercise in geometry: the twin triangles of the collar state a theme that is repeated in every detail. Bad painting serves the artist's ends as much as good: that Mrs. Pollard's far cheek is given too much roundness creates a sharp triangle that completes the design. Leaving visual realism behind, the artist produced the most realistic picture of his time and place. However, the Pollard limmer's ordinary protraiture carries no conviction.

Painting in New York was a fortunate exception due to a different European background. Although New Amsterdam fell to the British in 1664, its fundamental Dutch character was too deeply engrained to be extirpated. And Holland was Europe's one middle-class nation.

Serving a self-made population, its portraiture stressed not social status but individual personality. The likeness painted in New Amsterdam of the crusty Governor Peter Stuyvesant shows one side of his mouth pulled up and one eye partially closed in an expression of fierce disapproval.

As engravings and influence came in from England, the literalness of the Dutch painters vanished but not their integrity of approach. During the 1720s there appeared in the Hudson River Valley what I identified as the earliest school of American artists. I labeled it "the Patroon Painters." While accepting the iconography of the international court style, they simplified technique to what they could completely master. Sincerely and without self-consciousness they juxtaposed flat masses into designs that had inner validity. Colors became lyrical hues used broadly. The mood of the painters was innocence and joy. The rainbow's end seemed, to those who had prospered here, to have been discovered in their burgeoning land.

*

Entering the second quarter of the eighteenth century, I came on the precursors of West and Copley, men whom I had dealt with quickly in *America's Old Masters* but now discussed at greater length and in their own right. Then on to West and Copley viewed from the point of view of their work rather than biography. The book ended with Copley's sailing for England in 1774.

I devoted to West's and Copley's American years almost the same amount of space as I had in *America's Old Masters*. In the succeeding volume of my history I was to deal, for a second time, with the remaining two-thirds of West's career, with half of Copley's, and all of Peale's and Stuart's. How did it happen that, to the best of my memory, I was never attacked for being repetitive?

I was saved, I believe, in this and other situations* by my aiming narratives directly at my objectives. *Old Masters*, being a compendium of biographies, I dealt with the paintings as major evidence for the understanding of each creator. Now my overriding concern was

---

*I was to recount four times—in *The Traitor and the Spy*, the long and the short *Washington*s, and *The Young Hamilton*—the stirring drama that at Washington's headquarters accompanied the discovery of Arnold's treason.

with art and its reflection of society. The difference between these two approaches altered length, emphasis, pace, sequence, background, interpretation. Furthermore, I had perpetually in mind the need for freshness. I sought different leads, different scenes to dramatize, different metaphors, alternative quotations from documents. This variety enhanced my own interest as I hoped it would my readers'.

*

As I prepared the book, which I came to call *First Flowers of Our Wilderness*, I was faced with the quandary of following two contradictory purposes. One was my almost evangelistic mission to overturn the lethargy, even scorn, of the American people toward their own art. The desire to create a text that would attract readers at large also served my literary intentions and ambition. But, as I was (particularly in the first half of the book) pioneering on murky ground, it was necessary to include detailed justifications that would repel all but specialists and also play hob with my literary effects. The best solution I could puzzle out was to establish, between the main text and the conventional back matter, a separate section of "notes" that came to occupy forty-five pages.

When the time came for me to prepare the manuscript to go to Viking, making sure that everything was legible and that all the pages were there and in proper order, my troubles with the Library of Congress came to the front of my mind, raising qualms that I should have felt much sooner. Viking had contracted for a complete history. How would they react at receiving a volume extending only to the Revolution and implying further volumes?

Enter a letter from my longtime editor and presumed friend Marshall Best. Not content with stating that the book did not follow my contract, which called for a complete history, he stated that they had shown the manuscript to a well-known painter and art historian who had said that if it were published it would destroy my reputation forever. This was an attack which would well destroy a writer who had put his best for two years into the manuscript.

Not immediately, but soon after, during an opening at the Whitney Museum, Walter Peas, a distinguished painter and writer who fitted in with Best's description, walked over to me and said that my book

had been submitted to him by Viking, that he had been greatly interested, and had urged its publication, he feared, vainly.

But I had not had to wait long. As I was reading Best's letter, I
knew that I had a fail-safe that might make Viking's turndown to
my advantage. Egged on by Esther Forbes, the novelist who had won
a Pulitzer Prize in History for her biography of Paul Revere, Lovell
Thompson, the director of trade books at Houghton Mifflin, had
been mourning my contract with Viking and wishing that some way
could be found to break away so that he could publish the book. I
had hardly finished reading Best's letter when I was on the phone
with Lovell in Boston. "I think," I said, "that I can get my book
away from Viking." Lovell cheerily urged me to put the manuscript
instantly in the mail, and within forty-eight hours he was on the
phone complaining that it had not yet arrived.

Houghton Mifflin was soon boiling with enthusiasm. Lowell wrote
me, "*First Flowers* will be one of the really exciting books we have
published, and we are very proud." In addition to agreeing to a
handsome advance, they awarded me their Life in America Prize
(administered by Esther Forbes) of $2,300.

I seemed to be out of the woods, but who knows where an un-
walked path will lead.

29

BREAKUP

*

AGNES having no Frick Art Reference or anything absorbing to do, having exchanged a substantial house with resources and groups of friends for local isolation in a narrow walkup, had a major change of heart. She resolved no longer to focus on her relationship with me, but to become a career woman in her own right. Her suggestion was that she and I should find separate apartments in the same building where we could keep in close touch, but pay no attention to each other's activities, comings, and goings. This would have been, under the circumstances so long developed, impossible for me.

Agnes soon arranged to walk out of our apartment and live, at least temporarily, with her brother, but at my dismay she abandoned the idea. Another plan we did carry through. She would join some friends in New Mexico for three months. As I wrote my sister-in-law, "A major objective was to break by absolute necessity my continued dependence on her presence which she had, in the early years of our marriage, so fostered, but which she had come to find unbearably confining. It was agreed that I would not descend upon her in New Mexico or even call her on the telephone, but I could write her (as I did daily) as long as my letters were absolutely self-controlled, containing (although I could say that I missed her) no lugubrious self-pity or request for pity. I absolutely struck by the rules. But there was no rule against love letters."

Agnes was to come to her own conclusions as to how we should reorganize our marriage, and return to New York at the end of three months. We would then work things out. There was no mention of divorce.

I saw her off at Grand Central Station and was walking disconsolately home through Central Park when I heard someone call my name. It proved to be an old friend of whom I had seen little as she and Agnes could not get on. Informed that Agnes was not around, she said, "I'm giving a cocktail party this afternoon."

As I entered the door, I saw standing before me a resplendent beauty who might well have been the girl I had observed setting out from Sutton Place. She was accompanied by a fat Frenchman to whom I took an immediate dislike until he looked at his watch and departed. Courtesy dictated that I take Beatrice Hudson out for dinner. She told me that she had lived on Sutton Place.

Although she gave me her telephone number, I could hardly believe that so ravishing a creature would remember our chance meeting. I was greatly relieved to have the woman who answered the phone— it proved to be her mother—say, "Oh, you're the man who has a cat who talks with a southern accent." Beatrice clearly had not forgotten. And she agreed to meet me for lunch.

Looking back, it seems surprising that I did not feel impelled to invite so fine a bird to some fine place. Instead, I invited her to Joe's, an unpretentious restaurant on Third Avenue which I frequented. (Had I had the wisdom of a serpent I could not have done better as she was bored by men who felt that they needed to make an impression by "putting on the dog.") However, when I waiting at Joe's, a sense of incongruousness swept over me, and I felt sure that she would never appear. Of course, she was late (she was *always* late), but at last I saw her coming through the door, looking, it seemed to me, even more ravishing. She was stylishly dressed, wearing furs, a hat, and gloves. However, as she sat down beside me, she did not seem out of place since she was fundamentally what she was and Joe's was fundamentally what it was. We got on famously, greatly enjoying each other's company. After that, we saw each other with reasonable frequency. But we both thought of me as a husband eagerly awaiting the return of his wife, and behaved accordingly.

*

When the three months of separation were nearing an end, Agnes wrote me that the friends with whom she had been staying were leaving Albuquerque and that, before she came home, she would do a little exploring, by automobile, of New Mexico. She would send me the license number of the car and her itinerary. But when I went to my letter box the next day there was no communication. And the following day, and the day after that. On the morning of July 9, I wrote to the last address she had given me to repeat that I had received no letter. "I do hope you are all right." Maybe I'll get a telegram saying that she was safe back in Albuquerque. In a postscript I said that I had waiting around for the late morning and then the afternoon mail but still nothing. "I can visualize heaven these days. It is a white air-mail envelope with an address on it in your writing. If I knew what gods to pray to, I'd pray that you are all right."

I could not believe that Agnes had voluntarily not written. She knew too well my haunting fear: my pathological terror that my world would vanish. She must have suffered a dreadful accident. Sometimes it seemed that such news would be less wounding than to have her just disappear.

Dr. Rennie saw in the situation so much danger that he strained his schedule to see me not only on my weekly appointment but every day.

*

Eventually there was a ring on my doorbell, a voice calling my name from downstairs. I dashed down the three flights. A postal messenger stood in the dingy front hall. He handed me a registered letter addressed in Agnes's handwriting. I had first to sign the receipt. Evidence of how convulsively I then opened the letter remains: only a corner of the envelope is torn. I extracted a single sheet of paper written on both sides.

"Dear Jimmie," it began. "I can't come back to you. . . . The time for debate is over." Her efforts to persuade herself to make another try had been "catastrophic. . . . I wanted too much to please you and did not know when to take a stand for myself . . . become mistress of myself. . . . I beg you not to punish me by letting yourself be *very* wretched and making it appear to yourself or me or to others that I have let you down. I would indeed have let you down, damaged you perhaps irrevocably, if I had stayed with you and continued to go to pieces." She described herself as my "very loving friend," accused me of having tried to "own me entirely," said I could communicate to her through her mother, and gave me the name and address of her lawyer.

I had a date with Beatrice that night. One can easily imagine how a romantic novelist would dramatize this situation. Beatrice is waiting in her sitting room routinely as I dash in, my face working with emotion. I stammer out my news demanding sympathy, and this as a friend she does her best to give. But in both of us there is an opposite drive, the realization that the walls have fallen down, there is nothing now to keep us apart. The orchestra—I have changed to grand opera—revels in both motifs, appearing alternately louder and softer, opposing each other, merging together, leaping apart, returning again until at last all is harmony. And, as the curtain drops, Beatrice and I fall into each other's arms.

What actually happened is that, having mounted the stairs to my apartment in shock and sorrow, I called Beatrice on the telephone, giving some trumped-up excuse for being unable to see her that night.

I got in touch with Agnes's mother, who had down the years of my marriage become my very good friend. I did not ask whether she knew where Agnes was; nor did she volunteer any information. But she did not hide her strong disapproval of what her daughter had done. Recognizing that I was in a very bad state of mind, she felt it her duty to pick up the pieces. For the next month or so she was my sustaining companion, even staying with me for a little while in the cabin on the seashore I had rented for Agnes's return.

*

In mid-July, Agnes arranged through her mother to come—my absence having been stipulated—to our old apartment to pick up some of her possessions. She left a little note, the first communication I had received from her. I replied that it had "moved me deeply. Topsy's [the cat with the southern accent] fur was soon wet with tears— perhaps for the second time in a few hours. (She did not catch cold.)

"That it has taken me more than a week to answer your letter is not a sign of lack of desire to communicate with you, but of too much desire. I have so much to say, and I may say so little. That I

[286]

miss you from the bottom of my heart, you must suspect; that my emotions, which have been over-emphasized so long, must now be ignored, I know.

"I could write you a hundred pages, so much has happened that cries to be shared with my girl. I suppose I should think of you as my girl no longer—God knows I have tried!—but love and hope die hard. I still love you, but I know there is nothing I can do about my love for you at the moment except try to have it inspire me to the most perceptive kindness of which I am capable. . . .

"The candle still burns in the window—the door is on the latch. If you ever decide to return, Topsy and I will greet you with tears of joy, and a little grey ghost [another cat who had died in her absence], hovering overhead, will purr until he almost chokes. But I do not urge you to return. If you ever do so, it must be altogether at your own volition.

"Indeed, I would not want to re-live the last few years. We must only re-establish our marriage if both of us can enter into it with a new spirit. You have not given me a chance to show you what I accomplished in three months of vigorous self-discipline while you were in New Mexico. Since then, the need for self-discipline has become even greater. I tried, while you were in New York, to behave exactly as I guessed you wanted me to behave. If I did anything wrong, it was because—or so I believe—lack of communication with you kept me from knowing what you wanted.

"Perhaps when you get back to New York you will feel strong enough to have some dates with me, to let me chase you in your old role of a seductive and uncaptured virgin. I would like to discover whether my hand has lost its skill. But this too is altogether up to you. I will not pester you.

"Don't feel any necessity to make any comment now on the above—there are years before us, and time is a great resolver of confusions. But should you care to drop me a gossipy line, I should be glad to receive it."

In another letter, I urged, "We cannot reach any conclusion intelligently until we have a chance to talk to each other. The determining factors in this situation are our mutual states of mind—there are no issues between us that are not psychological—and I submit that we are in complete ignorance about each other's state of mind. I believe that I myself have been greatly changed."

Agnes replied that she hoped "eventually," after the divorce, to "see you often and hear about your work and all you are doing. . . . Since you are still the most important thing in my life, it would hardly be expected that I would stop suddenly being on your team." She needed money not only at once, but an allowance that would prevent her from being forced to take a job that she would not do well because it would not match her interests. "So, pip pip, and love, Aggie."

*

I came to understand that her objective had not been to ameliorate my behavior or seek a compromise, but to push me aside as an obstacle to her making herself over into an up-to-date career woman. That she had felt this need was understandable and forgivable, but how had she gone about it? Although I had abided strictly by the rules during our separation, she had consulted a divorce lawyer without giving even a hint, in our voluminous correspondence, that she might not return. Then she had chosen to make the break by using knowledge gathered during our long relationship to hurt me the most. All she would have had to do as she set out on her motor trip was to scratch a line saying that I should not expect to hear from her for a while. She knew exactly what her disappearance would do to me. Rightly or wrongly (although we eventually established agreeable relations), I was never able completely to forgive her.

30

BEATRICE AND NELLIE

*

BEATRICE had been away from New York during the summer months when Agnes had so determinedly repudiated me. By the time Beatrice had reappeared, all impediments that had stood between us were down. Love sprung up like a fire smothered under debris now opened to the sky.

Dr. Rennie had warned me against getting involved with another woman on the rebound. He studied the photographs I had brought along of Beatrice intently for a good quarter of an hour. Then he asked me many minute questions. A couple of sessions later, he said that he considered it no longer necessary to continue. Although I was not altogether cured, I could proceed on my own, without any crippling or too grievous distress.

Rennie had undoubtedly taken seriously the profound difference between my relationship with Agnes and that which was growing up with Beatrice. Where Agnes had encouraged me to be dependent on her, the much younger Beatrice—twelve years my junior—who had been tossed around by the world, was drawn to me, with loving admiration, by what she considered was my strength to create for her a happy life and a safe haven.

*

Beatrice was exotic, not incongruous within my previous environment. She had gone to the "best" girls' schools: Brearley (where my first cousin, Millicent McIntosh, was headmistress) and then Chapin.

However, her mother, Lotus Robb, had been a successful actress, having played the ingenue in Theatre Guild productions, and opposite George Arlis in *The Green Goddess*. Beatrice's father had also been an actor. They both had deserted the stage: Robert Hudson to become one of the most beloved habitués at the bar of the Players Club, and Lotus to marry a very rich man. Beatrice was an only child.

Beyond conventional schooling, Lotus's desire had been to expose her daughter to the very best. As a medium-sized girl, Beatrice studied the harpsichord with Wanda Landowska. Her tutor in French literature was Clara Berman, who also instructed the Rockefeller boys. Lotus taught her daughter that culture was centered in Europe, which might seem an augury for trouble between us, but may have made things easier because of my need to keep my writing separate from my daily life. We were to enjoy many European trips together, during which I profited much from her knowledge and taste.

Lotus, having divorced her millionaire, quickly squandered a munificent settlement, and married, as a third husband, Marvin Ross, an historian of medieval art. Fascinated with her somewhat younger new husband, she had left her beautiful daughter, who was then eighteen, more or less adrift.

Not sent to college, Beatrice took private lessons in piano and voice. She did make a stab at theater, appearing in the great hit musical *One Touch of Venus*, but she lacked the sharp elbows needed for success on either the theatrical or the concert stage.

Instinctively, she and I never sought details concerning each other's previous lives. Beatrice never tried to find out where my marriage with Agnes had gone wrong. I silenced all gossips who wanted to inform me about Beatrice's earlier years. It became manifest, however, that these years—lived as a tremendously attractive, gentle, young woman left by herself in the rough and tumble of New York— had not been tranquil and without adventure. It was also clear that she had been disturbed and unhappy: a Catholic priest sustained her for a while as father confessor, and she had as friend and sanctuary a young actor who was safe for her because he had no sexual interest in women. But he had his own problems with alcohol. The bottle had been the bane of the world in which she moved—Diana Barrymore was her close friend—which was plagued by suicides. This was a much more lurid world than I had ever experienced.

The amazing aspect was that Beatrice had not been, to the smallest degree, corrupted or hardened. She was, indeed, purified by a determination never to summon up again those dark years. Alcohol she held in control. During all the years of our marriage, my beautiful younger wife never gave any true cause for jealousy.

*

That while I was still married I was visibly separated from Agnes and often seen in the company of so alluring a younger woman stirred up gossip. The obvious conclusion that Beatrice was breaking up Agnes's marriage seems to have been battled by Agnes herself, who wanted to be regarded as a pioneering career woman, not a jilted housewife. I did, of course, come in for some criticism. It came mostly from couples unhappily married. What was their motivation? Was it outrage that I was betraying a difficult cause, or just plain envy?

Beatrice's mother, now feeling a responsibility to keep an eye on her daughter, was sharing an apartment with her, although she wished she could spend all her time with her husband in Baltimore who was a curator at the Walters Art Gallery. While expressing regret that I was legally married to someone else, Lotus soon decided to entrust her daughter to me. On our own, we preserved all visible proprieties. Renting out part of her apartment (she was thus to acquire her lifelong best friend, Vincent Youmans's daughter Cecily), Beatrice held on there. My apartment was inhabited by Topsy, the family cat Agnes had left behind. I liked, in later years, to attribute my subsequent remarriage altogether to the cat who, so I said, had looked over the girls I brought home and decided which one she wanted: "I never had a chance." But actually I never brought another girl home.

For country outings, we frequented an inn at Tyringham in the Berkshires. It was owned by a rich couple who, I concluded, kept it as a tax dodge since, although they welcomed Beatrice and me, there were rarely other occupants. We, of course, had occupied separate rooms. When we later arrived there for our honeymoon, our hosts made a little ceremony out of ushering us into a common bedroom that they had festooned with flowers.

*

The Christmas season of 1948–1949 had seemed to us to have been
especially created to celebrate our getting together. I remember the
excitement of riding, with her beside me, in a taxi down Park Avenue
between the decorative lights, all the more delightful because Agnes
and I had so parsimoniously avoided taking cabs that I had not even
realized that a light on the roof signaled that the taxi was empty.

Once, while Beatrice still had a chance to escape, I did reveal to
her my crassness. She had a phobia about putting on weight. As we
drove along on country outings she would get me to stop the car so
that she could go into a drugstore and stick a coin into the scales.
On one occasion, she jumped backward as if a snake had bitten her:
the needle was rising, higher and higher. When she discovered that I
had put my foot on the scales she was outraged, but we often laughingly rehearse the incident as an example of our camraderie.

In one direction Beatrice was incredibly naïve. For all of her knowledge of the capitals of Europe, the opera houses, the fine hotels and
restaurants, she had never been in any countryside that was not part
of an ornamental garden. I was able to reassure her in the presence
of a cow, to show her how to follow a trail through underbrush, to
help her cross a mountain stream on rocks and fallen trees. Her
delight in the succession of new discoveries made me think of Daniel
Boone entering for the first time the Ohio Valley. In this manifestation, I called her "the brave Daniella."

*

It was during the Christmas season, after Agnes's departure from
New York, that Beatrice and I acknowledged what we already knew:
we wanted to get married. One midnight we made a gleeful ceremony
out of carrying a letter to Beatrice's mother—we could have telephoned or stuck it in a letter box—downtown to New York City's
central post office with its grand three-storey columns. I had only
slight qualms for fear that Agnes, who had so insisted that she wanted
a divorce, might reneg since her pursuit of a career was not going
well. But she agreed to go where the law made divorce easy—the
Virgin Islands—and since there were no children involved, we had
no quarrel over terms. She received a sizable but not unreasonable

lump sum and small payments for five years to help her get started on a career that suited her, and the house in the country with all that had been left there when we had moved to New York.

On August 2, 1950, Beatrice and I were married by a judge in a municipal court. Now we could openly live together. My walk-up on Eighty-fourth Street was too convenient and cheap to be sacrificed, but Beatrice did not want to move in exactly where I had lived with Agnes.

I had a penchant for top floors since no one could stamp over your head, and the top floor had become vacant. We moved upstairs into an identical apartment.

The excitement of Beatrice's official arrival was dangling her huge grand piano—the second-largest size made—from the roof and maneuvering it into the narrow tenement window. It made itself at home, almost filling the alcove in our front room of the "railroad flat," and the number of doors that could be closed along the narrow interior hall which paralleled the stairs enabled me to write quietly in the again expanded back room while she thundered away.

*

If some unfortunate soul should someday decide to write my biography, he will be startled to find that there does not exist a single letter between Beatrice and me. I can see his eyes beginning to glow. For what dread reason did we destroy all our correspondence? I can visualize him whiffling around in other papers for hints of discord. He would eventually come to realize that he could find no letters because none had ever existed. Beatrice and I were never far enough and long enough apart—Beatrice visiting her mother in Baltimore or Washington; my giving a lecture or doing research or looking in on the shooting of one of my television shows—to summon up letters. We kept in touch daily by telephone.

It would be fatuous to assert that in the forty-five years between our marriage ceremony and this burst on the typewriter everything always went smoothly. There were, of course seasons and explosions of discord, chronic disagreements, and temporary fallings out. Once, the situation did become so heated that we decided to have recourse to outside help. Beatrice consulted her general practitioner, and he referred us to a team of matrimonial advisers: a woman for her and a man for me. After several separate sessions, all four of us got together. At some remark of mine, Beatrice sprang up to leave. If we had been by ourselves, I would have intercepted her, but our advisers did not move, and she was gone. I then rose and departed, fearing that all was lost. My route home was by Madison Avenue bus, changing at Eighty-sixth Street for the cross-town. Beatrice had not even gone home: she was waiting for me at the crossing. We were through forever with outside counseling. We are, as this is being written, advancing into the twilight and darkness of old age, hand in hand.

*

In 1952, after we had been married for two-and-a-half years, Beatrice became pregnant. This dictated, since we were up three flights of steep stairs, that we abandon our apartment and find one, within our budget, served by an elevator. After considerable searching, we were forced to accept what I remember as a monster, as it was a square, cut up into four rooms whose edges met in the middle. No possibility for me to write at home while Beatrice was playing her piano or a baby was howling.

Beatrice, so we were to discover, had got dates confused, since the birth became imminent some two weeks before schedule. Our obstetrician announced that this proved what he had guessed: we would have twins. And my mother-in-law was furious, suspecting that she had been given the wrong date to keep her from being present. Beatrice herself, when the moment came for her to set out for the hospital, sat on her bed polishing her toenails and stating, "This is our time; nobody can hurry me."

We did get in time to the hospital and a private room. As she was being wheeled to the delivery room, the doctor assured me that as soon as the baby was safely born, I would be notified, and it would be some time before Beatrice reappeared.

Time passed, and more time passed. I began pacing the hall always within sound should my telephone ring. Eventually I met a Catholic friend who was a veteran as he did not believe in birth control. Stating that doctors often forgot and that he knew from experience what to do, he led me to his room and gave me a stiff drink of whiskey.

Beatrice, when she reappeared, brought with her the news that we had had a daughter.

At one end of the hall, the hospital had a sort of a stage behind a plate-glass window on which the newborn babies made their utterly sanitary debut. Outside was a cluster of adults saying "Couchee-couchee," "Isn't he sweet!" etc. As for my daughter, she was demonstrating that, having no fear, she could by widely opening her mouth, cut her hand almost in half.

We named her dynastically Helen Hudson Flexner. However, "Helen," which had so suited my mother, with her soft southern charm, proved unsuited to our energetic daughter. She chose to be called by the nickname Nellie. Although she told me that she raised a certain amount of hell at the Chapin School, she demonstrated so much tact within our family circle in getting her own way that I have no memory of any ructions. At Brown University, to our extreme amazement, as she had never shown any religious interests, she majored in Comparative Religions. She explained that she wanted to ascertain what people believed and why.

During her summer vacations, I secured for her fill-in jobs with publishers. How things have changed! The best opportunity for females were then in publicity. Not realizing that I was throwing a fish into the water, I found openings for her in public relations.

After graduating in 1975, Nellie got a job in the publicity department at Dial Press. There she met Adrian Desmond, a British science historian in America to publicize his first book, *The Hot-Blooded Dinosaurs*. In 1977, she moved to England with him. She started her publishing career in London at Victor Gollancz Ltd as an editorial assistant; ten years later, she became publicity and marketing director. In 1990, she and Adrian had a son, Harry Flexner Desmond. Adrian was just finishing his award-winning biography of Charles Darwin, and Nellie was Publicity and Marketing Director at Michael Joseph, a hardback imprint of Penguin Books. They now live in the country outside London in a house with five acres of woods for Harry to roam in. Nellie continues her job part-time, and Adrian is writing the second volume of a biography of T. H. Huxley.

31

SEESAW

*

DURING my honeymoon with Houghton Mifflin, which began in 1945, Van Wyck Brooks's succession of volumes on American literature were eating up praise and selling heavily. Lovell Thompson and Esther Forbes, dragging along the editor-in-chief Paul Brooks, decided that they had in the making a similar series on American art. Wishing to control my by-line as a writer on painting, they bought from Viking the rights to *America's Old Masters*, which, although it was being published in German by the War Department, was out of print here. One evening at a dinner party, Esther had an inspiration: instead of reviving *Old Masters* as a reprint, why not divide it into component parts. I should enlarge the accounts of West, Copley, Peale, and Stuart into short but full biographies that would be published separately though in a uniform large format with many illustrations, thus setting in motion a series that could be continued indefinitely. How many of the books I would write myself in the long run was not clear, but it was agreed that I should begin with Copley and Stuart. Contracts were signed with an advance of $500 each.

*

No longer alone as in a desert, I had stepped under a waterfall. I had to postpone the work I had begun on the sequel to *First Flowers*. *First Flowers* itself was in the full freshet of production. This was the more time-consuming because when I brought in to Lovell a list of a hundred illustrations, he asked whether this was as many as I could find? We ended up with 157 in black and white and eight to be printed in color by that expensive process: sheet-fed gravure. The designer determined that giving a full page to each of so many pictures would be monotonous (particularly because they were mostly portraits). Reproductions would be spaced on the same pages as the text. This required laying out separately opening after opening. Regularly consulted, I had to write many detailed letters: the designer was in Boston and I, New York. Then there was the usual authorial labors of reading galley proof and page proof, not only the text but the back matter; correcting errors and filling in gaps. I had resolved to make the index myself and did so.

As if this were not enough, *Copley* and *Stuart* were sniffing at my heels. Expecting that *First Flowers* would knock down the barriers against popular interest in American art, the publisher wanted *Copley* and *Stuart* to come out before the excitement faded. My need was to expand the texts in *Old Masters* by half again. To do so without repeating or anticipating what I had written or planned to write in my historical volumes, *First Flowers* and its sequel, raised a serious quandary. However, it was easy to select different paintings for illustration, and I sought new approaches by aiming my new text directly at these. Backing me up was the different psychological effect of perusing a separate biography rather than part of a larger book.

It took me about four months to complete the enlargements of each volume: *Copley* was sent to Houghton in February 1947; *Stuart*, in June. I was collecting illustrations for both short biographies and even reading proof for *Copley* before *First Flowers of Our Wilderness* was officially published on November 12, 1947, more than a year after my manuscript had been completed.

*

First Flowers was copiously reviewed. Writers primarily concerned with American history without exception welcomed the "dual point of view of an artistic and social historian." *The New Yorker* commented that *First Flowers* "upsets many of our fondest beliefs about the life and habits of our pre-Revolutionary forebears." Allan Nevins wrote, "This book is indispensable to any student of our civilization. . . . It gives us reasons never before properly presented for valuing our cultural heritage. . . . Will be a rewarding experience for any American."

The less specialized writers on art lined up, as with *America's Old Masters*, on my side. Thomas Craven, whose popular reputation was the greatest, added to the list of major writers with whom I had been equated—Sinclair Lewis, Hemingway, Plutarch, and Jane Austen— the name of Balzac.

At the head of the old-timers concerned with American art was Fiske Kimball, the director of the Pennsylvania Museum. He defined the earlier paintings I discussed as rubbish not worth writing about. Insisting that the only important issue was in what way the paintings were so different from the European as to be truly American, he took my statement that more needed to be known about English provincial art as admission of a "fatal" flaw that made my book useless. When we next met, he taunted me with having given him the ammunition to shoot me down.

This was my first lesson of a danger very sad for the advancement of knowledge. If, as I think an honest scholar should, you acknowledge holes in your evidence, you clear a road for attack, often by academics bucking for tenure who want to demonstrate that they are smarter than the author.

*

Each of the small coterie of students of American art had nominated himself or herself as the successor of Sawitzky. I had, with the assistance of the librarians at the Frick, endeavored to soothe them by listing them all in my "acknowledgments." But there had been a dreadful lapse: the most aggressive of them all, George Groce, had been forgotten. He undertook to lead the pack who would disgrace my book as theft from Sawitzky. With the cooperation of Donald Shelley, the curator of painting at the New-York Historical Society, it was agreed that Groce should write a long and lethal attack for the Society's *Quarterly Bulletin*.

I found in Shelley's office Mrs. Sawitzky in a state of hysteria. She had been urged by the conspirators to lead the attack on me as a plagiarist. But she was attacking Shelley, who was cowering behind his desk. Over and over she vociferated that I had been her dead husband's friend, colleague, and favorite disciple; that he had found

comfort in regarding me as his successor; and that plotting villains—
a reiterated killing stare at Shelley—were trying to use her sainted
husband's name to destroy me. Having enjoyed the occasion for a
while, I then went upstairs to see the editor of the *Bulletin*. From his
battered state, I concluded that Mrs. Sawitzky had already called on
him. He said that he could do nothing since Groce's piece had been
commissioned, added a lecture on the freedom of the press, and then
asked me to call off Mrs. Sawitzky. Having treated him to a lecture
on the freedom of speech, I departed and was glad to see, as I passed,
that Shelley was still getting it.

Since the plagiarism charge had to be dropped, Groce, so I was
told, was now trying to demonstrate that *First Flowers* was a cesspool
of inaccuracies and lies. He would send his manuscript to the *Bulletin*
and then call it back to add more accusations. To Agnes who was
then in New Mexico I expressed to some perturbation: members of
his pack kept warning me of dire consequences. However, Groce
labored so long that the review appeared almost a year after *First
Flowers* was published. It ran to innumerable pages and was devoted
to stating that I had neglected to pay attention or obeisance to various
sources, most of them irrelevant, a good many by Groce himself. At
least one member of the pack stated that the review was the best-
ever publication on early American art, but to wade through page
after page required prior conviction.

*

The long-range and indeed almost devastating problems of *First
Flowers* was caused not by too little but by too much enthusiasm.
Had Houghton Mifflin slipped it out quietly as Viking had slipped
out *America's Old Masters*, it would have floated comfortably along,
but Lovell had brought Houghton Mifflin's powerful engines to bear:
mailing lists, quotes from the important, autograph-signing parties.
The salesmen were instructed to persuade bookstores to order quantities of copies, pile them in plain view, feature them in window displays. Full-page advertisements and many smaller ones appeared in
a wide range of media. Publication date was supposed to unleash a
stampede. But alas! Few buyers of expensive art books were shaken
out of their conviction that no one of any taste could possibly be
concerned with American art. The piles of books for sale did not

diminish, to the angry dismay of the booksellers. Books in quantities were returned to Houghton Mifflin, drenching the ledgers with red ink.

*

By the time the fiasco had developed, *Copley* was well along on Houghton's production line, flaunting a similar binding that had been intended to hook on to *First Flowers*'s galloping coattails. Although E. P. Richardson to my surprise wrote me, "Your Copley book in simplicity of form and eloquence seems to me perhaps the best thing you have done," the book got little review attention. Sales were so pitiful that Lovell expressed regret at having contracted to publish the *Stuart*. I agreed that if he would let me keep the advance (I had written the manuscript) I would not insist on publication.

The manuscript went into my metaphoric "bureau drawer." Six years later, I received a letter from Knopf, who were publishing a series, *Great Lives in Brief*, asking whether I would like to do Whistler. Calling on the editor, I said I would rather do Stuart, and, pulling papers out of my briefcase, stated, "and here is the manuscript." It happened that the editor was behind schedule; a manuscript already prepared was a gift from heaven. And a peculiarity of the Houghton Mifflin project fitted for an opposite reason into the Knopf project. Lengthy discussions of the paintings to be illustrated which I had originally added to swell the text now compensated for the lack, in the little Knopf volume, of any illustration. As part of a series, *Gilbert Stuart* was published in 1954 along with some other volumes. It was allowed to go out of print in 1959. As I write this it is returning to print. In company with a new edition of *John Singleton Copley*, my *Stuart*, under a new title, *On Desperate Seas*, is currently in print under the auspices of Fordham University Press.

32

A ROCKY ROAD

*

WHENEVER opportunity had offered, I had been working on the second volume of my projected four-volume history of American painting. What was eventually to be published as *The Light of Distant Skies* was devoted to the earliest major interrelationships between American and European painters. This involved two generations, the first so fruitful that the American artists, often resident in the London which was then the art center of Europe, led in many directions the development of European art well into the nineteenth century. West, Copley, and Stuart became internationally famous. The second generation became altogether subservient to existing European taste. On returning to the then burgeoning United States, the three leaders—Allston, Vanderlyn, and Morse—lost their ability to paint. Allston's American years were haunted by his inability to complete a huge canvas of *Belshazzar's Feast* which he had brought back from England almost finished; Vanderlyn concluded that no one but an artistic quack could paint in America; and Morse strayed away to invent the telegraph.

My explanation for this double phenomenon was that the earlier triumphant generation—West, Copley, Trumbull, Peale, Stuart, and others—were, although only Peale actually fought, members of the endlessly creative Revolutionary generation which was putting into practice ideals that were part of the international heritage, but were growing faster in America. Expressing their American environments, the painters stepped naturally into the forefront of European libertarian development. But painters of the second generation felt self-conscious at being representatives of a new nation, and wished, like freshman members of a prestigious club, to show that they could behave just like the old members. Their plight was deepened by the excesses of the French Revolution and the Napoleonic wars which created in Europe a virulent reaction against the conceptions that had inspired the American Revolution and the American republic, while the United States, as it expanded westward, was moving more and more away from Europe into its own orbit. The painters were at home nowhere.

It became an axiom of my studies that an artist cuts his roots only at the greatest peril. This does not mean, of course, that he had to stand, like a great oak, where the acorn falls. He can be like a vine that, while keeping in contact with the earth that nourishes it, seeks sunlight wherever the sky opens over his forest. My first generation profited from wider expanses of the heavens; the second cut their roots and withered.

*

Light presented much more perplexing problems of organization than had *First Flowers*. Then I had needed to concern myself only with developments on a long, narrow strip of half-settled seacoast. Now, all the more because West and Copley were so influential as international innovators, I had to survey the whole flow of Western European painting during more than a half century of political and artistic revolution. My early earned familiarity with Italy and its old masters was to be of great value to me, but even more important, since so much of my action was laid in London, was what I had learned from my mother about English mores, and from my own varied adventures while living there. I was, on the other hand, very fortunate in being a birthright inhabitant of the American seaboard who had already written extensively on the American past. This double view comprising both sides of the ocean did give valuable headstarts not shared by other scholars in the field, but it vastly complicated my text which threatened to have as much cohesion as a handful of marbles.

I was, of course, very much concerned with the specific actions and achievements of individual men. They criss-crossed with each other, sometimes walking in the footsteps of elders, sometimes cooperating and tussling with them and each other, sometimes flying off, momentarily or permanently, on personal tangents. And there were crowd scenes supplied by the Royal Academy and the incipient institutions of America.

In addition to the normal hazards of a writer concerning the past, I had to reckon with protagonists who had left behind physical incarnations that needed to be found and dealt with. I refer to, of course, the paintings which were for my study the most important characters of all.

*

Chronology is the backbone of every historical sequence, but the different chronologies in my book did not obligingly lie down side by side to form a railroad track on which I could speed along. I was forced to leap back and forth from one time scheme to another while giving the viewer the impression that he was being carried smoothly ahead.

The answer lay, as I had learned from *Steamboats*, in a combination of opportunism and organization. Opportunism enabled me, as I proceeded, to insert seemingly stray material where it would fit and quite possibly enhance the effect of the passage to which it was joined. Organization required the establishment of common denominators. Thus, by entwining in a single chapter the portraitists who worked in America during the first of my two generations, I brought unity and contrast to what might have seemed a scattering of artists, and was enabled to end on the high note of Stuart's practice after he finally returned to these shores.

The efforts to found academies could be grouped with other aspects of patronage and sales, while naïve art happily occupied a chapter of its own. Under the title "Eccentrics," I housed two artists who came from altogether different backgrounds and worked with altogether different subject matter, but were linked by using with tremendous effect the episodic techniques of naïve painters: Hicks of the *Peaceable Kingdom* and Audubon with his birds. Had chronology not forced him into my third volume, George Catlin, the painter of Indians, could have been included.

*

When, a year or so after *First Flowers* had been published, I had brought *Light of Distant Skies* so far that I felt ready to submit it to Houghton Mifflin, I telephoned Lovell. Having expressed the greatest enthusiasm, he made an immediate appointment for me to bring the manuscript to him at Houghton Mifflin's New York office. He received the two cardboard boxes with as much ceremony as was possible between two friends in a business environment, and riffled through the manuscript like a child anticipating candy. Springing up, he said he would telephone his editor-in-chief, Paul Brooks, to give him the good news. I listened to his making a triumphal announcement. Instantly, he was interrupted by a voice at the other end of the line, delivering a tirade alive with energy and emotion (I could not hear the actual words) that continued for a long time. Lovell seemed too stunned to interrupt. Finally, he put down the receiver and said with great embarrassment that he would have to look into the matter further. We had intended to lunch together, but the tension had to be broken. I took my hat from the rack and departed.

I was soon notified that Houghton Mifflin could not afford to continue losing money on my art books. I would have to discover some way to make them sell.

*

As I was aimlessly wandering on New York's Lexington Avenue, I strayed into a drugstore to kill a few minutes by examining the rack of paperbacks. In between the garishly decorated covers, I saw one that was mysteriously quiet and pulled it out to hold in my hand, *The Pocket History of Old Masters*. It was by the well-known critic Thomas Craven. My amazed eyes saw many excellent full-page reproductions of works of art, the price given as twenty-five cents. Why not a *Pocket History of American Painting*?

Bitter experience had taught me that the fortresses of esthetic-intellectual snobbery—polite society, art facilities, critics, museums, collectors with their attendant dealers—would not let their drawbridges down to admit American art. They had a perfect formula: American art was worthwhile only if it resembled European art, and those Americans who imitated European models, of course, were inferior to what they imitated. I had long had a feeling that if it were possible to get around these citadels which blocked the way, the broad American public would enjoy and admire the art that had grown up around them. And I knew that Pocket Books had achieved the largest circulation in the United States.

It seemed a wild chance, but having ascertained the name of the editor-in-chief at Pocket Books, Freeman Lewis, I wrote to him introducing myself and arguing that the American people, if given the opportunity, would gladly pay their quarters for a book on American painting. And it would be a noble act to give them this opportunity.

In the minimal possible time, I received a phone call. I soon found myself having lunch in a larger, noisier, and more expensive restaurant than I had ever been taken to by a publisher or gone to by myself. The Pocket Book editors were delighted with the idea of demonstrating to the snobs (who looked down on them too) a grass-roots (should I say asphalt?) appreciation of American art.

After I had a chance to show them *First Flowers* and some sample illustrations, the fervor at Pocket Books rivaled what had once been the fervor during my honeymoon at Houghton Mifflin. But I had moved from the staidness of Boston Brahmins to the unabashed energy of entrepreneurial New York. The pace and efficiency of Pocket Books was greater than I had ever encountered anywhere. My being a strange fish in their environment, instead of turning them against me, made them more eagerly cooperative, almost affectionate. They took me with them to their parties. I was as fascinated as when, in writing a book, I achieved access to a new environment.

They enjoyed lavishing on our project the highest standards permitted by their mass-media formats. Their four sixteen-page signatures of black-and-white illustrations were printed—one painting to a page—in that expensive process—sheet-fed gravure—and were, despite their small size, among the best plates I have ever received. The color illustrations on all four sides of the jacket were adequate. The signatures of my text, which alternated with the illustrations, had to be twenty-four pages, but they allowed me to insert an extra one at the end, getting up to about forty thousand words. One picture by every painter that I discussed was illustrated—forty-eight in all—and I linked the text to the illustration.

Pocket Books did not hang around. The contract was signed on June 1, 1949. The manuscript was to be delivered (as it was) in time for publication in 1950.

I felt no need to change, for the tremendously larger audience I now hoped to reach, my habitual directions, which reflected the normal focus of living. "While looking at the pictures," I explained, "we shall not forget their [the painters'] personalities, and we shall examine the civilizations that shaped them into the kind of people they were." My recognition of a different audience took the form, primarily, of explaining as simply and clearly as I could achieve, and in the minimum number of words, historical, art historical, and environmental considerations which to a greater extent I could assume were already known to my previous audiences.

I was well primed concerning the epochs covered by *First Flowers* and *Light*. However, concerning the Hudson River School of which I was to become so passionate an advocate, I repeated the then reigning conception that the landscapes were provincial, too big, inferior to more introspective work of the more Europeanized Inness. Heading the chapter "Towers of Achievement," I really put my mind on Whistler, Eakins, Ryder, Homer. Entering the twentieth century, I was competent with the Eight, with Burchfield, and dramatically successful (as we shall see) with Hopper. From the generation that was shaken up by the Armory show, which brought European modernism to America, my favorite was Marin, who I am pleased to see coming back into favor. Realizing that I was on uncertain ground, I depended heavily on advice, particularly from Dorothy Miller at the Museum of Modern Art. She and I had a real falling out over Benton—she threatened never to speak to me again—who had so ribaldly thumbed his nose at the modern art establishment in New York. I could not, I felt, omit him and other "regionalists" of the Middle West, however unsympathetic I was to their type of nationalism. I included the modernism of Davis and Weber, the social protest of Shawn, the ponderousness of Albright, the delicacy of Graves, the tempered cubism of Sheeler, and so on, without finding any common center. Had I been writing a few years later, after the Abstract Impressionists had emerged, I would not have had to end so inconclusively. My last two sentences were evasive: "All over the United States talents are maturing according to their individual needs. The harvest will be ready in season."

After I had informed Houghton Mifflin of my project with Pocket Books, Paul wrote me that he would like to buy sheets, add a hard binding, and issue *A Short History of American Painting*. I expressed a lack of enthusiasm, not wishing to get this quick, overall summary mixed up with my projected series, but Houghton decided to go ahead anyway. The first result was an acrimonious argument between "Doc" Lewis at Pocket Books and Lovell about rights, which I found extremely embarrassing. Then Houghton got their production so tangled that their edition came out after the paperback which could not, because part of a mass-market operation, be postponed. The *Short History* was hardly reviewed. It proved unalluring in bookstores, adding to the list of failures in Houghton's efforts with my art books.

Pocket Books's first shipment to their outlets in drug- and cigar stores, etc., was 300,000 copies, and they were soon busy replacing copies on the racks. My hope that the broad American public would be receptive was proved in spades. Pocket Books's symbol was a reading kangaroo, and when a book sold a million copies, the author would be awarded a silver statuette. I was told that I was in the running, but I never added a kangaroo to my souvenirs.

I liked to think that the *Pocket History of American Painting*, through its huge circulation as it was reissued in various guises, had a significant effect on the slowly rising interest in American painting. It even invaded the hostile citadels: although not mentioned by professors, it infiltrated campus bookstores.

More remarkable and altogether unexpected by me was the *Pocket History*'s international career. I received a letter informing me that Pocket Books had granted "a continuing option" to the United States Information Agency (a branch of the federal government entrusted with global propaganda) for the translation and publication in the following languages: "Arabic, Assamese, Bengali, Bicol, Burmese, Cambodian, Cebuano, Chinese, Farsi, Greek, Gujarati, Hebrew, Hiligaynon, Hindi, Hungarian, Icelandic, Ilocano, Indonesian, Kachin, Kannada, Korean, Laotian, Macedonian, Malay, Malayalam, Marathi, Oriya, Polish, Punjabi, Romanian, Serbo-Croatian, Sindhi, Sinhalese, Slovenian, Tagalog, Tamil, Telugu, Thai, Turkish, Urdu, and Vietnamese."

Of course, this whole menu was not served up, but I kept receiving copies, paper binding or hardcover, in languages that I had to look up in an encyclopedia. I was regularly informed that they were spoken by many millions of people. Other translations arranged for either by Pocket Books or my own agents also appeared in less exotic languages. Estimating twenty translations, I dreamed of outdoing Mark Twain's *Jumping Frog* by having the same paragraph translated from each language into English for comparison, but I could not organize this noble experiment.

*

Reveling in the *Pocket History*'s tremendous circulation, I was disappointed in the low earnings based on a royalty of less than two cents a copy. This was serious, as the cost of my divorce was much greater than in my darkest moments I had foreseen. I complained to Harriet that what I had already paid out was more than what it cost me to live for a year. Trained by my parents never to dip into capital, I borrowed from the bank, putting up what was left from my lifetime savings as security. "I fear," so I continued to Harriet, "that books on American art are too expensive a luxury for writers like me."

In need of a good seller, I undertook a subject that I had long dreamed of tackling, Benedict Arnold's treason. I parked *The Light of Distant Skies* on a siding as I opened my main track to what was to be published as *The Traitor and the Spy.**

*

After the passage of two years, *Traitor* steamed off in search of a publisher, leaving my main track open for *Light*. I procured a small grant from the American Philosophical Society and then a Guggenheim Fellowship. Things were stirred up to such a point that Paul Sachs, the Harvard professor whose all powerful course on museum management I had failed to take, arranged for me an invitation redolent with old New England intellectual tradition: I should deliver sections from my manuscript as a series of Lowell Lectures.

These lectures had been high moments during the New England Literary Renaissance. When Emerson had spoken, the police had to

---

*See Chapter 34.

be called out to handle the crowd. Complimented at being invited, although the stipend revealed Yankee tightness, I agreed.

I took six weekly trips to Boston for the mid-afternoon lectures. Always, as the train pulled out of Providence, it began to snow. I could always expect a warm welcome. In a manner most ecumenical in Boston publishing, I was regularly put up by the director of the Harvard University Press. Since the century-old Lowell Lecture routine omitted introductions, I had, as I began my series, to walk out by myself onto an extensive stage bare except for a lectern. Quickly looking around, I saw that the first two rows were filled from wall to wall with those dowdy, impressive old ladies who are a speciality of Bostonian upper classes. They were leaning forward as I appeared with an eagerness amounting almost to hunger, which I considered complimentary until, as I started to speak, they all relaxed back and, with a common sigh of satisfaction, went to sleep. Since this phenomenon was duplicated at each of my lectures, I concluded that insomnia was endemic among the most blue-blooded Bostonian dowagers who could nonetheless, ever since the days of Emerson, count on being able to get some sleep during a Lowell Lecture.

I was at first annoyed, but I became grateful for these old ladies since the auditorium as it stretched far behind them was, from my first lecture to my last, almost empty. An interest in American painting had obviously not made a dent in Bostonian higher thinking!

*

By the time that *Light* was completed, *Traitor* had been published by Harcourt, Brace and had become a strong seller, thus filling my double need to revive my bank balance and my commercial standing as a writer. Not wishing to let me go, Harcourt undertook to publish *Light*, but, as I was soon to discover, without any enthusiasm. Eugene Reynall, the head of the trade department, who had appointed himself editor for *Traitor*, handed on *Light* to Robert Giroux. Giroux's specialty was avant-garde literature but not too avant-garde for a good sale. Regarding the American art I had written about as so far beneath him that he felt besmirched, he made no effort to hide— although he was eventually to boast of having been my editor—his resentment and disdain. I was not informed of the decision to emasculate *Light* by printing two thousand copies directly from type, which was then distributed, thus saving the cost of plating but making a second printing impossible. However, when the volume emerged, there appeared amazing symptoms of a thaw.

The Light of Distant Skies was chosen by the Carnegie Corporation for distribution in the Commonwealth countries, and, with great publicity, for President John F. Kennedy's "White House List" of some two hundred volumes recommended as essential to the understanding of American history. Even more remarkably, considering the small number of copies there had been for sale, *Light* was selected by the American Publishers Association as one of two hundred "best and most important titles published in the U.S." during the four-year period, 1953–1957.

33

Hopper and de Kooning

*

It had begun, shortly after the *Pocket History* was released, with a phone call. The voice identified itself as Edward Hopper's wife. Her husband had been so pleased by what I had written about him that he hoped I would come to see him so that he could thank me in person. Knowing Hopper's reputation as a recluse, I was puzzled as well as delighted. Having made an appointment for mid-morning (the time Mrs. Hopper always suggested), I got down a copy of the *Pocket History* to ascertain what I had written. Because Hopper endorsed so strongly my summary of his career—and because the result was to be so fruitful in my own life—the two paragraphs seem worth quoting. The previous sentence is "We admire Sheeter's paintings but are not emotionally stirred.

"Edward Hopper (1882–) strikes richer overtones. Trained not in the estheticism of Chase but the humanism of Henri, Hopper thinks technical experimentation an empty exercise unless it grows from an artist's urgent need to transcribe his most 'intimate impressions of nature.' However, he has not worked in a traditional manner. Unlike his fellow student Bellows, he could not make the methods that they had both learned from Henri express his own emotions. While Bellows turned out a flood of art, Hopper engaged in a lonely search to find himself. As impervious to outside influence as was Winslow Homer, he adopted no ready-made recipes, either French or American. His technique and his vision matured together with the slow certainty of organic growth. Bellows was almost at the end of his career when

Hopper emerged from retirement, the possessor of a major and original style.

"Hopper had discarded Henri's romantic outlook and dramatic brushwork for a firm, laconic realism. He depicts American cities with love, and yet with unflinching exactitude: the garish stores, the jumble of architectural styles, the contrast of brightness and shadow on blank or overdecorated walls. When he shows people—diners at an all-night restaurant . . . a woman undressing under the glare of an unshaded bulb—we see them in a flash, as if we had gone quickly by a lighted window. The pictures are alive with the mystery and loneliness of a great city. In landscapes as in urban scenes, Hopper gains solidity from geometric compositions similar to those Sheeter borrowed from cubism, but he denies any borrowing: 'Angularity just comes naturally to me.' Living in the same age, he had reached some of the same conclusions as the Parisian masters. Like theirs, his art is moving and forceful because it evolved from his own temperament and his own experience."

*

When for the first time I had mounted three or four flights of stairs in an old house on Washington Square, and nervously knocked on a door, it was, as it was always to be, opened by a small, talkative, almost over-eager woman. Mrs. Hopper ushered me into her own studio. Its walls were crowded with her paintings of objects particularly of interest to her, including cats. Hopper himself was standing there. After Mrs. Hopper had explained who I was, he greeted and thanked me with Old World courtesy. His face seemed to remain expressionless, but even to my first glance it communicated depths moving within.

After I had admired, as was always expected, Mrs. Hopper's paintings, something remarkable happened, although I did not then know that it was remarkable. A door was opened, and I was ushered into a large room with bare whitewashed walls. No furniture except an empty easel in a corner and two plain wooden chairs placed in the middle of the bare floor. I was later to discover that almost no visitor, even fellow painters who were old friends, was allowed to penetrate into the studio where Hopper painted. His wife had to rustle up a third chair.

After a short time, Mrs. Hopper—as she was to do during my subsequent visits—rose and left me alone with the painter. This abandonment of her habitual role of chatterer protecting Hopper's wordlessness was also phenomenal.

Interviewers who with great difficulty succeeded in getting access to Hopper were infuriated—I remember particularly the art critic of *Time* magazine—because, although the painter would be visibly sitting there, his wife answered all the questions. If she had to step out, the interviewers would turn their faces to Hopper with great anticipation, sure he would leap on this opportunity to express himself. He silently awaited her return. The word went about that Hopper was hopelessly henpecked, but her role was essential to her man.

At the last Whitney exhibition of Hopper's work during his lifetime, he remained seated while Jo Hopper prowled before him. I watched Alfred Barr, that powerful director of the Museum of Modern Art, trying unsuccessfully to get by her in order to talk to Hopper. Finally, he declared in a loud voice, "I am proud of having been the first to discover your husband." Jo paid not the least attention. "Surely," I said, "you know Alfred Barr." She replied, "Any friend of Jimmie Flexner's is a friend of mine." There was nothing for Barr to do except turn on his heel and walk away. This was one of the few times I ever saw a grin invade Hopper's face.*

*

During the almost ten years of our friendship, which continued until his last illness, I would periodically sit in silence side by side with Hopper in his empty studio. These sessions were among the most remarkable experiences of my life. I am by nature a talker—since childhood I have been accused of talking too much—and, as a writer, my medium is words. Hopper had no use, beyond routine necessity, for words. During those voiceless sessions, which could last for an hour or more, the same tremendous power that Hopper exerted through his painting so reset my mind that our mutual silence became

---

*Barr did have some claim since his influential institution had helped Hopper's career along with a one-man show in 1933. Yet, in adopting that tone, particularly with the proudly self-reliant Hopper, Barr revealed the lack of human understanding which got him fired from the museum he had created, although they needed him so badly that he was always called back.

a medium for profound communication. I felt a warm intimacy grow between us, understanding perhaps deeper than speech could achieve.

I came to understand why, concerning paintings that seem to many viewers completely extroverted, he insisted that his subject was "me." He denied that he had been influenced by cubism or any of those aspects of modern art which he violently denounced. All his shapes, angles, and tensions, his vast subtlety in painting light, were means of expressing his own moods and emotions. His paintings were never (despite what is often written) brutal or sardonic. They were taciturn, even as he was, inspired by a loneliness that is perceptive, not sad, not edged with protest,* but illuminated, for those who can see, by the mystery and even romance of human existence.

How close to me he had come to feel was revealed when in 1961, at the age of seventy-nine, he feared that his powers were failing. He wrote me that he had sent a canvas, which he felt was the best he could now do, to the Whitney Museum, and wanted me to see it and write him frankly what I thought. Frankly! I realized that whatever I thought, I would have to be encouraging. What was my joy to see that the painting—it is now called *Summer Sunlight*—ranked very close to his best work! He was so pleased with my letter of praise that, in a manner that seemed completely out of character for him, he sent a copy to Lloyd Goodrich, the director of the Whitney: "Since I took the trouble of having the photostat made, it may indicate that I am not so modest as I am said to be."

Time passed. Hopper died, the Whitney put on a huge retrospective, and published an elaborate catalogue in which the author, Gail Levin, used this Hopper-Flexner-Goodrich correspondence as its climax. But I was not invited to the opening and heard of the catalogue use from Kurt Vonnegut, who had attended it. I went to the Whitney to check the catalogue, and telephoned up from the desk to Ms. Levin. When I told her my name, she gave two successive gasps: the first, because she thought I was dead (as she admitted), and haunting her from my grave; the second, because, if I were alive, she should have gotten my permission to quote me and had treated me with great rudeness. But, more amused than otherwise by this reflection

---

*During my intimate seances with Hopper, I never perceived even a hint of "social consciousness."

of how far back my concern with American art went, I took no offense. She took me on a private view of the show, along with Helen Hayes (to my great pleasure), and I contributed an article on my friendship with Hopper to the memorial number of the *Art Journal*.

*

My wife had never been invited by Jo to my seances with the Hoppers, but we invited the Hoppers to a dinner party which my wife has never forgotten. As by far the most distinguished guest, he was seated at her right, but he upset her and the whole table by never saying a word. Very different was our experience with de Kooning.

He was a big man, not as tall as Hopper but much heavier. When the other guests left, he stayed behind, lounging on our sofa and becoming increasingly prone as the hours passed. As the hours passed! He became drunker and drunker—we tried to hide the whiskey but he ferreted it out—and talked without stopping, his Dutch accent, always a little difficult to follow, becoming so thick that there was no understanding what he vociferated. Since when dawn came up the following morning he was not there, he must have departed somehow.

My other most vivid memory of de Kooning was that he said to me mournfully, "I have two wives (a wife and a mistress) but neither of them can cook." Could this be an explanation for the ferocious pictures of women he painted, bloated and brutally dismembered?

*

My principal recollection of Rothko was his describing, with tremendous intensity, his outrage at being unable to convince a grocer's clerk that there being an article about him in *Life* magazine was more impressive because he was a painter not a baseball player.

As the reader has made out, I was not a devotee of the Abstract Impressionists, although I acknowledge that they were the most effective American painters of their generation.

34

TREASON MOST FOUL

*

IN my studies of early America I had become convinced that the most dramatic episode of those years and one of the most melodramatic in all our history was Benedict Arnold's treason.

A druggist and disreputable horse trader, Benedict Arnold made himself, through inborn talents, the greatest combat general who fought on either side during the American Revolution. He married as his second wife Peggy Shippen, a disgruntled Philadelphia aristocrat, beautiful and much younger than he. Hardly were they married before they secretly got in touch with a poetic English soldier with whom Peggy had flirted when the British had occupied Philadelphia. John André was rising with startling rapidity to the important post of adjutant general of the British army.

In coded letters carried at great risk by secret agents, Arnold offered to sell his soldiers with the key fortress of West Point, and to deliver to the enemy, dead or alive, the indispensable commander in chief of the American cause, George Washington. The plot promised to destroy the American battle for freedom, with all its implications that were to ring down the corridors of history.

On September 22, 1780, André rowed ashore from a British warship for a secret rendezvous with Arnold. Thus was set in motion ten days of wild action which proved again that truth is stranger than fiction.

Here is a story which could have been chanted, exactly as it was inscribed by Nature on the authentic tablets of history, in ancient times by some heroic bard. Even blind Homer might not have scorned a drama so rich in events and personalities. On an exalted stage where moved the destinies of empires and perhaps the future liberties of all mankind, two able men and a gifted woman were drawn, by flaws in the very characteristics that had raised them high, into mortal danger. And Nature, not like lesser artists afraid of the extremest melodrama, lavishly interwove into her saga coincidence, extended suspense, struggles to escape, and exalted tragedy.

*

Eyeing this subject as I was writing my early books, I realized that if I were ever to be ready to tackle it the time was not yet. I was thus grateful that the possibility was blocked for everyone.

In 1925, the Clements Library at San Marino, California, had acquired the headquarters papers of Sir Henry Clinton, the British commander in chief at the time of Arnold's treason. In the vast archives were the essential documents concerning Arnold's secret negotiations with André and the events that resulted in his being hanged as a spy. Also documented was Arnold's escape and his subsequent adventures as a general in the British army. As long as this material loomed, no writer could tackle the story.

Much to my satisfaction, the Clements Library was in no hurry. They refused to release the material until they had found the perfect historical writer. I hoped the decision would be postponed long enough for me to have developed adequate skill and reputation to be in the running.

Finally, the announcement came: Carl Van Doren. I had to admit that he was an obvious choice, but felt nonetheless jealousy tinged with irritation.

I remember well my first sight of Van Doren. I was doing research for *Doctors on Horseback* in the American History Room at the New York Public Library when there appeared in the movement of persons up and down the central aisle a handsome man, over six feet tall, who carried such an air of distinction that I stared. I watched him approach the desk, say a few words to a most respectful librarian, turn and walk out of the room. To my amazement—I had never done anything like this before—I found myself on my feet. I went up to the desk and asked who was that resplendent figure? The answer was Van Doren. Carl Van Doren.

Viking was Van Doren's publisher as well as mine. Thus I was invited to a luncheon of celebrities Viking staged to celebrate their publication of an anthology of his works edited by himself. On one side of me was the popular writer and public figure Christopher Morley. We could find nothing to say to each other until, having been a Baltimorian, he realized who my grandfather was. His face lit up with pleasure as he told me that his own father had used the silences in Quaker Meeting not to commune with the Lord but to solve chess problems. In excitement, he would enunciate "check." According to Morley, all the other Quakers regarded this as a variety of religious experience, but my grandfather, knowing enough to understand, threw Morley's father out of meeting. This established a bond between us.

But I was disgusted with Van Doren because, although he had started publishing books at an early age, he included in his selection nothing that he had written before he was well established. Thus slighting your own younger years seemed to me as a young author the act of a pompous ass. And in my own relations with him—we kept running into each other here and there—he always treated me with the toploftiness of a professor to a graduate student, and not a very bright one at that. He would ask me what I was writing and then, the next time we met, say that he had checked what I had said in the *Dictionary of American Biography*, and was happy to tell me that I had been correct.

Time changes roles. Some thirty years later, I was commissioned by the Book of the Month Club to write an introduction for a new edition of Van Doren's *Benjamin Franklin*. I did not have to consult the *DAB* to conclude and state that he had written a major biography.

*

When in 1941 advance notices revealed that Van Doren had chosen as a title for his book based on the Clements Library papers a title that bypassed the treason: *The Secret History of the American Revolution*, I was considerably bucked up. It developed that he had devoted only some 300 of his 520 pages to Arnold's treason. Arnold's previous adventures were condensed into only twenty-two; André was entirely unintroduced, and Peggy's past was given a couple of pages. Furthermore, Van Doren had adhered conscientiously to the institutional distinction between history and biography. He cluttered emotional effect with detail following more detail, equally weighted. All the more because the essential documents were printed in a long appendix, the *Secret History* would, I concluded, facilitate rather than get in the way of what I wanted to do.

However, I did not leap into action. I had no really serious doubt that the basic conception of modern biographical writing—fidelity to fact as recorded in primary sources—could be applied, if the material warranted, to an epic drama. However, I was still not sure of my readiness to undertake so demanding a task. Would I make a fool of myself, perhaps call back my writer's block, if I attempted a theme that blind Homer would not have scorned? Better to wait until I was more experienced!

*

I might have procrastinated even longer, continued my painting history with another volume, had not Houghton Mifflin turned down *The Light of Distant Skies.* On the face of it, this failure would seem calculated to bruise my confidence and thus further impede my taking at long last the hazardous jump. But I blamed the turndown altogether on publishers' economics. The solution was to make my next book so foreseeable a smash hit that it could carry *Light* piggyback onto some publisher's list. I should summon up my courage, undertake the treason.

*

Research persuaded me that Arnold had been a classic example of the hero in the Wagnerian sense, a man of physical prowess and derring-do who found consummation in that activity which most tests bodily skill and fortitude: battle. Battle, not war: there were many aspects of war to which Arnold was unsuited and which he resented because they interfered between the hero and the exalted exercise of his gifts. Arnold could not understand policy beyond the scope of his eyes and his sword; nor could he feel idealism beyond the idealism of the body. He could kill the strong, spare the weak, succor the wounded. He protected women (eventually to the further souring of his entire career), but he could not understand what the American Revolution was all about. He was like a great tower that had been built to withstand gales from only one direction. When the hurricane shifted, the mighty structure crashed to the ground.

Even as a tree can reach its ultimate dimensions only in an open field, so Arnold was born in a place and time that uniquely permitted the characteristics of such a man to develop without check. He was among the first officers in a previously nonexistent army that was serving a nation not yet born. Any traditions he followed had to be applied from other contexts. His loyalties could not be due to habit and training; they had to come from circumstance and will. He taught himself to fight, and his military rise was beyond the most extreme possibilities in organized armies. The span of time from the day he joined the Continental Army as a captain to his commission as major general was less than two years—but even at that he had reason to feel aggrieved because officers of lesser ability had risen in this improvised army even more rapidly. Hardly sustained or molded by any institutions outside himself, Arnold remained solitary on a crowded scene.

There have been modern generals with many pyschological resemblances to Arnold. But how different their development! At an age when Arnold captained small merchant ships as an over-aggressive businessman, such modern fighters were gathered into a military establishment, educated at institutions like the United States Military Academy at West Point. They moved on routinely into the long-established army of a long-established nation, a meticulously charted world where there were laid out roads designed by generations of experience to take maximum advantage of the gifts that a born fighter possesses. There were roads of promotion up which they could travel with little resentment or controversy. Men especially trained for such occupations handled aspects of war with which the fighters were not equipped to cope. "Heroes" did not find themselves, as Arnold did, their own recruiters and supply officers, commandants of cities without aides trained in military government.

Such modern fighters were sustained on the sides of their natures where their own foundations were weak not only by elaborate organization, but also by conditioning and traditions often stronger than their characters. They have broken out in little ways, but they were isolated from such excesses as brought Arnold down.

In ancient times, Achilles shared much of Arnold's temperament. He brooked little interference with what he pleased to do, but his passions were sustained, as Arnold's were not, by social structure. Although he was titularly under the command of Agamemnon, he was the leader of his own tribe in what was a loose alliance. When Agamemnon pre-empted a slave girl he felt he had a right to, he sulked in his tent in a manner that would in a modern army have made him liable for a court martial. But his own followers felt that they were insulted by the insult to him. He could have marched to his "tall ships," perhaps even made his own peace with the Trojans, without being guilty of treason.

Since Arnold represents the full flowering of aggressive characteristics that exist to some extent in us all, all can to some extent identify with him. He is far from being an unsympathetic character. His bravery, his ability to lead men are sure and clear, and the picture of the wounded hero struggling with ingratitude and injustice which he lacked weapons to overcome would be touching were it not for his final, desperate act of betrayal.

Despite my fascination with Arnold, he presented me with problems. Being not myself an admirer of warfare and acts of death, I could not foresee devoting to him a full-length biography.

In this quandary, my propensity for multiple biographies, in which I tell two or more life stories separately until they merge in common action, came to my rescue. John André, the British officer who negotiated with Arnold, conferred with him on the banks of the Hudson, was captured on his way back to the British lines, and was hanged as a spy, added balance, the more satisfactory because Nature, in arranging complicated events, does not act at random.

Despite great and obvious variations in experience and character, the young British officer had weaknesses that dovetailed with Arnold's even as their tragedies eventually dovetailed. Thus, on a pyschological as well as an historical plane, the two lives drew together.

Where Arnold was from the start a physical man designed for derring-do, André began life as a delicate dabbler in the arts whose friends could not imagine him as a soldier. Yet he chose, although there was no such tradition in his background, to be a soldier. This was partly a conscious posturing in the presence of the old heroic tales that Arnold was from his own inner nature to re-enact. André also had worldly motives similar to Arnold's. He was, it is true, an inheritor of money as Arnold was not, and his family was higher in the mercantile scale, yet trade was considered in eighteenth-century English aristocratic circles an occupation unworthy of gentlemen. André's military achievements brought him, as Arnold was brought, into contact with social superiors who would otherwise not have countenanced him. Yet, like Arnold, he was resented by some as an upstart. He had failed, when ambition led him into his final gamble, really to achieve acceptance.

Fighting, killing, conquering came naturally to Arnold, but when the pageantry of British military life swung over into actual warfare, André was far from edified. He became, after unhappy experiences as a prisoner of war, a soldier by intellectual conversion. Not a fighter, but a staff officer, he was nonetheless more brutal than Arnold. Where Arnold killed as an aspect of the game of battle, André schemed killing as terror. Yet he held on to romantic ideas that Arnold never consciously harbored, setting out with a blithe sense of adventure to a rendezvous that was for Arnold soul's torture. If André (as seems possible) gained his ascendancy over the British commander in chief, Sir Henry Clinton, partly through homosexuality, this adds to the picture a not incongruous note.

That I would find a third protagonist did not come clear to me until I was some distance along in my researches. Chivalry (or male chauvinism, if you please) had cast Arnold's second wife, born Peggy Shippen, as a stock figure, a mere tear-jerking victim of Arnold's treason. I was the first to examine her past, study the development of her character. This led to the recognition of her major role in the treason. Being thus supplied with a beautiful villainess did much to heighten the story I had to tell. I should have had the perspicacity to change my intended title, *The Traitor and the Spy,* to the more salable possibility *The Traitor, the Beauty, and the Spy.*

Although Peggy was young and small, and fair and femininely appealing, there was more iron in her makeup than in either of the men's. The treason may well have been, in the first instance, her creation. Her sleepwalking scene was not the result of a "mind diseased" by horror and guilt. Long given to using hysteria to achieve her ends, she excited the emotions of Washington and his aides by, in her "distraction," revealing her young body almost nude. Not for her the lines, "All the perfumes of Arabia will not sweeten this little hand." She put that hand to work to make the best of the situation in which the treason threw her and her children.

*

The Traitor and the Spy was my first project which historical fashion had not largely ignored. Foreseeing well-marked and -paved roads to speed on, I was amazed. The very problem that had daunted me—the sensational, epic nature of the story—had scared away respectable historians and biographers. The best existing life of Arnold had been published in 1880; the only (and unreliable) life of André in 1861. But this did not mean that there had not been a flood of publication. The story had attracted, like a bowl of honey, every variety of fictionizer, romantic fool, etc.

Beyond what Van Doren had published, there was so much unpublished or only partially published manuscript material that I sometimes despaired. Making myself more trouble, I sent a notice to relevant newspapers and magazines asking for documents. The most important result was a letter from a research worker in London who was typing and classifying a large collection of family papers belonging to Group Captain A. R. Arnold. If I wished, she would ask permission to send me carbons. A large packet arrived greatly elucidating the Arnolds' lives and emotions after the treasonous couple had fled to England.

My adventures in serving André papers could be considered bizarre. It all started at a literary cocktail party in New York City when I told an old friend of mine, the poet Horace Gregory, about the book I was writing. He looked upset, walked off, and returned to tell me that his wife, Myra Zaturendska (who had once won a Pulitzer Prize for poetry), nurtured an imaginary love affair with André ever since she was a girl and had for years been collecting material to write his biography. With some trepidation, I followed Horace across the room to speak with her. Instead of looking angry and perturbed, she looked grave and sad. She realized now, she said,

[323]

that she would never do the book on André, but she did not want to have all she had discovered go to waste. She would tell it all to me.

I took her out to lunch at a very nice place, and she talked and talked. It did not take long to realize that she had created with her poetic imagination an André of her own fashioning, but I did my best to take what she said seriously. I even jotted down some notes. Her only statement that interested me was that in a certain church in Bath, where the André family had settled, there hung a portrait of Major André's mother.

I wrote to the rector. He replied that they had no portrait, but that one of his parishioners—he could not remember which one—had told him that she owned André's sword. I wrote him back urging him to wrestle with his memory: she might also have papers. He did locate her. She had no papers but supplied the address of Mrs. Louis J. André in Sussex.

Mrs. André sent me, carefully copied out in her own hand, a quantity of those personal documents which are of so much use to a biographer. Also photographs of comic drawings made by the major. In reply to my questioning about other descendants, she wrote that there had been a black sheep who had gone to Australia in the nineteenth century and with whom her husband's family had lost contact. I begged her to try to find an address, and she came up with one some fifty years' old: the name of a town. The renegade was said to have become a sheep farmer.

Assuming that sheep farmers are moored to their land, I sent a communication addressed to any descendant of the lost André. Back came a letter from one James André who was clearly enchanted to receive this sign of recognition from the outside world. He had no papers, but he had portraits of the Major. He sent me excellent photographs including the miniature of André which became a feature in my book.

Time passed, and Queen Elizabeth was to be crowned. I received a letter from James André stating that he and his wife would pass through New York on their way to the Coronation. Might he bring his wife to call on me? Of course, I replied, "of course."

My wife and I were full of curiosity. Through our door came a large, courteous, outdoors man—he told me that he herded over a thousand sheep—without city guile. When I warned him that he

Drawing by Alexander Archipenko, given to the author by the artist. (All works
illustrated in this section are from the author's collection.)

Composite silver lion; the head and body are 13th- or 14th-century European. A hole in the belly indicates that it was originally mounted on a staff. The tail and legs are believed to be of 16th- or 17th-century French origin. 3 1/2 inches high. Photo by Byron Bell.

"The Great Stone Face," so-named by the author because of its force. Tianon culture, Arawaka Indians of Hispaniola or Puerto Rico, who became extinct within a hundred years of the Spanish Conquest. 6 x 4 inches, less than one inch in depth. Photo by Byron Bell.

"Fifi": chief's seat and fertility goddess, carved from a single block of wood. Found in a Paris flea market in a pile of discarded chairs. Boule, Senegal, West Africa. Photo by Byron Bell.

Monochromatic drawings by different amateur artists: versions of Youth, after Thomas Cole's *The Voyage of Life*. See pages 379-80.

New England village green.

Desolation. Monochromatic drawing, found in New Haven, Connecticut.

Balloon Ascension.

The Magic Lake by G. L. Cummings.

Sarah Hobbs. Life-size oil portrait found rolled up in a chest. See pages 381-83.

might not be delighted by what I wrote about his illustrious ancestor, he replied that it was my duty to publish what I believed.

Discovering that he had altogether lost track of his English family, I took it upon myself to write him a letter of introduction to Mrs. Louis André. I was to receive a document, signed with many names, thanking me for having brought the sundered family together.

*

The resemblance to traditional epics of the events I was portraying could not be, as I sat at my typewriter, ignored. It would be in the reader's mind and must therefore be in the writer's. Passages that would not seem flat in some other kind of narrative would fall flat. The writer must sometimes do his best to buckle on the wings of Pegasus. Yet those wings are dangerous appendages, paradoxically the more so when the call for them is so obvious. I had every reason to fear that in dealing with events supremely romantic I would fly too high. Verisimilitude could easily disappear into what would seem conventional posturing.

All the great universals of humanity are clichés, and thus the closer a literary passage approaches exalted themes, the greater the danger of sideslipping into the sentimental, the shrill, the obvious. Yet an amulet exists against this danger. Although there is no greater cliché than love, no such thought will occur to a lover who is holding in his arms the woman he most desires. Love can be reborn in all its original ardor by the immediacy of the situation. The universal ceases to be a cliché when it is specifically applied. It follows that the harvest from historical scholarship can be, if properly handled, of great assistance in achieving elevated effects.

I found Nature endlessly indulgent. As the narrative became more exciting, requiring, therefore, to be more firmly rooted to detail, the record expanded to satisfy the immediate international concern. Long letters were written by those who had been on the scene, and there were no fewer than three court trials with recorded testimony, questions, and answers.

The personalities as well as the action that were revealed surpassed my greediest hopes. Not even Shakespeare could have conceived a more effective and perfectly integrated comic relief than that supplied by the two yokels who resentfully rowed the boat that brought André and Arnold together. It was a perfect stroke to have the brutish shrewdness of these low-comedy boatmen warp dangerously the elevated conspirators' history-threatening plans.

In addition to clinging doggedly to detail, the biographer dealing with events of the most throbbing emotion should use extreme literary restraint. Although the great scenes must be carefully prepared for, so that their significance will be completely manifest, once the horses start galloping, the author must step backward. His style should become stark, laconic, purely factual. It would be courting disaster to report with more than the greatest sobriety Peggy's hysterics with which she bamboozled Washington into believing her a victim, not a promoter, of the treason. It would be a desecration for the author to interpose his own sentiments between his readers and the nobility with which John André, when the hangman's rope swung above and toward him, conducted the fatal ritual of his own execution.

*

My friend Herb Alexander of Pocket Books was warning me that the salesmen at Houghton Mifflin had been embarrassed before their clients by being induced to load the bookstores with copies of *First Flowers* which had proved to be a dog on the market. Things had not been helped along by the non-performance of *Copley* and the belated publication of the *Short History of American Painting*. The salesmen would never, Herb concluded, take any book of mine seriously. I should move to another publisher where I was not stigmatized.

I was too pigheaded to take Herb's warning seriously. How right he was became clear to me when, having sent *Traitor* to Houghton Mifflin, I received a phone call, not from Lovell, my champion, but from Lovell's enemy Paul Brooks. He said that they would be willing to publish, but could not foresee many sales: I would have to accept a very small advance. This made doubly impossible my hooking on, as I had hoped to do, *The Light of Distant Skies*. Paul did not argue when I said I would go elsewhere. After a certain amount of unnecessary fiddling due to my having employed an agent (whom I soon fired), *Traitor* ended up with Harcourt, Brace, who also agreed to publish *Light*.

*

Published in 1953, *Traitor* sold better than any of my previous books except *Doctors*. Recommended by the Book of the Month Club, featured in *Life* magazine, it became the basis of a television show over CBS, partly written by me.*

The critical reception was as enthusiastic as I could hope. My fellow historian Carl Briedenbaugh stated, not untypically, "Mr. Flexner has perceived a romantic plot that far surpasses the invention of most novelists. Furthermore, he succeeds brilliantly in recapturing the tensions, the drama, the sordidness, and yet the occasional nobility . . . without the slightest departure from the truth. . . . The absorbing recital has the inventiveness of Greek tragedy."

Harcourt, after the same palace revolution that was to throw away their option for *Mohawk Baronet*, allowed *Traitor* to go out of print. It was picked up as a paperback by Collier Books, reprinted in a handsome hardcover edition by Little, Brown, and in 1991, was reissued by the Syracuse University Press. It trots along cheerfully while I hobble on a cane.

---

*See Chapter 51.

35

WILDERNESS ADVENTURE

*

IT would seem a natural progression to follow my account of Arnold's treason with the man generally considered to be the major villain during the early years of the nation. And there hung over Aaron Burr an aura of fascination. I began an exploration to discover what really was his nature and how I could handle it. The first discouragement was that his letters were utterly without fascination. He must have exerted only man-to-man the magnetism that had brought him power. What about women? True fire in that direction was revealed by the fire's having been extinguished. Burr's executors published a statement to reassure American womanhood: all his letters from females had been destroyed.

I found it no encouragement that all the major Founding Fathers, not only Hamilton whom he had killed, but Jefferson, Madison, Adams, etc., despised and distrusted Burr. Where Arnold had grandeur, Burr was sleazy throughout. Unless a writer was willing (as Gore Vidal was to be) to reverse the historical record, showing white as black and black as white, the Burr story narrates how a cheap and shoddy individual with no real convictions or abilities beyond the push to elbow himself ahead could successfully insert himself on the same stage as great men at one of the great moments of history. A truthful account of Burr could prove a fruitful subject only for a Balzacian biographer, and my interests are not Balzac's.

My next thought was to follow Arnold, the greatest Revolutionary fighter on land, with the greatest naval fighter, John Paul Jones. But

I quickly concluded that while Arnold was to some extent exonerated by the rigors and risks and triumphs of battle, Jones was by nature a brutal killer. He had murdered a man and fatally beaten another before he came to America. Having hesitated even about Arnold before I had found the poetical André as a foil, I shuddered away from John Paul Jones. (Samuel Eliot Morison was to find, in what he labeled "a sailor's biography," relief from Jones's character in his own passion for describing sea warfare.)

Directions pointed by *The Traitor and the Spy* having proved barren, I determined to take a leap into what had long been for me an imaginary realm. Like every American boy, I had been fascinated by the interaction on the frontiers between whites and Indians. We had dressed up as Indians and practiced marksmanshipn with bows and arrows. Why should I not carry my research into that enchanting land? I was less worried by my ignorance of the subject—learning was basic to my technique—than my needing to find a protagonist who offered a broad enough view and had left behind enough papers. The Daniel Boone type of pioneer, the semi-literate homesteader or fur trader, would not serve. Nor did I wish an Indian-hater, as I intended to present both sides of that irrepressible conflict. I was almost despairing when I happened on Sir William Johnson, a frontiersman-made-British-baronet, who offered biographical and historical possibilities far beyond my most sanguine hopes. That I had to search to find him signaled a need for such a book as I wished to write.

*

In 1738, at the age of twenty-three, William Johnson had emigrated to the edge of the wilderness from a farm near Dublin. Prospering on the banks of New York's Mohawk River, he came to combine, more than any other American who ever lived, Indian and white power. As Sir William, he represented his colony and then the British Crown itself, becoming official ambassador to the tribes. As Warraghiyagey, an adopted Mohawk and the adviser of many Indian nations, he kept burning in his personal backyard the council fire that was the capital of the wilderness, of a territory many times larger than all the white settlements. To his forest mansion, there journeyed from the east royal governors and colonial statesmen; from the west, sachems who ruled in savannahs no white man had ever seen. All were received hospitably. Johnson could entertain more than a thousand guests in a style both rough and grand. Through the fur trade and through the colonizing of western land he had made himself one of the richest men in America.

Content in forests, Warraghiyagey was uneasy in cities: he was a true frontiersman. Although he never visited London and avoided the colonial capitals, the letters he dispatched from primeval forests could make or destroy officials in gilded rooms. Warraghiyagey spoke to his white brothers with the force of his personal Indian alliances: the menace if need be of many thousands of raised tomahawks.

Because of his military successes during the French and Indian War, Johnson became known, to the despite of English regular officers, as "the heaven-taught general." He was one of the two Americans to be created Baronet by the British Crown. Twice he broke a British commander in chief; often he created imperial policies that His Majesty's government had no choice but follow. In 1768, he overruled the Crown and personally added to the Thirteen Colonies the area that now comprises all of Kentucky, a corner of Alabama, much of West Virginia, and Tennessee.

In character, Sir William was gargantuan: physically overwhelming, of tremendous appetites. His prowess in drinking is testified to by his death from cirrhosis of the liver; rumor asserted that he had fathered seven hundred children on women Indian and white. He was addicted to the outdoors, hunting, fighting, and fishing, but also to the arts of peace. In the wilderness, he planned for the settlers who were to clear his acres efficiently organized agricultural communities. A tyrant in his own bluff way, he could not, within his own domain, be gainsaid. Violent upon occasion, he was also benevolent, surprisingly tender to anyone, white or Indian, who was wounded or sick or bereaved, or for any other reason in need of aid. Those who were dependent on him felt toward him, for the most part, a passionate loyalty. Untutored, he was highly intelligent, able to defeat not only regulars in battle but politicians in the schemes of power.

Johnson's gifts of leadership were crowned with a mental dichotomy which in its extent and depth may well have been unique: he was able to be at home equally in cultures that were, within the development of human institutions, thousands of years apart. Sir

William was an able European man; Warraghiyagey thought and acted as an Indian. These two personalities lived together without strain in a keen mind and a passionate heart.

One of the most determining events in the history of the American Revolution took place eight months before the fighting began: Sir William, who was a staunch supporter of the Crown, died when only about sixty years old. Had he drunk less and survived, the Revolutionary War would surely have gone very differently, perhaps ending with a British victory. To give one example: had Warraghiyagey brought to Burgoyne's assistance the military might of the tribes, the surrender at Saratoga could not possibly have taken place. Burgoyne would successfully have entered New England through the back door, and cut in half the rebellion by establishing the Hudson as a British river. The French would not have been encouraged but discouraged about entering the alliance on which American victory was to depend. But Johnson's Indian wife and his white heirs were only partially able to muster his power.

*

Delighted by what I had discovered, I did not puzzle my head to wonder why so great an opportunity had remained open for me. A man so rare and picturesque and also so determining in the history of America should certainly have long occupied one of the most brightly lighted niches in American historical memory. How could it be that Johnson was only well known to experts? It was only after *Mohawk Baronet* had been published that I worked out an explanation.

National historical memory repudiates figures who do not fit accepted national preconceptions, unless, of course, the deviants were punished by failure. Sir William prospered, although he did not conform. His sexual activities have horrified. (Flamboyance in that direction is permitted to literary but not historical figures.) Among the deepest of American shibboleths is the belief that the frontier was by its very nature a spawning ground for egalitarianism. How shocking to realize that the most effective of all American frontiersmen had not been an egalitarian, not even a Tory in the conventional sense, but a feudal chief! Sir William was closer to Achilles than Daniel Boone, to King Arthur than to King George III or Benjamin Franklin.

But the most serious impediment has been that a truthful account of Warraghiyagey's career explodes those myths about the American Indian which were fabricated to justify conquest and virtual extermination, and are a cherished part of American legend. Johnson's adventures reveal that the Indians were not a stupid, incompetent, treacherous, sadistic race who needed to be purified by Christianity, justified by welcoming the stealers of their land, and, during the eighteenth century, given respectability by servile assistance to the British-American forces in their battles with the French from Canada.

Johnson's career can be understood only if it is realized that the Indian natives could be no more accurately defined as "French-Indians" or "English-Indians" than the settlers can be considered "Huron-Whites" or "Iroquois-Whites." Sachems and chiefs, like colonial governors and assemblies, were concerned with the welfare of their own nationals, and when the Indian leaders changed alliances as their national interests seemed to change, it was no more "treacherous" than the similar shifts—say, those of Prussia and France after the Treaty of Westphalia—that European statesmen were at their historical moment making.

If the Indian policies usually attributed to childish waywardness are examined with an effort to discover their logic, logic can usually be found. The tribes were in a situation like that of the Balkan States before the Russian conquest. All small and mutually hostile, they were caught between great powers. They tried similar maneuvering to ensure their safety and failed no more dismally.

It is common for historians to write that the Indians' military power should not be underestimated, and then, because of dedication to white thinking, white testimony, and the usual archives, blithely to underestimate. (Thus, Pontiac has been considered the greatest Indian warrior of the mid-eighteenth century for the very reason that made him one of the most incompetent: he tried to fight in the white manner.) Complete acceptance of the fact that in forest warfare one Indian following "savage" strategy was worth ten conventionally drilled white regulars upsets accepted explanations of the French and Indian War and Pontiac's Conspiracy. Debates around council fires loom as important as debates in legislatures; and Sir William Johnson, the man who brought Indian power to the English side, rises to his actual historical stature.

*

Respect for Indians brings to the fore impressive personalities. Tiya-noga, the Mohawk sachem known in English as Hendrick, was a statesman of rare perception, subtlety, and gifts, worthy of a place in histories of diplomacy. And the woman who was undoubtedly the most powerful member of her sex in America during the Revolutionary period (and later?) comes into focus. She far overtops the currently accepted heroine Abigail Adams, who has become a cult figure because she occasionally and ineffectually expostulated to her important husband about women's rights. Degonwadonti, also known as Molly Brant, the Mohawk wife and then widow of Warraghiyagey, was a major military commander: she controlled the Indian armies that, as allies of the British, fought the revolting whites, decimating the Mohawk and Wyoming Valleys. "One word from her," wrote the colonel officially in charge of His Majesty's Indian forces, "goes further with them than a thousand words from any white man without exception."

In addition to unearthing heroes, the Indian view reveals previously unrecognized villains, most conspicuously Sir Jeffrey Amherst. Through his injustice and savagery to the tribes, Amherst incited Pontiac's Conspiracy, even as he subsequently was to play, as adviser concerning America to the British government, an important role in defining the policies that detonated the Revolution and then lost the war that followed.

*

When I got down to work, there existed only two unexciting biographies of Johnson,* one a century and the other a generation old, that were worthy of serious consideration. The Indians, having no written language, left no such records. However, the huge archive of papers Johnson left behind—more than four million words—threw so much light on the conflict between England and France in the

---

*William L. Stone, Jr., *The Life and Times of Sir William Johnson, Bart.* 2 vols. (Albany: J. Munsell, 1865); and Arthur Pound, *Johnson of the Mohawks: A Biography of Sir William Johnson, Irish Immigrant, Mohawk War Chief, American Soldier, Empire Builder* (New York: Macmillan, 1930).

eighteenth century for the control of America that their importance as historical source material could not be overlooked. To my vast satisfaction, all of Johnson's known papers—letters to him as well as from him—had been or were about to be published. His own voluminous collection had been acquired by the New York State Library in Albany, and in 1921 publication has been inaugurated there. Twelve volumes, extending to his death, had been published by various editors. Dr. Milton W. Hamilton, who had been responsible for the last two, was gathering what had been missed for a final volume.

I would, of course, have to consult the unpublished material. To request access did not trouble my conscience as Dr. Hamilton was employed by the New York State government to make the papers available. But I knew enough of human nature to realize that he would not be pleased at my coming in from left field. I was not surprised when I received no reply to my letter.

*

Dr. Hamilton's office was hard to find in the many-corridored New York State Library, but finally I was knocking on a door labeled "Johnson Papers." I could see a human shadow through the frosted glass, but my knocking was ignored. Finally, I decided to try kicking too. At this the door opened revealing an angry woman who I judged was a secretary. "What do you want?"

"I have come, as I wrote you I would, to consult the unpublished Johnson Papers."

"Impossible," she replied as she tried to close the door on me. I pushed by her.

"I wish to speak to Dr. Hamilton."

"Impossible! Dr. Hamilton is a distinguished scholar. He cannot be disturbed." But at that moment there appeared through an inner doorway a middle-aged man with a smug expression somewhat disguised by irritation.

"What's all this noise about?"

Putting on my most courtly manner, I stretched out a hand, "Dr. Hamilton, I presume."

He ignored my hand. "What do you want?"

When I repeated my request, his face hardened. "The papers are not made available before publication."

"But I have to see them."

"Why do you have to see them?"

"I sent you a letter stating that I was writing a biography of Sir William."

Dr. Hamilton's smugness was entirely obliterated by rage. "How dare you! That's preposterous."

"Allow me to introduce myself," I said. "My name is James Thomas Flexner."

"Never heard of you." This from Dr. Hamilton.

"Perhaps you have heard of some of my books." As I named them I judged from the uneasiness that came into his eyes that he knew of some of them. But he took refuge behind a stock defense. "We want no popularizers here. The information has been reserved for the truly qualified scholar who will prepare the definitive life."

"I assume you mean yourself."

His answer was to maneuver around me and open the door into the outside corridor.

I reminded him that he was a state employee paid to make the papers available to the public. Then I amused myself by informing him that I had been a schoolmate of Governor Rockefeller's. "He's so busy, poor fellow, that I had not intended to bother him, but I suppose I will have to now."

Hamilton walked around me and shut the door.

I had won the battle but not the war. If I am ever called on to describe the plight of a soldier occupying a conquered city, I shall have memories. Everything I specifically asked for I was, with manifest ill-will, allowed to see, but I was offered no help, given no suggestions. I already knew so much about Johnson that I was not particularly upset.

*

When I called on Dr. William Fenton, the accepted expert on the Iroquois, in his office at the State University of New York, the hostility with which I was greeted indicated that he had been tipped off by Hamilton. He gave me a freshman lecture on the Mohawks. I retaliated by citing opposite information I had gleaned from Johnson's writings.

I had previously examined publications by Dr. Fenton and others on Indian culture, and in particular the Iroquois, to discover that the anthropologists had applied generalizations concerning primitive peoples to the interviews that they conducted on reservations with Indians separated by generations from their ancestral life in the forests. I had been puzzled by the extent to which their findings disagreed with what I learned from the Johnson Papers. Sir William could not possibly have achieved his power with the tribes without a profound understanding of their culture as it was practiced around him. His conclusions and activities from day to day, usually directed at specific situations and checked by the practical outcomes, were voluminously reported in his papers. He often tried to educate his associates in the colonial government and the British army, or his own subordinates, by explaining to them. This seemed to me infinitely more relevant evidence than reservation interviews. As for what had been Indian culture before the white men appeared, Sir William had stated that white influence had for generations been so great that it was impossible to reach any sound conclusions. In any case, the issue in no way affected my efforts to follow eighteenth-century Indians on warpaths and sit cross-legged at council fires where policy was made. I did not realize that in following what I considered my authentic sources to the despite of anthropological theories I was clamping a hornet's nest on my head.

*

Because what I had to report and interpret was so far from what I already knew, I spent more time on *Mohawk Baronet*—four years—than on any of my previous books. Harcourt Brace was still my publisher. They had condescended to bring out, after the success of *The Traitor and the Spy*, *The Light of Distant Skies*. However, they did not wait to receive the manuscript before they informed me they were not interested in *Mohawk Baronet*. Michael Bessie, a leading editor at Harper's, was a friend of mine. He offered to publish but warned me that there was little interest among his colleagues. I should, of course, have gone on, but I was sick of peddling manuscripts. I assumed that Bessie would see me through. But he soon decamped to help found a new publishing house, Athenaeum. His departure was by no means amicable—Harper's president Cass Canfield felt he had been betrayed—and the bad odor clung to Bessie's leavings. I was assigned to a just promoted editor who was bewildered and frightened as a lamb suddenly separated from his flock. It was clear that I could achieve nothing without maneuvering around him.

It had been part of my regular technique to achieve broad contacts in a publishing house on the theory that no one was as concerned with my book as I, and also because it was useful to keep the various departments informed of what the others were doing. But now, when the need was greatest, I was stopped dead. Harper's enforced a rule that the assigned editor could not under any circumstances be bypassed.

This induced various minor irritations, and then came the "lulu": I was shown as already approved a jacket for my book featuring a nubile Indian girl naked to the waist. I knew that according to long tradition and the law what would be taboo for a white woman was acceptable for a non-white. But the application to *Mohawk Baronet* was such a belittling of the tribes as my whole text fought against. And I would be misrepresented as seeking sales by being salacious.

I did succeed in getting my editor to raise the question. He reported back that his superiors had admitted that the use of such a jacket by a cheap publisher could be misunderstood, but no one could attribute low motives to Harper & Brothers. I was, of course, not placated, but my white rabbit would do nothing more than wring his paws.

The jacket did, in fact, greatly damage *Mohawk Baronet*. The readers it attracted were disappointed, while readers who might have been interested never picked up the book at all. Even worse, the jacket played into the hands of those who wished to convict me of unworthy popularization. Even favorable reviewers disapprovingly attributed to me overemphasis on Johnson's sex life.

Harper's strictly enforced the lack of enthusiasm of which Bessie had warned me. Johnson was still very much of a hero in the Mohawk Valley partly because association with his memory was used by the older families as a touchstone with which to exclude the more recent immigrants, mostly from central Europe, who had been imported as factory workers. An author's tour through the valley would surely sell books, but Harper's refused to put up a penny. I decided to go at my own expense. An energetic member of the Montgomery County Historical Society, who had on my previous exploring trips taken me under her wing, arranged for lectures and autographing parties in the combined book and periodical stores that dotted the valley. Appearing at the first, I was received by a proprietor both apologetic and angry.

She had ordered books from Harper's. None had arrived. There were no copies to sign. Telephone calls to other stores revealed the same situation. I made an enraged call to the sales department at Harper's which elicited neither apologies nor promises. Yes, the orders had come in, but since the stores lacked established charge accounts, no books had been sent or would be.

*

I shuddered to see that the review in *The New York Times Book Review* was by Dr. Fenton. It did contain a lengthy diatribe upbraiding me for not recognizing that anthropologists had the answers, but in describing the book as a whole he revealed that the subject matter and treatment were exciting. So did other reviews even where anthropologists carped. Although the original edition (1954) did not bring in a pile, the earnings were adequate to keep me going.

There have been subsequent editions. The extra-illustrated printing by Little, Brown (1979) was marred by an editor who changed the title to what he thought would sell better, *Lord of the Mohawks*, thus throwing away what momentum had been achieved by *Mohawk Baronet*. There was a German edition. In 1991, Syracuse University Press brought out *Mohawk Baronet* as part of an academically approved series. On the popular side, audio rights have been bought by Books on Tape. On the scholarly side, *New York History* summed up: "Though some specialists have argued with Flexner's interpretations, none have disputed the overall value of this work which has become a standard entry in the bibliography of Colonial New York."

36

THAT WILDER IMAGE

*

AFTER *The Light of Distant Skies* had at long last been published and *Mohawk Baronet*, which I had undertaken in the meanwhile, had been completed, I resolved to write what would be the third volume of my intended four-volume history of American painting. I, again quoting from William Cullen Bryant's sonnets, settled on the title *That Wilder Image*.

At the conclusion of my previous volume, I had depicted American painting on its most elevated scale as ailing because the generation of Allston, Vanderlyn, and Morse had failed in their efforts to acclimate European conceptions to a United States that was looking westward and aggressively going its own way. The new volume would be aimed at the next two generations, when, partially due to the unfortunate example presented by their predecessors, the artists created what I called "The Native School of American Painting." During the "era of good feelings," when the Monroe Doctrine warned Europe to keep its distance, the leading painters based their art on their own combined observations and on vernacular styles developed in their own homeland.

At the center of the movement were the Hudson River School landscapists. In writing my *Pocket History*, I had adopted the then accepted denigration of that school, but now major concern opened my memory and my heart. My childhood experiences when summering in countrysides the painters celebrated—Chocorua and the Hudson Highlands—rushed back, and I felt again that passion for American light which had called me home from Europe.

I found it highly significant that the Hudson River School constituted the only art movement in all American history which appealed to the whole spectrum of American life, from connoisseurs to ordinary citizens, all of whom enjoyed and acquired what pictures were within their range. Was this not a good augury for my continual desire to introduce the American people to their art? Perhaps this book would be a catalyst, supporting on a more sophisticated plane the crusade I had undertaken with my *Pocket History.*

*

By the time the Civil War cut its bloody wound through American society, the landscapists who led the Native School were middle-aged, with established points of view, techniques, and markets. They continued their approach with only minor changes. But the rising generation of painters, disillusioned by the horrors of the war, repelled by the upward march of industrialism, fled, before they had learned to paint at home, to the studios of Europe. There, they picked up the latest artistic fashions, bringing back wave after wave of foreign influence.

I laid aside for my projected fourth volume direct discussion of this development. Its impact on my current labors was the reiterated vilification of the Native School by generations of returned art students. A devotee wrote typically, "Nothing more alien to recognized art everywhere, outside of England at least, has existed anywhere than the now defunct and moribund school of landscape painting." This fitted in with the endemic obeisance of esthetically minded Americans to everything European, creating a still reigning prejudice that I would do my best to overcome.

The Native School pictures were unable, despite their onetime great distribution and popularity, to testify in their own defense since they had been expelled from sight. Occasional breakthroughs were short-lived. The ever-innovative Museum of Modern Art staged an exhibition of "American Romantic Painting." The Whitney Museum in 1945 staged a small exhibition of Hudson River School landscapes. The great figure there, Lloyd Goodrich, stated that, although he appreciated the Hudson River artists' "simple and unpretending companionship with nature," he found their canvases "unpleasantly hot

in color, thin in texture, and meagre in form . . . painfully limited."
In his widely admired history of American painting published in
1956, Edgar P. Richardson did not even acknowledge the existence
of the Hudson River School, although he discussed various of the
painters in various other categories.

*

Employing my best energies, connections, and know-how, I found it
by no means easy to locate the pictures I needed to write about. The
older museums did have some neglected canvases usually hanging in
storerooms or back corridors, and only half visible under discolored
varnish. Two museums, the Brooklyn, led by John I. H. Baur, and
the Detroit, led by Richardson, were buying American nineteenth-
century art, but their holdings were incomplete and small. The best
collections were not in art institutions. The New-York Historical
Society had preserved landscapes along with furniture, etc., and the
Century Association, a private club partly founded by the Hudson
River School artists, had preserved their works as an expression of
fraternal piety.

There were various flukes. A successful shoe manufacturer named
Ward Melville lived in Stony Brook, Long Island, where he set up a
local museum. Informed that the community had contained an artist
named William Sidney Mount, he notified dealers that he would buy
his work. There being no other market for the achievements of this
able genre painter who was closely linked to the Hudson River
School, pictures came streaming in. Thinking that Melville might
have collected information about Mount, I called at his office. He
was complimented by my interest, but knew only that the artist had
been a local boy. However, Melville had, by buying when no one
else would, established such a corner on Mount that, when the artist
finally became greatly admired, there were almost no pictures for
other museums or collectors to acquire. Any that could be purchased
brought tremendous prices.

Maxim Karolik was the second Russian, following Sawitzky, to
play a major role in the discovery of American art. A prominent
opera singer, he had fled to New York and fallen on hard times. He
was, according to the story that circulated, sleeping, as a homeless

man, on a bench in Central Park when a passerby, who had been a devotee of opera in Russia, recognized him, took him home, and presented him to New York society. He married an elderly Bostonian spinster named Codman, rich and of the best lineage. The fine New England furniture she had inherited fascinated him, and he decided to make it the nucleus of a collection. With great perspicacity, he worked in conjunction with Boston's Museum of Fine Arts, taking advantage of its expertise and donating the objects as they were acquired.

His furniture collection completed, Karolik started another: nineteenth-century American painting. Perhaps because of the bad name that had been given to the once-leading painters, Karolik decided to seek out little-known artists. This was, by its emphasis, to have a quirky effect on subsequent scholarship, but he did exhume two landscape painters of great ability: Martin Johnson Heade and Fitz Hugh Lane. Most of the huge collection was still in a basement storeroom. The Boston Museum helped by being the most generously trusting of any I ever encountered. I was ushered into the storeroom, shown the telephone which I could use when I wanted to be let out, and then locked in to prowl, unsupervised and undisturbed, wherever and for however long I pleased.

Karolik, known to us as "Uncle Maxim," was a big, endlessly effervescent man, with a huge voice and heart of gold. I got into a bind with a pathological collector from which Uncle Maxim could help me disentangle. When I reached "information" in Newport, the operator, as soon as I had said Maxim, supplied the name Karolik, which I interpreted as fame. And when I reached him, he boiled over with enthusiasm, assuring me that on any occasion when I could use his help—anything whatsoever—I could rely on him.

*

The most authentic and influential statement of the Hudson River School doctrines was *Letters on Landscape Painting* (1855) by the then leader of the school, Asher B. Durand. He stated that it was pernicious for a beginner to accept any instruction beyond routine technical information about paint and canvas, and dangerous for him to look hard at pictures by other hands until he had evolved his own way of seeing by solitary study with the legitimate teacher: Nature.

Only after he had finally established his fundamental style should a painter consider emendations and improvements gleaned from the works of other artists.

Since in my own role as a writer I believed that artistic treatment should grow from what you wish to express rather than be imposed from outside, I was in complete sympathy with Durand's advice. But, of course, no doctrine could be more opposite to the convictions of the Europeanized young lions who pursued "art for art's sake." They regarded subject matter as no more than a vehicle for expressing their own sensibility and virtuosity.

Durand's advice might seem a prescription for each painter's going off on his own tangent, but it did not turn out that way. The basic craft instruction of the painters had been the same. Poor boys who needed to make their livings, almost all had from an early age been employed in engravers' workshops. Deprived of color by the medium, they had imbibed reliance on what are called "black-and-white values." Gray, Durand wrote, although never visible in a landscape painting, was of fundamental importance since it modified all colors "without dissipating them." The gradation of values, caused by a lesser or greater accumulation of atmosphere, indicated distance, the darks becoming lighter, the lights softer and weaker, until the mingling of dark and light implied infinity. Morning, evening, rain, mist, or complete clarity required different value sequences. Light, as it entered all parts of the picture, threw shadows and was reflected back by earth of different consistencies, water smooth or wind-blown, rocks, wood, foliage, and the creations of mankind. Aerial effects were thus built into the basic structure of the painted view. Atmosphere, Durand wrote, "carries us into a picture instead of allowing us to be detained in front of it." This created the sense, inherent in Hudson River School landscapes, of space that implied the size of the American continent, even when the scene actually shown is restricted.

*

The Hudson River landscapists were, as I was to point out in a speech I gave at the Vatican, in essence religious painters. "Nature," Durand wrote, "in its wondrous structure and functions that minister to our well-being is fraught with high and holy meaning only surpassed by the light of Revelation." This conviction inspired not imaginative flight but ecstatic selection. As Durand put it, the artist was given "unbounded liberty to perceive in the infinite beauty and significance of nature . . . the time and place where she displays her chief perfections." Should that be found, "the artist will have no occasion to idealize the portrait."

However, Durand denounced "servile" imitation of Nature as "in every way unworthy. The artist as a poet will have seen more than the mere matter of fact but no more than is there and than another may see if it is pointed out to him." The painter carried his viewers closer to the divine by presenting truthfully those aspects of Nature that most elevated his own emotions, which were more sensitive than the emotions of those not esthetically gifted, but in essence the same. It was as if a preacher inspired his congregation from applying his deeper understanding to expounding God's word.

Statistics reveal that during the mid-nineteenth century, church attendance across America was greater than at any other epoch. Religious revivals moved across the land. A significant reason for the great popularity of the Hudson River School was the feeling that a landscape over the mantlepiece was supplemental to the Bible on the table. This phenomenon outraged the next generation of painters: "The American savages in art," like aborigines, "draw their religion, from woods and waterfalls."

A corollary from the Hudson River School's reverence of Nature as God's handiwork was that, even as a preacher would be blasphemous if he rewrote the Scriptures to suit his own ends, the painter should not seek self-expression by inserting his ego between the viewer and "types of divine attributes." Artistic skill was shown by so subordinating means to ends that the viewer feels he is looking at Nature's own face. No doctrine could be less hospitable to the displays of personal refinement and exquisite brushwork valued by the next generation of painters.

*

The returned students employed small canvases where finesse could be top dog. Thus, they most abhorred and fashioned into weapons with which to belabor the Hudson River School the huge landscapes created by Frederick E. Church and Albert Bierstadt. That down the decades the attackers never bothered really to look at the pictures is revealed by their failure to notice that the artists they thus bracketed together worked in basically different styles. One did not even belong to the Hudson River School. The German-American Bierstadt was in his own generation considered "the most successful Düsseldorf artist in America." His grandiose studio concoctions, related to theatrical scenery, had no particularity although labeled as showing the Rocky Mountains.

Church, who belonged to the high Hudson River School generation, was anything but a slovenly generalizer. He practiced a virtuosity far beyond the skills of the returned lions although aimed in the opposite direction: to reveal, with the utmost accuracy and versimilitude, Nature in all its variety in miniature. Miniature? Church's tremendous canvases were in the foregrounds and, to a lesser degree, in the middle distances compendia of innumerable, exactly rendered details. The whole was held together by stunning light effects that strained naturalism to the limits but not beyond.* In England, he was often more admired than Turner, since he did not allow earth to be dissolved by light. Church thought of himself as a scientific recorder, but he encouraged critics who sought out and expounded religious interpretations.

*

The most extreme deviation from Hudson River practice was due to "a dreadful disease." George Inness was an epileptic. He could not explore wild nature with the other painters; he could not hold himself down to detailed representation. Add that, never having worked as an engraver, he was not held back from a pure coloristic style by black-and-white values. He did paint some major panoramic landscapes, but as he grew older, he employed small canvases and depended more and more on the evocation of mood and emotion by saturation of light. He had spent some years abroad, and accepted, toward his own ends, enough influence from the Barbizon School to

---

*I cannot resist quoting Henry James on Church: "It is the kind of art which seems perpetually skirting the edge of something worse than itself, like a woman who has a taste for florid ornaments, who would dress herself in a way to make people stare, yet should really be a very respectable person."

enable the returning lions to consider him one of their own. But he always insisted in the Hudson River School manner that he was self-taught. When Impressionism began making its impact on America, Inness was outraged that he was considered "so lacking in necessary detail that as a legitimate landscape painter I have come to be classed as a follower of that new fad." Monet was either a humbug or needed an optician.

*

The taboo against the Hudson River School, shared by his biographer Lloyd Goodrich, had impeded understanding of the early development of Winslow Homer's art. Although, since he was the greatest artist of them all, the luxuriance of his growth rose higher and in wider directions, the Hudson River School fundamentals remained. It was my good fortune to present this new insight as the climax of *That Wilder Image*.

Homer could have been quoting Durand when he stated, "If a man wants to be an artist, he should never look at pictures." Homer did go twice to Europe, but a friend commented that his "difficulty in taking impressions from foreign art is almost ludicrous." His work had no more than coincidental resemblance to that of the young lions who were during most of his career (he did not die until 1910) streaming back from Paris. Henry James wrote that if Homer only had "a good many more secrets and mysteries, and coquetries," he might, despite his lack of "fancy," be "almost a distinguished painter." Like the Hudson River artists, Homer believed that nothing should stand between the artist and the subject he wished to express.

*

Although landscape painting occupied the starring role in *That Wilder Image*, I devoted to it only eight of the nineteen chapters. Next came genre with three, foreign influence with two, and with one apiece, portraiture, still life, and efforts to revive the high style. There were two portmanteau chapters: artist life and also "Popular Art, Prints, and 'Folk Painters.'" I was much concerned with the invasion of picture making by a revolutionary new device, the camera.

Diversity was more easily handled than in my previous books because the terrain was so much larger. When roads entangle on a narrow isthmus, you find yourself puzzling your way at many a crossroad and sometimes not even sure on which road you are traveling. But, in the mid and late nineteenth century, high roads tended to run, even if somewhat parallel, at some distance from each other.

The bigger scene was inhabited by many more painters who were important enough to be discussed, if only briefly. The Frick had files, sometimes rather skimpy, on them all, but finding authentic canvases was hard and tricky. Probably I would have done better had I been satisfied with only mentioning a name when I could not get my feet solidly on the ground—my greatest gaucherie was concerning Blakelock whose work had been so adulterated with fakes—but I was lured ahead by developing a technique by which I could with great rapidity master the scattered printed sources concerning lesser artists.

*

In honor of a deceased trustee, the Rockefeller Foundation had financed at the New York Public Library the Frederick Lewis Allen Room, a high-ceilinged, ground-floor facility containing eleven semi-independent working areas for writers.

Those admitted were all professionals, and we developed a warm esprit de corps, having coffee breaks and lunches together, forming the little informal club which recently (May 19, 1995) was described in *The New York Times* with great nostalgia by one of America's major biographers, Robert Caro.

We did have a certain number of agreeable flirtatious young ladies, but one of the workers was a middle-aged woman who did not often associate with us. Once she did drink coffee with me. I asked her what she was doing. She replied that she was writing a feminist book and outlined for me her major arguments. Feeling increasingly sorry for her, I interjected, "Betty, you'll never make an impression with that. It is just what I used to hear my mother say a generation ago." Betty Friedan persevered, publishing *The Feminine Mystique.**

---

*Another example of my perspicacity took place when I was swimming in a rocky Connecticut gorge along with Lawrence Langner of the Theatre Guild. We had never gotten along well together since, when he had been showing off by lecturing a group of reporters on the medieval theater, I had used my Harvard erudition to correct him on the difference between miracle and mystery plays. Now he told me that the

*

A glory of the Allen Room was that you could summon materials from anywhere in the library. The Art Room had collected catalogues and clippings which they filed under the artists' names. As I prepared to write about a relatively obscure painter, I would secure his file. Selecting the publication that seemed most inclusive, I would read it with great care, taking notes. Then I would skim the other publications, trusting to catch as I ran my eyes down the page any information I had not already noted. This method enabled me to complete in an inclusive manner in a single day my research on an artist. And, for those who did not know the secret, a listing of the sources gave an impression of weeks of digging. Even the dourest disapprovers of *That Wilder Image* could not help being impressed by my source references.

*

When, after three years of work, *That Wilder Image* was completed, I had no choice but to send it to the editor who had been so inadequate concerning *Mohawk Baronet.* He received me, after reading the manuscript, with what I can only describe as a fishy look on his face. A fine book! So well written! But, Harper's could not foresee enough sales to justify publication. However, and here he smiled, if I would write a one-volume history of American painting, they would be glad to give me a contract. As I quietly picked up the two typewriter-paper boxes that contained my manuscript and made for the door I looked back to see that his expression had changed to pity.

*

I was meditating on what book I should write with such obvious sales possibilities that I could attach *That Wilder Image* to its tail when soon I was accosted at a cocktail party by a man as short and stocky as I am. He introduced himself as Alan Williams of Little, Brown. He had, he explained, been assigned to find an author for a

---

Guild was planning to base a musical on the play *Green Grow the Lilacs.* I felt it my duty to warn him: "Don't do it! You'll lose your shirt. *Green Grow the Lilacs* was one of the worst plays I have ever seen." The musical was called *Oklahoma.*

[348]

one-volume biography of George Washington. My ex-wife had suggested my name; he had read some of my books; and could offer me a contract.

I had during my years of living vicariously in eighteenth-century America met Washington a good many times, at different places and under different circumstances. Never had the person I encountered matched the "Washington" who matched what I had been taught by "common knowledge" or through reading biographies. I had become increasingly convinced that there was a need for a more valid interpretation and dreamed that, when I was old enough, I might undertake it. Now tempted, I concluded that I was old enough.

When I made it a condition that Little, Brown undertake *That Wilder Image* and proceed quickly with its publication, not the slightest objection was raised. There was even enthusiasm—they produced (1962) an over-sized volume that was the handsomest I ever received—which I liked to interpret as a sign that my crusade was moving on. The Society of American Historians found themselves, to their amazement, honoring a book on American art, giving me my first major award, their Parkman Prize.

37

EXPLOSION OF AMERICAN ART

*

WHEN I signed the contract for a biography of Washington that included publication of *That Wilder Image*, it had been my intention, once the one-volume Washington was completed, to write the fourth volume of my history of American painting. But the *Washington* had expanded to four volumes which, with the addition of a one-volume condensation, occupied my major attention for some fourteen years, from 1962 to 1976.

During this period, I had not abandoned my concern with American painting. My colleagues in that field still occupied an important part of Beatrice's and my social life. I was amenable to writing off-springs of my previous studies, most conspicuously a short book, that was to be very widely distributed by Time, Inc., as part of a mail-order series: *The World of Winslow Homer*. I delivered so often lectures summarizing one or another of my painting books that the texts probably earned more per word than any of my other writings. As the interest in American art increased, my painting volumes reappeared in paperback. Continuing to write for magazines, being consulted by museums and for restorations, I had kept my hand in. But when my Washington project was finally completed, I found that my most intense interest had shifted to American Revolutionary experiences. And there was no further need to push the interest in American painting along.

The situation had been changing to an extent and so rapidly that, had my colleagues and I not dug the foundations, would seem inexplicable. Colleges and university art departments which had sneered at American art, could no longer dare not to present a bouquet of courses. The opportunities thus being opened attracted Ph.D. candidates who, without abandoning their superciliousness, climbed on the bandwagon, scattering theses and monographs. The values of the paintings, even many formerly almost unsalable, were approaching the stratosphere and still rising. Big corporations were beginning to sponsor lavish exhibitions and applying publicity money to the publication of elaborate, color-illustrated catalogs.

What credit or responsibility can I claim for this stupendous phenomenon?

*

As a biographer, I have examined hundreds of autobiographies, and have come to regard as a demonstration of human frailty the almost unanimity with which the authors present themselves as prime movers in whatever events they have been concerned with. In myself essaying autobiography, I have come to realize that this reflects more than ego: the distortion is inherent in the medium. Autobiography sacrifices its particular value as literature and as source material if it becomes a compendium of research that some outsider could have achieved. The more widely and perceptively the autobiographer looks around him, the more he gathers in evidence to refine his vision, the better the result. Yet the base of that vision has to be, like the beams given off by a lighthouse, the position he himself occupies.

Only concerning American painting have I been actively engaged with fellow workers in what came to be a mass movement. As I trembled at the thought of trying to assess my contribution, I came on a description that fellow worker Charles Coleman Sellers wrote for the *William and Mary Quarterly* in a review of *The Light of Distant Skies* (1954):

"The field of American art history is still in its vernal season. A large and varied company roams its verdure, while a few school-trained specialists endeavor ineffectively to herd the band along. In such a situation, there is always the one who runs ahead of the other, finding and shouting and raising the whole level of excitement. This one is James Thomas Flexner. His work runs boldly ahead of detailed individual research from which history must be written. But it is by no means premature. It has advanced and stimulated the whole body, strengthening by its popularization."

In 1973, some twenty years later, Russell Lynes, that knowing and genial writer on American cultural life, wrote of me, "It seems that almost single-handedly he revived an interest in nineteenth-century American painting." But the greatest accolade I received came from Lloyd Goodrich in a most peculiar form.

*

From his post at the Whitney Museum, of which he was to become the director, Lloyd Goodrich had long been the institutional figure most concerned with what interest in historical American art was then being pursued. As we have seen, Goodrich scorned the Hudson River School. He was making deep studies of Eakins, Homer, and Ryder, and it was with this triumvirate, who lapped over into the twentieth century, that his usual backward look began. It was fortunate for my relationship with Goodrich that I did not proceed to my fourth volume as I would surely have run afoul of him—he did not take competition lying down—but he tolerated my approach to Homer—through the Hudson River School—as too far away to collide with his ideas.

It must have been in the 1950s that Goodrich got on an Eighty-sixth Street crosstown bus and sat down beside me. Suddenly, he said, "It's funny to think that if this bus was wrecked, the two greatest students of American art would be killed." I glanced at him to see if he was joking, but he looked as serious as he always did, except after several drinks when he became surprisingly hilarious. Now he was clearly dead sober.

That he should assign so high a position to himself was remarkable only in his choosing this moment to mention it. But why link me in? I finally concluded that he was breaking American painting in half, establishing his claim to the more recent achievement and handing over the first two centuries to me.

*

Allan Nevins wrote me, "You have added a new dimension to our knowledge to the appreciation of American history. That is a memorable achievement."

*

But trouble lay ahead.

38

THE ART MARKET PLACE

*

THE community of art dealers has been eager to take a lion's share of credit for the revival of interest in American art. They do have a claim.

The basis of their trade is, of course, to buy cheap and sell expensive. Pictures already highly prized are procurable at prices payable only by major dealers who need to sell them to buyers capable of large outlays. But small dealers are susceptible to small currents, and it was thus they who were given to recognize that the value of American art was on the rise. They began stockpiling canvases while selling what made for them a nice profit. As the stakes rose higher, enter major dealers like Knoedler and Wildenstein. There can be no doubt that in our capitalist society, when the values of the canvases rose, so did the prestige.

At every advance in value, the profit motive sent out more human bloodhounds to smell out possible merchandise. "Lost" paintings came down from attics, up from basements, were lifted off obscure walls and into the ministrations of conservators. Engaged in my research, I would periodically drop in on those dealers who I knew were concerned with American art to examine what they had acquired since my last visit. Thus, as I moved through a small area in New York City, I was in effect touring the nation, since what the dealers were gathering in and pulsing out were filling in the vacuums in museums and collections everywhere.

When I entered a dealer's emporium, I could count on being favorably received. Although I did not publicize any of their pictures unless one happened to fit in with what I was writing, I was encouraging a favorable climate for American art. I was careful to keep myself clear of any financial connection—never purchasing or even asking a price—which meant the dealers and I could relax together, enjoying a similar interest, exchanging information. If I appeared in the late afternoon, they would unsheath a bottle of whiskey. I was entrusted never to carry tales from one gallery to another.

*

That the dealers were concerned with selling pictures one by one presented me with superlative opportunities for my extended scrutinies of canvases. On a simple easel or one upholstered in plush, whether in a reasonably comfortable room or one tricked up to a millionaire's taste; whether the canvas was carried in by the dealer himself or a liveried lackey, the painting was so placed and so lighted as to be perfectly visible. Under these favorable conditions, I was able to see much that would under ordinary circumstances be almost or completely invisible.

Concerning John Quidor's *The Wall Street Gate*, which I studied at Hirschel & Adler, I wrote: "As we examine the picture closely, hillocks in the foreground form themselves into a giant lying on his side and comfortably observing as he smokes his pipe. More staring brings out a gun beside him and then a huge dog—could it be Rip Van Winkle's Snyder?*—who barks at the movement of the normal-size people. Finally, another tremendous figure appears to complete a frieze across the whole front of the picture, this one sound asleep, perhaps Rip in another manifestation. Raising my eyes again to the concourse of burghers parading through a normally shaped world, I realized that they are all touched with madness. The three boys in the foreground carry mischief beyond sanity, and the horse's eye belongs to a wizard."

*

---

*Quidor painted a continuing epic, very different from Washington Irving's, although drawn from *Rip Van Winkle*.

My greatest good luck took place at Knoedler's, where I had got into the habit of wandering unannounced into the second floor-quarters of the American department presided over by Davidson. His secretary usually smiled a greeting, but one afternoon she leapt up as if to get between me and some pictures hanging on the walls. I saw at a glance that they were renditions of Indian life by Alfred Jacob Miller, although far superior to any of his work I had previously seen. Assuming from the secretary's manner that when Davidson appeared I would be shown out, I stared as hard as I could.

Enter Davidson. To his secretary, he said, "Since Mr. Flexner has seen the pictures we can't deny that we have them." Then to me, "If you promise to say nothing until I give the word, I'll show you all we have. What you see here is the beginning."

I was ushered into a back room containing only a table a chair and a lamp. The door was locked behind me. After a while, the key was turned and on the table was placed a pile of irregularly shaped sheets of paper, uneven in size but all small, with pasted-on corrections, spotted, torn, and stained by travel. Clearly, these were the original watercolors Miller had made on his trip far beyond the white settlements during which he had first created an image of the Rocky Mountains!

Miller had been a greenhorn, a minor Maryland portrait painter gathered up by an aristocratic explorer who wished to have large oil paintings of his adventures executed for his castle in Scotland. That the watercolors I was examining had been regarded by the artist as no more than rough notes explained, so I came to realize, their fascination and esthetic value. Confident that the images would be civilized before they faced the criticism of the knowing, and working too fast for thought, he had surrendered totally to the lust of the eyes, the exhilaration of his adventure.

Watercolor was not in Miller's day practiced as an art in its own right: its function was coloring drawings. The effects that could be achieved by allowing light to be reflected through the medium from the white surface beneath were not to be regarded as an asset for another fifty years: Miller had laid his watercolors on heavily as if they were oil paint, achieving his brilliance by laying gemlike hues against opaque blacks. Working to rapidly to mix colors or even select a wide variety, he employed a few tints in their pure state, keeping them separate and often touching in highlights with Chinese white. The stronger foreground colors reappeared in the distance, not reduced in brightness but diminished in size, becoming at last clearly visible only through a magnifying glass.

His object being to make models for large oil paintings in depicting often crowded scenes, Miller included in the utmost miniature everything he would then need. Combinations of background streaks unrepresentational from a reading distance became, if more closely scrutinized, men or horses. Although I could not identify tiny dots of color in the deepest distance, so strong was the artist's conviction that I was sure they represented something that was there. Impressionism without the Impressionist technique! I was never in my long life to experience any other pictures as I experienced these.

When I returned to the large room where hung the watercolors Davidson thought most enticing, I was flabbergasted. Up on the walls, framed, matted, and under glass, the pictures had lost their tremendous immediacy. Realizing that soon all the sheets that I had examined would be flattened out, repaired, and at least matted, I recognized in a surge what a sensational privilege good luck had given me.

*

Since attribution to a particular artist is the pillar on which the art trade rests, it has to be defined for a purchaser and the public at large as a solid pillar rooted in firm ground. But, of course, there are quicksands. Stylistic judgments depend on acknowledged definitions of style—the "experts" often disagree—and must then acceptably be applied. There is the question which rises with any prolific artist as to what extent the pictures were painted by studio assistants before being touched up (if at all) by the artist himself. Paintings (unlike sculpture) have always to appear complete, without blemish, which calls in, to a greater or lesser extent, restorers who are also repainters. Even if the picture is not an outright forgery, there may be little of the master there. But the value of the picture depends on a resolute attribution to the master.

In the "corpus" got together by a scholar, all variables can be given consideration and noted. Such a writer as I can elude most of the uncertainty by referring only to the pictures that stand on the solidest ground, and even then, if I feel the necessity, expressing unresolved doubts. But when considering whether to buy a picture, the dealer is allowed little time for waffling, and his answer has to be a positive yes or no. Although his pocketbook and possibly his reputation are at risk, if he habitually steps away when not altogether convinced, he can leave himself with nothing to sell, while less finicky competitors gobble up the market. And dealers with any breadth of merchandise cannot exert true expertise. Acquiring a picture involves optimism, and, once the picture is bought, the optimism must be turned into conviction that will allow the dealer forcibly to persuade a purchaser.

Early on, I had expressed doubt concerning a dealer's attribution and found that I was no longer welcome. My indiscretion had had two negative effects. It had embarrassed the dealer in his own conviction and, more seriously, put his integrity to the test. If an acknowledged expert had expressed doubt, could he honestly, or at least safely, not thus inform the prospective purchaser? One word of warning was enough to make me more discreet.

A dealer would be enchanted, of course, to have me endorse his attribution, but this was not expected. Endorsements were worth money, and to be known to give them carried an implication that a scholar was selling his integrity. Concerning attribution I never opened my mouth, although I would express esthetic interest, as this was personal to myself.

The instability of attribution, a menace to the entire market place, fostered an informal conspiracy of silence. Dealers of reputation were loath by attacking each other to lower public confidence. Collectors did not wish to impugn their taste or lower the value of what they had already bought. Museum directors and curators, who had persuaded their trustees to appropriate large sums, did not relish admitting that they had been fooled. Art museums tried to protect donors. The National Gallery in Washington urged experts not to dispute attributions in the Chester Dale collection, which they were exhibiting on loan until Dale had died and they had inherited.

Since even the most reputable dealers had to take risks, the situation encouraged a quiet bravado. I was amazed at the amount of carelessness that lay around. A small dealer showed me a photograph of a Patroon portrait in bad condition, with half the face missing.

He had handed the canvas on to a major dealer for restoration and sale. Following it there, I arranged to have it brought to me in one of their elegant showing rooms. Not a blemish was visible. Interested in some details, I picked up the ornamental phone that was by my elbow, explained what I had in mind and asked for a copy of the photograph taken before restoration. "Restoration?" came the reply. "Restoration! The portrait is in absolutely mint condition."

Even more brazen was Edith Halpert of the Downtown Gallery, the most important dealer who specialized in American art. She showed me an early New York portrait bearing an inscription which, visibly to the naked eye, had been written over a different one. When I asked Mrs. Halpert whether she had deciphered the one below, she asked indignantly how I dared suggest that there were two inscriptions.

This may just have been putting me in my place as a nosy scholar. I was glad to have an opportunity to put her in her place. Among her major clients was Mrs. John D. Rockefeller, Jr., who, partly because of her influence, had established a museum of folk art at Colonial Williamsburg. As I drifted into the Downtown Gallery, I saw that the exhibition room had been rehung with folk art and that Halpert was ushering around Mrs. Rockefeller. As I started to saunter in, Halpert turned on me with an angry face. She was gesturing me away when Mrs. Rockefeller spoke. "Why, Jimmie! How nice to see you!" Halpert almost tore her features apart by the speed with which she rearranged them.

*

Mrs. Halpert became the storm center of the most widespread brouhaha that involved many more institutions and important persons than any other that arose through my many years of involvement with American painting. It all started in 1935 when an itinerant "picker" brought into the Downtown Gallery a remarkable picture signed with a name unknown to the art trade: "W. M. Harnett, 1890." It depicted an old-fashioned revolver hanging aginst a battered door. The rendition of texture—rust-flecked gun barrel, stained and cracked ivory stock, battered brown wood door marked with nails and nail holes, and an old clipping glued thereon with one edge turned back; its wizardry in duplicating narrow space—all made it

[358]

almost impossible for the eye not to register that it was observing reality. A masterpiece of American folk art, it invoked the emotions inspired by contemporary surrealism. Mrs. Halpert realized that the painter, if more works could be discovered, would resemble a gold mine. She sent out via the moccasin telegraph of the art jungle a message that she was in the market for any paintings signed "Harnett." A surprisingly plentiful supply streamed into her gallery.

Harnett's most celebrated painting in his lifetime had been *After the Hunt*, which hung for a quarter of a century in Theodore Stewart's New York saloon. Some six feet high, it depicted objects relevant to the theme—dead game, a rifle, a bugle, a power horn, a crushed felt hat, etc. They were depicted hanging on a door with ornate hinges. In faraway London, the *Commercial Gazette* described how regular patrons fleeced "gentlemen from the country and particularly from Chicago," who "declared that no one could take them in and the objects were objects hung up with the intent to fool people." After the bets had risen as high as the stranger would go, he was urged to try to swing a jug hanging at the bottom of the composition.

A California newspaperman, Alfred Frankenstein, applied for and was granted a Guggenheim for a book on Harnett. He hurried to New York. Completely an outsider to the art world there and without an eastern suavity, he was received by Halpert without too much enthusiasm. He was always burrowing, asking questions, looking at pictures with an inquiring, skeptical eye. That a certain number of the "Hartnetts" were forgeries was general knowledge. However, it seemed to Frankenstein very strange when, within the artist's universally accepted oeuvre, he diagnosed, despite overlapping subject matter and composition, what he considered two very different painting styles. He called them "hard" and "soft."

The hard style, which included the revolver and *After the Hunt*, showed a "fanatical" concern with texture. Every object was depicted with the utmost clarity, and spatial relationships were firmly defined. But in the "soft" pictures, no effort was made to differentiate textures. There was an overall "muted, radiant, powdery surface" that reminded Frankenstein of Vermeer. Instead of achieving tactile sensation there were brilliant contrasts of color. This soft style was less powerful but had more esthetic appeal.

Frankenstein's concerns grew when he realized that postage stamps realistically portrayed in pitures attributed to Harnett had not been issued until after Harnett had died.

In his general research, Frankenstein had found mention of a still life painter named John Frederick Peto. He sniffed out that Peto had lived in a little village on the New Jersey shore. Questioning at the local post office directed him a house still occupied by Peto's daughter. She led him to an adjoining barn where he was stopped in his tracks by seeing "on ledges, shelves, and wall brackets" objects that had been featured in "Harnett's" still lives. He was trying to puzzle out how they could have got there—there *had* been a sale of Harnett's effects—when he turned his attention to the rest of his surroundings and saw hanging on the walls many excellent examples of still lives in the "soft style." That during the lengthy furor about Harnett no one had ever considered the possibility that two painters had been involved made Frankenstein, as he stood there in the deserted barn with Peto's daughter beside him, unable for a minute or two to draw the obvious conclusions. Then he almost danced with delight. What a scoop! A double scoop: esthetic and crime reporting.

Forgery! He had a hard look at Peto's daughter. She was a simple country woman who said that she had been very pleased, her father having been so neglected as an artist that he made his living playing the cornet at religious revival meetings, to sell his pictures to any comer for a few dollars. Someone more lurid had to be the mastermind of such a forgery ring as Frankenstein, utterly unfamiliar with the baffles of the art trade, visualized. He did not have to search for what seemed to him an obvious answer. He bought a Peto, added identifiable marks, photographed rear and front, and floated the picture on the art market. He kept calling on Mrs. Halpert to ask whether anything new had come in, and then one afternoon, she boasted to him that she had just acquired a first-class Harnett—and there was his picture with Harnett's monograph added. The case seemed closed.

Frankenstein was a journalist and recognized that he had lived a fascinating detective story. He wrote it up and sold it to *Life* magazine, which then had a tremendous national circulation. How directly he implicated Mrs. Halpert it is impossible to reconstruct, but he was worried when he was told that she had a weak heart. A nice boy as well as a naïve one, he ascertained the name of her doctor, called on him, received as he believed a promise of secrecy, and asked whether the exposé would kill her. As soon as he had walked out of the office, the doctor called Mrs. Halpert. Then the fur began to fly.

Mrs. Halpert was "fit to be tied." That there could be two painters where she had observed only one seemed to her inconceivable! Since, furthermore, implications that she was involved in a forgery ring not only were, she insisted, outrageous, but violated the gentleman's agreement in the art trade of mutual defense against any such charges, she alerted the trade association of the major dealers: mud slung at her would, because of her conspicuous position, tarnish the whole market place. *Life* was inundated with protests.

Not only were the dealers' reputations endangered. If Harnett really had two heads, all the scholars, museum personnel, collectors, etc., who had raved about Harnett for more than a decade and seen nothing peculiar, had made fools of themselves. Wherever the profession got together, growling was heard. It did not help that Frankenstein, finding himself cast not as a savior of truth, but as an intruder, complained loudly that he was being persecuted.

Halpert challenged him by putting on at the Downtown Gallery a "Harnett" exhibition that freely mixed both styles. I found Frankenstein there, sneaking around like a detective in a cheap melodrama. To me he whispered, "Don't say a word." I gathered that he thought that Halpert would somehow hear what was said. As I was subsequently told, she was in her office which had an inconspicuous window from which she could overlook her gallery. Seeing Frankenstein behaving so peculiarly, she telephoned her psychiatrist, imploring him to hurry over so that he could testify that her enemy was insane.

Carrying a large briefcase swollen with his evidence, Frankenstein became a modern ancient mariner reaching out for any listener he could snare. It took him much more than an hour to show all his photographs and papers and in so doing he put you in the embarassing position in relation to many of your associates of being completely convinced. Alfred Barr, the august director of the Modern Museum, complained to me when we had lunch together that he was being torn apart. His closest colleague at the Modern, Dorothy Miller, was married to Holger Kahill, who was a semi-secret partner in the Downtown Gallery. Dorothy was passionately pro-Halpert, but Barr did not doubt that Frankenstein was right.

A further complication was that the Gardiners, a husband-and-wife team, both curators at the Metropolitan Museum, were preparing for publication a book about Harnett on which the faintest shadow of Peto had not fallen. They persuaded Francis Taylor, the impetuous director of the Museum, who came charging out into the arena like a wild bull.

The situation was getting utterly out of hand when a quiet voice was heard. Henry Allen Moe, the great conciliator, was president of the Guggenheim Foundation. Frankenstein had been working under a Guggenheim Fellowship. He called a conference of the leading exponents of both sides. At this meeting of the high institution brass I was not present, but I heard it had got nowhere because both Halpert and Frankenstein had brought lawyers who did all the talking. But Moe was at his best operating behind the scenes. He worked out that the *Life* article be scrapped. The foundation would put up the money for Frankenstein to expand his researches to all the American still life painters of the Harnett period, and would pay for a handsome book publishing the results. No attacks by anybody on anyone.

The resulting volume, *After the Hunt*, was published in 1953, to become a major contribution to the study of American art. Frankenstein led off his "Acknowledgments" as follows: "First and foremost to Edith Gregor Halpert, Director of the Downtown Gallery, without whose interest this book could not have been written at all."

As for Peto, he now occupies in the pantheon of American art a separate niche, beside and level with Harnett's.

39

CATHOLIC FRIENDSHIP

*

WHEN I was a baby, my Catholic German governess was haunted by the belief that should I die without having been baptized, I would go straight to hell. Lacking the courage to defy my parents by carrying me to a church, she, after a long session of prayer, baptized me herself in the bathroom sink. I was to speculate whether, according to Catholic doctrine, this baptism had any validity. Informed friends told me that in a mortal emergency, as when a newborn child was unlikely to live, any Catholic could baptize in the absence of a priest. However, they were doubtful that this could apply in my case. But perhaps something did stick. As an agnostic, I have again and again down the years found favor from some aspect of the Church.

Although my only mention of Catholicism quoted Voltaire as urging Dr. John Morgan, "Above all, hate priests," *Doctors on Horseback* appeared, surrounded with lives of saints, in a reading list promulgated by New York's Cardinal Hayes. As long as Cardinal Hayes's annual reading lists were issued, my successive books appeared.

After Cardinal Hayes had vanished, I was taken up by the Christophers, a Catholic order devoted to encouraging, apart from religious doctrine, wholesome expression in the mass media. They hired annually, for a month or so, a first-class television studio where a suave priest and a charming middle-aged woman conducted every day a number of half-hour interviews. The Christophers thus honored several of my books. The tapes were widely distributed free of charge to television stations across the nation. Useful as fillers, they appeared irregularly on all but the biggest stations. I received fan letters from the strangest places.

The Christophers staged an annual ceremony at which they presented well-designed bronze medals depicting St. Christopher, with a staff, carrying the Christ Child on his shoulder. Recipients were actors and producers, advertising executives, magazine editors, and writers. They honored me for my *Indispensable Man*, and a year or so later they asked me to act as master of ceremonies, and hand out the medals. All seemed to me to have gone very well, but my ignorance of Catholicism must have broken out somewhere. I never heard again from the Christophers. But I did hear from the Vatican.

*

His Holiness Pope Paul VI nurtured a desire to revive the spiritual mission of the artist, the earlier fruits of which were so stupendously present in the Vatican. In 1973, he had added to the existing Vatican Museums a "Collection of Modern Religious Art." To help raise funds, His Excellency, Terence Cardinal Cooke of New York, had sponsored "The Committee of Religious Art in America," which was administered by one of the monsignors in his office. Very active was the pope's dealer in New York, Lawrence Fleishman, of the Kennedy Gallery. In 1976, they resolved to call attention to the pope's effort and encouraged American donors by staging at the Vatican a three-day seminar on "The Influence of Spiritual Inspiration on American Art." The pope was to participate, and impressive American sponsorship was achieved by securing as co-sponsor with the Vatican Museums the Smithsonian Institution in Washington. I was invited to be one of the seven speakers, my subject being "Spiritual Values in Early American Art." Publication in book form was anticipated, and in advance speakers were asked to submit their texts, to be sent to the others.

The pope's contribution was a brief opening statement eloquently concerned with an inherent problem. The works of art to be honored could not be, for effectiveness in these diverse times, limited to the production of Catholics or even Christians. Many of the objects already acquired were by Jews, and the donors invited to the symposium included many Jews, who had been lured (I suppose) by the opportunity to establish a Jewish presence in the Vatican.

"Oh, how much," Paul VI wrote, "we would like to convey to all artists who are at this moment in the throes of giving material expression to the unutterable intuitions of their spirit a word of sincere respect and deep sympathy. They are, perhaps even without knowing it, on the way that leads to God. . . . With their works, let them urge others too to start out with them towards a meeting which alone can be really satisfying for a being like man who is constitutionally a pilgrim towards the Absolute, whether he knows it or not."

*

Arriving at Rome on July 18, 1976, Beatrice and I were put up at the Grand Hotel. Our room was to be described by Beatrice, whose account of our stay which will often be quoted here, as "luxurious and quiet, looking out on a tawny courtyard with red flowering plants in the center." A knock at the door. A maid staggered in bearing "heroic pink roses" on what resembled more "a sapling trunk than a stem." There was also a fat envelope addressed to me. It proved to contain a wad of lire, large denominations and small. I remembered that when I had complained to the managing monsignor of low pay, he had said something about enabling me to tax-deduct my expenses although while they were paid by the Church. Here in my hand was untraceable currency. With what indignation my anti-Catholic mother would have exploded! But I found it piquant that so mighty an organization, on so high a level, would engage in such tricks to avoid giving unto Caesar what is Caesar's.

*

On the following morning, so Beatrice wrote, "we were bussed through the Swiss-guarded gates and around beyond St. Peter's so that we could admire Michelangelo's grandiose apse façade from the Vatican garden." Having always thought of St. Peter's, facing its tremendous columned square, as a geographic climax, I was intrigued to see the ancient Vatican City open up before us. From where the bus stopped, we walked through several courtyards—"very severe," Beatrice noted—and then downstairs into Synod Hall, a fifteenth-century meeting place. Beatrice ruled that it was hardly larger than a very big living room. Since we were underground, no windows broke the unvariegated brick walls.

It seemed incongruous to see before every chair a pair of earphones. Since conferees came from various parts of the world, simultaneous translation (in this case, only Italian and English) was often required. But our need to project slides of paintings seemed to have been alien. A medium-sized screen dangled dubiously from a roller attached to a pole, and at the rear of the center aisle, resting on uneven legs, was a projector that might have dated from Charlemagne had he gone in for such things. When an operator appeared, he viewed the device with alarm. He got a slide into a slot, but could not get it out again. Fortunately, an efficient museum curator rose from our group to get things moving.

*

As a world capital, the Vatican must have had an expert staff for entertaining delegates: each at the right level. We were surprisingly, so I judged from what happened, rated at least a B. This was undoubtedly because of the pope's personal concern, which was also demonstrated by the presence at our meetings of a decorative sprinkling of red robes, cardinals who could not have had any interest in American art.

Since there were only eight speakers and one discussion period in three days, there was much time to fill in. Most incongruous was a reception given by the Iranian ambassador. Beatrice's summary: "Champagne flowed into graceful, beautifully cut glasses but caviar was scarce." Several times we were bussed out for lunch or dinner to elaborate estates from whose gardens we saw sensational views of the *campagna* and the City of Rome. I had a fine time when seated next to Cardinal Cooke whom I had known only casually as a fellow trustee of the New York Public Library. Beatrice flirted so effectively with the American ambassador that he opened doors for us into various private collections—and was very useful after Beatrice's passport had been stolen.

*

I cannot say that the speeches at the seminar were particularly enlightening. What most interested me were the maneuvers of the two

Catholic theologians, one from Notre Dame University and the other from the Vatican itself, as they held forth on spiritual inspiration to an audience containing so many Jews whose object it was to please. The speakers found themselves stating that if a human being should delve prayerfully deeper and deeper, what he would reach at last was spiritual. Mother would have been gratified to hear doctrine that came so close to the Quaker doctrine of the priesthood of all believers. Did this mean that if Fräulein had been pious enough, my baptism would have worked?

We had, of course, to examine the pope's Gallery of Modern Religious Art. Although it seemed to New York–bred eyes unexciting, I felt it my duty to hang around and to seem impressed. Beatrice felt rebellious—when she thought of all the wonders in the Vatican she could be seeing. She did lure Archbishop Giovanni Fallani into leading us quietly to see the paintings she most wanted to see: "We went along after His Excellency," Beatrice wrote, "to the clicking of heels and salutes of the Swiss guards."

*

The climax of our seminar, of course, would be the speech by the pope. He was in his summer residence, Castel Gondolfo, but there was no facility there large enough to receive such a crowd as ours, some 150 people. The pope would come to us, which I was told was a great honor.

Beatrice remembered, "Quite a long wait, during which I looked forward to being regaled by his approach, possibly, I hoped, with a fanfare, through the rooms in Synod Hall, of which I had a good view from where we sat. No. The doors were now closed, a short wait more, and then opened, and he was on the threshold. He came in with one or two inconspicuous attendants. With a self-deprecating smile, he made his way to the dais. There he divested himself of his brilliant red silk cloak and stood for a moment in his heavy, severe, immaculate white. After some words of respect and gratitude from Cardinal Cooke, the pope addressed us on the subject of artists' devoting themselves to spiritual themes, remarking en passant with a modesty that could be achieved only by the pope, that 'nos altri,' we others, have the promise of Christ. His talk was ad lib, much longer than the printed text we had been given. His wax-white face and hands, and his thin, husky voice expressed intense enthusiasm for the cause of artists evoking spiritual truths, and for those present who partook in or encouraged his work, 'Bravi!' Then, with a smile he said he hoped we were numismatists and proffered to Cardinal Cooke a case of 1976 papal medals which he blessed before they were given to us. As soon as he had crossed the threshold, the doors were shut behind him."

*

Like a fool, I had so enjoyed the spectacle that I hardly listened to the speech, assuming that it would replace in the final report the statement printed in the advance proceedings. Not so! His Holiness had obviously enjoyed the luxury of speaking without notes and without record. I wish I could report what he *did* say.

*

Beatrice's and my visit to the Vatican was among the most agreeable happenings of our lives. I had foreseen stiffness and conscious grandeur, but we could not have been treated more graciously. Completely guarded in their ancient city behind St. Peter's, their authority going back almost two thousand years and extending around the globe, their basic convictions absolute, those who entertained us could feel no pressure to prove themselves, and condescension would have been looking too far down. As long as we did not presume or argue, and you may be certain we did not, benignity flowed without a ripple.

40

COLLECTING

*

ONE summer, when I was old enough to walk by myself within a restricted range, there was within that range a village store window that displayed in its window among other odds and ends a tribe of cats hardly larger than an adult's thumb but elegantly furry and standing on toothpick-like legs. Although I bamboozled my mother to buy me first one and then another, beyond that she would not go. True collectors are not so easily baffled. I would stand on the street staring longingly into the windows as pedestrians appeared. Kind ladies would ask the cute little redheaded boy what he wanted so much. The saleslady did not give me away, as she took the fee from one donor after another. But my mother recognized that my cats were multiplying in an unnatural manner. She intervened while allowing me to keep my holdings.

My next effort was inspired by Father's international contacts which brought in foreign stamps. What the mail would yield was a perpetual excitement that set me waiting for the delivery and then dancing around while my parents went through the pile. I mounted my catches in an album according to nations, enjoying the competition between the different pages of black paper. But then a family friend bought me an assortment of several hundred foreign stamps. I can still see the hateful transparent envelope containing an abundance that mocked my irregular, exciting, random yield. I abandoned stamp collecting.

My next collection could not be thus vulnerable. I resolved to dig out and buy first editions of standard authors.

First editions of standard authors on an allowance of less than fifty cents a week? This was possible in view of what someone had told me: If the printing date and the copyright date were the same, the book was a first edition. My method was to examine the bins outside secondhand bookstores where volumes considered of very little value were lined up, one row behind another, their spines kept visible. The succession of such bins on Fifty-ninth Street was considered close enough to our Sixty-eighth Street address for me to be allowed to go alone. More distant paradises were the more numerous and larger stalls at the secondhand bookstore center on Second Avenue above Fourteenth Street. Sometimes as a treat, Mother or Father would take me down there and watch as I prowled.

My method was to extract, for my comparison of dates, books with old-fashioned bindings that bore on their spines the names of authors I had heard of. If a volume looked really old, I would examine it anyway. Some of these finds were years later authenticated by an expert at the New York Public Library, although he said they had little value. Most often, I found "first editions" of works by the mid-nineteenth-century sacred cows of the New England renaissance: Emerson, Longfellow, Whittier, Holmes, etc. The explanation was, of course, that their great popularity inspired large printings in the year of publication. That not all were bona-fide first editions was brought home to me by the discovery that Longfellow changed a word in *Hiawatha* from "dove" to "dived" (or vice versa) which separated off the earliest valuable printing. I hurried to my bookshelf and discovered that my "first edition" had the wrong word. But I was unwilling to let my fun be spoiled by the niceties.

Although I learned to identify and pounce on the characteristic bindings of the Boston publisher Tickner & Fields (whose successor, Houghton Mifflin, was to be for a while my publisher), I did not as a reader relish the New England school. I learned as a joke to make conversation in the rhythm of *Hiawatha*. I was more pleased to get books by Mark Twain—they too had tremendous first printings— and an occasional Poe item in a "gift book." These were anthologies, usually with elaborately decorated leather bindings, published annually to be Christmas presents. I hardly noticed the illustrations that reproduced works of painters who were greatly to occupy my attention decades later.

When I located a prize, I carried it into the store and often tried to bargain on the price. The booksellers must have been both surprised and amused to see so small a collector, and they were often inspired to take off a dime or two. They also gave me advice, steering me to items not particularly salable. But they had to be careful not to condescend. One, when I tried to chisel him down from fifty cents, replied that he'd give the book to me for nothing, upon which I laid down the book and never visited the store again.

But I welcomed first editions as Christmas and birthday presents. Budgets for gifts to children not being munificent, I did not receive much to cheer about or even remember. However, Aunt Lucy did give what I still consider a treasure: a three-volume, leather-bound first edition of *The Monk* by Matthew Gregory Lewis. That in this Gothic tale the devil tricks a great preacher (based on Savonarola) into raping an innocent girl who proved to be his sister was considered shocking by historians of literature I took in my stride.

My first-edition craze lasted only until I became completely absorbed in school, but I remained in memory so fond of what I had so happily acquired that I could not bear to discard any of the collection. My favorites have remained on my book shelves as I have moved from one place to another. The other hundred or so volumes were stored in cartons which deteriorated down the years but which I never lost track of. Finally, in 1988, I gave the contents to the New-York Historical Society Library with permission to throw out or otherwise dispose of what they did not consider worth keeping. To my amazement, they sent me an appraisal that totaled a thousand dollars.

*

I was in my mid-twenties when I met at the Paris Flea market a naked woman. She was black, explicitly female, liberally tattooed, about three feet high, and carved out of wood. In those days, avant-garde French artists were much excited by African primitives, but Fifi (as I came to call her) must have entered the wrong circle. Perhaps it was the importer's outraged womenfolk who sold this very naked female to a junk man. I found her in a jungle of battered furniture and paid for her only a small price.

My worry was how I could get her into the United States. The

McCarron Act, which had outlawed Joyce's *Ulysses*, forbade the importation of what was considered obscene. Fifi's large, conical breasts, liberally tattooed, stood out straight, and there was a visible crack between her thighs. The obvious solution was to persuade Jack, who was sending some purchases to the Metropolitan Museum, to let them be chaperons for Fifi. He refused, but he did help me get her safely packed. I was not pleased that the result was so bulky that it would have to be conspicuously carried separately.

On the New York dock, the eye of the customs inspector was immediately caught. "Open that!" As he stared, I was horrified to see that Fifi had indiscreetly allowed a bit of sawdust to adhere like pubic hair in the wrong (or right) place. But the customs inspector laughed. "Boy, when you get that home, your mother will make you throw it out."

Thus, Fifi became an American citizen.

*

Once Fifi had found refuge in my apartment, all impropriety vanished. There is nothing salacious about her. She is a fertility symbol honestly doing her duty. Self-contained, preserving her own integrity, she has been a valued member of my household for some sixty years. From a little pedestal I made for her, she is observing me as I write these lines.

Her strong legs divided slightly as if she were carrying a heavy weight, Fifi is robust. Over her head she is holding, with both arms outstretched, a substantial flat disk which indicates her second role: a chief's seat or throne. Artistically, her amazing trait is that the sculptor so elongated her head from front to rear that, if the eye subtracts the upright arms, the head seen in profile is normally proportioned. According to Eliot Elisofen, a collector of African art, Fifi is Boule, from Senegal in French West Africa.

*

Fifi encouraged me to seek more African primitives, but this was hardly practical in New York where there were almost no examples except those specially imported for individuals of advanced taste and with larger pocketbooks than mine. I did acquire several minor objects and also a large wooden baboon mask that was lowered to my price range by having lost one ear. It had slits beneath its sculptured eyes to look through, but is so heavy that it must have been very uncomfortable when ceremoniously worn. It hung (as it still does) on a wall near Fifi. According to Elisofen, it came from Dan between the Ivory Coast and Liberia.

Girls I brought home after dark were or pretended to be frightened by the mask. I considered having a button I could press as we entered the door that would turn on a spotlight as the heavy mouth opened and said in a deep voice, "Hello, folks!" I even dreamed of having smoke emerge from the slits below the eyes. But somehow I never got around to any of this.

*

Spain, when I visited with Jack, proved a treasure trove for rummaging around. I decided I would rather buy a typical artifact than postcards. Assured by Jack that it was authentically seventeenth-century, I picked up a small statue carved in heavy wood. That it represented a saint was demonstrated by a hole drilled in his shaved head over his tonsure which had been used to attach a halo. The rest of him proved, when washed, that he had not heeded Christ's injunction to "give all to the poor and follow me." He wore a surplice of yellow gold treated to glow in candlelight, and had deeply folded over his neck and hanging over his back almost to his heels a dark purple cloak richly embroidered in gold. He was much too elegant for his environments when I got him home, but standing self-confidently on a table, he ignored everything around him, becoming eventually a favorite of my second wife's.

Another find raised reverberations. In a junk pile, I found a medal depicting Marie de Medici. Although it was lead, not silver, Jack asked (vainly) that I give it to his museum. Research was to reveal that it had probably been awarded to a writer who had won it in a contest the queen annually staged for the best poem in praise of the Virgin. And now it had become the possession of another writer. Hands stretched across the centuries!

*

My major junk pile discovery in Spain was a flattish, heavy oval stone, so small that I could cover the surface with my hand. One side was uncarved, although slightly rounded. The other was incised in the lowest of low reliefs—hardly more than a quarter inch from high to low—with the essentials of a human face. The entire surface was subtly modulated and dominated by a design made up of an arching hairline; two ovals with slightly raised edges that indicated eyes; and a larger such oval for a mouth. A narrow vertical nose widened to represent nostrils. That was all! Yet the result was so powerful that I came to call it "The Great Stone Face."

Nothing could be more certain than that this was not a random creation. It had to represent some mature tradition. But what culture? Search as I could, I could find no answer.

After having settled near New Haven. I invaded Yale's archeological Peabody Museum. I fought my way to a Dr. Rouse, who informed me haughtily that it was not his job to inform strangers. But getting a look at the Great Stone Face, he reached out his hand. After ten minutes of scrutiny, he smiled and congratulated me: It was good enough for the museum to accept as a gift.

For what collection, I asked? He replied grudgingly, "West Indian." But he soon found himself explaining that it was a Zemi, a supernatural being with magical powers, dating between 1300 and 1400, an example of the Tianon culture. Tianon culture? says I. There was no help for it: he had to specify the Arawaka Indians who had inhabited the Island of Hispaniola and part of Puerto Rico, but had become extinct within a hundred years of the Spanish Conquest. Then he summoned his secretary to bring a deed of gift.

I told him I was very sorry. My sculpture had the responsibility of keeping the roof on my house. Surely he would not want the roof to blow off my house!

When Dr. Rouse and I passed on the street, we did not notice each other.

*

Another mysterious object came to me in an altogether different way. Aunt Carey had a passion for buying bibelot all over the world. When, after she had retired from Bryn Mawr, I called on her with my brother and his wife, she gave me a nondescript bronze bird with dangles and William's wife a small silver lion. We eyed each other's gifts enviously for some time before we got around to a swap.

The lion is very small, three and a half inches, and his body is incised with decorations that, although effective, have no relevance to his lionhood. A thin tail curls over his back and ends with a little design of its own. He had a protruding tongue shaped like the spade on a playing card. His four legs are attached to a silver base. There is a seemingly inexplicable hole in his belly. Tiny as he is, he has dignity, charm, and authority. Like the Stone Face, he certainly exemplified a tradition, but again I could find no hint of what the tradition was.

Years passed, until I saw in the *Metropolitan Museum Bulletin* for May 1948 an article by my friend James Rorimer, entitled "A Treasury at the Cloisters." The illustrations showed "aquamaniles," decorated ewers for carrying liquids. They were thirteenth- or fourteenth-century, and, although obviously serving another and much larger purpose, they resembled my lion.

Putting the lion in my pocket, I hightailed it for the Metropolitan. Rorimer accepted the resemblance and the date-span. I then amused myself by showing the lion to whatever other curators might be concerned. They disagreed, as have other experts to whom I have shown my lion down the years, only on more specific dating and places of origin in Eastern or Western Europe. It was a decorative arts curator who diagnosed that the legs and the base were a later addition, probably, she said, eighteenth-century French. This explained the hole in the lion's belly: my lion had originally topped a ceremonial staff. Thus, he had a relationship with Fifi, who had also played a ceremonial role.

I was happy to feel that my lion, after half a millennium, was safe in my custody. However, silver appeals to silver polishers. The first one disattached the spade-shaped tongue, but fortunately she preserved it. When the director of the Brooklyn Museum was having dinner in our apartment, he offered to have his restorers put back the tongue. They used wax.

Enter another silver polisher. She put the lion in hot water, melting the wax. The tongue went down the drain. The lion and his tongue were thus separated after five hundred years! This I consider one of my worst sins.

*

I am in the habit of advising people who have cherished heirlooms not to try to find out too much about them. My particular example was a Spanish refugee from Franco. He liked to complain about the loss of his Velázquez and his El Greco. When I asked him how his family had come by them, he replied that his father had got them as payment for a bad debt. He should have been grateful to Franco!

I have had my own hard times. What had been my excitement at finding in a bin in front of a New York City shop a large, first-class drawing by Burne-Jones which someone had signed "Rossetti." Examining in bright sunlight, I could discern no hint that it was not an original drawing. I paid out a small sum.

My next step was to examine the Burne-Jones photographs at the Frick. The drawing was there, with an exciting notation that it was lost.

Agnes Mongan, the curator of drawings at the Boston Museum of Fine Arts, was then doing research at the Frick. She carefully studied my "Burne-Jones," said she could see nothing wrong with it, but added that she had a memory of there being something peculiar about Pre-Raphaelite drawings. She advised that I take it to Murray Pease, the chief restorer at the Metropolitan.

Murray was a good friend of mine. His examination with a magnifying glass raised no questions. "But, just for fun," he said, "let's try a microscope." Alas! Had Burne-Jones made strokes with his pencil, the scratch would have ever so slightly abraded the paper. My drawing showed no such abrasions. It was an old, contemporaneous photograph.

Here was a nice issue! Since the picture could be distinguished from the original only through a microscope, for the viewer it was an equivalent of the original. Why, then, was it worthless? But the scorned picture committed suicide. The old cardboard to which the photograph had been glued was unable to stand up to so much handling. It gave way, tearing my "Burne-Jones" to shreds.

*

All my art collecting so far described in this chapter had depended on chance encounter. But Agnes and I, when we were living in the Connecticut countryside near New Haven, revived the method I had followed in New York when a boy seeking "first editions." Then I had walked the streets scanning racks outside secondhand bookshops for volumes thus displayed because they were considered of almost no value. Now we scoured the roads seeking nineteenth-century works by local artists which were then admired by only a few eccentrics. Had our automobile been a horse who could read, it would have automatically stopped at the sight of a sign reading "Antiques."

I always felt a surge of excitement as I walked over the threshold not knowing what we would find. The shabbier the shop, the more promising. Having in those years almost no competition from other collectors, we could set our top price at twenty-five dollars. We rarely spent as much as ten.

There were of course other sources than casually visited antique shops. We so educated local dealers that they brought down from attics what they would otherwise have left behind. Stores that were outlets for charities offered what old families discarded as worthless. Auctions held on the lawns of old houses that were being vacated were, particularly in nice weather, good fun even if we found nothing. And exhibitors in pretentious antique shows sometimes filled empty space around what they were featuring with the lesser merchandise we sought. I remember one miraculous afternoon when I found in corners at a major antique show on New York's Madison Avenue not one but two pictures I greatly prize.

*

After Agnes decamped, I continued my collection more on my own since Beatrice's artistic interest, although she sometimes came along for the ride, was concentrated on music and European masterpieces. Down the decades, I must have examined many thousands of possible purchases: sometimes twenty could be seen hanging in one cranny or another of a disorganized antique shop. I could scan rapidly since I had only one criterion for selection: what sparked my esthetic taste. But very often, after my eye had been caught, I could not be sure. Many a picture had been so neglected that even if I secured the dealer's permission to take it out into the sunlight, I could not discern enough to reach a conclusion. But lowness of price enabled me to take chances.

Once a picture had been brought home, the more intimate labor began. Wherever I was then living, I managed to set up a workshop:

in the country expansively in a barn or garage, in the city temporarily, available when needed.

The first task, the cleaning off of loose dirt and easily removable surface grime, supplied immediate disappointment or more eagerness to go ahead. I had learned, from books and my museum friends, in what directions and how far I could proceed without damaging various varieties of pictures. My efforts were enlivened with suspense. Sometimes, the more revealed, the less satisfying. The picture would then be returned to the antiques market. Other pictures, as they blossomed under my hands, inspired me with mounting affection.

Framing was the next problem. Sometimes existing frames needed no more than cleaning and shoring up; other times such was the battering the pictures had undergone that I often had to start anew. Both economy and my need for frames apposite to the periods of the pictures induced me to seek out in junk shops piles of discarded frames. I picked out those large enough to be cut down to size. What a task! Fashioning the main segments, each pair identical in length, presented problems, but was child's play compared to cutting four pairs of diagonals so accurately that every corner would neatly fit together. The smallest irregularity reveals itself in disfiguring cracks. I eventually bought an all-metal miter box, with a built-in saw that could be firmly fixed at the correct angle, but if anyone ever tries to sell you a Flexner frame with flawless corners, don't buy it. It's a forgery!

*

Not created for a larger world, to rival other pictures in exhibitions, to march down the august corridors of history, the works I collected were painted for the use to which I was to put them: to be enjoyed in a domestic setting. Were I somehow to bring home a great painting, it would overwhelm domestic peace, as if a virtuoso were perpetually thundering an instrument in my parlor.* I did not feel deprived. Did

---

*The one sure major masterpiece I unearthed was Benjamin West's *Agrippina with the Ashes of Germanicus*, which had been a milestone in the development of late eighteenth-century neoclassicism; and had brought to West the patronage of George III. I found the canvas leaning on the floor at an obscure gallery in New York City— it was almost too large to hang. So habituated to my determination as a scholar to keep clear of personal financial considerations I did not even ask the price which perhaps I could have reached then living near New Haven, I informed the Yale

I not vicariously come to a possession, sometimes with more intimate an understanding than most of the physical owners, of the major paintings I wrote about and occasionally reproduced in my volumes?

My busman's holidays did not by any means carry me into esthetic slums. I claim that every picture I discovered, preserved, and cherished has true artistic integrity.

Although I was occasionally lured into doing research and even reproducing some of my finds in one of my books, that I usually did not do so makes me feel, in some ways, closer to my domestic companions.

*

My roadside collection was somewhat menaced by an aspect of the antique trade: "Pickers" scoured the roads as I did, and bought from humble shops what they could sell at a profit to more ambitious dealers. Usually, however, they passed by what I wanted. I was not in competition with high-flying dealers in "folk art," who specialized in cute confections (usually by children) for Philistines, and, for the more serious minded, on coincidental resemblances to sophisticated, often European, modernism. Seeking the best examples of what local American amateur or artisan creators themselves sought to achieve, I was carried into many media: oil, watercolor, black-and-white compositions, needlework, paper cutouts and, although this was not part of my main search, woodcarving. I found one silhouette, dated 1808, fashioned in low relief on marble. I can claim to have rediscovered a lost mid-nineteenth-century female art. It was called in instruction books "monochromatic drawing."*

These pictures, although often of substantial size, were considered so worthless (they are still undervalued) that antique dealers, when they ransacked attics, automatically left them behind. The difficulty was that the pictures could be dismissed as copies, since they often resembled popular engravings after well-known paintings. It was necessary for me to train what dealers I could to extract them for me.

The monochromatic method was taught in young ladies' finishing

Art Gallery, where the picture still hangs. Had I been a fool not even to consider financial opportunity?

*The pictures were called in the trade: "sandpaper drawings."

schools because, as with finger paint, it was easy to achieve a passable result. Small engraved reproductions were displayed on copying racks. The girls placed little piles of black pigment on flat, slightly rough, white surfaces and then pushed it out to create forms and shading. White lines were drawn by scraping with an edge of hard leather to the surface beneath.

Talented young women, who would today become professional painters, continued to use the monochromatic technique which, because of its simplicity, was highly suited to untutored inspiration. Since detailed drawing was impossible, large shapes were dictated; and the lack of color encouraged dependence on black-and-white values to indicate position and distance. All the more because they tremendously enlarged their sources, usually page-size illustrations, the abler women recast their compositions according to their own emotions and inspirations, creating original works of art.

Among my favorite possessions are two very different versions of Thomas Cole's tremendously popular *Youth* from his series *The Voyage of Life*. One version stays moderately close to the original, although landscape details—foliage, rocks, declivities—which Cole depicted realistically, are enlarged and altered to serve design, rocks and hills fantasized. The artist did not hesitate to have the river, on which "Youth" (here turned into middle-age) floated, flowing in the distance uphill.

The other drawing is so morbid that my wife will not let me place it in the front part of our apartment. Cole's composition, although recognizable, is so overwhelmed by ominous shadows and shapes of the artist's own devising that Cole's allegory of youthful hope is transmuted into neurotic nightmare, including frightening, phallic shapes. However, the girl's family cannot have been upset, since I found the picture elaborately framed for display.

*

Most of my pictures, created by rural artisan painters, were scaled to fit the small rooms of farmhouses. However, the artists had no use for miniature views. Like the expansive painters of the Hudson River School, wayside painters responded to the wide spaces of our continent. They scorned abbreviation or generalization. Even if less than an inch in height, human figures have hats on their heads, visible arms and legs in motion. Horses have harnesses, heads, and tails. Although a viewer may not specifically register such details, some of which can be appreciated only through a magnifying glass, this multiplied presence contributes to verisimilitude, drawing the eye in rather than catching it from without.

A black-and-white, which I have entitled *Winter in the Country*, summarizes, although measuring only 13 by 11 inches, activity on a dark winter's day brightened by fallen snow. We see a frozen pond with three boys skating and another fallen on his back; a sledge with driver behind two horses promising warmth with its load of firewood; two horsedrawn sleighs, one containing a single driver and the other a couple; a road curving between fences to houses so shrunken by distance that the farther one is no bigger than the top of a thumb tack. To the far right a tall tree with elaborate visible roots and contorted bare branches cooperates with another tree rising from behind the middle-distance farmhouse to hold the sky and land together. The sky, occupying nearly half the background, is dark and marked with lines so faint that the viewer cannot be sure whether or not snow is falling. The larger farmhouse—occupying two inches—is so skillfully out of drawing that the eye is not bothered to see simultaneously the façade and one side. In no sense episodic, *Winter in the Country* presents a strong, coherent image.

Of necessity altogether different in technique is a rendering in color of Bish-Bash Falls, a favorite subject for Hudson River School paintings. My version of this imposing natural phenomenon is ten inches high and six in width. No small details here! To communicate power, the artist has, without altogether sacrificing verisimilitude, abstracted (the word would have meant nothing to him) the cliffs on the two sides of the ravine into ponderous sculptured solids. Being unwilling to eliminate altogether the clinging patches of vegetation, he had painted them so lightly on the heavy surfaces that, when you become conscious of their presence, they seem hallucinations.

*

The star of my collection is the most enigmatic and also the most celebrated as it was borrowed and displayed by the Metropolitan Museum.

The opening gun was a phone call from a nearby Connecticut

antiques dealer saying that he had something peculiar to show me. He had been summoned to an old farmhouse near Portsmouth, New Hampshire, that was to be offered for sale, to handle the antiques. He had found on an attic floor a lengthy, unpainted wooden chest that proved to contain, among other discarded objects, a roll of green cloth. Unrolling it, he was amazed to see, on the inner surface, a life-sized half-length portrait of a woman in elaborate Victorian costume. He could find no indications that the portrait had even been stretched for framing or otherwise displayed.

Hurrying to his shop, I was impressed and more puzzled by the picture. That the bare green cloth of the background had been used like the silk of a Chinese ancestor portrait made some sense in that Portsmouth had been a center of the China trade. I knew that sailors had sometimes taken with them snapshots to be enlarged by Chinese painters, but the costume dated the picture before there were large enough photographs. The artist's painting style smacked of Chinese craftsmanship but just as much of American "wayside art." Most surprising was a distortion of the somewhat enlarged face, which, although impressive to eyes trained by modern art, would have horrified Victorian and (I suppose) Chinese taste.

This bouillabaise should by all rights be an incoherent hodgepodge, but I can testify through living with the portrait that it is an impressive work of art: handsome, powerful, and in no way incoherent.

The dealer gave me the telephone number of the family descendant who was selling the house. He was pleased by my interest and met me there. He had, he told me, known from childhood about the hidden-away portrait and who it represented. He took me to a little family graveyard in the woods and showed me her gravestone: Sarah F. Hobbs Died Nov. 3, 1884, age 83 years. So far so clear, but the inscription added another enigma by making no mention of a marriage. Had Sarah Hobbs never married or had there been a marriage in her younger years that the gravestone had surpressed? Was there hidden here an explanation of why so strange and elaborate a portrait, although never destroyed, had never been hung? My guide offered no clarification.

I have made my amends to Sarah (as I presume to call her) by displaying her portrait in a conspicuous position for more than fifty years wherever I reside.

*

As our daughter grew up and spent her summers elsewhere, as my tennis game deteriorated with the passing years, as New York City became more and more our residence, and when Beatrice and I abandoned the care and feeding of an automobile, my active collecting almost altogether came to an end. But this did not mean that the pictures I had accreted down the years passed out of my affections or my life. On the walls of the good-sized New York City apartment I inherited from my parents, some forty old comrades are in place. Beatrice, having put her foot down, there are only three large ones in the living room. In the dining room, the figure jumps to four. The master bedroom four, and the master bathroom only three. But the back hall houses eleven smaller pictures arranged in two tiers. These are reinforced by nine fellow pictures in the back bathroom where the shower over the tub has forever been disconnected. There are more in the closets which sometimes emerge, but on the whole the pleasure I achieve is from continuity. Home is home, and I walk the halls surrounded with friends who bring back happy memories of old times and excitements achieved.

I have not encouraged my acquisitions to go again out into the world. Although I have lent single pictures to museums—Metropolitan, Whitney, and so on—I have never let them accompany traveling exhibitions. Only once has the whole picture collection gone visiting: some two miles to the Century Club, which is for every member a home away from home.

I would, of course, like to have my collection of Wayside Art kept together. This concern has been shared by various visitors, partly because of its interest in relation to my career, and more because the artistic effect is more in the sum than in the parts. Queries have come in from various institutions, but I have preferred to procrastinate.

41

SEEKING GEORGE WASHINGTON

*

LITTLE, Brown's request (1961) that I undertake a biography of George Washington fitted in with a long-range idea of mine. In almost all the books I had published, I had found myself wandering around in late eighteenth-century America. In one context or another, at various lengths—he had been a major character in *The Traitor and the Spy*—I kept meeting Washington. Watching him in action, I had again and again been amazed that, were I to apply to what I saw any of the accepted visions of Washington, they would blur or distort the actual record. Clearly a new, more perceptive biography of Washington was needed! I had been fascinated by the idea of attempting such a work when I was old and wise enough. Alan Williams's proposal had made me decide that I was old and wise enough. I was all the more tempted because Little, Brown had agreed, it seemed to me with some enthusiasm, to bring out *That Wilder Image*.

*

The landscape of writings on Washington stretched back more than 150 years, a terrain as various as you could imagine: hills and hollows, mirages and booby traps, and enough vegetation to block the eye in every direction. But, some thirty years ago, there had stretched across the landscape a high mountain range: Douglas Southall Freeman's seven-volume (the final one by his successors) life of Washington. In its vast documentary importance, it threw a shadow backward over all the works that had preceded it, and as it had frowned down on the years since 1948, it had scared away other biographers of any stature. The resulting lack of any generally accessible biography of Washington had inspired Little, Brown's desire for a one-volume life.

It was not in my nature to be frightened by competition, since I always felt that my ideas would end up differently. Where I made my mistake was in obediently signing Little, Brown's contract for a single volume. I soon realized that my fundamental desire to veer from the traveled high roads and beat my own paths to a newly visualized Washington would require much more space.

With a shudder, I compared the magnitude of what I had undertaken with that faced by Lincoln biographers. Washington had lived eleven years longer than Lincoln. While Lincoln was a major national figure for only some seven years (from the Douglas debates to his assassination), Washington was for twenty-four years (from his election as commander in chief to his death) the most conspicuous and influential man in the United States. For seventeen of those years, comprising the war, the Constitutional Convention, and the presidency, he was from day to day actively engaged in great events. Before all that, his role in the French and Indian War made him internationally known when he was hardly twenty, an age at which Lincoln was still an obscure frontiersman. And the scope of my studies was almost doubled by a determination to describe Washington's indispensable role in the creation of the United States and yet not lose the man in the leader. Events indicative of character were as important to me as world-shaping decisions. I had put myself into a pretty pickle.

I knew that Little, Brown was bringing out Dumas Malone's life of Jefferson in individual volumes as they were completed. I should have to persuade them to do the same for me. Toward this end, I arranged to have lunch with my editor. We were having a convivial time until I made my suggestion. Then Williams behaved as if I had thrown a bomb in his lap. The comparison with Malone, he contended, was ridiculous since Malone was playing Freeman's role! An attempt to try to compete with Freeman would be idiocy. My reply that I would need only three volumes not Freeman's seven did not in the least placate Alan. Little, Brown had recognized a need: there existed no post-Freeman accurate and readable one-volume life of Washington. He had been assigned to find someone to fill that gap; he had found me, and I had signed a contract. I had received an advance. To defeat the objective was inconceivable. He would not even mention my suggestion to his superiors in Little, Brown's Boston office.

Being neither willing nor capable of creating a book in which I did not believe, I had no choice but to go over Alan's head by writing to Arthur Thornhill, the president of the firm. Arthur saw a way out of the dilemma. Avoiding the dreaded competition with Freeman of a new multi–volume work, I would be permitted to produce as long a manuscript as could be bound under one cover, which could well be above one thousand tightly printed pages. There was no suggestion of a larger advance for so much greater and longer a labor, but, as at various other times in my career, my small but adequate private income unlocked confining fetters. Although it was to my mind a clumsy solution, it was a solution that would enable me to get going on what scale seemed to me best.

*

Having in essence gotten my own way, I had knocked down all protective walls that shield a restrictive project. I was standing in the open in the midst of a vast historical expanse, committed to recreating one of the most celebrated Americans—perhaps the most celebrated—who had successfully carried through a war of independence and then presided over one of the most important governmental experiments in the history of the world. And I had to conquer by my own strength alone: not an institutional credential, no funds for (what I did not want anyway) a research team.

Although the metaphor did not occur to me at the time, I was much in the position of Faust after he had rashly invited "the stone guest" for dinner. How was I to conquer the traditional "marble image" of Washington which had clumped its way some distance even into Freeman's august volumes? I could almost hear its heavy footsteps approaching my door.

*

Even if I were somehow to end up with multiple volumes, the existing compromise could be an advantage since I had to visualize Washington's life as a whole.

My obvious first port of call was the catalogue room of the New

York Public Library. I discovered that the cards gathered under the heading "Washington, George" filled three deep drawers. Fetching a ruler, I measured how many cards to an inch and how many inches. Multiplication gave the figure as 2,997 cards. And this included only book-length publications classified under Washington's name. How many thousands more?

The only way I could deal with this phenomenon was to turn my back on it. Since my book was to close with Washington's death, what had been fabricated about him in subsequent generations was hostile to my purpose. Even more dangerous to me were the misconceptions that had invaded my own mind during more than fifty years of living which could raise a fog between me and the original sources on which I wished my work to be founded. To clear my vision, I determined with an act of will to conclude that I knew nothing, except what I had already in my own previous researches ascertained, concerning Washington.

When I mentioned my resolve, I was likely to arouse skepticism. How was it possible, I was asked, to ignore matters so entangled with our culture? In fact, I was merely giving rein to the skepticism I had been trained to have at home and in school, to what came naturally to my temperament. As a biographer, I had always sought security, as my eyes turned in various directions, by being certain that my feet were solidly on factual ground. And always I wanted to achieve a clear view, unobstructed by later events, backward to the happenings and psychologies I needed to understand.

*

My determination not to mix up the issues of Washington's lifetime with the current events of my own lifetime was made more feasible because, ever since I had discovered biography, I had kept my writing as independent as I could from the world specifically around me. I found strength in living in other worlds.

The greatest temptation to intertwine my narrative with current events came when I was writing, during the Vietnam War, about Washington in the Revolution. There were many parallels, the Americans now the equivalent of the British and the Viet Cong of the patriots, which would have made my book a best seller and, by my appearing on major television shows (I was invited), brought me into the limelight. But I was too dedicated to my ideals as a biographer. And in the long run I was rewarded for my abstinence. Had I served current events my series would have become obsolete when the events were no longer current. It would not, after three decades, still dominate the field of Washington literary biography. Television presentation on a grandiose scale would not in the 1960s have come banging at my door.

I was, as a denizen of the Northeast, helped in the understanding of Washington and his Virginia world by a trick of inheritance. My mother's Thomas family had been among the early settlers of Maryland: their geographic base had been close to Mount Vernon. On his way to the Constitutional Convention, Washington had spent his last night of freedom in the home of one of Mother's great, etc., grandmothers. True, the Thomas family had exiled themselves from plantation life in 1810 by, as a matter of Quaker conscience, freeing their slaves, but they had carried to Baltimore and my mother had carried to New York much of the social sensibility that I was to find again in Washington, who also freed his slaves.

*

People enjoyed asking me how I could possibly expect, after two hundred years of research, to find enough new information to justify a new biography? My answer has been that the rediscovered tidbits which scholars revel in are more likely to confuse the record than elucidate it, since spotlights shine on their findings not because of the importance of the discovery but because of its novelty. Better to examine the voluminous record as a whole for a more profound insight and understanding.

For my part, I made a beeline for original documents and those secondary sources that authentically elucidated them. Because of the importance of what I was studying, there existed a reassuring if daunting flood of documentary publications. All of Washington's writings that had come to light by 1944 had been brought out by John G. Fitzpatrick in four volumes of his diaries and twenty-eight of his other writings. Many Washington documents which had subsequently appeared were published or in identified collections. A cascade of contributory contemporary material—official papers, the collected papers of individuals, letters of groups like the members of the Continental Congress—filled volume after volume. Encouraged by the far-ranging format which had been forced upon me, I resolved to postpone digging up unpublished manuscripts until my researches would enable me to determine the importance of whatever scattered documents I might find.

*

Of biographical publications, Freeman's *George Washington* was, of course, the most important. Freeman had been a formidable individual. The abbreviated listing of his institutional positions filled more than half a column of small type in *Who's Who*. His four-volume life of Robert E. Lee was regarded as almost sacred scripture in the South. This he had followed with two volumes on *Lee's Lieutenants*, other generals in the Confederate Army. Then he was somewhat at loose ends. His admirers saw as his natural next step a biography of that other Virginian, General Washington.

Foundation funds showered upon him enabled Freeman to avoid all drudgery of research. He had completed six extensive volumes when he died in 1953. A seventh, the largest, was prepared by two of his former assistants.

My own personal run-ins with Freeman had not been particularly salubrious. Despite my experience with important men, both in life and in research, I had never come across another who garnished his greatness with a pretense of humbleness. Whenever we met, he would address me by name, and then modestly announce himself as Douglas Southall Freeman. This farce reached its climax when, in working on *The Traitor and the Spy*, I uncovered a fact—the place and date of John André's birth—that he wanted for his account of Washington during the Revolution. He asked me whether I would not generously share this knowledge with a lowly fellow scholar. I was tempted to answer with the New York colloquialism based on the rivalry of two department stores: "Does Macy's tell Gimbels'?" But I suspected that Freeman would not relish this; I merely said that I was saving my discovery for my own book. I could not foresee how grateful I was to be to Freeman for both the weaknesses and the strengths of his biography.

A basic weakness was caused by the backfiring of what had seemed so advantageous a mating: a Virginian famous for his biography of

[389]

another famous Virginian writing about a third. The catch was that Washington would surely have been outraged by Lee's efforts to tear apart the nation he had done so much to create and cement together. Furthermore, Washington evolved so far away from Virginia mores that the major opposition to him, especially during and after his second term, came from more faithful Virginians like Jefferson. Freeman was too worldly and too scrupulous an historian to allow any bias to come to the surface except occasionally, as when he expressed shock at Washington's indifference to his ancestors, but the fact that the great Virginian was untrue to the society Freeman adulated had to militate against sympathy and understanding.

In any case, Freeman's conception of "scientific history" made him separate the presentation of what he defined as fact from concern with personality or psychological motivation. When informing readers about the contents of letters, he avoided actual quotation, conveying the meaning as he saw it in his own words. My belief that personalities should be permitted to reveal themselves through extensive quotation marked a profound difference in our intentions.

Freeman ended his second volume with a safely isolated appendix in which he summarized aspects of his protagonist's character under a series of numerical headings. There was an essay incorporated into the ending of his fifth volume. Much of what he stipulated was cogent, but there was no continuity to give a sense of a life being lived. Freeman intended a final character summary for the end of the final volume, which he did not live to write.

I could be very grateful that my august predecessor so skimped two major directions I pursued—character delineation and evocative presentation—that no one with more on his shoulders than a pumpkin head has ever accused me of being an imitator. But Freeman's massive work was nonetheless of tremendous assistance to me. It was as close as such an effort could be to an original source.

Freeman had kept in his office in Virginia several desks, each assigned to one of his various activities. When he sat down at his Washington desk, he found laid out by his assistants source material which was chronologically applicable to that day's writing. He justified this piecemeal approach with the truism that Washington himself did not know what was later to transpire. Freeman proceeded step by step alongside his protagonist. Whatever else may be said about this method, it suited my purposes wonderfully because I could make myself a third in the procession, while at the same time pursuing my anointed task of surveying Washington's total career.

I was able to poach, so to speak, on Freeman's foundation-supported research team because listed on the bottom of every page were the sources they had considered worthy of laying upon his desk. What they had selected helped guide me through those almost endless cards at the New York Public Library. Another advantage I got from Freeman was that the existence of his monumental work continued to keep the coast clear of any new biographies that might rival mine. Furthermore, Freeman's well-indexed pages absolved me of any responsibility I might have felt toward including details for the record's sake.

Had I been able to foresee, I would enthusiastically have supplied Freeman with the date and place of André's birth, and anything else he wanted.

*

I shall never forget my first trip, undertaken in January 1964 (three years after I had begun working on Washington), beyond the libraries, out into what remained of Washington's world. I began, of course, with Mount Vernon. I was overwhelmed by how strongly the spirit I had sought on paper still reigned there.

Almost never have a great house and its grounds been so entirely an expression of its inhabitant. Jefferson's Monticello was a perpetually revised hobby of a man who was deeply versed in architectural books. Washington blithely admitted that he had "no knowledge of the rules and principles of architecture." He was, indeed, tempted to regard these rules as being for America a kind of pedantry. His statement that he had "no other guide than my eye to determine my choices" has gained him little renown among architectural historians, and even less with architects, who find it intolerable that this amateur should presume to build so extensively without consulting or hiring professionals. These authorities further believe that nothing could be more reprehensible than enlarging a small house by adding one piece after another instead of following a total concept.

Mount Vernon grew organically like a flower or a tree. In the very center of his mansion Washington had left embedded the humble and clumsy farmhouse where he had played as a small child. This determined the eventual width of the finished mansion house and dictated that most of the rooms be small. There was no possibility for an extensive and decorative entrance like the one a professional architect had designed for George Mason, Washington's neighbor. Mason had torn down his older building when erecting his Dunston Hall, which is so much more conventionally admired than Mount Vernon.

In preparation for his marriage to Martha, Washington had literally raised the roof, inserting a second storey between it and the original farmhouse. In 1774, when he was entertaining numerous visitors, he extended the house southward to create a private wing for his own family. Then, feeling a yen for an elegant two-storey banquet hall, Washington built a balancing wing to the north, putting in false windows where necessary to make the façade symmetrical.

But Washington's eye told him that he had created a new problem. The long house, extending in a straight line and only two stories high and two rooms deep, lay on the ground like a huge wooden beam. To establish a central focus, he was to erect in the middle of the roof-line a modest triangular pediment, without decoration, that pointed up toward an hexagonal cupola. After the Revolutionary War had been won, he topped it all with a weather vane that depicted a dove of peace.

Although Mount Vernon's basic form enabled more rooms to have river views, the fact remained that the house was too narrow for its length. To solve this problem, Washington developed two expedients. On the mansion's inland side, he built low colonnades arching out from the far corners of the main block to connect with outbuildings which gave further depth by being set at right angles to the house. On the river side, he constructed a portico along the whole length of the building, freestanding columns rising to meet an extension of Mount Vernon's roof. Supplying ample space for outdoor relaxation and entertaining, this was based, as were so many of Washington's revolutionary and political achievements, on enlightened pragmatism. Washington's invention became a characteristic feature of pre-Civil War architecture in the South.

*

The visitor to Mount Vernon can share the pleasure Washington himself felt in the grounds that he designed and carefully tended for a half-century. As if foreseeing greatness, Providence, in which Washington believed, had placed his childhood home in a beautiful setting. The "mount" on which the house stands is only two hundred feet above the Potomac, yet the surrounding countryside is so flat that this seems a commanding height. What Washington called his "perspective view" is magnificent: the river is some two miles across and makes a wide curve so that it seems to embrace Mount Vernon. Providence, still on the watch, has taken care of the far bank. Although only a short distance from the city of Washington, it has remained so relatively undeveloped that it has been possible to return most of the land that Washington saw from his portico to its original bucolic state.

To fully understand Mount Vernon and what it tells us about our first president, we must realize that from the end of the Revolution to Washington's death in 1799, this house was the most conspicuous and the most important structure in the United States. The officers of the central government, including Washington, lived and worked in rented quarters. There was no Capitol and no White House. Furthermore, not only was George Washington the most popular symbol of the new nation, but he was internationally considered one of the greatest men in the world, since it was believed that he had opened up a new and better era for all mankind. One would expect that so important a structure would be replete with grandeur.

But while accepting the responsibilities that devolved upon him, Washington resolutely preserved Mount Vernon as his private residence. The interior expresses his domestic life with Martha. This did not mean that either wished to retire into solitude; both relished the extensive entertaining traditional to the Old South.

The series of ground-floor rooms combine modest elegance with domestic ease. Although interior doorways are flanked with columns and topped with broken pediments in the eighteenth-century style of Robert Adam, the pictures on the walls are personally relevant, and the graceful furniture was built for comfort.

Only the banqueting hall, two stories high and dominated by a huge, elegantly stuccoed Palladian window, was designed by Washington to be formal and to be, as far as he could discover, to the

latest taste. The room breathes a touching simplicity. There is eagerness rather than pretension. We sense and share Washington's own
pleasure in having realized a personal vision.

Compared with the great mansions of Europe, Mount Vernon is
tiny. No note of pomp or grandiloquence is struck anywhere. The
house and grounds reveal a human warmth that, for those who have
the heart to feel and the eyes to see, registers on the senses as beauty.

Driving along the shore of the Potomac after my first, deeply moving visit to Mount Vernon, I saw before me the great capital city
that bore my protagonist's name with above it the tall spire of his
monument. The sense I had felt at Mount Vernon of being an interloper in Washington's private world became mingled with an almost
overwhelming sense of presumption. However, there could be no
turning back. I could only dedicate myself more devotedly to my task.

*

Always the curatorial staff of Mount Vernon were understanding.
They realized how crucial it was for me to become at home in the
environment which was in effect Washington's self-portrait. They
enabled me to reverse the old boast, "George Washington slept here."
I spent many nights at Mount Vernon, not, admittedly, in the mansion
but only a few hundred yards away. If I wanted to wander the estate
at night, I would telephone the security office to call in the guard
dogs. After being assured that it was safe to go out, I would walk
around at will, solitary except for the ghosts who talked to me.

I remember particularly an evening when I carried my cocktails
and supper out onto the portico. While I sat there watching, as Washington had so often done, the moon rising over the Potomac, I was
struck with an esthetic revelation. The tall columns that Washington
had proportioned in accord with the interior space and the deep vista
beyond rose in sequence with the majesty and beauty of a great
classic colonnade. This effect was all the more remarkable because
Washington had resorted to no such classical quotations as Thomas
Jefferson would have considered necessary.

*

Washington was not considered by John Adams an educated man.
He had, indeed, less formal education—not beyond today's sixth-

grade level—than any other president of the United States (even Jackson and Lincoln studied law). He was not a great reader. His education came from communication with other people, and, more fundamentally, from his own reasoning powers and experience.

Washington's transcendent gift for learning from experience made personal happenings, failures as well as successes, part of the main historical flow. This doubled my determination to sweep nothing under the rug.

There was his dark love for Sally Fairfax, the wife of his neighbor and best friend, that entangled years of his young manhood. The evidence is clear, although usually toned down if not denied, that a major motive for his marriage to Martha was a desire to break away from this fascinating and wounding obsession. Although there were strains at the beginning, Washington came to write of marriage as the most important event in a man's life. Martha had become his great emotional resource, the one individual to whom he could reveal the tortures and weaknesses in his character. This triumph of reason over emotion was to be a lodestone, leading his entire career.

*

Those who think of Washington as an old man with ill-fitting false teeth will be amazed to hear that he was one of the most precocious of Americans. At the age of twenty-one, he was chosen to head a diplomatic mission through the wilderness to warn the French out of the Ohio Valley, which George II claimed as his own. Only a few months later, Washington made an appearance—not to his advantage—in world history. He triggered the Seven Years' War, that embroiled Europe, by mistakenly firing in the forest on a French diplomatic mission. For some years Washington was in command of the Virginia Regiment trying to protect the frontier from French-inspired Indian raids; he took a prominent part in two expeditions by British regulars. leading the escape of what remained of the British army from Braddock's defeat by the Indians. Entrusted again and again during the French and Indian War with more responsibility than he was truly competent to handle, the very young man was given in this forest university happy and unhappy lessons that were to serve in the creation of the United States. Washington was indeed the only one of the major Founding Fathers to have felt the totality of the continent through deep personal experience in the wilderness.

On being elected commander in chief of the Revolutionary Army, Washington confessed to the Continental Congress that he felt himself unequal to the task. Consulting refugees from the British regular army, he tried at first to match his farmboys against professional soldiers in the conventional manner. The farmboys had to rely on their agility in running away. Learning rapidly, Washington developed methods of guerrilla warfare so well suited to the American terrain and the American genius that he outlasted four well-trained British commanders in chief and won the war.

*

During the Revolution, the Continental Congress was a raggle-taggle body, in part because the alliance of the states had been an emergency measure never really defined, in part because there existed no executive branch. Often problems that required immediate attention were handed to one of the committees which had become so numerous that a congressman could be a member of a dozen or more. But Washington regarded the Congress, since it presumably represented the people, as his superior to be obeyed. He pleaded for orders, although they sometimes never arrived or came so belatedly that they were already out of date. Twice, when Philadelphia was menaced by the British army, the congressmen fled in confusion, over their shoulders (so to speak) according Washington dictatorial powers. Not pleased at being thus burdened, he applied the power charily, mostly for the twin ends of encouraging continental unity and winning over Tories rather than punishing or exiling them. As a military commander, he did his best to make the required operations of warfare as undamaging to non-combatants—particularly women—as was feasible. Washington realized that whatever happened on the battlefields, the British could conquer America only if they could get the American public on their side.

*

The most dangerous situation for the future of American freedom (and the world's) arose when, although no peace had yet been signed, the fighting had ceased. Feeling their burdens lifted from them, the various state governments turned their eyes to their own affairs, leaving the Continental Congress without funds to pay even interest to the financiers who had lent money to the cause, or long-overdue pay owed to the soldiers. Pressure was put on Washington to lead the army in reforming the dilatory, wobbly civilian governments, and there were even threats to remove him, if he refused, from command. The road to become king or dictator beckoned Washington. Jefferson remembered, "The moderation and virtue of a single character prevented this revolution from being closed, as most others have been, by a subversion of the liberty it was intended to establish."

*

Back at Mount Vernon after the peace, Washington resolved to remain a private citizen for the rest of his life. But this did not mean that he sat in a rocking chair admiring his Potomac views. His energy spilled over in many directions. He was a successful farmer on a large scale and in many ways an agricultural experimenter. He was his own architect, patron of the arts, a breeder of foxhounds and mules, and was considered the most graceful rider in an age when everybody rode horseback. He had a passion for building canals that he hoped would tie together the eastern seaboard and the new settlements in the Ohio Valley.

Although not given to prying into other people's affairs, both embarrassed and resentful of curiosity seekers, Washington was gregarious, enjoyed drink without too much drunkenness, told jokes and appreciated a good anecdote. He no longer danced as when he was a young man, but he still enjoyed the company of attractive women. He manifested an almost hypnotic appeal that enabled him to lead armies and overwhelm elections. But he was far from glad when the call came for him again.

Across the nation, chaos was on the rise. The various states and economic classes squabbled with each other, threatening the continental unity which Washington had felt in his bones among the endless forest glades. Indeed, the recently settled new West was threatening to revolt and peel away. It was to face this crisis that the call went out for the Constitutional Convention. Washington's sense of duty carried him there, and he became president of the convention. He was not the theorist as Madison was, but he was the bedrock.

Madison wrote that it was only because of the people's faith in Washington that the states ratified the Constitution. He had no choice but to accept the presidency of the new nation.

Washington's new task was infinitely more important for the future of the human race than winning the Revolution. The American experiment, altogether new in the history of the world, could disprove or prove the age-old maxim that the people, incapable of ruling themselves, had to be controlled by aristocrats. The task was made more difficult because many Americans were themselves nervous about the newfangled government—two states had not even joined the union.

Seeking the unanimity that was necessary if the Constitution would unite the nation, the convention had left vague the most controversial considerations. However, if the government was to function, the gaps had to be filled. This was the labor of Washington's first year—I called it the second constitutional convention. He was successful because it was his gift to exhume fundamentals with which all sides could agree. Jefferson, on his belated return from France, expressed astonishment that the opposition to the new government had "almost totally disappeared." He credited Washington.

*

The basic schism—it was to cause the Civil War—was between the agrarian, slaveholding South and the mercantile Northeast. Washington secured for his cabinet the leaders of both sides: Jefferson of Virginia, Hamilton of New York. He succeeded remarkably in keeping these adversaries, despite much neighing and bucking, in double harness.

Then the wars of the French Revolution exploded. Their eyes on Europe, Jefferson believed that if the British won, America would become a monarchy; Hamilton believed that if the French won, guillotines would be set up in American squares. Each wanted to risk American neutrality to help his side. Convinced that the United States could take care of itself, Washington insisted on true neutrality. Looking westward, he believed that America's contribution to Europe should be to offer asylum and prosperity to those who fled the European burning.

Washington was forced to accept a second term by both Hamilton and Jefferson, who agreed that otherwise the nation would split apart. But at the end of his second term, Washington was adamant. Although the Constitution provided a presidential election every four years, it was assumed that a successful president would die, like a king, in office, the vice president having been provided to step in like a crown prince.

But Washington wished to demonstrate that a free people could establish succession regularly and peacefully, by the ballot box. And so it was. Success for the popular government had been established for all the world to see.

But from the controversies of his second term Washington did not emerge unscathed. Both Hamilton and Jefferson had resigned from his cabinet, the more avidly to pursue their opposite paths. Although in modern terms Washington was not an old man when he retired, he was no longer sure-footed, lapsing into periods of senile confusion. He allowed himself to be caught up in the controversies on the Hamiltonian side, endangering his position as the beloved hero of the entire nation. But when the Hamiltonians wanted to run him again for president, he replied that to do so would convict him of pure idiocy.

I was to title my fourth and last volume *George Washington: Anguish and Farewell.*

*

As I had explored the fields and forests of Washington research I came on a wall, shutting off a large area, the gate fastened by chains and locks, some rusty with age, others shining new. In the two-volume index of Fitzpatrick's huge edition of Washington's writings, all proper names were listed except those of blacks. Scholars of all persuasions had been afraid of investigating Washington and slavery for fear of what they might discover. But I was wafted over the gate by my self-imposed mission to pursue the truth wherever it might lead.

As a young planter who had been brought up to slavery, Washington at first felt no guilt. But before the Revolution broke, he had become so unhappy about trafficking in human beings that he could no longer bear to sell a slave, although natural increase was giving him a larger work force to support than he could profitably employ. In 1774, he wrote, drawing no racial distinctions, that if the white Americans submitted to British tyranny, "custom and use shall make us as tame and abject slaves as the blacks we rule over with such arbitrary sway."

*

Washington's stint as commander in chief kept him in the North most of eight years. Recognizing in a business economy a viable alternative to the slave-based agrarianism of his own background, he seriously considered disentangling himself from what he could not justify: he could sell his slaves and use the proceeds as investment capital. But such sales, which would separate the slaves from the only things they had, their familiar environment, their families and friends, would have bothered his conscience. And he had been buoyed through so many hardships by the dream of reclaiming the peace he had known as a planter at Mount Vernon.

The Revolution won, Washington hoped that the American experiment—new, radical, unique—would serve as a model for the freeing of nations from kings and tyrants. Proving this contention required national unity—and no issue could be more divisive than slavery. Putting first what he considered the more comprehensive battle for freedom, Washington limited himself to secretly slipping some slaves into freedom, stating privately that if an authentic movement toward emancipation could be started in Virginia, he would spring to its support. No such movement could be started. The best Washington could do was to free his own slaves in his will.

The thinking of Virginia's favorite leader, Jefferson, had moved oppositely from Washington's. In his younger days, Jefferson had urged practical steps toward manumission, but, as he grew older, he receded into purely verbal libertarianism. He bred slaves for sale, and never freed more than a select few related to his family by blood. History has not realized that Washington's support of Hamilton's financial schemes was partly motivated by his unwillingness to agree with Jefferson on the sanctity of the slave-dependent Virginian way of life.

When an old man, Washington told a visitor, "I clearly foresee that nothing but the rooting out of slavery can perpetuate the existence of our union, by consolidating it on a common bond of principle." He foresaw the Civil War. Although exile from his ancestral acres would have torn his heart, he confided to an intimate that if the issue became inescapable, "he had made up his mind to move and be of the Northern."

*

As an honest biographer, I could not be immune to Washington's charisma, which had in his lifetime been manifest (even if resented) to almost everyone. I believe a biographer could hardly be more foolish (although it is often done) than to depict his subject as an individual who could not achieve what the protagonist did achieve. Another advantage of my recognizing Washington's greatness may seem paradoxical: I felt no qualms about seeking out and revealing flaws. Washington's shoulders were plenty broad enough to bear them, and they brought him closer to the rest of mankind.

*

Early in 1965, four years after the contract for a single volume had been signed, I submitted to my editor a completed manuscript covering Washington's life from birth to his election as commander in chief. This so obviously—it was to print up to 390 pages—made a book unto itself that Little, Brown capitulated and drew up a new contract for three volumes, the second to deal with the American Revolution, the third to cover the rest of Washington's life. I suspected that the last volume would have to be twins but decided it would be discreet to keep my mouth shut.

When I finally informed Little, Brown that I would need that fourth volume, there was not even a squeak of protest since the series not had only proved salable but had been widely praised. No effective competition had appeared to lap up the cream Little, Brown had feared I had spilt when I had deserted their desire for a single volume.

*

As the volumes successively appeared,* my interpretations of Washington seemed highly original, but this was only because the record

---

*George Washington: The Forge of Experience, correctly titled for my intention, was published in 1965; George Washington on the American Revolution, in 1968. Then came George Washington and the New Nation (1970), which dealt with his seventeen years as a civilian between the wars, and his first term as president. Anguish and Farewell, in 1972, brought the biography to a close with Washington's death.

of Washington's life had been so distorted or buried. The picture I presented, being based almost altogether on documents from the period, showed Washington as he had acted surrounded and observed by his own contemporaries. Since I depicted Washington in all his weaknesses as well as his strengths, I expected to be attacked from the right for besmirching the spotless image. Instead, the attacks came from the left. I assume that this was because those who value our American past were glad to have the Father of Our Country presented as the roundly attractive figure he had been. But the left, who like to despise and make fun of the Founding Fathers, were outraged.

As was to be expected in so roiled a scene, where so many reviewers had their own prestige and positions to defend, the hundreds of reviews—each of the four volumes stirred up its own batch—showed much inconsistency. But under the breakers, the movement of the tide was strongly favorable.

The completion of my project threw the series into the arena where major prizes lurked. Already a considerable number of specialized awards had come, but the big ones were still in the cards: the National Book Award and the Pulitzer Prize. The National Book Award was announced first and came through satisfactorily. But the biggest fish was the Pulitzer.

*

A trustee of the New York Public Library as the representative of the writing profession, I was a thorn in the side of the Librarian, who believed that the function of trustees was to raise money, and resented my using my knowledge to interfere with him. One afternoon, he informed me sullenly that my fellow trustees were planning a cocktail party to celebrate the Book Award. I, of course, expressed pleasure. Then he named a date which happened to be when the Pulitzer Prize was to be announced. Wishing, if things worked out well, to be then generally available I suggested a change of date. His sour look broke into a smile. "We'll have to forget about the party then," he said and tried to make an exit. I agreed to his date.

As guest of honor, I would have to be present from the beginning. But my wife, who always preferred to be late for everything, agreed to listen at home for the telephone until politeness absolutely insisted that she set out. My editor would man the phone at Little, Brown until the news, good or bad, came in.

On that day, I was lunching at the Century Club when I was called to the telephone. A voice I did not recognize said, "You'll be happy before nightfall," and hung up. A tip or a hoax?

At the party, I had one eye on the guests and the other on the door through which my wife or editor would appear. My wife came in. She had heard nothing. Enter my editor looking depressed. The prize winner for biography had been announced. He was someone else.

Nothing to do except have another drink and respond heartily to congratulations on the Book Award. Then a door I had not watched opened, and an excited secretary appeared to announce, "The *Chicago Tribune* is on the phone for Mr. Flexner. He has won a Pulitzer Prize."

I was rushed to a phone in the director's office. All I could make out as the voice asked me various questions was that I had won some rarely given special prize which my interviewer regarded as the Pulitzer's greatest honor. When I got back to the party, I discovered that my editor did not understand any better than I did. But we agreed that the *Tribune* call was undoubtedly for real, and that I had every right to celebrate. Which I did, nonetheless getting home safely.

I found an explanation in the *Times* on the following morning. What I had received, a "Special Pulitzer Prize Citation," was given at long intervals—seven years had passed since my predecessor—for achievements not provided for in the Pulitzer gift. A requirement was that all books honored had to have been published during the previous year. The judges had wished my award to include all four of my volumes. It was not until 1991, when the Pulitzer was celebrating its seventy-fifth anniversary, that I learned that in all those years there have been only five or six such citations.

Concluding my last volume I had written, "One advantage a biographer has over a novelist is that, while a novelist cannot spin out of his imagination a character whose dimensions are larger than his own, the biographer may stretch towards comprehension of an individual much greater than he. Although in this task the biographer cannot hope altogether to succeed, he need not altogether fail, and it is a fascinating adventure."

During twelve years I have on most mornings woken up anticipating association with an endlessly complicated and various individual who, so I became convinced, was one of the greatest men in all history. This is a privilege hard to relinquish."

But I found a way not to relinquish it.

*

Like a snake biting its tail, I returned to the very beginning of my project. Then I had considered the single volume Little, Brown had wanted an impossible task. But now I concluded that my previous efforts would make it possible for me to distill what I had discovered into a single volume. Knowing that further facts, more personal details, deeper analyses, and also justifications for my conclusions were available in the four volumes, I could move from one high point to another, reaching a broader public.

What I had in mind was not an abridgment but a condensation. I had no intention of extracting cogent passages from my four volumes, and then supplying transitions to bridge gaps. That would result in a hodgepodge without literary quality which could carry no conviction. An altogether new text was required.

I spent a long summer typing away in the garage adjacent to my summer house in West Cornwall, Connecticut. My friends asked me whether I did not find what they assumed was a routine exercise a terrible bore, but I never had a better time. It was a pure exercise in literary expression. I needed to do no research. My scale was pre-established: one-quarter of what I had already written.

I was perpetually exhilarated by the way that this change in scale, with its concomitant new sequences and new summations, created new inspirations. Action, character depictions, conclusions, were in essence the same but differently coined. Thus, I was free to dash on, without new research, absorbed in literary expression. However, the book was by no means skimpy: over four hundred pages.

Never being accused of limping along in the shadow of the four volumes, *Washington: The Indispensable Man* (1974) has lived a very active life of its own: three separate times distributed by the Book of the Month Club; once out simultaneously in four different editions. Many more than a million copies have been distributed.

My publishers and I were worried lest the single volume push the four into shadow. It seems to have had the opposite effect, encouraging readers to examine further. And with Freeman looming in the background, my four volumes occupying the middle distance and my one volume prowling the foreground, there has been little room for new biographers to maneuver. Most of the serious publications that have emerged have attempted no panoramic view, either being even shorter than *The Indispensable Man* or zeroing in on specific aspects of Washington's character and career considered by the author of special importance.

*

As I was completing my fourth volume, a new mighty force emerged on the Washington landscape. With copious foundation support, Mount Vernon and the University of Virginia inaugurated a gargantuan documentary project. It would make Fitzpatrick obsolete by including all Washington's writings subsequently discovered. More stupendous was the intention of publishing the tens of thousands of communications that had been addressed to Washington. Each document would be accompanied by a scholarly, often lengthy, note. The resulting volumes would be issued in different chronological series, and it was acknowledged that the effort would not be completed until well beyond the end of the twentieth century.

However much possible rivals to my own *Washington*s were scared away, I was not frightened by this brontosaurus snuffling at my tail. The vast majority of the letters addressed to Washington would be of value only to students of the writers, and I was confident that almost all papers directly of importance to the study of Washington had already come, one way or another, into my ken. It would take a discovery of blockbuster impact—it was hard to conceive where it could come from*—that would do more than change details in a study like mine already grounded on so various an accumulation of evidence. Since there was no explosion, the total effect was to my advantage. As Freeman began to fade, his volumes going out of print, this new uncompleted project frightened away any competition on a large scale.

---

*The most piquant direction would be the discovery of a long-secreted packet of passionate love letters written by Washington to someone else during his marriage to Martha. Since, according to my analyses, the possibility was very small, I would have had to re-examine my analyses.

The cherry-tree Washington, the marble image, even Freeman's austere hero, had not inspired dramatic presentation. But it did not take television long to recognize that the Washington I had presented, who had been the most popular man in his time, would again have a wide appeal. I had by no means said goodbye to Washington.*

---

*See Chapter 51.

42

ALEXANDER HAMILTON

*

WHEN I had completed *The Indispensable Man*, I was back at my old dilemma of finding a new subject. I would have loved to have taken on a biography of Jefferson, and I might have dared had I been younger. The very situation that fascinated me mined the ground. It seemed to me that Jefferson's attitudes and behavior had in many important directions—consistency, the treatment and rights of women, of Indians, of the blacks; the freedom of the press—been very different from what his admirers admire. Of course, I had been closely associated with Jefferson only as far as his character and career impinged on Washington's, but what I had seen implied the need for a new biography independent of his posthumous reputation. Malone had gone further in this direction than Freeman had for Washington. But he had said to me that he was leaving to younger scholars Jefferson's attitudes and behavior toward slavery, and that he was proud of writing as a Virginian. To tamper with myths so passionately believed in—more so than the various Washington myths—was more than I felt I could undertake. And Malone was my good friend.

The obvious subject was pushing at my elbow: Alexander Hamilton. On the issue of length, Aaron Burr with his bullet had made a great contribution, and Hamilton's most historically important activities were part of the panorama with which I was already familiar. Furthermore, Hamilton presented a more direct narrative than Jefferson did since his mind did not sprinkle around but was limited to a few overwhelming drives.

There existed a bushel basket of biographies of Hamilton. They were almost all dedicated to a myth even more preposterous than those that trailed after Washington and Jefferson. Hamilton, it was insisted, had personally created the United States and charted its beneficent future course. Attributed to him were the Constitution and all the achievements of Washington, a dullard who would have lost the Revolutionary War and bungled the presidency had Hamilton not told him what to do. Hamilton had, furthermore, saved the nation from being destroyed by a replay of the French Revolution.

I was puzzled by this endlessly reiterated hype which went so far beyond Hamilton's true achievement—which was rooting in a too exclusively agrarian nation the financial institutions needed for balance—until I realized its genesis and purpose. At about the time of the Civil War the capitalists who were finally conquering America were being attacked by the agrarians as interloping outsiders. Their response was to insist that they were the true creators of the nation because of the contributions of their own Founding Father, Hamilton.

Before this campaign began, there had been no biographies of Hamilton: his widow had sat on the papers. Her son, John C. Hamilton, "an eminent member of the New York Bar," finally led the parade by basing "the history of the Republic" on his father's writings. The Jeffersonians, of course, yelled their heads off, but who north of the Mason-Dixon line would bother with such rebels, and the myth was perpetually repeated by biographers eager for sales to capitalists with heavy pocketbooks.

*

As they rose to economic dominance and built their palaces in prestigious imported styles on major thoroughfares, particularly New York's Fifth Avenue, the capitalists wished to be accepted as America's upper class. It was, alas, impossible to hide that their Founding Father had been an immigrant from the West Indies. (There was subversive evidence that Hamilton had been illegitimate.) However, it was possible to fabricate for him a background of grandeur. His mother, it was decided, belonged to the aristocracy of St. Croix. Her "first" husband was a high-born Dane who had introduced her in his own homeland into the most exclusive circles. But back in St.

Croix, he treated her so cruelly that the saintly woman had to flee. She eventually sought refuge with a Scot named Hamilton with whom she had two sons, one named Alexander. Alexander's own son wrote that his father had perpetually eulogized his mother as a saint. She, in fact, was never mentioned in her son's voluminous writings.

Having decided to deify Hamilton's mother, the propagandists missed an opportunity that would have delighted them. To justify her abandoning him, they depicted Alexander's father as a rotter. Though exiled for some unknown reason, the father had been in fact an aristocrat, a younger son of an important branch of the great ducal family of Hamilton. When Alexander married into New York's powerful Schuyler clan, he tried (in vain) to find his father in order to have him live with them. That the incompetent aristocrat he had loved and admired had received such a beating in the brutal West Indies was a bitter memory and affected Hamilton's career.

*

A newly opened sugar island, St. Croix was inhabited by speculators who, if things went favorably, could become millionaires almost over night, but might find themselves in debtor's prison. Debauchery, murder, theft, endless lawsuits were the order of every day. The slaves were so badly treated that calculated into the purchase price was the probability that they would not live ten years.

Hamilton's mother had come from an ordinary family. The man she married was not the aristocratic Dane of legend, but an incompetent plunger. She had been imprisoned for adultery and, upon being released, had disappeared onto other islands. As soon as she managed to get under the wing of well-off relations, she threw Alexander's father, with whom she had been living, out and returned to her married name, making it clear to all that Alexander was a bastard. When she started a little store, Alexander's precocious abilities undoubtedly made it prosper, but when she died, a son from her legitimate marriage appeared from nowhere and took everything. Legally classified as an "obscene child," Alexander had no legal rights. From the age of eleven, he was altogether on his own.

Once the squalor and degradation of Hamilton's early years have been allowed credence, we realize to how startling an extent his desperate efforts to handle the situations into which he had been by birth thrown created his adult points of view: his low opinion of his fellow human beings which could mount almost to hatred; his unsympathetic myopia to the loyalties and prejudices of his neighbors, which both freed his mind and earned him enemies; his view of himself as a loner, not expecting to be popular but obsessed with a need to exert power, to demonstrate himself superior; his conviction that the best way to lead men was not through their affections and virtues but by either persuading their intellects or satisfying their weaknesses; his industry and efficiency, which also served to drive from his mind painful things; his passion for overcoming disorder with order, for building sound institutions, and his belief that order must be imposed on his fellow men rather than built in cooperation with them; his nationalistic yearning to create a powerful, honorable, and internationally admired state as an object of pure, abstract beauty—he was not inspired by any love for America or its inhabitants. He was a nationalist, but he never felt that warm springing of the heart which is patriotism.

Fired by genius, this constellation of traits enabled him to recognize in the structure of the emerging United States serious weaknesses which he had the ability and drive to cure. But, as my research went on, I diagnosed a streak of madness which led him to perverse acts that damaged the creations of his genius. To the Constitutional Convention he proposed the establishment of what would be in effect a republican monarchy: the president and senators chosen for life by a limited electorate. There was no possibility of the plan's being ratified, but that he had promulgated it impeded his whole future career with anti-royalist distrust.

Then there was the time, at the end of the Revolutionary War, when he tried to persuade Washington to lead the army, to secure the pay that was owed it, against the civil government. He darkened his future, when John Adams had been nominated to succeed Washington as president, by publishing a violent attack on Adams and then lamely urging votes for him anyway because Jefferson was even worse.

Most grievous for the future of the United States was his preparing the ground for the Civil War by his refusal of any concessions that would make his necessary financial reforms palatable to the agrarian South.

*

It was surely not coincidence that Hamilton operated most effectively only in tandem with a more stable collaborator. He wrote the *Federalist* in conjunction with Madison. His two highest periods, his role in the Revolutionary War and his financial inspirations, were carried through under what he himself called the "aegis" of Washington.

Hamilton could never be ignored but he could never be loved. The tragedy of his life was that unlike Jefferson, who remained powerful through the succeeding presidencies of his disciples Madison and Monroe, Hamilton had no personal followers of political stature. He had given Adams, who succeeded Washington, good reason to hate him. He practiced law, stirred around in New York State politics, and faced death too successfully (was it suicide?) in an unnecessary duel.

*

My publishers had made the mistake, which I was not astute enough to pick up, of leading off their jacket copy by calling my book "a psychological biography of Alexander Hamilton." This was not an untruth, but in those years the words "psychological biography" were taken to imply an effort to psychoanalyze. I had never opened a book by or about Freud, and considered that my approach was, as practiced by Shakespeare in *Hamlet*, as old as literature. Yet I was read lectures by several reviewers reminding me that I had not been able to get Hamilton on an analyst's couch. True Freudians, of course, laughed at such claims, but had a tendency to accuse me of trying to join their group under false colors. But these did not scuttle my volume.

Considering how original and unconventional it was, *The Young Hamilton* was surprisingly well received. Most reviewers were Jeffersonians and thus gratified. The devotees of the Hamilton myth regarded my book as too preposterous to be bothered with: it was not even mentioned in their bibliographies. Since I had emphasized the strength of Hamilton's genius, the more enlightened business publications were not outraged but fascinated. *The Economist* considered *The Young Hamilton* "up to the standard of literary elegance, psychological penetration, and historical scholarship that Mr. Flexner's massive life of George Washington has led everyone to expect." Little, Brown has kept the book in print for nearly twenty years.

*

In some four years of labor, I carried Hamilton to the epoch that had ended the first volume of my *Washington:* the successful completion of the Revolution. Ahead lay one more volume, perhaps two, but I found myself wondering whether I really wanted to proceed at such length. My manuscript had turned out to be, more than any other of my biographies, a psychological study. And, in that endeavor, I felt that my objective had been achieved.

Hamilton's character, unlike Washington's which was always growing, remained constant, the same forces playing over and over, even as his influence enlarged and as circumstances changed. Would it not be most effective to devote a final chapter to revealing in a brief chronological narrative how his psychological fix shaped the triumphs and failures during the rest of his career?

This could be considered a very foolhardy thing to attempt, since Hamilton's most significant achievements lay ahead, but when I got down to actual writing it came very easily, a good omen, since I can drive fast only when I encounter no major roadblocks and can see ahead clearly.

Although *The Young Hamilton* stirred up considerable controversy, my summary treatment of his last twenty years fitted the book so well that it came in for no literary criticism.

43

JOHN ADAMS AND
STATES DYCKMAN

*

The Young Hamilton being, as far as my labors were concerned, put to bed, I was returned to my reiterated problem: what should I do next? The format of *Hamilton*—carrying a protagonist through his early life and then in a summary chapter revealing how identified traits determine the rest of his career—seemed to have worked well. It was, indeed, generally approved. Why not do the same, as it would be suited to my age, with another Founding Father?

Were I to hold myself to the most important, it was a small group: only four, excluding Franklin of a previous generation. Washington and Hamilton I had already dealt with. Jefferson still seemed to me, even more now that I was sixty-nine, beyond my possibilities. That left John Adams.

My cousin Catherine Drinker Bowen had published a book on Adams, which ended with the Declaration of Independence, and had been highly successful. However, one reason for her perpetual success was that she wrote eloquently in a female voice, falling in love, so to speak, with her male protagonists. I was unlikely to fall in love with John Adams. My problem would, indeed, be the opposite. When writing about Washington I had come to dislike John Adams.

Because of his agitations at the Continental Congress while Washington was under consideration for commander in chief, Adams persuaded himself that he himself had personally created Washington.

Feeling, despite his lack of actual military experience, within himself great gifts as a soldier, he came to disapprove of Washington's generalship and, as a leader of Congress, meddled as much as he could. A Harvard graduate, he regarded Washington, who had had no formal education to speak of, as an uneducated lout. Adams found it infuriating that, as the years passed, even when he was being inaugurated as president, whenever he tried to bask in the limelight, the light shone instead on the tall figure of Washington.

My previous studies had revealed Adams as amazingly inconsistent. During the Revolutionary War, he had postulated, on democratic principles, that any free citizen could, without training, become an invincible soldier. He hampered Washington's efforts to recruit a regular army. General officers, Adams believed, should be elected annually by Congress. But he insisted, as the federal government was being organized, that the presidency (to which he hoped to succeed) should be separated off from the rest of humanity with a grand title. Adams plumped for "His Most Benign Highness."

*

With what might be ruled egotism worthy of Adams himself, I believed that, if I undertook a biography of John Adams, I could by an act of will, wipe out all preconceptions and start out with a blank screen. I felt further reassurance because among the wide cast of characters I had delineated down the years, without getting into trouble, were many not to my taste. I had, indeed, found them especially interesting, since comprehension pulled my experience in wider directions. But this had always been on a small scale. Could I really sail on an even keel through such a biography as I now projected?

It was encouraging that I was by personal experience more familiar with the world in which Adams grew than I had been with the environments of any other of my major protagonists. Had I not spent four years at Harvard and season after season at Chocorua, a summer colony of Boston Brahmins? And there existed, since Adams was always fascinated by his own states of mind, quantities of personal material contained in diaries, letters, etc. I was not taken aback by the fact that he wrote three different sets of reminiscences in different handwritings. Did he think of himself as three persons? "Okay," I thought. I accepted the challenge to pull them all together.

I completed in about a year, also dedicated to further research, what I considered an adequate draft of seven chapters carrying Adams from the beginning to his first manhood, reveling in what seemed to be intimate revelations that included an almost day-to-day account of his almost broken heart concerning a flirtation. Then, in a thunderclap, I realized that his confessions, his self-revelations completely omitted his courtship of Abigail Smith, the woman he was to marry and who remained the lodestone of his life. Did this demonstrate an existence of a fourth, deeper flow, hidden below what he had recorded in any of his different handwritings? Had he been fooling me with poses?

To find that deeper flow was certainly my major task. Reading over what I had so far written, I now diagnosed triviality in Adams's self-revelations that I had copiously quoted. I also noticed that I had instinctively reached for more depth by placing heavy weight on his environments: the family going back four generations on the same farm; his parents; Harvard as it was lived during his years there. Since he seriously considered going into the ministry, I made a detailed study of the ecclesiastical situation then rampant in Massachusetts. Also, the nature of law practice as he was undertaking it. These essays were in themselves interesting but did not bring me any closer to the fourth voice I now realized that I had to comprehend.

I was led to the inevitable conclusion that, perhaps all the more because I had not altogether overcome my dislike of him, I was failing to understand John Adams. From that there was an inescapable corollary: I would have to abandon the project on which I had been laboring for more than a year.

My determination was far from satisfactory to my publishers, who had foreseen another success that would enhance the value of my byline. A new editor to whom I had just been assigned demanded to see the manuscript as far as it had been written. I had never shown an editor an unfinished manuscript, and I was sure that he would cause trouble by insisting that I continue. I did not escape trouble. He was furious. Although I remained assigned to him, he set in motion the machinery that was eventually to shatter my long relationship with Little, Brown.

Providentially, as Adams faded away, there appeared a project which might have been designed for my situation. I was offered a large stipend (I would have to return my advance to Little, Brown) and an unlimited allowance for expenses to write from an extensive unused archive of personal papers a biography of an almost unknown Loyalist called States Dyckman, who had been employed by the British military during the Revolution in a manner that had enabled him to make two fortunes and to build on a shore of the Hudson a great manor house, Boscobel.

After so long following the footsteps of the great, it appealed to me to follow an altogether untrodden path, all the more because it would, by leading me into the British side of the Revolutionary War, satisfy my predilection for new horizons. I had no way of realizing at the start that this adventure would unfold in stunning detail an emphasized unrecognized cause for the victory over the British of the American rebels.

*

On the east bank of the Hudson, a few miles below my family's summer house, Rock Neath, there now stands Boscobel, an architecturally exciting, very early-nineteenth-century mansion named Boscobel. It had originally been downriver. Its site had been acquired by the United States Veterans Administration for a hospital. The old house being in the way, they had sold it to a wrecker for thirty-five dollars. After neighbors lay down in front of the bulldozers, Boscobel was then taken apart, the pieces stored in local barns. Enter Mrs. DeWitt Wallace, co-owner with her husband of *Reader's Digest*, who re-erected Boscobel in its present location.

Boscobel was a freak among major Hudson River mansions, because it had represented no dynastic family. Its builder, States Dyckman, had been born inconspicuously in 1754 into an ordinary family on the northern tip of Manhattan Island. At the start of the Revolution, he had been arrested as a Tory. Having escaped to British-held New York, he had been employed in the Quartermaster Department of the British army, had accompanied his employers to England, and had returned after the peace with a fortune which he squandered.

Going again to England, he came home with another fortune with which Boscobel was built. Despite his being utterly unknown to history, he had left an archive of papers worthy of a major historical figure.

A squabble between the trustees of the Boscobel Restoration Inc. had prevented the papers from being examined, but a way out had finally been discovered and I was offered a generous grant to unravel the mystery and write a book. Despite my innate curiosity, I might not have been tempted had I not thrown away a year's earnings with my abandonment of John Adams. I would have leapt with joy had I foreseen that these unconsulted papers contained a major explanation of why the American colonies had won their freedom from Great Britain.

The Quartermaster Department that Dyckman joined supplied the horses and wagons that enabled the British army to be mobile. His first task seems to have been to use his Tory connections in Westchester County to find farmers who would, invisibly to Rebel eyes, sneak teams to Hudson River coves where they were picked up by the British. But soon his employers recognized Dyckman's great skills at so inventing or doctoring accounts that the quartermasters were able to put into their own pockets (according to States's estimate) three-quarters of the huge sums paid by the Crown for the land transport of the largest expeditionary force sent out in the eighteenth century. This was to make an important contribution to American freedom since the financial weight on the British government of continuing the war had been a reason why the British finally accepted defeat.

States's shenanigans were made possible by a fundamental aspect of British society. Primogeniture, which awarded major inheritance to eldest sons, spawned bevies of younger sons who had to be provided for in a manner suited to their station. Ordinary methods of making a living, such as trade, were considered below their rank. There existed, beyond marrying heiresses, three acceptable directions: the Anglican clergy where appointments were frankly called "livings," government, and the armed forces. Since it smacked of trade for gentlemen to receive more than token salaries, the draining off of "perquisites" (what our plebeian society would call "graft") was necessary to the system.

Any official designation of a code for the lining of pockets would acknowledge the practice and question the integrity of gentlemen. Each official was entrusted to make his own decisions. The higher his social rank, the larger the sum that was considered legitimate. The Quartermaster Department, with its necessary direct financial dealings, being almost an aspect of trade, was looked down on, and thus States's employers came from secondary families. However, presented with great opportunities, they were very greedy, creating a situation that was to make for Dyckman two fortunes and sink the war effort.

*

I have occasionally amused myself with the idea of writing an equine history of the Revolutionary War. On the horse front, the Rebels had many advantages. Controlling most of the countryside and also the loyalty of the inhabitants, they had little difficulty in procuring horses and wagons. And they had much less need. Dependent on little equipment beyond what they could carry on their backs; having lighter artillery which men could pull along; fired with zeal to fight on empty stomachs; able to live off a friendly land, they had little need for transport. But the British army was so dependent in every service upon horse transport that when a division retreated from Philadelphia through New Jersey to New York, the wagon train stretched for twelve miles. An effort early in the Revolution to import from England, at a cost of £100,000, a wagon train had achieved almost nothing: the horses had become sickly on the voyage and many had died, while the wagons proved too heavy for American roads. The lesson was that wagon trains would have to be put together in America.

The resulting problem had struck hard during the French and Indian War: farmers hid their teams in the woods when they saw redcoats approaching. It proved more feasible for the quartermasters personally to buy the teams, cash down, and hire drivers, often slaves. But official regulations provided only for daily payments to owner-drivers. By signing receipts with uncheckable names or illiterate crosses, the quartermasters reimbursed themselves over and over for their original outlays.

This practice, vastly enlarged, was still in effect when Dyckman joined the Quartermaster Department.

To begin with, Dyckman demonstrated a gift for straightening out the fraudulent records, which had been kept carelessly on the march. He saw to it that no blemishes—such as having wagons appear from nowhere or receipts bearing signatures for the same name in different handwriting—would appear on the surface. To keep up appearances was, at first, all that was necessary, since the supervising officials who checked the accounts wished to seem assiduous while not interfering with the system on which aristocratic prosperity was grounded.

There was a reason beyond "perks" (as they were affectionately called) why the system was condoned. To hire wagons by the day from hundreds of owner-drivers offered little possibility for the efficiency that military campaigns required. As it was, the Quartermaster Department was extremely efficient: whenever and wherever land transport was needed, at however short a notice, it was supplied.

Each quartermaster, as he was succeeded in the job, handed in his own accounts, and all had to be passed not only in New York but also in London. As States graduated from detailed doctoring to larger issues—did, for instance, some of the wagon trains charged for actually exist?—he found himself drawn to England, where he was constantly and profitably employed.

His task was not made easier by the quartermasters who, after themselves returning home, were far from discreet in splurging their gains, and, as the war went increasingly badly, tempers soured. To make States's problems more serious, the wagon issue got involved in the fight as to whether General Clinton, as commander in chief, or Cornwallis, who was actually forced to surrender, was responsible for the crushing defeat at Yorktown. Cornwallis had opposed, while Clinton overlooked, the quartermaster's illegal private ownership. The situation became so much a public scandal that Parliament felt it necessary to overrule the war department by sticking onto the issue its "Commissioners Appointed to Examine, Take, and State the Public Accounts of the Kingdom."

In their report, no bones were made about the ownership or the tremendous personal gains of the quartermasters. At the "highest price," the commissioners reported, a four-horse wagon would cost £20 and each horse £15. The proprietor could recover this money in three months. Then, if he possessed fifty large wagons and two hundred horses, he would make £9 885 8s. 4d. a year. (Multiply by several hundred for current value.) But, having huffed and puffed, the Commission pushed to one side the basic issue of "how far such profit belongs to the public" by stating "could a single instance of fraud be discovered, such a discovery would so vitiate and corrupt the account as to subject the whole to revision and unravelment." This reinforced the importance of States's contribution as one quartermaster after another presented accounts which, within the unwritten rules, had to be sanitized.* Although by no means regarded by his employers as an equal, Dyckman was well paid.

*

With the return of peace, Dyckman was consumed by a desire to dazzle his family and old environment with his upper-class manners and purchases. The majority of Tory refugees also wanted to go home. The New York Coffee House, which States frequented, was swept up by waves of anxiety, hope, or despair as boats from America brought varying information on how deserters from the cause were being received by triumphant Rebels.

Although studies on Loyalists tend to dwell heavily on public policies, statutes passed by legislatures, etc., according to the evidence I found, determining issues were likely to be local or personal: whether members of their still-resident families were eager to welcome or reject; how former neighbors felt; and whether a man's property had been confiscated and granted to a Rebel who would not be pleased to see the old proprietor sniffing around. And there was always the question of what the Tory had done in England during the Revolution. States's quartermaster activities had been sub rosa. He had owned no real estate that had been confiscated. And his relations,

---

*The issue raised by the quartermasters' perks remained an open wound all the more inflamed because the war had been lost. Although the quartermasters had been not well enough born and too greedy, to demand, in the public eye, that they give back what they had appropriated would have opened the whole issue of the underhand prerogatives so basic to the aristocratic system. On the other hand, what had been done could not be publicly vindicated. The issue became frightening to the upper class when the French Revolution had broken out and threatened to cross, in one way or another, the Channel. Eventually George IV's brother, who was titularly commander in chief of the army (and whose wife was reputed to sell commissions) abolished the charges.

who had been staunch Rebels, received him gladly. In January 1789 States Dyckman reached home.

*

The emotional center of States's life had been his sister Catalina, thirteen years his junior. When he departed for England, he had left her a spacious allowance, eager to keep her from crossing from British to Rebel-held territory, thus breaking contact with him. But she had found his attention oppressive. She did move, and, when she married one Daniel Hale, made no effort to inform States. But Hale immediately got in touch, wishing to borrow large sums without interest or security.

When States reached home, he discovered that Catalina, having been prescribed laudanum for "a painful indisposition," had become addicted. The result was a wrenching battle, with Catalina torn in the middle, between her husband, who accused her of willfully shirking her marital duties, and States, who wished to cure her under his wing. States himself was badly stricken with gout, then an epidemic disease, extremely painful and potentially fatal. He married a much younger woman, the granddaughter of a onetime semi-legal pirate who despised him. The girl, however, adored him as the height of sophistication. She welcomed Catalina into her care. To impress them, and even more to please himself, States spent more and more on luxuries. Had not his quartermasters promised to pay him large annuities? But feeling that they needed him no more, they overlooked their obligations.

As the months stretched into years, States dispatched across the ocean legal drafts that were always protested, indignant letters that remained unanswered. In order to protect himself from New York's debtors' prisons, he found himself selling off painfully, one by one, under the eyes of his neighbors and his wife's hostile family, the aristocratic purchases that had been so great a source of pride. He skirted in his anguish the very edge of madness.

But he did have a weapon. Giving as his reason a need to clear up matters in the United States, Dyckman had brought home with him from England the extensive archive of incriminating papers that I was eventually to find so revealing. However, this insurance against

neglect by his employers was useless in America. So in 1799, Dyckman packed up his papers and set out with them to England.

*

Whether because of his eleven years in equalitarian America or the
result of rage (probably both), States was not, as he had previously
been, the obsequious employee. Now, in writing the quartermasters
(or their heirs), he referred to himself as their patron, their benefactor,
who had preserved for them their gains. This did not go down well
with the toplofty Britons, but the investigations were not altogether
quiescent, and there could be no doubt that the papers Dyckman
held were dynamite. Once again, they made him a rich man. He
promised to destroy the papers but again broke his word.

After his return to America in 1804, States resolved to claim
equivalency with the great ancestral Hudson River families by erecting a mansion that would rival those they had inherited. But he
harbored an even more grandiose vision. By deciding to call his mansion Boscobel, the former Tory was draping himself in the mantle of
British royalty. The house he was planning was to be his refuge from
the tumultuousness of the world. The original Boscobel had played
a major role in English history as the refuge of the legitimate mon-
arch, later to be crowned George II, from an effort of the Cromwelli-
ans to find him so that they could behead him.

States did not live to preen in his mansion. The foundation had
barely been dug when he died of gout (1806). Yet the house, after
going through its own tribulations, now stands resplendent as a memorial to the little man who had, by helping to augment the ruinous
cost of the war to the Crown helped the cause in which he had not
believed: the freedom of the United States.

*

When the forthcoming publication was announced, the squabble over
who really owned the papers re-emerged. To my dismay, lawyers
prowled. However, the Boscobel trustees achieved a compromise: my
publication was accepted, but the papers were to be put under lock
and key. The monopoly thus created added to the importance of my
book, but the person at the Library of Congress who decided under
what categories the book should be catalogued did not even mention

the American Revolution, burying the perks of the quartermasters and the deadening effect on the British war effort.

Published under the title *States Dyckman, American Loyalist*, the book was anything but a success. I learned the idiocy of assuming that curiosity concerning an interesting character who had been newly discovered would attract purchasers. The thousandth biography of George Washington could beckon, but a strange name, except in the title of a novel, appeals to no one. And States was not low enough in the social and economic scale to attract the proletarianists. Add that Little, Brown, having indulged me by publishing a book they were sure would not sell, made no effort to prove themselves in the wrong. But to paraphrase the Salvation Army, a book may be down but not out. At the end of 1991, eleven years after *Dyckman* had been published, my phone rang, and the director of Fordham University Press expressed dismay that I had not answered his request—the letter must have got lost somehow—that he might republish *States Dyckman*.

44

THE METHODOLOGISTS

*

I have envied preachers who are traditionally empowered to kick off their sermons with quotations from the Scriptures, being thus supplied with a prefabricated "lead" around which they can elaborate at whatever length they feel they can get away with. Only once in my long career has fate allowed me such a quotation, if not from the Bible at least emerging from a Valhalla of academic art historians, the *Art Journal*, published by the anointed College Art Association.

The *Art Journal* condescended in 1984 to devote an issue to American art. In the opening "Editor's Statement," Jules David Proun, a Yale Ph.D. and professor, paid his compliments to my generation, who were "not trained as art historians," by stating that we had studied American art for unworthy reasons: nationalistic, genealogical. He and his fellow Ph.D's had subsequently made the study of American art "respectable."

Proun, and his fellow academic Prometheuses, had emerged after my colleagues and I had over some two decades nurtured the admiration for American art which had finally opened up new jobs in the universities and art museums. Lapping up the cream, the Ph.D.'s. held on to their belief that the field of study was inferior to the study of European art. They would elevate it, as far as was possible, by applying to it the scholarly "methodology" that had in the 1930s been brought to the United States by German professors fleeing Hitler. Wanting to make out that these German paragons were not too far away from American creation, Proun wrote that "perhaps in gratitude to their adopted country, they sought and found value in [America's] indigenous art." To prove his point, Proun named William Sawitzky and Oscar Hagen. Readers of this book need not be reminded that Sawitzky (despite his name's being similar to that of the German émigré leader Panofsky) had been a Latvian ornithologist. As for Hagan, although German, he had been in America for many years before this new influx. His contribution, *The Birth of the American Tradition in Art* (1940), had been one of the worst ever written on the subject.* Spinning fine theories, he never lowered himself really to examine the paintings.

The German refugees were gathered into the New York University Institute of Fine Arts, whose director, Clarence Cooke, was a friend of Jack's and mine. I met the immigrant professors. They could not hold in their disdain for the nation to which they had been forced to flee. They announced that since noble Germany had succumbed to Hitler, America would, of course, succumb to something worse. They considered American art beneath contempt.

Cooke's own field was Spanish art. He prepared for Jack and me, when we were planning our trip to Spain, a guide to the cabarets in Madrid, telling what time to arrive at each and which girls to ask for. His taste in female beauty was impeccable, and I could not help wondering how his Germanic scholars, if they found themselves in our lack of shoes, would, with their "formal analysis," have explained the beauty we saw so opulently displayed.

*

By the time Proun wrote his "sermon," the N.Y.U. Institute was far along in dominating the study of American painting. Its appeal was that its teachings enabled the scholars to practice what Proun called "orthodox art history," examining the artifacts just as if they were studying European art. This, of course, was a replay of the desires (which usually eventuated in feebleness) of American portrait sitters to be depicted as if they were English lords, and of American painters, back from foreign studies, to paint just as if they had not come home.

Cooke had been succeeded as Director of the N.Y.U. Institute by

---

*The professor had made recompense to his adopted country by giving to the American stage a charming daughter, Uta Hagen.

Craig Smyth, who felt that an outside influence was needed and that the Institute could not indefinitely scorn American art. He asked whether, if he could pry open a way, I would join the faculty. More devoted to writing, I was not too enthusiastic, but agreed that Craig should go ahead. He did succeed as far as to have his faculty agree to forget that there was no such thing as American art and also that I had no Ph.D., but it was assumed that I should teach according to their methodology. To this I could not agree, as I was convinced that their methodology, however useful it might be to European studies, was made largely irrelevant to our art because of the givens of American civilization (which Proun and his successors were delighted to ignore).

I have occasionally wondered whether I had been "chicken" or too conscientious and too dedicated to my writing. If I had taught American art from the sacred halls of the N.Y.U. Institute, could I have bored from within to keep the study closer to American realities? I doubt it. The senior professors would surely have caught on and given me the bum's rush. If nothing else was achieved, to be able to cite in my curriculum vitae a seat in the Valhalla of methodology would have been good fun, and might have ameliorated attacks.

*

A different opportunity, more suited to my maverick's propensity for going my own way, opened to me.

In planning its hundredth anniversary celebration (1970), the Metropolitan Museum decided to make a big splash about the nineteenth-century American art they had for so long neglected. They would stage a four-day gathering of "scholars, historians, critics, and collectors" to create "the first such formal exchange of ideas." Although it was almost ten years since Proun and his associates had marched on the field waving their Ph.D.'s, the committee that had been called to plan the occasion asked me to deliver at the opening dinner the "keynote address." To get my speech rolling I tried a little oratory: "We should not forget that one of the excitements felt by the Hudson River School landscapists was caused by their realization that they had an unhackneyed realm of nature to explore and express. Thomas Cole believed that the painter of American scenery had privileges superior to any other since all nature here was new to art. How fortunate we are to be able to share, in our own field of endeavor, the same pioneering excitement felt by the Hudson River School. Much of the painting it is our privilege to explore is new to art history. What a feast lies before us! From any position we care to take, we have only to look around us to see unexplored esthetic peaks and glades. Our task thus requires more pioneering than is called for in the pursuit of established European art history. We cannot proceed along highly cultivated ground sustained by a host of able predecessors in whose footsteps we can walk. We must blaze our own trails.

"When Worthington Whittredge returned from years of study in Düsseldorf and Italy, he concluded sadly that to try to paint American landscape altogether according to the techniques he had learned in Europe would result in blemishing distortion. To learn to paint American nature, he isolated himself for months in Catskill glades. Fellow scholars, we cannot study American art altogether in terms of the European! We, too, have a need for Catskill glades."

That so many of the most important American artists were to a considerable extent self-taught, that art in America had no strong artistic traditions to be followed or revolted against, played hob, I argued, with that major conventional technique which might be labeled as artistic genealogy: "who got what from whom?"

"All artists," I pointed out, "make choices among available alternatives. If artists have worked in cultural centers in an atmosphere of strong traditions, explanations for these choices may justifiably be sought in cultural terms. One can proceed along a methodological road, at least seemingly solid, paved with ideas gleaned from books, with sights and associations of studios, and with memories of past art. But in the study of American painting, if one tries to follow that road any distance, it soon shrinks to a footpath, and then vanishes in a tangle of wilderness, trees, and second growth."

It was my contention that the two most basic forces in effective American art were outside conventional art history: the personalities of the artists as people as well as painters, and environmental considerations not primarily esthetic. And there lurked the phenomenon that struck at methodology like bubonic plague: spontaneous invention. I even went so far as to say that a fundamental fallacy of our rising art historians was their almost total ignorance of American history, conditions, and popular culture.

I sat down to considerable applause. I felt encouraged to repeat the most cogent parts of the speech in a Foreword to the "deluxe" edition of *America's Old Masters* that was being brought out by Doubleday.

E. P. Richardson, of the Detroit Museum, that giant in my generation among students of American art, wrote me, "When I heard your talk in the colloquium at the Metropolitan Museum, it was like encountering an urbane man of the world among a crowd of undergraduates (some honorable exceptions, of course). It reads that way too. I was pleased to have the printed form. Thank you." However, my message raised the hackles of the graduated "undergraduates." Indeed, it dug a deep ditch between me and the young scholars and curators who were taking over the field.

*

Proun summarized what became the ruling attitude when he pontificated that "the study of art" dealt exclusively with "art: the study of patterns or causation, stylistic, iconographical, technical." Having succeeded in breaking away from regular history departments, the art historians dropped their own ladders into the past. They concerned themselves with stylistic influences from one painter to another, and influences from what written sources they did not consider beneath their own dignity to examine. They outlawed all suggestions that painters had lives of their own away from their easels, were more than painting machines.

Goodrich would not permit the *Magazine of Art* to include a photograph of an artist as part of a discussion of his works. What would happen to Methodology if it were considered possible that one of a painter's forms was influenced by his wife's new hat? How, indeed, could Methodologists be expected to sympathize with or understand artist life since their own sheltered, cerebral, tenured, institutional lives were so far removed from artist life.

*

The art historians' ignorance of American life on any level below their raised chins was revealed, to take one example, by their complete misunderstanding of the pantheism obvious in the Hudson River landscapes. That mid-nineteenth-century America was the scene of sweeping religious revivals, "camp meetings" in the country-side and successful urban crusades, was too far below their scholarly dignity to be noticed. But Emerson and Transcendentalism were magic words in the halls of academe. Although no evidence was presented either way, any admiration of Emerson from the painters, and admiration for the painters from Emerson—the Hudson River School, and particularly the brands given a label the scholars them-selves coined, "luminism"—was considered, although actually a re-sponse to American light, an offshoot of Transcendentalism. The two movements were, of course, somewhat parallel, but they had different followers: Transcendentalism by the intellectuals who read essays and attended lectures; the Hudson River School, ordinary citizens who, like the painters, responded emotionally to God in Nature.

*

My subtitle for *That Wilder Image*, "The Native School of American Painting," was like a red rag to a bull for the Methodologists whose stock in trade was diagnosing European influences. Theodore L. Steb-bins, of Boston's Museum of Fine Arts, attempted rescue by going through piles of photographs of nineteenth-century European land-scapes. When he came to one that somewhat resembled the Hudson River School, like Little Jack Horner "he put in his thumb and pulled out a plum and said what a wise boy am I." His essay was hailed as a major contribution. So pleased were the Methodologists that they ignored their own requirement that the presumed imitator be demon-strated to have had access to what he imitated.

I had in my own library two relevant sources: a biographical dic-tionary published in Boston in 1870, *Artists of the Nineteenth Cen-tury*, which boasted 2,500 names; and a mammoth three-volume set, *The Art Treasures of America*, published (1879) in New York by art dealers to flatter their clients, which included lists of entire collec-tions. In neither of these sources was there any mention of almost all the artists Stebbins had pointed to. He unintentionally supported that which he most shuddered away from: simultaneous invention.

*

More than my Methodological heresies outraged. The historian of American culture, Russell Lynes, wrote, "There are many art historians who resent him not only because he knows so much but because he writes so unforgivably well." My literary style was considered shocking, smacking of such horrors as Ruskin and Pater, when compared with the lackluster prose preferred for scholarly monographs. And my activities before the Methodologists took over got in their way. The index of *Art in America: A Bibliography* (1979) lists under my name ninety-two references. Scholars were only too likely, if they were so indiscreet as to have a look, to find that I had been there before them. The damage came to be defused by an informal conspiracy of silence. My publications were ruled too old-fashioned to be consulted or included in source references. I received no invitations to the opening of exhibitions featuring work that I was the first to write about. John Howat, who, wishing to be considered the discoverer of Kennsett and then the godfather of the Hudson River School, slammed the inner door to the Metropolitan Museum, through which for more than thirty years I had so intimately passed, in my face. An elaborate catalogue he issued of a Hudson River School exhibition at the Metropolitan mentioned *That Wilder Image*, without citing the title, only in a derogatory half-sentence.

I did meet the Methodologists at the luncheons of the advisory board of the *Magazine of American Art*, from which I had not been expelled. They grouped together in gossiping knots, but no one spoke to me, whom they considered a walking skeleton devoid of enough brains to get itself buried.

*

I confess that no tears came to my eyes when I was informed that the Methodologists are being elbowed aside by a new generation which evaluates paintings according to their own judgment of whether what the pictures convey agrees with their own position on feminism, racism, proletarianism, etc. This does get them away from purely esthetic natters, but gets them no nearer to my approach. They resemble the hundreds of biographers of Washington I had ignored as they warped the record according to their own religious or political ends. However, the Washington distorters fastened themselves to Washington's coattails seeking to trap his prestige, while the modern distorters preen themselves on what they consider their own superiority to the painters.

The new fashion will in due course give way to another, but with this succession my books need not be involved. My concern was to evaluate paintings in their own terms and the terms of their own generations. Although different conclusions may be drawn, the bedrock on which my books rest is a constant, untroubled by any temporary fashion.

America's Old Masters, which is just coming out in a new edition, and my three volumes of painting history have refused to die or even stay out of print. Along with my *John Singleton Copley* and *Gilbert Stuart* (now titled *On Desperate Seas*), they are navigating into their third generation. They comfort me in my old age, and I am confident that, when I am well under the sod, they will profit by suiting better the definition of classics.

45

OUT OF THE MELTING POT

*

I KNEW that what I intended to undertake after finishing *States Dyckman* would be, within the scope of American mores, dangerous. To write, as he had hoped, a life of my father would have been considered an admirable act of filial piety, but was, I felt, beyond my possibilities. Unless I had run into feminist objections because of my sex, I could have given in to family pressure to write a life of Aunt Carey. But to publish a family history that extended backward for generations would be regarded as a snobbish effort to establish social superiority. Indeed, after I had published *An American Saga*, I was besieged by people, often strangers, who felt a need to get even by telling me at length about *their* ancestors. Those who had no genealogy to offer were sullen and often rude.

What first lured me was finding, after I had inherited my parents' apartment, in the back of a closet a large suitcase that molted rotting leather, and was chock-a-block full of letters, often still in their original envelopes, dating back to the early nineteenth century. They were between members of my mother's family.

My next discovery was the determining one. I found, sidewise against the wall behind a row of books, a vellum-bound notebook in which my mother, then an instructor of English at Bryn Mawr, had practiced her pen with short essays. She had just jotted down a criticism of herself for always writing about landscape, not people, when she entertained at Bryn Mawr a man who seemed an excellent subject for her since he was an exotic from outside her natural world.

She thus described a Jewish professor of medicine called Simon Flexner:

"After he had left, I sat and thought about the little man with whom I had been laughing and talking for nearly two hours and I found myself admiring and pitying him at the same time. Admiring the courage and determination with which he was carving out for himself success in his own special line, and pitying him for what seemed the dreariness of his existence. . . . He could only be a skilled intellectual machine, a builder after designs of others, never in any, even the smallest, sense an artist, a creator.

"Two things I seemed to see at war in him: a downright self-assertiveness and belief in his own way of doing things, which produces the effect of impulsiveness, is perhaps accompanied by it, and, over against this, intellectual quickness to perceive where he has made a mistake and an intense realization of the necessity for being politic. Add to these things a keen sense of right and wrong, a deep moral seriousness, a feeling of moral responsibility. One can easily fancy what fits of despondency he must have to live through, how he must grit his teeth and curse his fate, and finally resign himself."

This equivocal account by my mother of her first rendezvous with the man she was eventually to marry set fire to an ambition that had long been incubating in my mind: to devote a volume to a basic aspect of American achievement—the sometimes tortuous growing together of old settlers and new, of people of variant backgrounds, economic, cultural, and religious. And where could I better exemplify this saga than on my home ground!

*

Ever since my unpublished first book, "Enter and Possess," I had been prone to plots that interwove two or more personal narratives. Now I would delineate two family lines widely separated until, in the middle of the volume, they came fatefully together. As I drew up a plan for the new project, I did not realize that what I was developing closely resembled the organization of a previous book of mine on an altogether different theme, *The Traitor and the Spy*. At the start, there had been no more connection between Arnold and André than between the family backgrounds of my father and my mother, the Flexners and the Thomases. In both books, the two narratives could be dealt with separately in alternating sections, each containing several chapters. Eventually, with the opening of the treason negotiation as with my parents' getting to know each other, the sections overlapped, now to be carried along by alternating single chapters. The true mergers came when Arnold and André had their portentous first meeting on the banks of the Hudson, when Simon and Helen became engaged. From then on, the action advanced in a single line to the closing climaxes: the discovery of the treason, Arnold's escape, and André's hanging; the marriage of Helen Thomas and Simon Flexner. For each book, I felt a need for a closing chapter summarizing the subsequent adventures of the Arnolds and the Flexners.

An advantage of this format was that it enabled me to carry out as effectively as I was competent to do my father's wish that I write his biography. I could deal at length with his life up to his assuming the directorship of the Rockefeller Institute, and in the concluding chapter give a bird's-eye view of the rest of his career. Aunt Carey could also be dealt with to some extent. But the plan, as applied to my new book, contained a perhaps fatal impediment that had not arisen with *The Traitor and the Spy*.

*

Since Arnold and André had been born within a few years of each other, their biographical accounts could start comfortably in tandem. But the Thomas family had appeared in America in the seventeenth century; the Flexners, some two hundred years later. How could I establish a stable structure with one leg so extremely shorter than the other? To condense the Thomas narrative to the length of the Flexner's would violate the theme of the project: the old meeting with the new. Not willing to abandon what otherwise seemed so effective, I decided to proceed with my research and hope that my mysterious longtime partner—my subconscious—would at its own time come to my rescue.

The solution emerged when I was surrounded with the most beautiful landscape I had ever inhabited. I was privileged to stay a month at the Rockefeller Foundation's Villa Serbelloni at Bellagio which occupied the steep height that separated Lake Como, as it flowed southward from the slightly visible Alps, into two separate watercourses that flowed on into northern Italy, each lined with variously shaped low mountains.

From the little balcony in front of my workroom, I saw below me to the left and on the right separate rivers, each reflecting sunlight from a different angle and mirroring its own surrounding hills. As I stared down one afternoon, I was interrupted by the mental flash I had been waiting for.

The salvation seemed to common sense ridiculousness itself. I should reverse chronology by starting my book not with the Thomases but with the Flexners. Then, after I had reached a suitable stopping point, I could depict the Thomases' preceding two centuries as a lengthy flashback. To get away with this would require considerable legerdemain, but had I not written for the *Saturday Review* an essay entitled "Biography as a Juggler's Art," which had been twice reprinted in anthologies? And I would be helped along when I reached the constricted chronology of the Simon-Helen relationship by her being some years his junior. My stratagem was to work out so smoothly that, to the best of my knowledge, no reader was conscious of peculiarity.

Writers of family history usually have great difficulty determining the adventures and personalities of their forebears. The muse of their adventures is typically a maiden aunt who claims a memory of what her grandmother told her, the entire narrative enhancing wealth, social position, worldly importance. But, in relation to my mother's family, the augury presented by the molting leather suitcase was confirmed in most directions to a startling degree. Her ancestors were inveterate scribblers. Biographies, long or short, of all four of her grandparents had been printed, as had an extensive family history. Furthermore, members of the family had been visibly involved in recorded historical events.

The original Thomas settler had been active in the first civil war in all American history: fought in the 1650s on the banks of the Chesapeake between a few hundred Puritans and Roundheads. During the Revolution, the Battle of Redbank was fought on a family farm: a Quaker ancestress defying the cannon balls, as a protest against war, from behind a spinning wheel. During the political confusions following the election of 1800, John Chew Thomas could, as a member of the House of Representatives, by his single vote have established Jefferson as president weeks before the technical tie with Burr had been straightened out. Later, John Chew Thomas, by freeing all slaves, had temporarily bankrupted the family, a situation handled by his son, Richard Henry Thomas (my mother's grandfather), who married in succession two heiresses. And Mother's father, James Carey Thomas, had played a major role in the establishment of Johns Hopkins University, the Hopkins Medical School, and Bryn Mawr College.

As I moved along, I came to realize that pursuing family history could be a literary form, supplying the opportunity that Chaucer had so effectively applied in his *Canterbury Tales*. The pilgrimage gave Chaucer an opportunity to bring together a very diverse group of people, each of whom had a story to tell, thus extracting a coherent narrative out of incoherence. The same opportunity is given to the family historian, all the more because family sequence is built into our culture.

But there were no *Canterbury Tales* for the Flexner family. My father's parents had been obscure Jewish immigrants who had come to Louisville, Kentucky, shortly before the Civil War and married there. Fortunately for me, their seeming obscurity had fascinated Father by adding puzzlement to his own upward trajectory from elementary-school dropout. Not given to huddling under unsolved problems, he undertook what researches he could concerning forebears in Alsace and Bohemia: he persuaded his mother to write down an account of her early years, and he himself jotted down, whenever the spirit moved him, his own experiences from as far back as he could remember. And once he was on the high road, exterior sources supplemented what he recalled.

It is natural for the human animal to aggrandize his memories as the years pass, moving himself more and more into roles of importance. But if Simon recorded the same experience in jottings some twenty years apart, he would tell the same story without variation. He was being as accurate as if he were recording a scientific experiment.

*

Fortunately for *An American Saga*, circumstances kept Helen and Simon from coming freely together from their first meeting, through courtship and engagement, to the brink of marriage. Also fortunately, the post office was infinitely more efficient in those days: it was possible to exchange four letters—two apiece—between Bryn Mawr and Philadelphia in one twenty-four hours. Further separation could be similarly bridged. The telephone did not intervene. Thus, the slow merging across several years of two individuals from such different backgrounds and with such different experiences could be perpetually followed often day after day. There were no gaps. As far as it is possible to judge, neither my mother nor my father destroyed a single document.

The main text of *An American Saga* reached its climax with the marriage of Helen Thomas and Simon Flexner. I added a brief appendix concerning their later lives which to some extent duplicates what was summarized here in the opening chapter.

*

The financial support I had been given for *States Dyckman* being now obsolete, I needed to find other sources. My application to the National Endowment for the Humanities elicited a snotty letter stating that writers boasting about their family histories should themselves pay. I turned to my old friend, the Guggenheim Foundation. After some hemming and hawing, they gave me a small grant. I came to realize that, although I much preferred to stand on my own feet, I would have to rely on sources primarily concerned with my father. I procured two annual grants from the Rockefeller Foundation, and a three-year grant for expenses, to be administered by Rockefeller University, from the Commonwealth Fund.

I had *in situ* a general contract with Little, Brown but I needed an editor. Roger Donald had, without consulting me, changed the title for their reissue of *Mohawk Baronet*. Also, Donald had put roadblocks in the way of *States Dyckman*. Since I refused to work with him any longer, Arthur Thornhill, the president of the firm, offered to fill in as my editor. This seemed ideal because Arthur, when speaking on occasions in my honor, stated I was the author of whom Little, Brown was most proud. (It did not occur to me that he might on other occasions announce different choices.) In any case, Arthur handed my manuscript over to a just-promoted editor. She decided that the manuscript was much too long—it was more or less my usual size—

and urged that it should concentrate on the Flexners, shrinking the Thomases and Whitalls to a sideline. When this I would not accept, she set out to abridge the whole manuscript.

Remembering my ancient pitfall with "Enter and Possess," not having as with *The Traitor and the Spy* the Revolution to hold the two narratives together, I had kept an eagle eye out, before Helen and Simon met, for any links I could manufacture between the Thomas and the Flexner narratives. The editor, with an equally eagle eye, scratched all the connections out.

The mails brought me batches of pages so mutilated that I often had to throw them away, substituting photocopies of the copy I had kept. After this charade had gone on for a while, she decided to wash her hands of the book, although it remained her responsibility as my editor to see it through the works. One result was that, although I had paid for the index, I never saw it until after the book was bound. It was a disaster. And it being the procedure for her to present the book to the salesmen, she also did her damage there.

Fortunately, I still had two devoted colleagues at Little, Brown: the copyeditor and the book designer. They saw to it that my volume was in good shape and elegantly dressed, one of the handsomest I had received in my long career.

An American Saga was published by Little, Brown in 1984, and by Fordham University Press in 1993. Reviews were scanty although adequately favorable. A statement by John Russell of *The New York Times* stood out: "*An American Saga* is my favorite book of the season. It deals with momentous events, both public and private. It touches on the life of the mind as it was led to a very high level. It is full of social comedy, subtly observed and no less subtly put down. Above all, it is that rare thing in the 1980's—a love story for grown up people."

*

My long association with Little, Brown came to an end when they remaindered, in almost the blink of an eye, *An American Saga*, along with *States Dyckman*. Both have been returned to print by Fordham University Press.

46

ASSAILING BIOGRAPHY

*

WHEN I was at Harvard, some individual of great perspicacity told me that if, during an examination, I could not find an answer to a question, I should write down the first thing that came into my head. This would allow my unconscious mind to throw up what my conscious mind had forgotten. However, if I let my conscious mind intervene, confusion would follow. When examination papers came back, I was sometimes amazed to see how much of what I had written down I did not know that I knew.

Hanging around the American Laboratory Theatre in my boyhood and around the Group Theatre during my young manhood, I had become familiar with "The Method" which they were in succession so effectively to introduce into American theatrical acting technique. Actors were encouraged to prepare for stepping on the stage by consciously culling from their memories happenings in their own lives that involved emotions similar to those they were, in their theatrical roles, to re-enact. But as a biographer I did not wish thus to summon up a particular personal experience that would overwhelm deeper comprehension.

At the end of a day's writing, I was careful not to bring the text to a sharp conclusion. I would leave open a coupling on which to attach my next day's work. The problems involved in that continuation would, when I got home, churn in my mind. However, I followed a prescription once given me by a doctor as a palliative for over-stress: I should use a drink of whiskey to drop a curtain on all further thought concerning my literary problems. On going to sleep, I handed the quandaries on to my unconscious mind.

If I had been engaged in a long, sustained, and all-absorbing piece of work, my unconscious mind was primed for seeking conclusions. (I could rarely achieve results if I were working on more than one project.) If single-minded, I was blessed again and again with formulations of comprehensiveness, depth, and subtlety my conscious mind might well never have reached. What had been going on within my skull in the hours of darkness, I can only guess from the results. It seems that my brain had drawn on and synthesized the impress of innumerable relevant experiences that had been stored there day after day, year after year.

An invaluable boon of the synthesis thus supplied me has been that my unconscious mind enforced no distinctions between my memories of actual happenings and the hallucinations, the terrors, that have besieged me with the emotional impact of reality. I have read somewhere that the inhabitants of certain islands, who lived in Elysium without actual menaces, kept a balance by suffering from dreadful dreams. My own life had been sheltered and privileged. Had my usable experiences been limited to what had actually happened, my scope as a biographer would have been catastrophically curtailed.

Also of tremendous value to me, particularly in writing about the protean George Washington, were the information and understanding fed into my subconscious mind by the adventures and reactions of my numerous and various previous biographical protagonists.

Drew Middleton, the veteran military correspondent of *The New York Times,* confessed to me that, knowing that I had never served in any war, he had been amused at my writing about Washington in the Revolution. He had picked up the book with the intention of teasing me, but was frustrated. Although unable to think of a reasonable explanation, he had found convincing my accounts of men in battle.

*

What my unconscious mind had stirred up during my sleeping hours or stretches of semi-wakefulness was by no means codified, presented to me as memoranda at waking. As I ate breakfast, shaved, and dressed, the night's harvest (if there was to be one) did no more than murmur behind closed portals. I knew from experience that the rustling would stop and the portals fail to open if my conscious mind became occupied with tensions raised by my own daily life. Down the long years, I have tried to persuade those with whom I have lived not to assail me with disturbing matters between my rising and my setting out for my day's work. Should this request not be honored, my labors for the day would usually be frustrated and come to nothing.

Even under optimum conditions I could not foresee as I put the first sheet of paper into my typewriter. Only rarely, despite the link I had left from my previous day's work, have I been able to start auspiciously. But I clack away. Very often, the first few paragraphs resemble warming up before a tennis game. They do not count in the score.

I remember that once, as I was living in the country, a stray cat had kittens in my barn. I put out food for the mother, but she would not approach it until I was out of sight. When the progeny were old enough to walk around, I determined to make friends with the family. They were occupying a pile of firewood at the back of an unused box stall. I sat myself just outside the door of the stall, put a dish of milk before me, and kept myself as motionless as I could. The mother crouched in a corner, eyeing me with fear, but the kittens were curious. After about an hour, one kitten approached the dish and even took a lap of milk. When I gently reached out a hand, the kitten rushed back to its mother, but it soon reappeared. Gradually, the kittens clustered around me. At long last, the mother came out, purred, and rubbed against my ankle. Thus, my courting of the unconscious mind.

*

Once in a while I would, as I fiddled with my typewriter, strike a gusher. Prose would pour out so rapidly that I could hardly keep up, my fingers dashing at the keys. Sometimes it seemed that my unconscious mind tapped what had been stored there during my early years as a poet: since what emerged became the most metaphorical and strongly rhythmical of my writings. The flow often ignored the barriers my conscious mind had set up, dashing off in directions that seemed to have no relevance to where I had intended to go. But I made no effort to steer, hoping that the strange landscapes into which

I was being carried would prove to have a relevance that my conscious mind would welcome.

My unconscious mind sometimes struck after I had left my typewriter behind and gone off by bus for lunch or home in the evening. These new insights could continue the work I had been doing, or they might concern themselves with those problems of structure, where to go from here to there, which perpetually haunt a writer who is not sticking to any premeditated design. As the inspirations started to appear in the bus or some other public place, I clutched at various parts of my body and drove my hands into free-swinging pockets. I would desperately search for something to write with and something to make notes on. I have learned that these inspirations, if not instantly written down, disappear like the impress of a dream.

How to protect the integrity of inspiration can only be signaled by inspiration itself. I learned that I had to keep my imaginative and cognitive interpretations of the inhabited landscapes I was trying to re-create altogether separate from the day-to-day life I was living, all the raw experiences that had not had time to ripen and broaden in my unconscious mind. This, of course, did not mean that I might not wander and experience in the reality around me. It did mean that I should never discuss what I was writing with anyone until I considered the book entirely completed. I showed not a chapter, not a page, not even a paragraph to anyone. Not to a fellow scholar working in the same or a contiguous field; not to the editor to whom the book would eventually be submitted; particularly not a member of my family who possessed another route, with its own disturbing overtones, to my subconscious. I permitted myself one exception which harked back to my early days working as a poet. I had then, as a substitute for publication, copied verses I felt finished into my private notebook. Now, when I felt that I could celebrate having a chapter completely finished, I handed it to a typist who made no comments.

*

During the isolated hegira when a book was in progress—it could extend to two or three or more years—I was never lonely. Was I not inhabiting the world I was re-creating, charting unseen landscapes, becoming intimately acquainted with groups of new associates? And around me in the very tunnel I was myself inhabiting, I felt the pressure of numerous invisible eyes and ears. These represented the read-ers for whom I hoped to re-create as truthfully, as powerfully, as I could, the world that was unfolding before me. It was as if I were creating a theatrical production. I knew that I could not reach every-body—I could not shout in the street—but I wished to attract as large an audience as I could while not outraging accuracy or art.

*

There was, of course, no way that I could deny or completely forget that, before I was to get together with Little, Brown, my completed manuscripts were habitually turned down by whatever publisher had brought out my previous book. I did not feel this deeply discouraging because I knew that I had invited it by refusing to walk a consistent path. I was like a surveyor beyond the frontier who, as he discovered and laid out good bottom land, felt that sooner or later settlers would flock after him. And who had, again and again, seen it happen! None of my books remained unpublished for long, and when reckoned not in terms of a single publishing season, many, as they passed from edition to edition, would rank as best sellers.

*

In a letter to my mother, Bertrand Russell defined effective writing as "the outlet of feelings that are all but overmastering but yet must be mastered. Two things to be cultivated: intensity of feeling and control."

My preferred method of control has always been revision. It is most needed for outpourings, but regularly basic to my method. I sometimes make changes while still composing a first draft, but if they start to impede momentum I dash ahead. My practice requires two rereadings, separated by time. This is basic. If I make a significant alteration on the third draft, I find it necessary to revisit it twice.

I am much disapproved of by writers and other individuals who have fallen in love with their word processors. The burden of their song is that you can write so much faster because it is so much easier to revise. They explain ecstatically that, as you change a word or delete a sentence, the machine will instantly banish the old and give you new copy which shows no sign of being touched. If you desire to move a paragraph, you press some buttons and it leaps off to land somewhere else. This, according to my view, is a nightmare.

When I make a revision, I write in the new copy without obliterating the old. Thus, when I come through again, the alternate versions are both before me on the same page. I may conclude that I did better the first time, or may combine the best of each version into a new one. If the page gets to look as if it had been walked over by a chicken, I copy it over myself, in the process encouraging further reconsideration.

As for moving passages around: finding and wielding scissors and paste, making room to insert the passage where you now want it to be, gluing or stapling are foreseeable nuisances that make me consider seriously before I undertake the change. Being forced to think two or three extra times has great advantages. Gilbert Stuart, when, as he painted a portrait, he found the image forming too easily, would roughen it up to force on himself more attention.

*

As I revise my manuscripts, sentences often ring untrue like a cracked bell. Then I change around by trial and error until I am satisfied. If I skip over a sentence that bothers me, thinking to myself, "what the heck, I guess it's okay," when I come to it again it bothers me again. Revealing how little I was practicing or wanted to practice a conscious style, I did not ask myself, as book followed book, what I was in fact doing.

The answer was brought home to me when some editor at Harcourt, Brace went through the manuscript of *The Traitor and the Spy* as it was on the way to the printer, and cut out words that seemed to him or her superfluous. As I started to read the galley proof, I was horrified to find sentence after sentence falling flat. Most conspicuous was the book's climactic sentence: "Pure villainy is forgotten, while we mourn a broken sword, tarnished honor, the glory that descended." The editor had scratched out "the," thus creating three ponderous footfalls. But the little word prevented the reader from coming down heavily on the word "descended." Thus, the sentence was enabled to toss the ending of the book upward into the air.

Eugene Reynal, the editor-in chief at Harcourt, Brace, was so conscious of the damage that he footed the bill for extensive resetting.

And it brought home to me that all the little revisions I had been making for years were primarily concerned with the weight of words and rhythm. I also came to realize that I mumbled to myself as I wrote, testing sentences as if they were read aloud. I had previously been surprised when people working beside me in libraries had asked me if I couldn't keep quiet.

*

I had not forgotten the lesson I had learned, when as a boy roaming the American Laboratory Theatre, that a word or phrase takes on its specific meaning from context.* This phenomenon makes it possible for a writer to force on the reader acceptance of his own connotations concerning a word which might be quite different from what the reader would have felt if left to himself.

I did not then draw the connection, but this explained something that had puzzled me as a youthful poet: I could make no effective use of rhyming dictionaries. I now realize that since the listed words were all without context, they were for literary purposes dead. As an experienced writer, I have found books of synonyms almost equally useless. The optimum situation is to have the wording appear in my mind along with the thought. The two have been, so to speak, forged together. Otherwise, I sit at my desk trying out in my mind this word and that until one clicks into place. If nothing effective comes, I make use of some obvious word and type over it a question mark, hoping for better luck during one of my revisions.

Although I find it an amusing pastime to try to guess or even look up the derivation of some words, as a writer I feel all this has little significance. My opinion could be attributed to my not having been taught Latin, but I doubt that one educated reader in a thousand can remember enough Latin to have it color more than a word here and there. And what about Sanskrit, Anglo-Saxon, early middle English, and all the geographic connections of modern times? You don't have to know that one is romance and the other Anglo-Saxon to appreciate the fundamental difference between "mansion" and "house."

I am not overawed by rigid dictionary definitions. If I do look up a word, it is to determine the perimeter (I have just looked up perime-

---

*The same is true of color in a painting.

ter) beyond which a word cannot be (except in extreme cases) intelligibly stretched.

My usages quite often raise the hackles of publishers' copy editors who write in the margins "Does this definition exist?" I used to reply in the margin, "It does now." Becoming more learned, I now write "neologism," which the copy editors find more soothing.

I like to quote "Dean Briggs of Harvard" who is reported to have said, "If the English language gets in my way, God help the English language." But this is for me just a flourish. I have reason to be grateful to those individuals who, in the manner of the Académie Française, labor to "keep the language pure" by establishing rigid standards of usage. I am immersed in the English language like a fish in a river, and can swim against the current only if there is a current to swim against.

The greatness of Shakespeare and the King James translation of the Bible can be to some extent attributed to their having been written when modern English was coalescing and its freshness had not been rubbed off by continual usage. I believe that it is still possible to freshen a word by an unusual application of a usual meaning. This can cause confusion when your prose is walking, or even jog-trotting. As the literary tension mounts, so does the usefulness of intuitive overtone, and the vocabulary begins to grow wings. At the close of a bravura passage, syntax can take on altogether the coloring of the imagination. You can describe the sun as black.

*

My greatest weakness is spelling. This I have attributed to what I laughingly called a family curse—neither Mother nor Aunt Carey could spell—and also the Lincoln School, where spelling, considered mechanical not intellectual, was almost ignored. A more basic explanation was indicated by a very embarrassing evening.

During my first marriage, my wife and I spent a weekend in Connecticut with a school friend of hers who had married Louis Kronenberger, the anointed deep literary thinker of *Time* magazine, a position of great pomposity. He challenged me to a game of ℠Scrabble, explaining that the combatants had words lying out before them. One would draw a letter and, if he could, by shifting the letters around, use it to expand one of his opponent's words, he had made a capture. My opponent quickly captured my stock of words, while I was almost utterly unable to retaliate. Finally, we gave up, enabling him to feel great satisfaction that he had mightily triumphed over me. I was chagrined, at a loss for an explanation since that there was such a thing as dyslexia was not yet known to me.

Although I had overcome this disability as far as reading and writing were concerned, remnants have remained. (These have grown in force during my later years: I have difficulty correctly copying a telephone number out of the directory and then dialing it.) That I was years before uneasy about my weak spelling is revealed by my carefully mastering one of the most irrationally spelled words in the language, "ecstasy," and then stumping generally good spellers.

Fortunately, my misspellings of dictionary words have almost never gottten into print. I encourage the typists who copy my manuscripts to correct as they go along, and further mistakes are almost always picked up by the publishers' copy editors. I have found an advantage in these misspellings, since copy editors, eager to express themselves by making changes, find so much opportunity in my misspellings that they leave my prose alone.

There was, however, an Achilles' heel: the spelling of proper names. Unless they are of well-known characters or places, there is no way typists or copy editors can correct. Realizing that I am on my own, I do my best to get the names right, but the invisible fingers of dyslexia often intervene. Most of the errors which eager reviewers were able to find in my books have been names.

*

After being subjected to my heretical statements about vocabulary, the reader may be surprised that I am a stickler in grammatical construction. This may seem the more remarkable because I was never taught grammar at the Lincoln School. I like to say that I do not know a preposition from a proposition, and, in truth, I cannot at this moment define a preposition. But this does not mean that I am not as accurate as a sharpshooter in using correctly whatever a preposition may mean. In the some thousand reviews I have received, I have never been admonished for grammatical inaccuracy.

English grammar means so much to me because it is the skeletal structure of clear writing. I do not feel that to fire the reader's imagination you have to write obscurely and I will not tolerate a wobble in my prose. I view the logic behind grammar not as an exercise but as a utilitarian necessity to which I scrupulously adhere.

*

My mother had impressed upon me when a child that a narrative should always flow like a river, even if it sometimes curved backward, parallelling itself. I have taken this so much to heart that I wish to make books or sections of books resemble what a bird would see if he flew over a river, which, draining extensive valleys, achieved more and more force as it penetrated nearer and nearer to the ocean.

The river flows between banks that in their confrontation temporarily determine its shape and direction. It might at its beginning be a confluence of major streams. It might divide for a time, flowing around variously shaped islands, to come together refreshed. The flood is swollen by tributaries large or small flowing in from other landscapes to become part of the main stream.

There are placid lakes where, as the banks widen out, the drive of the water slackens, and contemplation is summoned. Floods may submerge the entire landscape. I paddle bewilderedly until the pressure exerted by the slight emergence of a current indicates the way back to the main stream. As the terrain slopes downward, currents move so fast that you are in perpetual danger of striking submerged rocks. Waterfalls shatter your boat or inspire your prose. And there is always the faith that, if you can keep your vessel upright and afloat, the manuscript will slide at last into a safe harbor.

The infusions from outside which I have called tributaries must be, if they are not to seem digressions, brought into the narrative flow where the confluence comes most naturally. To achieve the junction without a contrived transition, I remember the burlesque theater I sneaked into as a boy. A skipped space in the text is the equivalent of a "blackout," setting the new stage.

Blackouts, as I came to realize, have a second contribution to literary structure. These sections of a chapter can assume their own entity: lead, content, climax. Of course, such subdivisions have to pile up like building blocks to erect the larger structure of the chapter. Only later, when I became involved in television production, did I recognize the connection with a practice basic to that medium and to film.

*

A biographer of considerable reputation boasted to me that he abandoned a subject in mid-course because of his horrified discovery that his protagonist had behaved in a manner that he could not, without besmirching himself, condone. In the opposite direction, a professor from Columbia University has a speech he often delivers on the presidency in which he demonstrates, to his own manifest satisfaction, his own superiority by mocking president after president as a fool. Muckrakers are building themselves up as they tear the respected down. On still another personal tack, biographers seek worldly position by associating with the colleagues and family connections of famous men recently dead.

Jeffrey Meyers, the editor of *The Craft of Biography* (Schocken Books, 1987), states that his contributors, professors of literature all, "define themselves as well as their subjects." In his anthology, Meyers reveals a succession of schoolgirl crushes that have gone over the edge into cannibalism. Using knives borrowed from Freud, his contributors cut their subjects up for the stew pot and chomp them down, convinced that in the eating they have acquired the reputations and the abilities of their victims.

Meyers confides, "My own claim to fame is that I found and held in my hands the brain of [the poet] Wyndham Lewis." This claim is, of course, extreme. However, Carl Van Doren's children accused him of taking over, as best he could, the mannerisms of Benjamin Franklin. It is rumored in literary circles that biographers of Lincoln stalk portentiously around waiting to be shot by John Wilkes Booth. What about me and George Washington?

*

For me to identify myself with any of my biographical subjects, large or small, would undermine the alchemy which came to my rescue when I discovered my aptitude for biography. I have in any case dealt with so many individuals that to explain my choices by personal identifications is to envision me outheading the Hydra. In choosing a theme, I have, of course, been concerned with the possibilities supplied to me as a writer by the cast of characters. However, should there exist enough source material, this is not as grave an issue as one might suppose. It has been my fundamental belief that the life of no individual can be, if imaginatively comprehended, uninteresting. There exists every kind of drama, from derring-do to entangled contemplation, and part of my pleasure is discovering the motivations whatever they might be. Most menacing is not seeming dullness, but too strong an immediate reaction on my part. This is not so serious if I automatically feel sympathetic: liking encourages understanding, and I am not given to going overboard. The problem rises if I find myself automatically hostile. Hostility must be overcome since it blocks understanding. If such an understanding is achieved, it brings a double reward: it expands my own horizons.

I have been able to interpret such a variety of persons because the impetus does not come from me to them, but from them to me. My insight, my imagination is directed to comprehending individuals outside myself.

*

As my long career has moved by, I have been amused to see the over-long, all-inclusive Victorian biographies against which Lytton Strachey rebelled, return in a different guise. It has become fashionable for biographers to cherish every morsel of information about their subjects—they are spurred on by electronic devices—which pour out by the bucketful. Publishers add to the effect by bulking up the books until they seem to be designed for doorstops. Certainly, such compendia do not make for vivid reading. I suppose that readers thus engulfed enjoy feeling that they themselves are living with a glamorous set.

However, authors of biography in the true sense must recognize that, although people do live from day to day, it is not wholesale that experiences are recorded in protagonists' memories. One happening that occupied only a minute or two can outshout a year of trivialities. Nitpicking biographers, having buried the steps that lead to a climax, can step over the climax without recognizing it. For my part, I have tried to extract from the welter of living the episodes and feelings that determine futurity. It is my desire so to approach a climax that, when it is reached, there remains no need to adulterate dramatic action by comment or explanation.

*

Opening at random the third volume of my *Washington*, I came on the following sentence: "The growing season at Mount Vernon continued, beneficent crops bowing to the wind in every field." It contains a statement of fact that you could find in any textbook. But the word "beneficent" incites (all the more because Washington was facing many troubles) human emotion. The second clause offers movement and visual experience without in any way violating historical integrity. This approach broadened and enlarged to whatever extent called for, applied to thousands of situations, can stand as an epitome of my biographical style.

Again and again vividness requires that a particular event be revealed in its setting. When I depict Sir William Johnson at a powwow or a war dance, accurate knowledge of Indian customs is invaluable. And I could count on any significant variation appearing in my specific sources.

I have never put between quotation marks my own rendering of what I knew had been said. However, not wishing to banish altogether the vividness of direct speech, I have quoted from a protagonist's reminiscences, the more avidly the closer in date. Going even further, when there had been an argument in an exchange of letters, I have presented contradictory statements as if in an oral debate. I have always indicated in my text what I have done.

Since I do not want readers to be perpetually interrupted by having to turn to the source references, I wish to communicate relevance more directly, by building into my texts indications of what sources I am relying on, to what extent, and also how solid I judge the sources to be. There are a thousand ways by which this, without monotony, can be done. "According to" can be made to refer to an historical character or a fellow biographer. If I wish to present a conclusion without committing myself, "historians say." And so on, and so on.

One might foresee that all this paraphernalia would put my readers off, but it can have the opposite effect. The reader feels that he is being given a fair deal, invited into the author's confidence. The warmth and conviction thus engendered is very important since I often wish the reader to join me in excitement, accompany me to heights where no dry-as-dust scholar would dare penetrate.

47

BIOGRAPHICAL TECHNIQUES

*

As time went on, my research methods became more sophisticated and more various. Variety was demanded because of my basic principle that technique should not be applied from above according to any pre-established and generalized conceptions, but should rise from below to express in the best way possible the material being presented. This pragmatic approach, plus my conviction that basic details have a greater impact than a sprinkling, enabled me to document so many different books in what an academic scholar would regard as an incredibly short period of time. The need to master specific phenomena gave focus to my research.

I might seem to be making trouble for myself by so often tackling subjects that were at the time when I wrote them outside the bounds of conventional scholarship. But this was often an advantage. We have seen how I had to struggle to disentangle myself from the snake pits of innumerable publications concerning George Washington. And it was to my advantage that my protagonists had lived before walls had been built between specialties and insignificant details had been piled high. Almost all of my characters, not excluding Washington, were particularly open to a biographer who was also teaching himself as he went along.

*

When, after having determined the subject for my next book, I start doing my research, I have to move slowly. Everything possibly of

Bust of the author by Richard McDermott Miller, 1986.

The author, being sculpted in bas-relief by Richard McDermott Miller, in Miller's studio, 1986. Photo by Joseph Noble, director of the Museum of the City of New York.

Barry Bostwick (as Washington), the author, script writer Richard Fielder. In background: reproduction of the original "Mount Vernon" for the CBS production of *George Washington*. Photo by Bob Greene/CBS.

On the *Washington* set: Patty Duke, Barry Bostwick, an unidentified man, and the author.

Left: Jaclyn Smith (as Sally Fairfax) and the author on the *Washington* set. Right: Barry Bostwick as Washington. Photos by Bob Greene/CBS.

The author, after receiving the Peabody Award for the Washington telecast. Left: David Gerber, producer of the CBS production. Right: John McNulty of General Motors.

The author on the *Washington* set. Photo by Bob Greene/CBS.

The author, his daughter, Helen Hudson ("Nellie") Flexner, and his wife, Beatrice Hudson Flexner. Behind them is a painting of the author's father, Dr. Simon Flexner, in his laboratory. The painting, by Adele Herter, is in the collection of the University of Pennsylvania Medical School.

With Beatrice on the streets of New York. The photo, taken without its subjects' knowledge, appeared the following day in *The New York Times*.

significance must be noted, or at least indexed so I can find it again. As I go on, I can be increasingly selective. A repetition can be omitted unless the new reference is more enticingly worded for possible quotation. Trivia should be, like mildew, brushed away. Fakes, myth, and false evidence become easier to identify as my knowledge of the subject increases.

Always in a hurry and eager to get to my writing, I am driven during my researches to take as few notes as possible, but I am held in line by conscience, by my hope that I will write a book both accurate and profound—and also by curiosity. This curiosity must be restrained from leaping fences into strange pastures, but there is always plenty of interest in the areas I am legitimately exploring.

The combination of knowledge and intuition needed to judge what is and is not worth noting has made me very wary, despite Freeman's example, of relying on research workers. My need was somewhat different from Freeman's, as he was building up the factual record while I was more concerned with insights that would light sparks. The nature of my need is hard to communicate, particularly as the academic mind does not turn easily in my direction.

For *States Dyckman* I was allowed unlimited funds for research. Since more of the material I needed was in England than I could cover during a visit there, I hired a highly recommended young scholar: a "triple first" from Cambridge. He was good at finding his way around, but it would have been easier to make someone stone deaf understand opera than to get into his head that in addition to containing facts, correspondence could reveal character. He was very toplofty with me, making it clear that he regarded my urging as historical charlatanism, and sticking to his principles by refusing to consult with me at the club where I was staying as he would have had to lower his ideals by wearing a necktie.

It is my habit to ask the research workers digging up material I cannot reach geographically to send me not their notes but photocopies of the documents they have unearthed. From those I make my own notes. I never photocopy material I myself can reach. That would be carrying home material undigested, not even chewed on. Passages that I would probably decide to quote verbatim I myself transcribe with pencil or typewriter. The task being laborious, I am encouraged as I go along to cut, laying bare the gist. Perhaps more important, by copying I key the material into my unconscious mind.

I do not slow down by transcribing with word-to-word accuracy, since I know that only a small part of what I copy will actually get into my text. One of the last steps in the completion of a manuscript is to compare all the quotations with their sources; my wife reads aloud from the original document while I follow along with what I have written down.

Being able to apply this method is only one of the shortcuts made available to me by my living not in the boondocks but in New York City. No other spot in the world could so facilitate my labors. Not even Washington, D.C., which does have the Library of Congress to match the New York Public Library, but almost none of the supporting facilities. I have almost never wanted any printed materials that are not available in New York City. Manuscript collections are always unique, but both the Public Library and the New-York Historical Society have great ones. The photograph collection of paintings at the Frick Art Reference Library has no rival anywhere else in the world.

Knowledge that I can easily and immediately re-examine what I want facilitates and speeds up research. One example: when going through a printed compendium of documents, I can postpone note-taking by indicating with light pencil in the margin what might prove, as I read on, trivial or better expressed in another passage. As I eventually erase the pencil marks I have sometimes wondered whether the library that owns the book would not rather have them left with an inscription in my hand stating that I had thus used the book— but I have never had the presumption to ask the question.

*

I always keep in mind that for me note-taking is not an end in itself but a preliminary step to writing. Involved is not only selecting but prescient labeling. On the top of every notation I add to the necessary bibliographical information whatever heading I prophesy will prove most helpful. If the drift of a document changes, I will start a new sheet under a different heading. As I have become more experienced, I have substituted for heavy filing cards paper from ordinary three-by-four blocks. This both reduces bulk and makes possible, if several headings seem to apply, making carbon copies to be separately filed.

I set up my files to follow, as far as I can foresee, the structure of my book. Notes on major actors are gathered together under chronological guide cards. When preparing to write, I extract all the sheets from the relevant chronological section and number the notations as they appear. Then I inscribe headings on a lined block, and write in the numbers I have given the relevant sheets, creating little indices. The sheets are now further sorted to be often intermingled with material from other files.

For each major actor there will be a second file classifying such matters as appearance, character, anecdotes, traits, relations with women. The sheets here arranged are usually carbon copies. These are consulted whenever wanted. Repetitions created in the main text will be later ironed out to leave only the insertion that is the most effective.

Secondary characters are filed alphabetically, those of enough importance with their own subheadings, the others put in haphazardly under the right letter to be dug out when needed. Background material has its own file, the headings chosen to indicate relevancy to the text. Whenever required, special markers will be inserted to indicate material discovered after the writing of early drafts, or material which was left out but should perhaps be eventually inserted.

*

Perhaps because of the example of my father, who presided over experiments that would go awry if there was the slightest error in the preparation, I have always been a stickler for factual accuracy. Without a Ph.D. or any academic positions, writing in a literary style that could be damned as "popularizing," I have been subject to much hostile scrutiny. Reviewers have, as is to be expected, disagreed with me on conclusions, but, despite their best efforts, they have been able to find only a thin scattering of factual errors, mostly misspellings.

*

Textual notes, whether printed at the bottom of pages, or with the backmatter either in special sections or interlarded with the source references, give freedom to speak in voices different from the main narrative. They can supply explanation that would otherwise impede the narrative flow; or inform the reader of information unknown by the narrative's characters; or express opinions either my own or of some character at the time or of a later historian. In some of my books the text notes were extensive. In some they did not appear at all.

In each of my volumes my fundamental approach of growing form from substance was applied in the backmatter. I did conventionally open with acknowledgments of help received from institutions and individuals. Then came a discussion of the most important sources which could be an essay covering several pages. Sometimes it would make sense to break the latter part of this discussion down under separate headings concerning the major characters and events involved. For some volumes, these special essays were interlarded with the source references. In all situations, identification was not strung out but kept to the intelligible minimum.

My attitude toward source references was very different from that of those scholars who wish to demonstrate assiduousness by piling up. The pressure on me was rather the other way, as was demonstrated by Harcourt, Brace's idiocy in trying to help *Traitor* become a best seller by publishing the source references in a separate pamphlet. However, my labors to be as concise as possible did not mean being skimpy. The combined source material for my four-volume *Washington* ran to some 120 pages. My responsibility, I believed, was no more and no less than to reveal the foundation on which my text was grounded. Let Ph.D. candidates and buckers for tenure do their own research!

*

It is a safe generalization to claim that the appreciation among scholars of my books increases with the stature of the reviewer in his own academic field and his public reputation. It is associate professors in jerkwater colleges who try to throw envenomed darts. Particularly moving and invaluable to me was the unfailing support of Jefferson's great biographer, Dumas Malone. And I cherish a letter to my publisher by the leader of American historians, Allan Nevins, concerning *George Washington in the American Revolution*:

"I would be happy to be quoted by you as saying that this volume maintains the remarkable combination of finished scholarship and impressive stylistic merit which Mr. Flexner exhibited in his first volume on Washington. And this book is even more striking in its qualities, for the story gains in volume and importance as Mr. Flexner pushes on to the very crisis of the Revolution; and his portrait of Washington as a personality, much the most convincing yet drawn by anybody, gains in every chapter in attractiveness and force. This is a book which no one interested in American history, whether student or layman, can afford to neglect; and it is one of the best additions yet made to the corpus of American biographical literature."

48

THE OUTSIDE WORLD

*

SINCE a maverick does not run with any herd, if he is not to be a hermit or at least a recluse, he has to seek companionship wherever he can find it. When I emerge from the solitude I require for my writing, I become very gregarious. To the dismay of my beautiful wife, who is so obviously attractive that she was taught by experience to be aloof, I have a habit of talking to strangers: from children to the elderly, on the streets, on buses, on airplanes, in fact almost anywhere that the opportunity comes naturally. I have trained my succession of poodles to be so friendly in my neighborhood that, as I walk along by myself, I am these days perpetually asked "Where is Sophie?" Readers of this volume have followed me into many different situations in the world around me.

Who's Who is, of course, an omnium gatherum of several thousand successful individuals from every walk of American life. I remember my great pleasure—it was during my troubles with Agnes—to be tapped, all the more because I was being gathered in with a broad spectrum of American life. I was again very pleased when, many years later, I was included in a two-page list, at the opening of one of the annual volumes, when some twenty people were especially honored—baseball players, singers, scientists, captains of industry, etc.

*

Although a maverick makes an incongruous president, or a powerful executive officer, the currents of life have more than once washed me up on such shores.

In 1954, I found myself president of the American Center of P.E.N., an international writers' club which had been founded, shortly after the end of World War I, by John Galsworthy and other leading English writers on the belief that "if the writers of the world could learn to stretch out their hands to each other, the nations of the world could learn in time to do the same." The American Center had come into being in 1922 with Booth Tarkington as its president. Centers also sprang up in many countries.

The American P.E.N. had down the years ups and downs, and was more or less somnolent when an energetic publisher, John Farrar, undertook the presidency and the task of rejuvenation. Regulations forced him to retire in 1955, and for some inexplicable reason I was elected in his place.

Since the international founders had believed that writers of achievement could most effectively shake hands across international boundaries, the American P.E.N., as I knew it (it has since become a mass organization), regarded itself as honorary. We had an admissions committee—candidates had to have published at least two books of merit—and a membership for the whole United States of about two hundred. But even these presented problems of keeping in touch. My contribution was on the gregarious side; I established weekly cocktail parties, all at the same place and time, without any reservations being necessary. These convivial occasions brought together at their convenience members from all over the wide New York area, and were an open door for members from other areas of the United States or visiting members from other national P.E.N.s.

A combination of being most concerned with the American past and my chronic fear of traveling kept me from grabbing a wonderful opportunity: attending, costs paid, the international P.E.N. conference, that year at Amsterdam, where I could have met leading writers from all over the world. In fact, my interest was fading. Since attending to organizational arrangements took too much time from writing, I resigned my presidency after one year.

Next came the Society of American Historians.

*

Led by Allan Nevins, Henry Siedel Canby, and Bruce Catton, a group of senior historian (I sometimes by chance listened in) were planning to found an informative historical magazine for the general public, and also a society that would bring together literary and academic historians. The outcomes were *American Heritage* and the Society of American Historians.

A contribution of mine appeared in the second issue of *American Heritage,* and down the years I was published there again and again. The magazine serialized extensive parts of my *Washingtons.*

I became, of course, a member of the Society of American Historians but I was not actively concerned until the bicentennial of the American Revolution loomed. Then I was invited by some of the leaders to lunch at the Columbia Faculty Club. They wished to reflect the occasion by making me, as Washington's biographer, president of the society. I was, of course, complimented. Since the secretary, a professor at Columbia, had a passion for running things, I lasted out my three-year term. But not without getting into some hot water.

The Society staged a dinner as its major annual event. I decided to use my position at the Century Club to give our membership an historical and artistic treat by opening to them the club house, a beautiful building designed, almost a century before, by McKim, Meade & White. The founders having included members of the Hudson River School and many subsequent members having been artists, the walls constituted a veritable museum of American art.

I had innocently stepped into a hornet's nest. As a son of Jews on one side and extreme feminists on the other, believing that it was the calling of historians to follow source material wherever it was to be found, it did not occur to me that *our* women members would resent being dragged to a club where they would normally not be admitted.

At the meeting one male supporter read aloud, entirely out of context, Abigail Adams's famous letter (which has made her modern reputation) to John urging the Founding Fathers to observe women's rights. I learned later that two of the Society's female members had loudly called two of the elderly Century members "Old Pussycats."

Of course, having been alerted, I should have consulted the board concerning the location of the next dinner, but I continued my course of opening to the Society landmark places. I secured admission to the University Club. It was supposed to be anti-Semitic, which did not bother me, but it certainly did not admit women members, which re-outraged the female historians. They even talked of a picket line.

Then a quiet voice spoke. Barbara Tuchman, the best known of female historians and a predecessor as president of the Society, said, "Don't be silly." The protest collapsed.

Having decided to let sleeping dogs lie, for my third and last dinner I chose the National Arts Club on Gramercy Park. It had on its walls an interesting collection of paintings, and had been founded precisely with the intention of being bisexual. Our female members were delighted, several appearing in tuxedos which were only separated off by wearing not tight but floppy bow ties.

Another of my indiscretions as president of the Society was inspired by a desire to help along the intention of the founders to encourage literary historical writing. I wished to urge the English departments in colleges and universities to raise their sights by including not only what was regarded as artistic writing—poems, essays, the novel, etc.—but also to promote good writing in such subjects as history, biography, even science. A voice much more powerful in academe than mine—that of Henry James's biographer Leon Edel—had put forward the same ideas but got nowhere. Obviously, I got nowhere. The trouble was that such a change would involve leaping over the fences between disciplines considered so essential to academic organization. And most of the senior professors were satisfied with the way they wrote.

At the end of my three-year term, I relinquished the presidency of the Society of American Historians without regret.

*

As time passed, I entered the zone of those eligible for election to the American Academy of Arts and Letters,* the most prestigious organization for writers, fine artists, and musical composers. It had been established in 1898 and was incorporated in 1904 by an act of Congress with a maximum membership of 250. Getting in was long and chancy since almost no one ever resigned, and the angel of death was very lenient with the academicians.

---

*The organization was then called The American Institute and Academy, there being an interior split left over from an old controversy. As a newcomer, I was elected to the Institute, but since then the distinction has been abolished.

I was first approached in 1962 by the then president, the operatic composer, Douglas Moore. He said he would arrange it, but after a considerable wait, he told me that neither the writers nor the artists would accept me as I was then considered a writer on art.

Time passed, and then my *Washington*s came sailing along the waves. Various friends of mine were now members of the academy. In 1976, I was elected.

I was to serve for three years as vice president for literature, and I was assigned the task (I had done the same thing for the Century Club) of writing a short account of the Academy for publication. The last such essay had been written by Jacques Barzun, the charismatic author and Columbia professor who had then been president of the Academy. Born in France, he wished us, like the Académie Française, to concentrate on keeping the language pure of innovations. But the freshening of words was basic to my style. I emphasized my own gregariousness by praising the Academy for bringing together artists of different persuasions.

*

Annually, the Academy awarded, by vote of the members, gold medals in two categories that appeared by slow rotations. In 1988 biography came up. A nominating committee was to present three names for a vote of the membership. Since I considered this the greatest honor available in America, I was all eagerness. Finally, the vote came in; I had won.

The Academy had an extremely large auditorium for its annual meetings at which, after other ceremonies, the two gold medals would be awarded. I would have to make a speech of acknowledgment. I was meditating on a short account of my travels down the years when one of my friends told me how an Englishman had laughed at Americans who on such occasions indulged themselves with long rigmaroles. I then remembered how as a lecturer I had captivated audiences by rising with only a small slip of paper in my hand. I decided that I would limit my speech to what would fit on the small piece of paper which I would display to the audience before I began to read:

"I am of course very grateful for the honor accorded me this afternoon by a vote of the writers, fine artists, and musical composers who comprise the Academy and Institute of Arts and Letters. It is a particular gratification to me that this medal, in conjunction with the medal periodically given to historians, testifies to the age-old conception that history and biography, far from being, as they are classified in many universities, aspects of social science, are essential components of the panoply of the literary arts."

Outreach

*

49

THE SPOKEN WORD

*

MY experience with radio broadcasting began when, as a twenty-three-year-old, I was scheduled to speak on noise abatement over New York City's radio station, WNYC. The studios were under the roof of the huge municipal building.

It was with a great deal of uneasiness that I set out with my much-worked-over speech grasped convulsively in my hand. The occasion was so important to me that I expected to be received when I arrived with much attention. But the one elevator that went so high disgorged me into a tremendous empty space, lugubriously lit, with a few dirty sofas against soiled walls and no human being in sight.

Empty, murky corridors went off in several directions. Dreading to be late, I feverishly sampled one corridor after another, banging on locked doors, forlornly rattling doorknobs. Finally, I sat down on one of the sofas, raising a cloud of dust. I was marooned in an atmosphere so depressing that even during subsequent years when I had become inured to radio, it never failed to lower my spirits. Now, terrified of disgracing myself on my first appearance before a huge audience, the more ominous because it would be unseen, I felt as if I had fallen into a morbid pit in my own psyche.

Finally, an oblong of light sprang onto the floor of one of the corridors. From the door that had been opened stepped a tall, willowy, immaculately dressed young man. Having approached me formally, he greeted me with all the ceremony I could have desired. I was led into a room furnished with a few rickety chairs and an oblong table bearing several microphones. My companion showed me how close I should put my mouth to the microphone, and asked me to say a few words so that sound could be adjusted. Then he spoke into his own microphone a few words of gracious introduction, and pointed to me.

My manuscript before me, I was reading smoothly, without any of the confusions or hesitations I had feared, when I felt a strange sensation on the top of my head. Something was happening to my hair. I felt that I should not interrupt my speech by turning from the microphone to investigate, but finally, as the sensation went on, I dared a quick backward glance. The announcer was running his hands through my curly red hair.

As I could not shout into the air waves, "Take your god-damned hands out of my hair!" all I could do, as I read doggedly on, was to shake my fist backward over my shoulder. This had no effect. The hand continued to move through my hair.

The instant I had got through my speech, I sprang up to face the announcer. He was talking into his microphone, gracefully closing the show. Having finished, he rose languorously, delivered in my direction a deep courtier's bow, and then dashed for the door, slamming it behind him. By the time I got the door open, the murky corridors had returned to their suicidal emptiness.

I have spoken on radio many hundreds of times, but never again with the drama of my debut.

*

Not an academic, I have never earned my living by lecturing to captive audiences. Making a public speech was so much of an adventure that I felt a need to rely on a written text. The demand came from museums, colleges, restorations, historical societies, patriotic organizations, etc. As each of the three volumes of my painting history was completed, I summarized it in a forty-minute speech. Since I delivered these talks over and over for decades, with only an occasional need to bring a few paragraphs up to date, they were, word for word, among the most financially rewarding of my writings.

I was able to borrow slides from the Metropolitan Museum. Then, as the interest in American art accelerated, the Carnegie Corporation decided to fill a gap at most institutions across the country by sponsoring a set of slides suitable for teaching. I was being consulted when the project was gobbled up by a dynamic, foundation-eating professor from the University of Georgia. I was invited to a meeting at which he would present his plans. He appeared late, in a great rush as he had to catch a plane for somewhere. He urged a new method for making color slides which he insisted were more accurate. A few impressive samples were shown. Then, before any doubts could be expressed, he bustled off, leaving behind him, to the irritation of those called upon to advise, a decision to proceed.

I laid in what slides I needed. The first time I tried to use them was at a club of the ancient aristocracy of Brooklyn. The occasion was proceeding with staid felicity when interrupted by animal screams from the hired projectionist. Having relied on a carousel to feed his machine, he had discovered that my new slides were too bulky to fit into the slots. I suppose, to stand up under careless treatment in jerkwater institutions, they had been bound not with the usual black tape but with some celluloid-like substance. Fortunately, the director of the Brooklyn Museum was present and could get into his institution at night. After a long stage wait, he reappeared with a larger carousel.

A slide finally being shot on the screen, I was gratified to see that the color was excellent. But as the old song goes:

> Oh, wayly, wayly,
> But love is bonnie
> A little while when it is new.

It was my habit, as I used no pointer and did not want to lose direct contact with the audience, when a new slide appeared behind me to merely glance over my shoulder to make sure it was the right one. I was thus surprised when, after several months, a member of an audience asked me whether all American painting was really brown. Sure enough, the fancy new method that had been sold to the Carnegie Corporation had addled. I, knowing my way around, was able to get replacements without cost, but I guess that in the boondocks a generation grew up believing that all American painters worked in sepia.

I have often wondered whether slides are really inanimate objects. They seem born with a monkey-like disposition to play tricks, in cooperation with projectionists who seem to have been recruited from institutions for the insane. Not only do slides appear on the screen only to dash instantaneously off again; not only do they sail in reverse or upside down; but often—and this is the killer—they have managed to rearrange themselves into the wrong order. Then under grand auspices, like the Grace Rainey Rogers Hall at the Metropolitan Museum, you can pick up a telephone and remonstrate with the projectionist who is far off and high up in a box. Usually, you shout at the man who is within hearing distance. This may straighten the situation out or incite the projectionist to hysteria: slides would appear on the screen as in a rain storm, the one you want passing by in a jiffy. Often the only remedy is to walk back to the machine and sort things out yourself.

Slides were not alone as my inanimate enemies. There is electricity. Projectors adore smoking menacingly, and particularly blowing out fuses. Not only in small institutions: the motto seems to be, "the bigger they are the harder they fall." My best-remembered incident took place at that major Texan institution, the Amon Carter Museum of Western Art. I had set up for them in celebration of the bicentennial of the Declaration of Independence an exhibition of portraits of the Founders. My own stipend was exuberant; I was given money to hire an expert assistant, Linda Sampter Bantel, now director of the Pennsylvania Academy. We were instructed to pay no attention to insurance costs, which enabled us to attract out of Boston, for the first time, Stuart's Athenaeum Portraits of George and Martha Washington. Deciding to use likenesses of Founders whether shown as small children or octogenarians, we were able to get together the works of three generations of American painters. We were to produce a book, *The Face of Liberty,* with many color illustrations, for which I did an extensive introduction, the whole published under my name.

My speech at Fort Worth had been planned for the exhibition's opening crowning occasion. The extensive main gallery of the museum having been cleared of exhibits, and a huge projector brought in on a trolley, the tremendous front wall became the slide screen. No need to strain your vision! Each painting was blown up to about ten times its natural size. I confess that I felt uneasy, as if I were standing under Mount Rushmore, as these vast effigies towered over me. A gargantuan Copley was staring down over my shoulder when, without warning, the whole museum was plunged into darkness.

An announcement reassured that everything would be fixed in a moment; there was much scurrying around in the blackness. It was only after about half an hour that someone remembered the existence of baseplugs, relics from an earlier time. They offered what feeble electricity they could. An ancient slide machine was exhumed, and I continued my lecture where I had stopped, the Copley having shrunk until it seemed on the huge wall no bigger than a postage stamp.

My own reaction, I will confess, was amusement at seeing Texas fall on its face. Except when slides get so seriously mixed up that there has to be a fifteen-minute scramble, I rather welcome contretemps: I quickly learned that if the speaker, instead of having fits, displays smiling good nature, he gets the audience staunchly behind him.

*

I never went far enough into the business of lecturing to hire an agent. However remunerative it might be, dashing around the countryside for a considerable time on a prearranged schedule did not suit my temperament or my primary concern with writing. Requests came directly to me. If they came from institutions where I had friends, the result could be conviviality. But at organizations organized to serve the snobbery of families who were older than their neighbors, it could prove very annoying that I was expected to be present for cocktails and dinner before my speech. Dinner was the worst, as I would be trapped at the high table facing the audience between two women who, priding themselves on being hostesses, would insist on trying to draw me out without any idea of what strings to pull on. My efforts to interest them were equally vain, and always, however experienced I became, I was a little nervous and anxious to get the speech over with.

At the pre-lecture cocktail parties, I was surrounded by strangers with whom I had nothing in common, and I had as the speaker to stay reasonably sober. I would try to tame drinks with canapes. On one occasion, as the cocktail session dragged along like a wounded snake, I despaired because there were no canapes. Finally, I was relieved to see appear beside me a black tray bearing candied fruits. I was just reaching down with outstretched fingers when I realized that what I saw was actually a flowered dress drawn tight over the rear of a fat woman who had dropped something and was leaning over to pick it up. If I had pinched that voluminous bottom!

*

When, in the mid-1960s, the subject of my lectures changed predominantly from varieties of American painting to George Washington, I felt it safe to launch on a different method of public speaking. As I associated with Washington year after year, he so occupied my conscious and unconscious mind that I felt no more need of written texts: I would speak extemporaneously.

This new departure, on which I embarked in my early fifties, brought a shower of advantages. It is amazing how much it impresses audiences when a speaker, with no more than one small sheet of paper before him, can proceed fluently for forty minutes without becoming tongue-tied or making a fool of himself. Secondly, having no need to look downward at a text, I could hold eye contact with the audience. Because what I said rose spontaneously into my mind, the talk communicated spontaneously. And, I was not trapped by a written lecture to any length or direction. Both could be modified, as I proceeded, to suit the particular audience I found before me.

The problem was to get started. I made it a practice to concoct in advance some gracious reference to the institution and the occasion. I discovered that, however banal the practice, it did relax the audience to start with a joke. I built up a considerable repertory of jokes. To prepare for the body of the speech, I harked back to my old newspaper use of a "lead" that determined direction and got the momentum flowing. Sometimes, I would jot an opening paragraph or two on the piece of paper I would take with me. Having thus gotten in motion, I could count on being able to continue since each idea summoned up a continuation.

Another advantage of talking ad lib is that it does not require, any more than a conversation does, a consistent structure. All that is needed is to proceed in a manner your audience finds interesting and conclude on some high note. I make it a practice to listen to sounds from the audience: if there is a creaking that indicates fidgeting in chairs, I quickly change my ground, or, if the speech has gone on long enough to make this feasible, come rapidly to a close.

So used have I become to this technique that I was driven almost crazy when I was speaking at the National Gallery in Washington. By intention or inadvertence, the door at the far end of the hall had been left open. Sightseers were continually coming in and, when they saw not another exhibit but a man shooting off his mouth, going out again. Although I fully understood what was happening, I could not prevent the swishing from setting off in my sensibility a succession of alarm bells.

My continual hazard was timing. I believe that the most self-destructive thing a speaker can do is talk too long, and regard the common tendency in that direction as proof of the supreme power of egotism. Usually where I spoke, there was a clock on the wall, and I did wear a wrist watch. I would try to memorize the time when I began, but my free-association method would drive out the memory. I would get worried and stop so quickly that the sponsors felt short-changed, or I would get excited and run on. The solution finally came to me. I bought a stop watch. I found it an excellent maneuver to display, as I was starting, the stop watch. Breathes there a man with mind so dead that he does not fear being trapped for life by a speaker? A stop watch in the speaker's hand is a preventive for the creaking I dread to hear.

*

As time went on, experience taught me that I could successfully address audiences without preparation on almost any subject not altogether alien to me. This was a great emancipation, and very valuable to those aspects of my career not directly allied to my books. I sometimes found myself called in purely because of faith in my ability as a public speaker, as when I awarded prizes for the National Book Award, and also for that Catholic organization the Christophers.

*

I was in my forties before there emerged a new medium that was to become a major force in American life and also in my career. I shall never forget my own first adventure with television when network telecasting was still in its infancy.

Called to the studio, not shortly before broadcast time as on radio but several hours in advance, I entered a wildly different atmosphere.

Everyone was excited and jittery, as if they had a half-tamed monster on their hands. I was used at most to someone's determining briefly what kind of questions I would like to be asked. Now the interviewer put me through what was almost a rehearsal of our some twenty minutes on the air. Although I had a touch of laryngitis, she was pleased with the result and made me feel quite a fine fellow.

The studio we entered took me aback. It was many times the size of a radio studio, but crowded with paraphernalia and people stepping over wires. There was a massive camera on a trolley and many lights on poles. I was sat down in a chair. The chair was moved several times. Someone fiddled with my necktie, smoothed out my coattails, and pulled my trouser legs down over my socks. I was told where to look and almost stunned by bright lights shining into my face. I had become very nervous. The clock moved, a signal indicated that we were on the air, and the interviewer asked me the first question. I found that my laryngitis had closed in. I croaked.

There was visible consternation, and then what seemed the head of a large snake rose from the floor close to my left shoulder. Looking again, I saw it was a human hand offering a lozenge. (The rescuer had crawled in under the focus of the camera.) The lozenge did the trick, probably because it took my mind off my nervousness. My voice came out clear as crystal.

*

Other opportunities to appear on television came along while the medium was still so new that I had rarely seen a television show—I had no set of my own. That my appearance was being reproduced through the atmosphere filled me, as I was being interviewed, with a vast curiosity to ascertain what I was being made to look like. Fortunately, or unfortunately, there was a way I could find out. A "monitor" was so placed that the interviewer could see what was being achieved. If I turned my head in that direction, I too could see, but this involved my rudely looking away from the individual with whom I was supposed to be chatting. I still feel, as I recollect, the strain on my neck as opposing nervous impulses tussled with each other for the position of my head.

Several times, after I had emerged on the streets from a television interview, I was embarrassed with amorous approaches. In the early days of television, no one was allowed to appear until his face had been powdered and colored to suit the prejudices of the lens. I kept forgetting to wash my face.

*

I have never, as the years rolled, come to regard appearances on television as an aspect of routine like talking over the radio. Since I could be seen as well as heard, I have always felt that, while I was being interviewed, I was engaged in a dramatic performance. The cross-talk acts between two comics so effectively achieved at the burlesque theater into which I had sneaked during my boyhood, came into my memory. Of course, my interviewer and I were not intentionally comical, although we cracked an occasional joke. Furthermore, our tempo had to be slower as our act occupied not only a few minutes but usually fifteen, occasionally a half hour, and several times a whole hour. But I felt that we had at whatever length to establish tempo and continuous contact.

The interviewer, so much more experienced, should of course set the situations with his questions or comments, but I felt I could wander afield while keeping my eyes on his face to diagnose when I should change my tack or shut up for the next question. Again, burlesque had taught me a valuable lesson: I was commonly thanked and complimented when we went off the air, and was told more than once by a veteran interviewer that I was one of the best subjects he had ever encountered.

50

OMNIBUS

*

OMNIBUS was an effort by the Ford Foundation to raise the standards of network television. The foundation put up part of the funding (assisted by a commercial sponsor) for a two-hour presentation, comprising several segments, aired over the CBS network on Sunday afternoons. The show was supposed to be a bellwether which, by competing successfully with commercial programs, would show the feasibility of high standards and would also develop techniques. All this agreed with my own conviction (or rather hope) that intelligent programming, if effectively presented, would attract wide audiences.

Omnibus dreamed up a new, presumably more accurate, format for historical drama. The dialogue, instead of being written for the characters, would be quoted in their own words from their writings. This would require a narrator to assist continuity, and Omnibus had, as its regular master of ceremonies, Alistair Cooke.

Their first theme, the relationship between Napoleon and Josephine, worked beautifully, since an exchange of love letters is in effect a dialogue. For their next attempt, they became more ambitious: they would deal with one of America's greatest historical dramas, Benedict Arnold's treason. I had just published *The Traitor and the Spy* and presumably had what they needed at my finger tips. I was called in and asked if I would be willing to prepare the script. I expressed enthusiasm. But then they had sober second thoughts. Had I ever written a play, and what did I know about television? I answered that I had never written a play and that I did not possess a television set. "But," I continued, "only a virgin can lead a unicorn." This so bemused them that they signed a contract.

When, however, they saw what I had written, they hired a professional scriptwriter. I was invited to be present when he presented his text by reading it out loud. Some twenty staff members were seated facing the producer, who was facing them grandly from behind a large desk. The writer stood in the empty space between them, and read the required twenty minutes' worth with vivacity and much intonation. He had planned for bells to ring periodically, followed by a statement of how much time before the treason. Not even a shred of my script was included.

After the author had finished, he laid the manuscript with a histrionic gesture on the producer's desk. The producer led applause and then a tall man arose in the middle of the room and insisted that my script was more promising. Andrew McCullough was listened to because (as I subsequently discovered) he was to be the director. When he pointed out that I knew the material so much better, the producer ruled that the scriptwriter should confer with me.

The writer told me that he had not been shown my script. Now that he had seen it, he thought basically it was better than his, although utterly naïve concerning television production. He would lay aside his draft and develop mine to fit the medium.

It was I who delivered our combined effort to the producer. He gave it a quick glance and then angrily accused me of trying to mislead him. He had expected to receive the professional's script with some historical additions, and here was my lousy script back again prettied up some! He could not believe that the professional had agreed to this. Interrupted, he gave me an appointment for the next morning.

The next morning, I found McCullough, his secretary, and some assistants waiting for me in the hallway outside the office door. He had not had breakfast and suggested that we should go to a nearby restaurant where we could sit around a large table. I had not the slightest idea that this was not the appointment I was supposed to attend, that I had been kidnapped.

We spent the whole morning at the restaurant and had lunch there, while McCullough and his cohorts went over the script. Only when we got back to the office, and I found the producer in a rage did I realize what had been going on.

The next event did not, in the general novelty of everything, enter my mind as a warning. The office more or less emptied out, as everyone went to a conference on my script—but I was excluded. Anyway, the result was from my point of view happy: McCullough carried the day.

I continued to be excluded from office conferences where major decisions about the script were made, but I was allowed to take part in carrying them out. Entitled "Treason, 1780," the show was presented with my name as author, although I could not conceivably have done it by myself.

*

Since the necessary recording devices had not yet been invented, nothing could be taped in advance. Scenery, lighting, acting, sound, and dialogue would be broadcast to hundreds of thousands exactly as they had appeared at the moment of shooting on one of the cameras. This required, when the show was actually on the air, a perfectly regimented (so we hoped) madhouse. Three-dimensional stage sets, each including its own retinue of lights, were spaced along the walls of a room as large as a gymnasium. The empty central area was haunted by three cameras that could travel on wheels and swing around on dollies. Elaborate diagrams had been drawn to enable everyone and all equipment to be at the right position at every split second.

For the actors, this involved much zigzagging across the open space. The actor playing Benedict Arnold had to be perpetually on the run as he was so often on camera. At one dramatic moment, the stage manager tried to send Arnold in the wrong direction. There was a short wrestle before Arnold could continue his intrepid charge.

During the showing, I had a seat in the projection room. Here was the only slight possibility of editing. Facing the director were three screens. He could instantaneously shift from one camera to another.

All in all, we got away with it very well: no serious blunders. Then, for the first time, I experienced the tremendous falldown inherent in airing television dramas—all the more poignant during those early years when whatever had gone on the air, to however large an audience, could never be amended, was absolutely final. After a lecture, if given to only fifteen people, there would be applause. After we had entered thousands on thousands of homes, there was no reaction from the world outside as we gathered in someone's apartment to drink and hash over what had happened. No sending out for reviews as after the first night of a play. Before advance showings were possible, television reviews were few, belated, and usually from the boondocks.

*

Although the producer from whose claws I had been kidnapped remained somewhat hostile, I remained a protégé of my director, McCullough.* And I became good friends (as I still am) with Mary Ahearn, who was the alter ego of the top producer, Robert Saudeck. My speaking style was too wooden, when I did not have my own prose to read, for me to be allowed on the air, but I worked spasmodically with Omnibus during several years, called on for this project or that.

Years before Boston Television produced their disaster on the same subject, Omnibus presented a series on the Adams family—separate episodes, concerning John, John Quincy, Charles Francis, and Henry. Our technique of authentic quotations was to be used, and the great historian Allan Nevins was to be adviser and also narrator. I was appointed to represent Omnibus in working with Nevins. Me to match Nevins! I could only view him with great admiration—and a certain amount of amusement. Nevins always operated on a hair trigger. He could not walk but had to run. If a group went upstairs with him, he would dash up each flight and then wait on the landing. When we needed some arcane quotation, he would grab a pencil and a piece of paper, disappear into the stacks of the Columbia Library at a trot, and reappear, it seemed almost before he had started, with

---

*McCullough persuaded me that he and I should collaborate on expanding "Treason, 1780" into a Broadway play, using the technique of authentic quotations. We worked together for some time, but not with enough intensity to make me take my mind off my biography of Sir William Johnson. The drama finished, McCullough interested a leading Broadway agent. I received a telegram jubilating that the play was as good as sold, but, although the agent is still friendly with me when we meet on a bus, that was the end.

what we needed. The amusement in relation to his Omnibus role was supplied by the fact that molasses on a cold day moved no more slowly than the television rehearsals.

Nevins was supposed to wait, in his chair behind a desk, for the moments when he was to interpolate his lines, but the moments seemed never to come. Because the shows were to be aired live, every instant of air time had to be worked out in advance. This involved seemingly endless conferences between the director, the cameramen, the lighting experts, the prop men, and the scene designers. Nevins was being forced to waste time! During the first rehearsal, he could hardly control himself. For the next he appeared with such a pile of books—he could extract the gist from one book in a jiffy—that when the cameras finally sought him, he was invisible behind the volumes. For the third rehearsal, he failed to appear at all. Finally, a system for warning him of delays was worked out, which gave me the delightful task of walking with him on the nearby streets, trying to keep him interested—I was twice as interested—with historical and biographical discussions. As a result, for the rest of his life he was my good friend and staunch supporter.

*

On the Monday before each Sunday show, the cast was brought together for the first rehearsal. The various actors read their parts. They were all fluent except for James Daly, who was cast as Henry Adams. He stumbled with the lines and seemed almost unable to read, making me wonder how such a clod had been given so sensitive a part. However, as the rehearsal went on, I realized that the others had been applying histrionic habitude, which Daly was trying deeply to understand. I was watching a great performance in the making.

On Sunday morning, when we went through the show as if it were on the air, he was magnificent. But when the show really went on the air, he seemed, to my horror, to have been extinguished. I found out later that his moustache had been glued on badly and was in danger of falling off. There was no remedy since he was almost perpetually on camera, and the continuing possibility broke his concentration. What should have been a triumph was turned into a disaster. The few of us at the dress rehearsal had seen an achievement that was forever lost to the world. Such was the irrevocability of live television!

*

My darkest adventure at Omnibus resulted from an effort to do a good turn for the Whitney Museum. Having abandoned the three linked houses on Eighth Street where I had spent so many happy hours, the museum was moving into a new building behind and connected with the Museum of Modern Art. I urged successfully that recognition of the occasion opened an opportunity for a discussion on contemporary American painting. I selected from the Whitney's permanent collection some dozen paintings that added up to a chronological sequence. Too conscientious to work from photographs, Omnibus borrowed the originals which they set up in a basement so that a camera could move from one to another. I prepared an accompanying text to be read by our master of ceremonies, Alistair Cooke.

All went as merrily as a marriage bell until, on the very evening before the telecast, our producer found himself sitting at a dinner next to Sir Kenneth Clark, then the director of the Tate Gallery, which could be considered an English equivalent of the Whitney. To Saudeck, this seemed providential. He invited Sir Kenneth to comment, as they appeared in sequence on the air, on the Whitney pictures. I was not notified.

My amazement, as I was watching the airing, at seeing Cooke step aside for Sir Kenneth turned to horror as Clark, with all the condescension the British enjoyed concerning American culture, sneered at picture after picture and ended up by saying that the only art America had ever produced was *The New Yorker* cover.

The Whitney and the insulted artists were, of course, furious. I tried to make amends by persuading Omnibus to offer air time to the museum and/or the artists for a rebuttal. But the Whitney refused to sully itself by engaging in television controversy. They focused their wrath on me. They could not prevent me from entering their museum as a member of the public, but they ostracized me in every way they could.

*

My close relationship to Omnibus—I was officially connected with seven shows and of two specified as the author—lasted for a little more than a year, and never took precedence in my mind over my labors on *Mohawk Baronet*. However, the studio was within easy walking distance of Beatrice's and my apartment, and even when I had no specific assignment, I would wander over. Allowed complete access, I achieved a broad view of the production procedures of what has become in television history the pioneer of high-grade network television. This gave me the comprehension and humility which was to serve me so well when, in my seventies, I was exploded into two major productions—twelve hours of prime time on the CBS network based on my *Washingtons*.

51

THE VERY BIGGEST TIME

*

GEORGE Washington had not been considered an available character for dramatic presentation. Neither the theater nor television had made any serious effort. Then my biography replaced the marble image with a warm and appealing human being. This was not lost on those who wandered through the wildernesses of television. Several projects were inaugurated that died aborning—one major effort was canceled on the very day when the contract was to be signed—and then, when I was in my early seventies, a Hollywood producer, David Gerber, got in touch with my lawyer.

It was by no means Gerber's intention to employ me as a consultant or in any other capacity. The contract with which I was presented built a legal palisade against interference by the author of the biography, even banning my making any public comments concerning the show or the contract I was to sign. I did look cross-eyed at this provision, but Harriet Pilpel, my lawyer, assured me it was routine.

After several months I found in my mail two cardboard binders containing typed script. A covering letter from Gerber informed the recipient that these were the first two hours of an eight-hour miniseries, carrying Washington through the Revolution, which was being prepared for CBS. There was nothing to indicate any connection with my biography. Gerber asked for suggestions but made no mention of payment.

At a cocktail party, I discovered that Professor Richard Morris of Columbia had received the same communication. He informed me that he had no intention of giving Gerber free advice. If other historians were also consulted, their reactions seem to have been the same. But, whether or not my role was acknowledged, I felt intimately involved, all the more because the script was firmly grounded on my biography, presenting Washington as I visualized him! The dramatization was surprisingly authentic; I believed I could help. I prepared a good many pages of typescript, mingling my suggestions with the praise I truly felt, and sent them off to the scriptwriter whose name was given as Richard Fielder.

Fielder's conclusion that my attitude was cooperative and my suggestions useful tore down a crucial section of the fence built to keep me out. Down the years of the project, Fielder and I were to work amicably together. I became tremendously impressed by his ability to simplify a complicated situation, which it might have taken me pages to elucidate, into a burst of dramatic action. We communicated by telephone or letter, and then he was sent to New York where we spent several days going over the script line by line. We ended up with as few disagreements as was under the circumstances possible.

*

A newspaper account was to state that Gerber had carried my four volumes to CBS, dumped them on an executive's desk, and shouted, "We must dramatize this!" Be that as it may, a usual procedure was followed. CBS agreed to pay for a year's preparation, peanuts for them since the only costs were Gerber's overhead, Fielder's salary, and a small option payment for me. At the end of the year, Fielder's unfinished script was submitted to CBS, who agreed to finance another year. I think at the end of the second year (although it may have been the third) the script was considered finished and the moment that determined failure or success came: CBS would decide whether to drop the extensive project—eight hours of air time—or put their resources behind it. Fielder warned me that a high proportion of the projects were rejected. I was nervous until a phone call told me that this hurdle had been successfully jumped. But there was another major hurdle: CBS needed to find commercial sponsors to cover a very large expense.

I was quietly reading at home when my telephone rang. The man on the other end identified himself as a vice president of CBS. It was urgent that he pick me up early the next morning and drive me to their studio. On the way, he explained that they hoped to sell the whole eight hours to a single sponsor, General Motors, which would have many advantages over piecemeal sponsorship. The automobile industry, my companion admitted, was not doing very well, but CBS would get GM to sign some kind of a guarantee for the many millions that would be involved. He also kept saying that my books, which the contract had scorned, were now the key to the project. This I neither understood nor believed. However, my errand was to tape an endorsement of the show to use in hooking General Motors.

At the CBS building, where I had occasionally gone for some talk show, my reception was as different as if I had suddenly become King of Siam. I was taken into a set made up as a living room and was seated in an opulent chair. There were not one but two cameras. The intention was that I should endorse the script. I said that the script was historically accurate and would be a contribution to American self-understanding, although there were a few weaknesses which I specified, adding that they could easily be remedied. I was made to go through it several times, and then I was allowed into a control room where a full hour was spent in piecing together the best version.

Eventually, I secured an explanation. The branch of GM with which CBS was dealing was concerned not specifically with selling cars but rather with enhancing the company's public image. The budget of the central corporation for that purpose would not cover the cost contemplated: production for eight air hours at two million dollars (when a million dollars was *real* money) an hour, and then purchasing the most expensive prime time for a total of eight hours on three successive evenings. It was necessary to secure support from similar funds at the subsidiary companies, Cadillac, Buick, Chevrolet, etc. To help achieve this was the purpose of the interview that had been recorded.

I was still puzzled as to why my endorsement was so required when I was invited to have dinner with some GM executives in the Oak Room at the Plaza Hotel. I then met the two men with whom I was to work closely, John McNulty and his top assistant, George H. Pruett, Jr. Also a grizzled vice president in charge of engineering who, I gathered, was there because he was a great power on the General Motors board.

It became clear as we talked that they were nervous at linking GM's corporate image with presenting to millions of Americans an image of George Washington. Enthusiastically accepted, their contribution would achieve the positive effect they sought, but supposing they were open to accusations of besmirching the Father of Our Country? The purpose being to humanize Washington, they did not argue for the marble image. Nor did they make the slightest suggestion of censorship. Their strategy was to find protection by standing behind me and the reputation of my biography. They wanted nothing to go on the air that I would not endorse. If I felt it necessary to bring an objection to them, they would back me to the hilt.

This approach was put on the record when Roger B. Smith, chairman of GM, thus publicly announced the project: "Historian James Thomas Flexner won a Special Pulitzer Prize and a National Book Award for his biography of George Washington. Next year, we plan to present Mr. Flexner's biography as a prime-time mini-series drama. It is a beautifully and precisely written work. . . . People *want* something for the time they give to television. We think they will want to see Mr. Flexner's biography of Washington." No mention of Gerber or Fielder or CBS.

*

As my education continued, I learned that, according to practice and perhaps law, a sponsor might not interfere directly with the content of a television production. GM would speak to their advertising agency, N. W. Ayer, which would speak to CBS, which would either suppress the objection or pass it on to Gerber, who might or might not agree. But all this would take time, and time wasted during a multi-million-dollar project cast a long shadow. It was, therefore, a very valuable asset that, being an individual with no official status, I could fly free across all taboos and, as I thought best, talk directly to anybody. This role gave me power.

I had seen enough of the world not even to hint at the promised complete backing by GM, but Chairman Smith's announcement had spoken in a loud voice. The cat was further let out of the bag when GM requested that Gerber rescind the gag provisions in my contract. Gerber even agreed to my speaking at will to the press, adding (I suppose to save face) only that I should notify him, when possible, in advance. I decided that it was never possible. Harriet Pilpel worried about conflict of interest when I accepted consultation fees from both Gerber and GM, but I am sure that both suspected the situation, agreeing that fair representation of my volumes was now an objective agreed to by all.

The issue that raised the most anxiety concerned Sally Fairfax. The young Washington had fallen in love with the wife of his best friend and neighbor, and for a period of years conducted a somewhat desperate flirtation reaching to historically undefinable limits, although George's friendship with Sally's husband was never broken. There is strong evidence that George had proposed to Martha Custis to escape from this dark love. Convinced that the happiness which had resulted from his thus abandoning passion for judgment had been a major steadying influence on Washington's career, I had given the affair considerable space in my book. This attention was increased further in Fielder's script somewhat to the dismay of GM, but, since truth and good taste had been adhered to, I successfully defended biographically this important episode which worked to heighten the popular appeal for our show.

The prominence of the somewhat lengthy scenes was greatly increased by Gerber's casting as Sally one of television's most celebrated beauties, Jaclyn Smith. A published rumor stated that this was my doing, and if consulted, as a susceptible septuagenarian I could only have cheered. Jacky and I became good friends, partly because we both kept poodles. An amusing possibility was created when Jacky, as I was on my way to return to New York, gave me a healthy kiss. Cameras being omnipresent on television sets, this was caught by three different ones, each from a different angle. Selective cutting and sequencing could make the kiss seem to occupy several minutes. I leave the prints to the discretion of my biographer if I ever have one.

*

The show was to be shot on location. I received a summons from Gerber, whom I had not then met, to join a several days' expedition through Virginia exploring for filming sites. He had been paying me only by the hour for consultation with Fielder, and he offered me for this trip a measly stipend. Encouraged by my anxiety neurosis about leaving home, I declined. I received an impassioned phone call from

Fielder saying that Gerber's feelings were very hurt. I was puzzled. Why should Gerber's feelings be involved? Only later did I work out that, when he had abandoned his principle of banishing authors, he had expected me to come catapulting in. Instead, he was made to plead and pay adequately.

This was not the last time that my chronic anxiety about traveling strengthened my role in the production. I categorically refused to fly to California and made difficulties about flying to Detroit, thereby, without any intention of increasing my prestige, forcing anyone from Gerber's outfit or GM who wanted to consult me to come to New York. And I was encouraged during the four months of filming not to hang around the sets often enough or long enough to have my presence become a routine of the production.

It had, however, been a good beginning when I allowed myself to be persuaded to go along on Gerber's trip. My friends in the television world had told me that Gerber was a man of culture and sensibility who put on the role of a tough, blatant Hollywood producer. He was large, noisy, and highly ebullient, surrounding himself with a wall of talk which you had somehow to get through in order to establish any communication with him. Then he was understanding and I would almost say sweet. I quickly concluded that he was just as concerned as the GM people with an authentic presentation of Washington, and that he also believed that this could best be achieved through sticking to my interpretation.

His reason for wanting me along on this trip soon became clear: needing permission to film at Mount Vernon and Colonial Williamsburg, he felt they would be reassured by my presence. Since I had had long relationships with both, this proved to be the case. For my part, I enjoyed, as an augury for more theatrical excitements to come, traveling in Virginia with the set designer seeking eighteenth-century interiors and streets. I was fascinated to learn that he could change telegraph poles into trees, shooting at such an angle that the connecting wires were not visible, and that he was not discouraged if one or two modern buildings marred an eighteenth-century row. He would hide the eyesores behind painted façades.

*

After Barry Bostwick had been cast as Washington, I was called to Alexandria, Virginia, to inform him. Much fuss was made about our having lunch by ourselves at a secluded table. But Barry had not had time to read my book and I could not make out much about him. Finally, he asked me, "What were Washington's five most important characteristics?" I was completely stumped: it was much too complicated. Later, after he had been playing the part for a while, he told me that everyone kept asking him, "What were Washington's most important characteristics?" He said he told them, "Washington was very tall." Barry was very tall.

Although not as resoundingly as Jacky, Barry greatly attracted the opposite sex. It was a somewhat embarrassing occasion when we visited together the huge General Motors office building in Detroit. Female employees poured out from every hallway to get his autograph. Not wishing me to feel upstaged, he directed them to get my autograph too. They had no idea who I was, but obeyed. I quickly discovered why celebrities develop monograms, since writing out "James Thomas Flexner" on the shoals of paper offered me was impossible.

Barry proved to be a great asset to the show, which he to some extent carried on his shoulders. To feel Washington in his own body, he had, in addition to what he learned from me, done a little research on his own, and had consulted Washington himself through a psychic medium. He came to feel so strong an identity that I was faced with a problem when we appeared together at interviews, live or on television. Knowing many times as much about Washington, I found it difficult to hold back when he gave what I thought were wrong answers and I had a real problem when I felt that in his performance before the cameras he had gone off base. I used all the tact I possessed, and we remained, for the duration of our common effort, good friends.

*

I was consulted on many aspects of production. One discussion was over how the actors should speak. Was John Adams to use a pinched New England accent, Washington and Jefferson a "you-all" southern intonation, and so forth? I argued that no one knew for sure how eighteenth-century voices sounded, and we could easily get bogged down in a cacophony of actors' interpretations. Let the Americans use the generalized accent usual on our current stage, and the English actors follow current parlance of their national speech. This would have the advantage of emphasizing the separation between the adversaries. This plan was agreed to and elicited no criticism.

*

When the actual shooting began, I was hesitant about invading the locations, until I was informed that my presence would be welcomed. I was amazed on being first transported from an airport to find that my destination was a mobile village standing in an empty Virginia countryside. Trucks and trucks and trucks. The cavernous interiors of two vans, I was to discover, were filled, almost to stiflement, with racks holding thousands of costumes. There were buses for transporting hundreds of people around the set; two mobile kitchens with serving counters running along their sides; a marquee stretched over an extensive dining area; elongated campers as temporary housing for leading actors, directors, cameramen, etc.

A courier automobile carried me to the shooting area: an extensive field smiling under summer sunshine. At the far end, behind a specially designed garden, I saw an almost unbelievable structure. Standing there was the one-and-a-half-storey farmhouse which had been the original Mount Vernon that had been two centuries before incorporated into the larger mansion house. When I exclaimed over this apparition, I was told I had seen only the beginning. I was reminded that in preparation for marrying Martha, George had raised the building to two-and-a-half stories. The extra storey was off to one side, waiting to be inserted after a crane had lifted the roof. Then the whole would be taken apart. It seemed to me sad that this mock-up, even if it was only partly three-dimensional, could not be given to Mount Vernon as an additional display, but I kept my mouth shut as this was not in my province.

*

Never had I been treated with such warmth, consideration, and admiration. On the various locations I visited during the four months of shooting, the actors were encouraged by the director, Buzz Kulick, to discuss with me the characters they were portraying. When one was called to the camera, another often sat down beside me. They had all read *The Indispensable Man,* so we had a basis for discussion. Often they had questions. Patty Duke, who was to play Martha, wondered what her fundamental attitude to George was. My assurance that she cared deeply for him, was a great strength to him, and greatly missed him when he was away led to a moving performance since Patty is a great actress. Jacky Smith wanted to know whether Sally had ever gone to bed with Washington, and managed to convey sensitively my belief that they had tottered on the edge year after year, obsession tempered by an uneasy sense of guilt, a relationship that would not have been greatly changed if they had sometimes slipped over the brink.

Authors and learned advisers typically have no understanding or respect for the television medium and nothing but disdain for its practitioners whom they ignorantly try to order around. The television professionals respond in kind. For the Washington show, to have only one individual to deal with, and for that individual already to have had enough television experience to understand and respect their skills and achievements, was such a boon that they almost fell over themselves to admire and cherish me.

The most comprehensive account of activity during the production was written by Edward Park, a contributing editor, for the *Smithsonian Magazine.* Although I was not around during his visit, he wrote that the set was haunted by "the miraculous Mr. Flexner." When he has asked for the justification of any episode, he was assured, "That's the way Mr. Flexner sees it." He quoted Fielder as saying, "During the shooting, everybody got sort of infected by Mr. Flexner." Gerber: "You know the author is sort of an uncomfortable addition to the set. But not this one. We kept asking him questions. After all, this was Washington." Park decided he had to come to New York and have a look at me. "Mr. Flexner," he reported, "at seventy-six is small and straight standing, with a wonderfully elfin look masked by mutton chop whiskers."

*

In a symposium on biography at the Library of Congress, I had my say (which was widely reprinted):

"Basic to my agreement with Dick Fielder and many others was a shared sense of dedication to what we all feel is a noble cause. As the project grew with production, this conviction went beyond Fielder to the producer, David Gerber, the director, Buzz Kulick, whom I have come to regard as my good friend, Barry Bostwick, who plays Washington, and the other actors, who have not only listened to my advice but asked for it, the executives at General Motors and their advertising agency, N. W. Ayer, and the personnel involved at CBS. We all felt that we were in a position to make a real contribution to American life.

"Behind the almost evangelical air that sometimes seemed to prevail as the screening went on is a conviction that the fundamental values of the founding fathers are invaluable today in the United States—and, indeed, the world—and are under serious attack. We are engaging in no propaganda or arguments but are aiming to present the truth in one specific but vital area. We are trying to give back to America the Father of Our Country as the person he actually was.

"The television show we have in preparation is not a history lesson, although it may well propel thousands of Americans to such lessons. It is an effort to delineate truthfully the character of a man who occupies a place in every American psyche, who is more than any other the human embodiment of the American flag. Away with the fallacious cherry tree, with wooden false teeth that never existed! We hope to reveal, in his youth and middle age, a man who was known in his own generation as 'amiable,' possessed of charm and magnetism and great physical prowess. A man who taught himself to be the person his highest ideals made him wish to be, who learned from experience to be a triumphant general and had within himself the possibility to become, as president, a leader for all the world to follow toward freedom, the democratic process, and the self-determination of peoples. A man who, although assaulted like all of us with the temptations of flesh and ego, achieved, through willpower and magnanimity, a greatness that when fully revealed will shine as a guiding light down the years."

*

The tremendous advantage of having only one sponsor rather than a chop suey of advertisers became evident as the power of GM was put behind our "Washington" in showers of advertising and publicity.

I became much involved in GM's decision to prepare a kit to be dispatched gratis to 75,000 secondary schools across the nation. Although related to the mini-series, it was to be in itself an historical source, boxed for preservation on library shelves. Thousands of letters from teachers were to thank GM for what many said was the first new material on the Revolutionary period that had reached their schools in many years.

The kit contained a small videotape from the show and a text to be read if the school did not have the necessary equipment; a paperback of the *Indispensable Man,* a teacher's guide, short essays on related historical topics on sheets of paper to be photocopied for each pupil. I was to write two introductory papers and supervise the whole.

A list of subjects to be discussed was drawn up in California by a panel of high school teachers and professors. When the result was sent to me, I was flabbergasted. The establishment of the United States was depicted as despicable. Subjects included persecution of Tories (nothing said about Patriots); Washington's enemies (nothing about his admirers); maltreatment of slaves; maltreatment of Indians; maltreatment (this was given two whole segments) of women. Nothing about the self-determination of peoples, the establishment of the first republic in the modern world, etc. The panel must have been made up of aging 1960s radicals. This was what they wanted to tell the children of America about their heritage! I had only to speak to have the whole thing turned around.

*

Fifty thousand copies of the *Indispensable Man,* featuring Barry Bostwick on the cover and an insert of stills, were distributed by Signet Books. The Book of the Month Club used my *Washington* three ways: the four volumes as a premium offer, *Indispensable Man* as a hardcover selection, and a quality paperback published as a selection of their paperback book club. I was copiously interviewed by the press, over radio and television, a heady continuation of the rejuvenation of a man in his mid-seventies.

The mini-series was scheduled by CBS on the most prime time: Sunday night (April 8, 1984) from eight to eleven, continuing on Monday from eight to ten, and on Tuesday, from eight to eleven. On Sunday, we were to follow "Sixty Minutes," the news show with the very highest ratings.

When I heard that "Sixty Minutes" was to feature Nixon directly before our "Washington," I complained to one of the reporters, Morley Safer, who happened to belong to my tennis group. He told me superciliously that we were very fortunate to inherit a large audience from "Sixty Minutes." After the event, I ran into Mike Wallace, the leading figure on "Sixty Minutes," who told me that we had outdrawn his show.

*

When the finished tapes had come in from California, Beatrice and I were given private showings—it took two afternoons—in a heavily upholstered room at CBS. I discovered that some changes I had not approved had been made during the actual filming and cutting, but there was nothing to get excited about. Beatrice and I emerged into the New York City traffic very pleased.

Since a television show had to be seen at the instant or not at all, reviews based on tapes had to be run in advance. I doubt if there was a newspaper of any importance across the United States that did not feature our show on the front cover of its weekly television section, and often also with several stories. I may well have received more publicity in that anticipatory week than during all my previous life.

As Beatrice and I watched quietly in our own television (formerly maid's) room, we knew that professional rating of the show was being determined by invisible electrical impulses going into machines whose verdicts on viewership were beyond question or appeal. If our experiment was to have, as we hoped, an influence on future programming, if the top brass at General Motors were to be pleased, the figures had to be very high.

We did have very high ratings. Thirty-four percent of the television sets in use were turned to our wavelengths. Sixty million viewers, approximately as many as voted at presidential elections. We were nominated for the top award in the industry, an "Emmy," and did win the major prize for high quality television, a Peabody Award.

*

The show was syndicated so widely that my friends liked to say, "The sun never sets on Flexner."* Our bagging the BBC was a trial to American public television, which, although they bought copiously from the British networks, had great difficulty selling to them any production of their own. However, our reception in England ran, as had my four-volume *Washington,* into anti-American prejudice. It was considered presumptuous for America to dare invade the British air with something that pretended not to be cheap and vulgar, and furthermore depicted their defeat in the Revolution. Television critics were beside themselves with rage. One writer for the *London Times* was so sure of what the show would be like that obviously he did not bother to view it. He had Washington going around saying "Call me George," and imagined a scene inserted to demonstrate Washington's sexual prowess.

---

*The following list was sent me in September, 1984: Armed Forces Radio & TV Service, Bahrain, Chile, Colombia, Costa Rica, Dubai, Ecuador, El Salvador, Italy, Japan, Korea, Kuwait, Namibia (S.W. Africa), Panama, Mexico, Saudi Arabia (ARAMCO), Trinidad/Tobago, United Kingdom, Uruguay, Zambia.

52

PRESIDENCY DISPLAYED

*

WE were encouraged to feel that we had achieved a seminal triumph toward opening American networks to important historical programming. (I liked to think how much my onetime colleagues at Omnibus must approve.) We resolved to repeat the demonstration. We would do Washington's presidency.

The old team was reassembled: Gerber as producer; CBS supplying seed money; GM, led again by McNulty and Pruett, foreseen as sponsor; Fielder as scriptwriter; Bostwick and Duke as stars; Flexner's biography as the source and Flexner (now from the beginning) as historical adviser. Since the time span to be dealt with would be reduced to the eight years of the presidency, we intended not an eight-but a five-hour mini-series.

Everything went as merrily as a marriage bell until the finished script was submitted to CBS. The moguls were horrified: no sex interest comparable to Sally Fairfax and Jaclyn Smith; no such violence as had been offered by the French and Indian and the Revolutionary Wars. Good God! Nothing but the building of the first republican government in the modern world; the feud between Jefferson and Hamilton that might have been interesting if one of them had been murdered. Efforts to keep the United States out of the fighting in Europe were so disgustingly successful as to prevent bloodshed. Was not CBS engaged in an all-important war of their own: with the other networks for ratings and the resulting revenues? What nerve to ask them to endanger their ratings and prosperity by sacrificing prime time to the crazy idea that the broad public would accept such namby-pamby gruel! Any sense of obligation because of their use of the air of the United States does not seem to have occurred to CBS. They indignantly repudiated the project.

*

I was invited to dine, again at the Plaza, with McNulty, Pruett, and some other GM worthies. They announced that if I so advised, General Motors would override CBS's veto and make their own arrangements with Gerber. If I advised the other way, they would drop the project.

I was astonished to have a great corporation seem to leave altogether up to me a decision involving their public image and millions of dollars. It all seemed squeegee. They knew I had been working with Gerber and Fielder; they knew that it would be much to my own advantage to have the show go on. They must have suspected that I was not working for Gerber altogether as a volunteer. I guessed that McNulty and Pruett took my approval for granted and had set up the formality to impress their own board. I was much complimented that high brass would be so much impressed.

What a terrible quandary I would have been placed in had I had serious doubts! However, Fielder and I had been working, as before, amicably together. I was able wholeheartedly to endorse the script. GM made its deal with Gerber.

*

But, alas, we were not really disentangled from CBS. As GM would pay for the air time, CBS did not altogether refuse, yet they would not promise what GM considered essential, such prime time as had been allotted to our first mini-series. Everything came to a halt. I was told that GM was toying with the possibility (which they considered dim) of getting what they needed from another network. Finally, CBS gave in but only on the condition that the script be cut from five to four hours. Gerber replied that this was impossible and said he would abandon the whole project—but, when the chips were finally down, he gave in to the inevitable.

I did my best to help Fielder, as he prepared the shorter script, but we could not prevent the condensation from being damaging from both an historical and an acting point of view. Patty Duke, for instance, complained that all the color had been removed from her part so that she had nothing to do except say, "Yes, George," and "No, George." However, there was enough strength and value left for me to urge and GM to agree that we be not daunted.

But CBS had not completed their mischief. Their continued procrastination prevented us from going into actual production. Gerber did manage to hang on to Barry and Patty, perhaps because of their loyalty to the ideals we were trying to exemplify, but when director William A. Graham (who had once worked for Omnibus) was hired, he had to accept being paid day by day. As for me, at seventy-six, I was getting no younger.

When CBS finally agreed that our mini-series could, like its predecessor, start on a Sunday night after "Sixty Minutes," they set the date (September 26, 1986) so short a time in the future that all production had to be cramped.

Casting, except for our loyal stars, was done on a crash basis. The casting agents summoned what experienced actors, usually with minor reputations, were available on immediate notice. To these, short scenes from specific roles were sent for study—without any context and often with only twenty-four hours' notice.

Gerber, some of his staff, the producer, the director, the agents, and I sat around a bare table in a large rehearsal room overlooking Broadway. I was much impressed by the respect the agents showed to the actors when they were called in one by one to read. When I arrived late for a session, I was banned by gesture from proceeding to my chair, having to huddle in a corner until an actor had finished his reading. As one of the agents read in an expressionless voice the other side of the dialogue, the actors, having had no opportunity to achieve deeper insight, read with considerable fustian. I had difficulty telling the renderings apart, and was thrown into a greater confusion when told that the actors might be cast for other parts than those they were reading. All this was well over my head, but one objection I did make.

All the male actors they had summoned were tall, robust, physically fit, with dark hair. Jefferson had had reddish hair and, in fact, slouched, but I made my pitch concerning the most extreme incongruity: Madison had been a small studious man with spindly legs. To honor this, I contended, would not only serve historical accuracy, but help with variety of appearance. Maybe they attributed my suggestion to the loyalty to his own size of a little man. In any case, I was silenced by the statement that there were no small accomplished actors except comedians. Time was to demonstrate that my desire for variety had not been foolish. Viewers complained that it was almost impossible to tell Jefferson, Hamilton, Madison, etc., apart.

*

Even actors cast for the major historical roles could be allowed no more than a day or so for preparation before they actually performed before the cameras. Never before in our productions had my advice been more needed, but the new director, unlike Buzz Kulick, did not want me to meddle in what he considered his prerogative to tell his actors what to do. The filming was almost all in Philadelphia. I received an impassioned phone call from Barry begging me to ask Gerber for permission to come and help. But the policy that had served me for so long of not pushing myself forward made me say that it would be better if Barry would do it. Since Barry felt he could not do it, this was probably a mistake as the actors remained only slightly informed.

When I was finally called to Philadelphia, I found none of the previous unanimity of spirit. Unity was impeded because the shooting was predominantly indoors in smallish eighteenth-century rooms. No sunny fields where we could be comfortable together. Actors not immediately required were away somewhere—the stars in their campers—while those waiting to appear hung around on doorsteps. Shooting space was so crowded with all the paraphernalia of high technology, and the plethora of workers required by the union rules, that there was hardly space to fit in anyone not absolutely essential. The director would ensconce me in his chair while he stood beside it. I was astounded by the disciplined organization when we operated in a small, boarding-house room. There was hardly space for the action, and most of the floor was covered with wires, over which no one tripped, a dozen or so men moving around without running into each other or clashing together any of the equipment they were perpetually shifting to serve different camera angles.

A step toward reviving the old spirit had been taken by firing the new producer and importing Fielder. But the director remained so at outs with the old team that he was reduced to begging me, when a dinner together was being arranged, to see that he was invited. He tried to ingratiate himself by paying the whole bill.

While the actors of the second tier, Hamilton, Jefferson, Madison, etc., were somewhat at sea but eager to cooperate, the stalwarts from the previous production carried the show. Despite her complaints, Patty warmed the heart with Martha's affection for Washington. Barry was on camera some two-thirds of the time. I had been worried as to how he would come over as president, because I felt that in the previous mini-series he had relied so much on his virile, athletic charm. But I could not have been more delighted. Probably because in the older Washington this youthful charisma would be out of place, he was inspired to dig deeper.

The last few days of shooting were in the country again, at Mount Vernon. The sun shone as of old. But a sinister note was struck when I was assigned to have lunch with a group of visiting television reporters and columnists. Led by a young man with a twitching face representing a major Los Angeles newspaper, they charged me with trying to palm counterfeit goods off on the American public. We were cheating the people by engrossing their atmosphere with a show that lacked sex and violence. We would not get away with this, they warned, with righteous indignation.

*

General Motors, I was told, was in such financial doldrums that they had, instead of as usual transporting their top staff to some Caribbean island for their annual meeting, remained in Detroit. It was considered menacing that, when told how much our Washington show was costing, Chairman Smith had remarked angrily that without that expenditure they would not have had to sacrifice their holiday.

Publicity and advertising appeared but not on the scale of the previous mini-series. In my own backyard, the New American Library abandoned their plan to prepare a tie-in edition of the paperback—leftover copies of the previous one would serve—and the Book of the Month Club bowed out.

For the formal opening of the previous mini-series, a one-hour condensation had been put together and was shown, with much fanfare at a theater in Washington. This time it was decided to stage the opening at the New-York Historical Society where excerpts would be shown on a battery of spaced television machines. I was in England when the plans were made.

On my return, I was surprised to find that the invitation read: "General Motors and the New-York Historical Society request the honor of your company at a reception and dinner to honor James Thomas Flexner, Pulitzer Prize winning biographer of George Washington and to preview GEORGE WASHINGTON: THE FORGING OF A NATION."

In smaller type on the facing page: "Among the guests honoring Mr. Flexner will be George Washington, Thomas Jefferson, Alexander Hamilton, James Madison, John Adams, Martha Washington, and other historical characters from the cast of GEORGE WASHINGTON: THE FORGING OF A NATION, as well as key members of the production team."

In my speech of acknowledgment, I said that I assumed that I was being honored as a catalyst bringing together the two groups represented at the dinner: network television and historical scholarship. I compared this to the confluence of Ohio and Monongahela rivers into the Mississippi. But would the Mississippi roll?

*

The ratings of "The Forging of a Nation" were respectable, no more. We had gotten by without destroying but also without speeding our crusade along. Really to make a dent in the television industry we would have to come up with another major hit.

Although I was outraged that the lack of sex and violence had proved so damaging, I felt that our whole effort to establish authentic historical drama should not be allowed to sink on that reef. I was encouraged to this conclusion by my having on the shelf of my own books an account of an historical drama that seemed to have everything that the most greedy network might desire. *The Traitor and the Spy:* Arnold, the greatest combat general of the Revolution; André, the charismatic spy; and Peggy, the beauty who used sex as a weapon.

Gerber had a wait-and-see attitude. McNulty and Pruett were much interested. Fielder was reported as opposed. There was an inherent problem. Sympathy could be built up for Arnold because of his unhappy childhood, the delays in granting him rightful promotion, his gallantry rewarded by a crippling wound, his great prowess on the battlefields. But then came a 180-degree change. Arnold's effort to sell his commander and his soldiers to the enemy could not, without condoning treason, be treated sympathetically. I could argue for the tragedy of the "fatal flaw," a broken sword, tarnished honor, the glory that descended; I could point out the many similarities between the Arnold story and Shakespeare's *Macbeth*, but no one was satisfied. Then Fielder came up with an idea: by making Washington a major character, we could present patriotism to contrast with Arnold's "treason most vile."

This was being mulled over when McNulty and Pruett were categorically informed that General Motors could not afford any more mini-series. The Mississippi that we had hoped to start rolling was thus blocked at the source. No longer held together by actual possibilities, our team fell apart.

*

April 30, 1989—I was eighty-one years old—was the 200th anniversary of Washington's inauguration as president of the United States. This called for national celebration. I was too used to being a maverick to expect to be tapped for any academic symposia or recruited by any official committee. The most obvious site for a celebration was New York City, where the inauguration had been. True, Independence Hall, where the ceremony had actually taken place, stood no longer. However, the cavernous Sub-Treasury Building, built some years later and now not in use, with its imposing front steps supporting a gargantuan statue of Washington, could be adopted as substitute. The celebration that would be held there was steered by a consortium of retailers eager to attract trade to the city. They made it clear that they did not want me around, and put the management in the hands of the Radio City Music Hall Productions, which was experienced in such ventures. The invited guests—I was not one—were shown to their seats by usherettes bearing a Radio City emblem.

My role was engineered by Sophie, my standard poodle. She played every morning in Carl Schurz Park with the dog of the woman who was handling the festival's promotion. When the three network news operations each wanted someone for their daily most major news half-hours, she could find no one connected with the New York Celebration who carried that kind of weight. Dog spoke to dog, and I found myself on two of the three networks. It was a weird experience. Much time and expense were lavished on interviews. At the big, lofty, Sub-Treasury Building, cameramen crawled around just below the high ceiling, but my appearances on the air in those half-hours, where every minute was worth thousands, came and went so quickly that before I could take a hard look I was gone.

*

In the bookstores, although years had passed, no real competition appeared for my volumes. The Book of the Month Club used *The Indispensable Man* as an alternate selection, and Signet Books distributed a specially prepared paperback.

My four-hour mini-series on Washington's presidency reappeared, as a "General Motors Mark of Excellency Presentation" on the PBS Network. The fact that no advertising interruptions were accepted on Public Television left a blank half-hour in each of the two two-hour presentations. These were filled by having Bill Moyers, that star of all interviewers, talk with me about Washington. The idea was that we would get together at Mount Vernon, but Moyers could not find the time so the taping was scheduled at Fraunces Tavern, where Washington had at the end of the Revolution said farewell to his officers. The tavern is down at the very bottom of Manhattan Island, and I was horrified to find that the driver of the car sent for me by Channel 13 had no idea where to go. It was late in the evening, and there was no one in that business district to ask: the buildings were shut and the streets empty. As we cruised around, getting later and later, I got as near to hysterics as I have ever done. We reached the tavern at last, and I entered full of apologies to find that Channel 13 had done the same with Moyers and that he had just arrived. The harm was that we had had no preparatory moment to say a word to each other before the taping had to start. But he is one of the most skillful of interviewers and I was hardly a greenhorn. Moyers was pleased and I was pleased, and my friends were pleased.

When the explosive outburst of the anniversary was over, I returned to writing the book that you, dear reader, are now holding in your hands.

Index

*